Interdisziplinäre Beiträge zur kriminologischen Forschung

Band 48

Kriminologisches Forschungsinstitut Niedersachsen e.V.
Lützerodestraße 9 – 30161 Hannover

Dr. Dirk Baier/Prof. Dr. Christian Pfeiffer (eds.)

Representative Studies on Victimisation

Research Findings from Germany

Nomos

The Deutsche Nationalbibliothek lists this publication in the Deutsche Nationalbibliografie; detailed bibliographic data are available on the Internet at http://dnb.d-nb.de

ISBN 978-3-8487-2984-5 (Print)
978-3-8452-7367-9 (ePDF)

British Library Cataloguing-in-Publication Data
A catalogue record for this book is available from the British Library.

ISBN 978-3-8487-2984-5 (Print)
978-3-8452-7367-9 (ePDF)

Library of Congress Cataloging-in-Publication Data
Baier, Dirk / Pfeiffer, Christian
Representative Studies on Victimisation
Research Findings from Germany
Dirk Baier / Christian Pfeiffer (eds.)
308 p.
Includes bibliographic references.

ISBN 978-3-8487-2984-5 (Print)
978-3-8452-7367-9 (ePDF)

1. Edition 2016

Table of Contents

1. Introduction

Dirk Baier, Christian Pfeiffer

Representative research on crime rates and their trends in Germany is sparse. To date there have been no regularly repeated victim surveys of the kind that exist in the US and the UK. Anyone with interest in nationwide crime data for Germany has to refer to the German Police Crime Statistics. As it is known, these statistics only give a small picture of overall crime. Not only do they fail to permit reliable estimates about the prevalence of victimisation in the German population, it is also difficult or impossible to make inferences from the Police Crime Statistics about questions such as what population groups face heightened victimisation risk, what other factors are determinants of victimisation, and what are the consequences of criminal victimisation.

A major research focus at the Criminological Research Institute of Lower Saxony (CRLS), which is where all papers compiled in this volume came from, is to address the shortcomings of the Police Crime Statistics, among other things using representative surveys. The institute was founded in 1979 as an independent research institute in the form of a registered association. For three decades now, CRLS has practiced what is the rule in the English-speaking world but remains the exception in Germany, where criminology is less well established in the university research landscape, namely interdisciplinary research. CRLS brings together legal scientists, social scientists/sociologists, psychologists and in some cases researchers from other disciplines on a project basis. This not only addresses a need in research related to victimisation. Other focuses of CRLS's work – including research on offenders, research on prevention, intervention and evaluation, and research on institutions – likewise benefit from interdisciplinary collaboration. CRLS is well equipped to foster such research, for one thing because it has a fixed state-funded budget enabling long-term appointments, and for another because it annually raises third-party funding, for example from ministries, foundations and other organisations, that makes it possible to employ other staff (such as doctoral students) for shorter periods to carry out research on specific issues.

One of CRLS's objectives is to perform applied research, i.e. research of use to practitioners. This is achieved, firstly, by selecting and addressing current topics of public interest. Secondly, CRLS aims to make project findings available to a broad public, using both the media and direct contact with interested citizens through lectures and podium discussions. Thirdly, based on project findings effort is made to infer ideas for the prevention of crime. This can lead to the development of specific prevention programmes and evaluation of their effectiveness. CRLS thus also serves as an intermediary organisation between criminological research, practitioners and policymakers, and contributes in this way to a crime policy along rational and science-based lines.

Alongside this applied research, CRLS also aims to undertake more basic research. This requires the presentation of research findings to the academic public. Suitable channels for this purpose include congresses and publication in academic journals. In the past, however, success in reaching an international audience has sometimes been limited. One aim of this book is to present findings of different research projects of the CRLS to an international audience.

This compilation is divided into four sections, each containing at least one paper. The primary aim of each paper is to provide a descriptive overview of a victimisation-related topic. All papers centre on the presentation of findings from empirical research projects. These include both large-scale standardised surveys and qualitative interview studies with small numbers of interviewees. A distinctive feature of the projects carried out at CRLS in recent years is the increasing use of both quantitative and qualitative methods to investigate a phenomenon. Where underlying project data allow, the papers supplement the descriptive findings with correlational analysis. This relates both to potential determinants of victimisation and to potential consequences. Nearly all analyses presented in this volume use cross-sectional data. A few studies recently begun at CRLS are at least long-term in nature but were not yet able to be included here. But a number of papers in this compilation are able to draw comparisons with predecessor studies. This allows trend analysis, enabling conclusions to be drawn on trends based on self-report data for selected victim groups and forms of victimisation.

In the first section, in a sense by way of background for all subsequent papers, which largely relate to self-report survey data, *Dirk Baier and Michal Hanslmaier* present a key, reported-data-based statistical resource, the German Police Crime Statistics. Among other things, the authors look at the composition of crime in Germany in term of offences and trends over time, which in some cases can be traced back as far as the 1950s.

The three papers that make up the second section are papers aiming to present information that is representative of the German population. *Dirk Baier, Michael Hanslmaier and Stefanie Kemme* first report what people think concerning crime prevalence and trends. For nearly all offences included in the analysis people estimate the number of offences to be larger and trends to be more negative than they really are. A key factor in people's (mis)judgement proves to be media use. People who frequently obtain their information from tabloid media and commercial television tend to be especially far from reality.

Dirk Baier and Susann Prätor examine violent victimisation in adolescence, using a very large sample of nearly 45,000 ninth-grade respondents. Among other things, adolescents are confirmed to face a very high victimisation risk: Almost one in every six adolescents have been a victim of a violent act in the past year. This risk has fallen, however, since 1998. Crime in Germany drops not only in terms of reported crime, but also on the basis of self-report data. This is also confirmed in the analysis by *Lena Stadler* and *Steffen Bieneck.* The authors concentrate here on sexual abuse against children and adolescents, using a sample of over 9,000 surveyed individuals aged 16 to 40. In total, one in every 25 respondents reported having experienced sexual violence with physical contact before the age of 16. Alongside the prevalence of the various offences, the authors also look at the trend in reporting behaviour and at the perpetrators of sexual violence.

The third section of this volume comprises studies dedicated to investigating the victimisation of various subgroups. *Karoline Ellrich and Dirk Baier* look at victimisation experienced by police officers, as does *Bettina Zietlow.* Ellrich and Baier relate their analysis to a survey of over 20,000 police officers in ten German federal states, while Zietlow bases hers on an interview study of 35 officers. Police officers are shown to be confronted very frequently in their work with verbal and physical violence. At the same time, between 2005 and 2009 there was a rise in violent assaults that left police officers unfit for duty. Both the analysis of the standardised survey and the in-depth interviews show that such assaults inflict a severe psychological toll and that greater support in coping with the aftermath of assaults would be desirable.

In their paper for this section of the volume, *Steffen Bieneck* and *Dirk Baier* investigate physical victimisation among prison inmates. The analysis is based on a standardised survey of inmates in northern and eastern German prisons. Almost one in every sixth respondents reports having experienced physical assault in the preceding month; every ninth inmate reports having experienced extortions, one out of 50 inmates at least one incident of sexual violence. The authors additionally analyse violent perpetration in prison. Regarding this, one finding is that perpetration is not only caused by individual factors but in part also by factors of the prison.

A further victim group is analysed by *Theresia Höynck* and *Ulrike Zähringer* in their paper on homicide of children. The research project is based on an analysis of files for almost all child homicide offences in Germany from 1997 to 2006. The findings show the greatest risk to be in the first year of a child's life, and over a third of the children killed died the day they were born. Major differences are found between the 508 cases ultimately analysed with regard to perpetrators, circumstances, etc., and an analysis is therefore performed with reference to a number of specific case groups. In-depth analysis is provided for cases of neonaticide, maltreatment, extended suicide, mental illness, purposeful homicide and neglect.

Sandra Fernau writes about another special group of victims: people who were sexual victimised by Catholic clergy. She did biographical, semi-structured interviews with 13 victims. Using these interviews she can demonstrate the interplay between sexual abuse in Catholic institution and religious socialisation. Among other things it is pointed out that victims suffer on fear of stigmatisation and negative reactions by their family or community; that is why the majority of them did not talk about their experiences until 2010. Additionally, the interviews prove that the perpetrators had special religious ways to legitimate their doing, and these legitimisations are often taken over by the victims. As one conclusion Fernau points out that religion has an ambivalent status: For some victims religion helps coping with the traumatic experiences, for others it impeded any coping with the abuse.

Although consequences of victimisation already dealt with in part in papers in the second and third section of this volume, the fourth section includes two further papers that deal exclusively with the consequences. Their focus is on topics that have attracted scarcely any notice in research to date. *Michael Hanslmaier, Stefanie Kemme and Dirk Baier* go into the question of whether experience of victimisation heightens fear of crime and lessens life satisfaction. Research into life satisfaction has attracted increasing attention in the social and economic sciences in recent years, but not yet in criminology. The authors show among other things that most of all, experience of violent victimisation reduces life satisfaction; additionally, individuals with greater fear of crime show lower levels of satisfaction.

Finally, *Bettina Doering and Dirk Baier* investigate whether victimisation affects individual morality. There are sufficient indications in research that experience of intrafamilial violence in particular can reduce self-control capabilities and enhance aggressiveness. Scarcely any research has been conducted, on the other hand, into whether such experience also inhibits the development of positive characteristics. The authors explore such relationships using a survey of adolescents. The main finding is that morality is not compromised by experience of violent victimisation, but at the same time it is an important factor in protecting against violent behaviour. It is concluded that the socialisation conditions for resilience factors are to be seen as distinct from the socialisation conditions for risk factors; in future, greater effort should be dedicated to investigate the factors determining positive personality traits.

The findings presented in the various papers relate to research projects carried out at CRLS in recent years. Victimisation research will remain a research focus at CRLS. For example, current projects include for instance victims of domestic burglary or human trafficking. The mental stress after incidents of domestic burglary is particularly severe because they involve strangers encroaching upon the victims' personal domain. Another research project is planned for victims of severe violent assault. Respondents for this project should be recruited in hospital casualty units. One of the objectives is to improve institutional assistance for victims of violence. In a similar way, the aim of future projects of the CRLS will be to investigate experiences of victimisation and their consequences as fully and comprehensively as possible.

Part I:
Official Crime Statistics

2. Crime in Germany as Reflected in the Police Crime Statistics

Dirk Baier, Michael Hanslmaier

2.1 Public crime statistics

This paper uses the German official Police Crime Statistics to draw conclusions on the prevalence of crime in Germany, the age dependency of crime, and crime trends in the last few decades. The Police Crime Statistics allow an analysis of crime that is finely divided by types of offence and in some cases reaches far back into the past. This advantage comes with a major handicap: The statistics cover reported crime, meaning that offences, victims and perpetrators are only included if a crime is reported or is discovered in police investigations. The statistics thus only reflect a fraction of all criminal activity. The size of that fraction varies from offence to offence: Offences with high reporting rates (such as robbery and murder) contrast with others with very low reporting rates (such as shoplifting or sexual assaults; cf. Schwind 2010, Schwind et al. 2001, p. 347). The ratio of reported to unreported crime also shifts over time: The proportion of crime that is reported is affected by rising or falling reporting rates, increasing or decreasing police density, changes in policing strategies and other factors. This paper cannot therefore aim to paint a full picture of crime in Germany. An analysis of the Police Crime Statistics is nonetheless provided ahead of the remaining papers in this volume for three reasons. Firstly, it makes it possible to analyse offences like murder and manslaughter that are not covered by self-report studies. Secondly, as yet there is not a self-report study in Germany that is repeated at regular intervals and provides information on victimhood and offending. The surveys that exist are repeated only sporadically in specific domains or for specific year. Thus the Police Crime Statistics are the only source that is able to give information on trends in crime and victimization. Thirdly, comprehensive analysis of the Police Crime Statistics allows a comparative discussion with findings from self-report studies and so makes it possible to identify strengths and weaknesses of the statistics.

Alongside the Police Crime Statistics, Germany also has other public statistics that record crime and formal social control. This paper, however, focuses on the Police Crime Statistics, as these in a sense form the basis for other statistics in that police investigations are usually the first step in criminal prosecution.[1] Besides the types and numbers of offences reported or recorded, the Police Crime Statistics also include sociodemographic information on identified suspects and victims (Rat für Sozial- und Wirtschaftsdaten 2009). The findings in this regard are discussed in the ensuing sections of this paper. Other criminal and judicial statistics published in Germany are as follows:

- Public prosecution service statistics *(Staatsanwaltschaftsstatistik)*, which record the activities of public prosecution services at upper regional and regional courts. The statistics count the highest outcome for each court case. They also include the number of individuals affected by investigations (Heinz 2012).
- Criminal prosecution statistics *(Strafverfolgungsstatistik)*, which provide information on criminal court decisions, i.e. sentencing and convictions of individuals and where applicable the nature and severity of sentences handed down. These statistics cover all accused individuals in respect of whom final sentences are imposed or main criminal proceedings terminated by judgement or dismissal of a case. The statistics thus provide an overview of trends in court-registered crime and enable an evaluation of sentencing (cf. Brings 2005, Heinz 2012, Rat für Sozial- und Wirtschaftsdaten 2009).
- Prison statistics *(Strafvollzugsstatistik)*, which provide demographic and criminological data, as of a specific reporting date, on sentenced prisoners and individuals in preventive custody. These statistics also contain information on crimes committed and expected duration of custody. On a quarterly basis, they additionally record prison occupancy, intake and releases in the reporting month, and prison capacity (Heinz 2012, Rat für Sozial- und Wirtschaftsdaten 2009).
- Probation statistics *(Bewährungshilfestatistik)*, recording all individuals assigned to a full-time probation officer in a given year. The statis-

1 The public prosecution service itself, however, initiates 17 percent of public prosecution investigations (Federal Ministerium of the Interior/Federal Ministry of Justice 2006, p. 536). Such cases are only included in the Police Crime Statistics if the public prosecution service involves the police in investigations (Kemme et al. 2011, p. 20).

tics include suspended sentences imposed and revoked (cf. Heinz 2012, Rat für Sozial- und Wirtschaftsdaten 2009).

A central point of criticism regarding the above statistical sources is their incompatibility. The Police Crime Statistics, for example, classify offences by a different system (a criminological classification) than the criminal prosecution and prison statistics, which follow the arrangement of sections in the German Criminal Code. Incompatibility between the different statistical sources also means individual offenders cannot be traced through the entire process of formal social control (cf. Entorf/Spengler 2005, Heinz 2012).

In the following, crime trends are analysed on the basis of the Police Crime Statistics. These provide the most detailed and comprehensive picture compared with the other justice statistics as no filtering is involved. The Police Crime Statistics report crime in three ways: Number of offences, number of victims, and number of perpetrators. The analysis in the following mainly focuses on the reported number of offences. This is justified in victimological terms in that most offences have victims. 'Victimless' crime (such as economic and drug crime) only accounts for a small fraction of offences. An analysis based on offences also has the merit of including cases where the perpetrator goes unidentified. The data on victims and perpetrators provided in the Police Crime Statistics are used in the demographic part of the analysis.

2.2 *Crime prevalence and trends*

A total of 5,933,278 criminal offences were recorded by the police in Germany in 2010. At a population of 81.8 million, this corresponds to a crime rate of 7,253.2 criminal offences per 100,000 inhabitants. Thefts make up the biggest share of criminal offences (38.8 percent, see Figure 2.1). This includes vehicle theft (mostly bicycle theft), shoplifting and theft from vehicles. Domestic burglary and car stealing only account for a small proportion of theft but are often a focus of public debate. The public consequently tend to significantly overestimate the prevalence of such crimes. A further 16.3 percent of criminal offences are fraud-related. This includes offences such as fare evasion as well as fraudulent failure to supply goods as agreed (merchandise fraud) and fraud using unlawfully obtained non-cash means of payment (credit card fraud). About one in eight police-recorded offences consist of damage to property (11.8 percent).

Far less common are offences involving physical assault of the victim. Assaults here entails offences by individuals where no weapon or other object is involved and no severe injury results. A total of 6.3 percent of offences come under this category. Aggravated assault is less than half as common (2.4 percent). This consists of assault with a weapon/object or by groups of perpetrators or with serious consequences. In the Police Crime Statistics, bodily injury offences of this kind are grouped with various other offences in the violent crime category.[2] All in all, 3.4 percent of offences recorded in Germany fall into this category. Offences involving severe violence are exceptionally rare. In 2010, for example, 293 cases of murder were recorded, four cases of sexual murder and 7,724 rapes.

Another major category of offences consists of drug offences, which made up 3.9 percent of offences recorded in 2010. Relatively frequently these are offences under the Narcotics Act *(Betäubungsmittelgesetz)* (mostly relating to heroin and cannabis) and drug dealing. A total of 19.5 percent of criminal offences do not come under any of the categories mentioned and are labelled other offences in Figure 2.1. These include a wide range of offences; relatively frequent among them are insults and offences against the Aliens Act *(Aufenthaltsgesetz)* and Asylum Procedures Act *(Asylverfahrensgesetz)*.

Figure 2.2 shows the long term development of crime rates (offences per 100,000 population) in Germany. So far, the analysis has covered the whole of Germany, however this figure is limited to Western Germany plus Berlin, because crime has not been reliably recorded before 1990, the year of German reunification, in the eastern part. It is necessary to state the number of offences relative to the population because the population grew in the analysis period from 53.5 to 68.9 million. It is also important to note that there were at least four major changes in the way offences are included in the Police Crime Statistics over time, as indicated by the gaps in Figure 2.2: From 1963, the statistics ceased to include road traffic offences, producing a drop in the total number of offences. From 1971, the

---

2 The violent crime category comprises the offences of murder, manslaughter and killing another at his own request, rape and sexual coercion, robbery, extortion accompanied by violence, and assault on motorists with intent to rob, bodily injury resulting in death, aggravated assault, extortionate kidnapping, hostage taking, and attacks on air and sea traffic (Bundeskriminalamt 2011, p. 16-17).

Fig. 2.1 Share of offences by type of offence in 2010 (in percent)

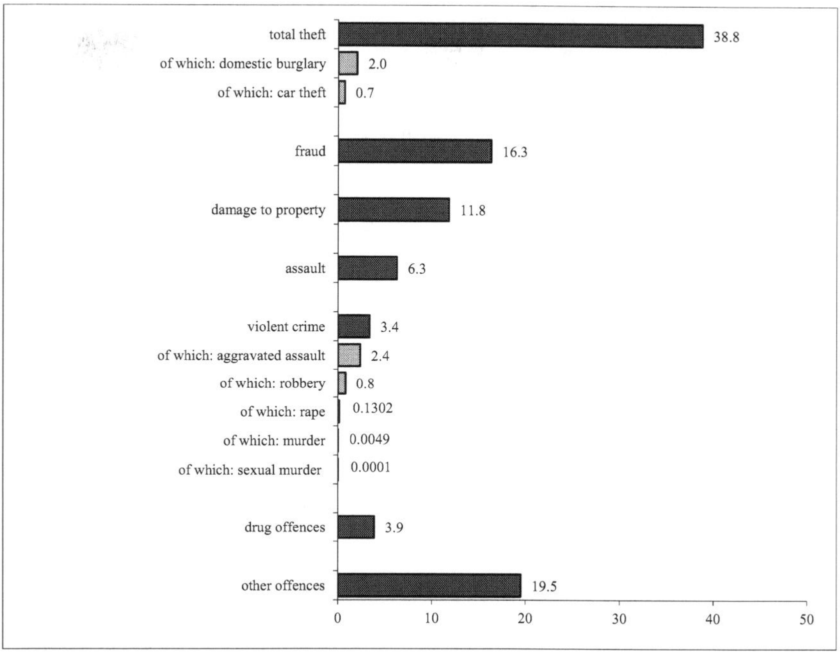

data began to be uniformly compiled on the basis of case outcomes, i.e. not included in the statistics until police investigations were concluded. Since 1984, perpetrators are counted once only no matter how many offences they are suspected of. In 2009, the counting method changed again to prevent double counting of perpetrators who came to the attention of the police in more than one of the Federal States. From 1991, the statistics for western Germany include Berlin as a whole and not just West Berlin; two years later, Police Crime Statistics were published for the whole of united Germany for the first time.

As Figure 2.2 clearly shows, the period between 1955 and 1993 saw continuous growth in crime within the German population. The crime rate for all criminal offences increased 2.7 times. Since then, the prevalence rate has stayed broadly constant or has slightly fallen. Whereas in 1995, 6.7 million criminal offences were recorded throughout Germany (including Eastern Germany), by 2010 the total was down to 5.9 million, as has already been mentioned; the size of the German population remained nearly constant during this period (81.5 million in 1995 and 81.1 million in

Fig. 2.2 Trends in selected criminal offences since 1955, per 100,000 population (Western Germany plus Berlin)

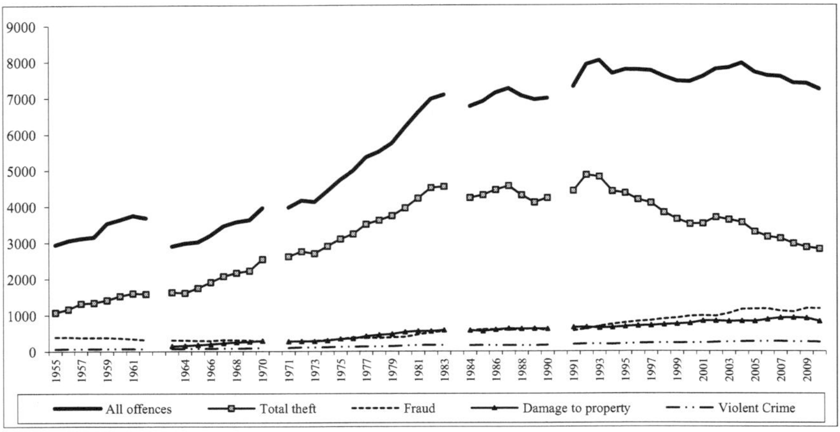

2010). The trend in theft is similar, with the prevalence rate rising 4.5 times between 1955 and 1992 but then dropping back again. Between 1995 and 2020, recorded cases of theft in Germany fell from 3.8 million to 2.3 million.

The remaining offences in the analysis show a rising trend that also continued beyond the early 1990s. The lowest prevalence rate for fraud-related offences was in 1966; by 2009, such offences had quadrupled. The upward trend is also visible in a comparison of the years 1995 and 2010: For Germany as a whole, the number of cases rose from 623,192 to 968,162. Damage to property has only been included in the crime statistics since 1963. That year also marked the lowest recorded prevalence rate, and 2008 the highest (6.2 times higher). 607,909 cases of damage to property were recorded by the police throughout Germany in 1995, compared with 700,801 in 2010. Finally, Figure 2.2 shows the trend in violent crime. While remaining at a low level overall, this offence category saw a fourfold increase in the prevalence rate between 1995 and 2007. There has been a sharp rise in case numbers since 1995: Whereas 170,170 violent offences were recorded in that year, in 2010 the number was 201,243.

The rise in crime cannot be solely interpreted as a rise in criminal inclination of German population. Certainly, changes came about during the period under analysis that may have resulted in an increase in crime. Sociocultural and economic changes are among the factors that can be pointed to in this regard. The emergence of new lifestyles and routines, like the shift of leisure activities into the public arena, is not without consequence for crime trends in society (cf. Cohen/Felson 1979). The loosening of traditional ties ('individualisation'), as reflected among other things in rising divorce and mobility rates, likewise alters the prior conditions for crime (cf. Sampson/Groves 1989, Shaw/McKay 1969). Similarly, by the logic of strain theory, rising poverty and unemployment may be reflected in the crime statistics (cf. Durkheim 1966, Merton 1968). Finally, the demographic changes since the end of the Second World War will not have gone without effect (South/Messner 2000). Such changes, however, are not enough to explain the marked rise in police-recorded crime. Other changes must also be taken into account: For instance, the period saw an increase in police density and thus formal social control. In 1964, West Germany had 210 police officers per 100,000 population; in 2005, the figure was 325 (Gesis-ZUMA 2007, p. 180). Crime reporting behaviour is also unlikely to have remained unchanged over the period. Unfortunately there are no comprehensive longitudinal data on this for Germany. Some empirical data, however, show a rising trend, for example with the reporting of assaults to police in the city of Bochum comparing the survey years 1975, 1986 and 1998 (Schwind et al. 2001, p.140-141). There is additionally a certain amount of change in what the law considers an offence, with some forms of behaviour being decriminalised and others criminalised.[3]

Figure 2.2 shows the trend for the main offence categories. Analysing individual offences separately yields the picture presented in Figures 2.3a and 2.3b, which show absolute numbers of offences for the whole of Germany since 1995. Case numbers are seen to increase for both forms of assault and for rape. As these are offences with low reporting rates, the rise is likely to be attributable to an increase in reporting to the police.

This does not reflect a general growing inclination towards violence in the German population, as the number of cases for other violent crimes demonstrate: Robbery has decreased by a quarter since 1995 and murder by more than half. The number of cases of sexual murder was 69.2 percent lower in 2010 than in 1995. Decreases in the number of cases are also seen for domestic burglary (down 42.5 percent) and car theft (down 79.2 percent).

---

3 Since the Federal Republic of Germany came into being, adultery and pornography have been decriminalised, for example, while various economic, environmental and drug crimes have been added to the statute books (Schwind 2010, p. 4).

Fig. 2.3a Trends in the numbers of selected criminal offences since 1995

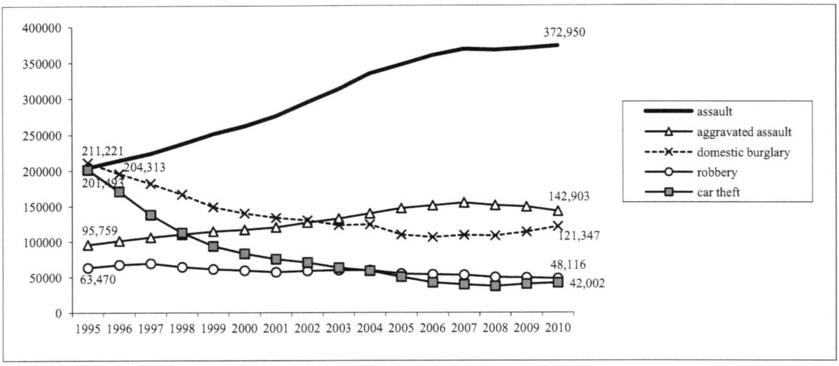

Fig. 2.3b Trends in the numbers of selected criminal offences since 1995

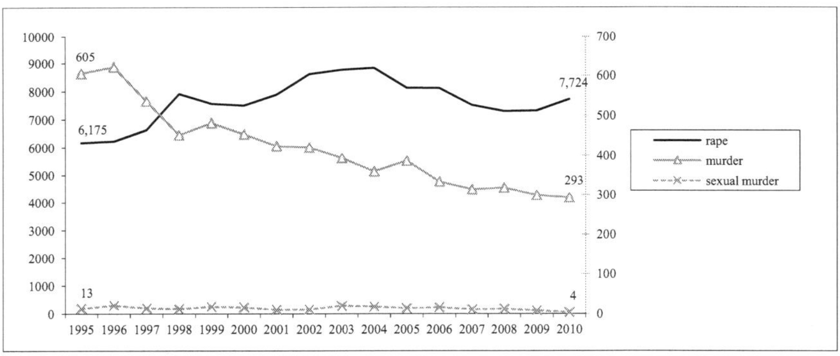

Looking at the last 15 years, crime in general is declining in Germany. Various developments can be pointed at to explain this (Baier et al. 2011, p. 21ff; Kemme et al. 2011):

- Germany is ageing: Between 1995 and 2010, the percentage of the population aged 60 or older increased from 20.7 percent to 25.9 percent. The share of older people in the population is thus increasing, and older people generally commit fewer crimes, while the share of younger people with greater affinity to commit crime is gradually shrinking.
- Immigration is falling: In 1993, 1.3 million individuals immigrated to Germany; in 2008, the total was down to 0.7 million. The large influx in the early 1990s was mainly related to 'Aussiedler' – people from

former Eastern Bloc countries claiming German nationality on account of German descent – and to asylum seekers, for example from war zones such as the former Yugoslavia. The immigrant population has since changed not just in number, but also in composition, with the great majority of recent immigrants coming from countries of the European Union. As analyses both of the Police Crime Statistics and of self-report studies show, immigrants on average have a stronger criminal inclination (cf. e.g. Baier/Pfeiffer 2007), so a decrease in immigration goes hand in hand with falling crime rates.

- Higher crime clear-up rates deter: One of the basic facts in criminology is that not only sentences or sentencing severity acts as a deterrent, but also the risk of being caught. This risk has grown in recent years, with the number of crimes cleared up rising from 46.0 percent (1995) to 56.0 percent (2010). A rise in clear-up rates of this kind can be seen for various categories of offence. The clear-up rate for murder, for example, has risen from 89.7 percent to 96.1 percent and that for theft (overall) from 27.7 percent to 30.0 percent.
- Technical precautions prevent crime: The trend in theft especially, and most of all burglary and vehicle theft, gives reason to assume that a range of technical systems are making it increasingly hard to steal. In the case of shoplifting this relates to merchandise security systems, in the case of domestic burglary to various door, window and patio door locking systems, and in the case of car theft to technology such as immobilisers.
- There is a spreading culture of nonviolence: Repeated surveys of school pupils support the conclusion that less use is made of violence today in child-rearing, that parents, teachers and others in the immediate social surroundings of adolescents increasingly disapprove of violence, and that adolescents themselves more frequently distance themselves from the use of violence (cf. Baier et al. 2009, p. 94ff). These cultural changes are likely to be important with regard to people's inclination to engage in criminal behaviour. They lead to a higher degree of informal social control; there is growing pressure to behave in accordance with the norm. And they lead to higher reporting behaviour, so that it is no contradiction that Official statistics on assaults increase whereas a culture of nonviolence spreads.

One distinguishing feature of crime as reported in the Police Crime Statistics is that there is apparently both an urban-rural and a north-south divide.

This is visible in a comparison of Germany's 16 Federal States (Figure 2.4). The prevalence rate for all criminal offences in 2010 is highest in the three city states. It is also higher in the northern States of Schleswig-Holstein and Lower Saxony than in the southern States of Bavaria and Baden-Württemberg. Even the five eastern German States show a north-south divide. To date there are few empirical findings from self-report surveys to confirm these differences found in reported crime rates. The findings available show the north-south divide to be largely accounted for by reporting rates, meaning that victims in the north more frequently report crimes to the police than those in the south (Pfeiffer/Wetzels 1994, Baier et al. 2011, p. 90f). Reporting rates are also found to be higher in urban than in rural areas (Baier et al. 2009, p. 42). Additionally, there are differences to be found with regard to other factors (such as unemployment, poverty, and composition of the population) between urban and rural and between northern German and southern German regions, and it cannot be ruled out that these also account for part of the statistical divides.

Fig. 2.4 Number of criminal offences per 100,000 population in the 16 German States, 2010

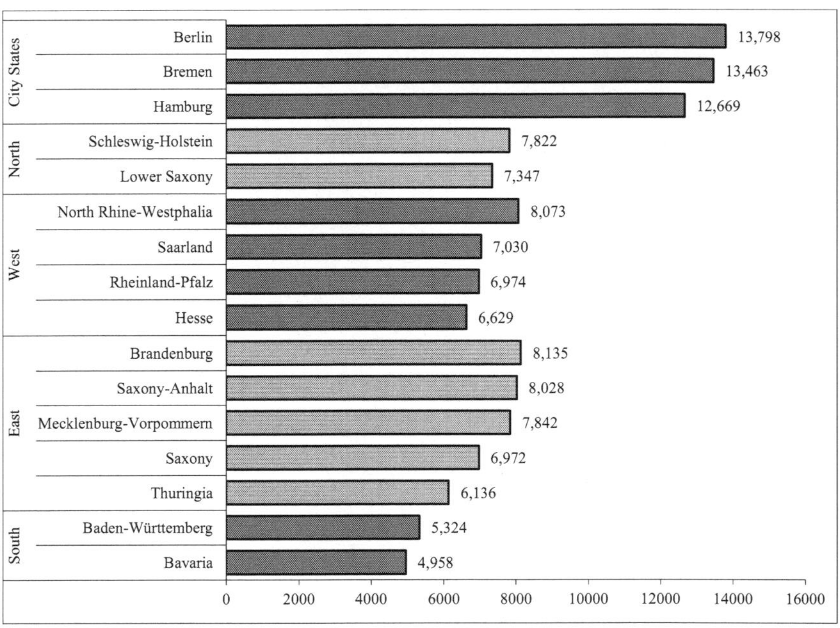

2.3 International comparison of crime figures

Comparing official crime statistics between countries is a difficult task. There are differences between the countries regarding the legal and crimal justice system. These differences include definitions of crimes, the practice of reporting, recording and counting crimes as well as differences in the reporting behaviour (Spark 2013, p. 2). Nevertheless scholars have attempted to assemble statistics on crime that are suitable for cross-national comparisons. In this chapter we give an overview on crime in the European Union; the data presented are based on Eurostat figures by Spark (2013). The interpretation must, however, bear in mind the difficulties arising from a cross-national comparison (e.g. Aebi et al. 2010).

Assessing the trend of total recorded crime from 2005 to 2010 we see a steady decline from almost 23.5 million offences to about 21 million[4]. Taking a closer look on the single Member States we see an increase in the number of recorded offences for twelve states. Germany and 15 other countries[5] show a decreasing number of total offences. These trends, however, are not the same for all types of crime. From 2007 to 2010 the number of recorded offences for domestic burglary increased by more than 7%[6]. For drug trafficking, violent crime and robbery the number of recorded cases dropped by 3 to 6%. By contrast motor vehicle theft decreased by 23% (Clarke 2013).

Figure 2.5 shows the total crime rates for the members of the European Union (EU-27) in the year 2010. Keeping in mind all the obstacles that come along with a cross-national comparison, we see quite a big range. The lowest crime rates are reported for the Baltic states, Cyprus, Bulgaria and Romania. The German rate is located in the upper third and similar to the United Kingdom and the Netherlands. The highest rates are shown for Scandinavia and Belgium. This results pin points at one difficulty arising from cross national comparisons of official crime statistics. Are the Baltic States really much safer than Scandinavia or does figure 2.5 merely reflect

---

4 These EU figures do not include Estonia, Ireland, Sapin, France, Latvia and Finland due to data problems (see Clarke 2013, p. 2.).

5 Scotland, England/Wales and Northern Ireland are treated separately as the have different jurisdictions.

6 These EU figures exclude Spain and Finland and additonally Estonia (violent crime), Cyprus (violent crime), Ireland (robbery) and Hungary (drug trafficking) due to data problems (see Clarke 2013, p. 1).

differences in reporting behaviour and recording practice? The problems typically associated with official crime statistics become crucially, when we compare different jurisdiction. Trust in police and national traditions for solving conflicts may affect the propensity to report offences to the police. Additionally the ways in which national police authorities register and count offences have an impact on the amount of registered crime.

Fig. 2.5 Number of criminal offences per 100,000 population in 27 EU member states in 2010

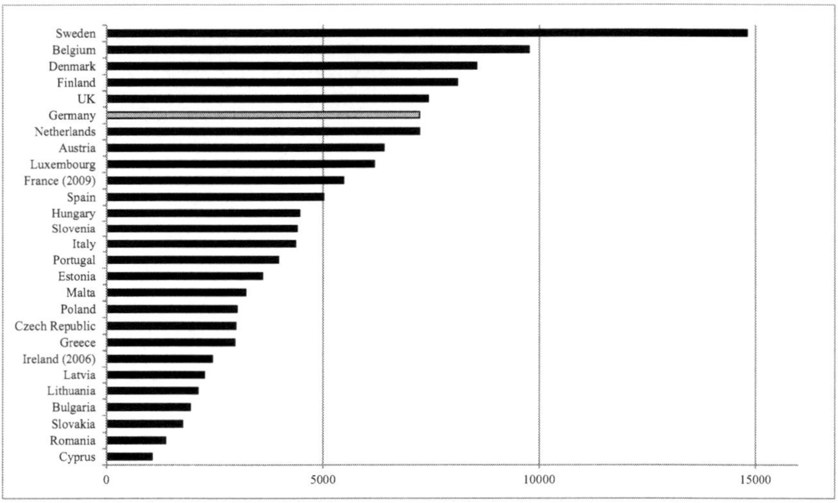

Source: Crime data from Clarke (2013); Population data at 1st of January 2010 from Eurostat; own calculations.

When we compare the crime rates for different offences, we see a similar picture (Table 2.1). The Baltic states and the new Member States in Eastern Europe seem to be relatively safe, compared to Western and Northern Europe. Disaggregated crime figures for Germany show that the rates for violent crime, domestic burglary and motor vehicle theft are in the midfield of the EU-27 rates.

However, one should not overrate those differences. Cross-national comparisons of crime figures should be based on data that is collected using the same methodology (e.g. data from cross-national victim surveys). Comparisons based on official crime statistics can only be meaningful interpreted, when the relevant circumstances are similar between countries or when we look at differences/ similarities in trends and not in the levels.

Table 2.1 Number of criminal offences per 100,000 population in 27 EU member states in 2010 for total, crime, violent crime, domestic burglary and motor vehicle theft

	Total Crime		Violent Crime		Domestic Burglary		Motor vehicle theft	
	rate	rank	rate	rank	rate	rank	rate	rank
Austria	6397	8	533	8	188	17	61	22
Belgium	9689	2	1130	3	630	3	183	11
Bulgaria	1944	24	120	21	317	8	6	27
Cyprus	1024	27	57*	26	395	7	295	5
Czech Republic	2983	19	178	17	96	25	125	13
Denmark	8511	3	478	9	809	1	375	1
Estonia	3607	16	399	10	238	14	65	19
Finland	8066	4	741	4	121	23	208	8
France	5472*	10	543	7	288	10	302	4
Germany	**7253**	**6**	**246**	**13**	**148**	**20**	**102**	**14**
Greece	2954	20	109	23	715	2	244	7
Hungary	4465	12	384	11	198	16	86	17
Ireland	2452*	21	272	12	569	5	255	6
Italy	4344	14	212	16	284	11	327	3
Latvia	2273	22	63	25	187	18	56	23
Lithuania	2121	23	111	22	147	21	62	20
Luxembourg	6081	9	661	6	296	9	71	18
Malta	3209	17	90	24	170	19	90	16
Netherlands	7195	7	680	5	620	4	100	15
Poland	3016	18	129	20	99	24	43	24
Portugal	3973	15	228	15	250	12	191	9
Romania	1364	26	26	27	66	26	12	26
Slovakia	1756	25	149	18	35	27	62	21
Slovenia	4372	13	136	19	125	22	26	25
Spain	4996	11	232	14	243	13	143	12
Sweden	14671	1	1213	2	212	15	375	2
UK total	7381	5	1624	1	456	6	190	10

Source: Crime data from Clarke (2013); Population data at 1st of January 2010 from Eurostat; own calculations.

* The values for France (total crime) and Cyprus (violent crime) refer to 2009 and the value for Ireland (total crime) refers to 2006.

2.4 Crime by age group

The age structure of crime in Germany follows the same pattern as elsewhere, with adolescents and older youths featuring disproportionately in the crime statistics. Figure 2.6 shows this by the example of violent crime. Victim statistics are published in Germany only in relation to selected offences and not for crime as a whole, hence the analysis is restricted at this point to the violent crime offence category; the perpetrator statistics, on the other hand, allow analysis for all criminal offences (see below). Of all victims of violent crime in 2010, 13.0 percent were aged between 14 and 17, and 15.1 percent between 18 and 20. Offenders account for an even larger proportion of these two age groups. Yet these same age groups respectively made up only 4.0 percent and 3.5 percent of the resident German population in 2010. In other words, these two age groups show at least three times as much involvement in violent crime as would be expected from their share of the population as a whole. The opposite is the case for the two age groups comprising the under-14s and the over-60s: These groups are significantly less frequently victims or perpetrators of violent crime than their share of the population would lead to expect. As the example of violent crime shows, victims and perpetrators differ little in age structure.

Fig. 2.6 Selected age groups as a proportion of all victims and perpetrators of violent crime in 2010 and of the population as a whole (in percent)

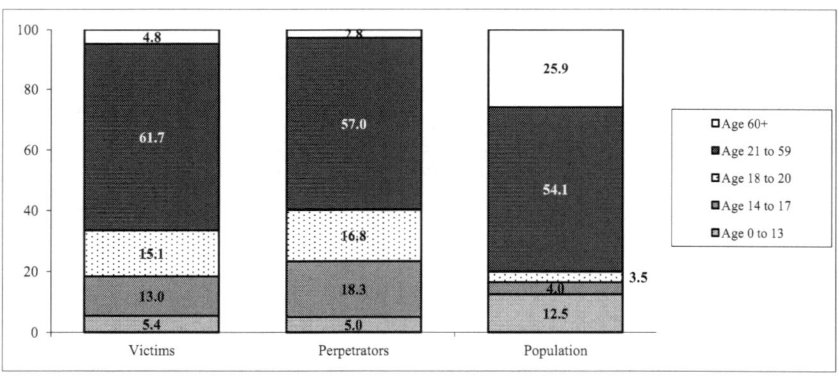

As the data on perpetrators are more finely divided by age and also allow more offences and categories of offences to be analysed, the focus in the following is on the offender statistics. Figure 2.7 shows crime levels in the various age groups for all offences using the number of police-recorded suspects per 100,000 in each age group. Comparing the male and female population, it is evident that women in Germany are increasingly rarely recorded as suspects, regardless of age group. The number of suspects per 100,000 men is on average three times higher than the number per 100,000 women, with the exception of the 12 to 13 and the 14 to 15 age groups where the discrepancy is only two times. The figure also shows that the age group with the highest crime level among men is the 18 to 20 age group, whereas for women the highest crime level is found at a younger age in the 14 to 15 age group. The difference can be explained by the fact that female offenders tend to commit theft-related offences such as shoplifting (Schwind 2010, p. 84) and such offences tend to be committed earlier in an individual's biography than other offences, in which men are significantly overrepresented. In 2010, for example, the number of suspects per 100,000 was only 2.3 times as high for men than for women when it came to theft, whereas the differential for violent crime was 6.4 times. The gender gap is particularly large for sexual offences (92.8 times for rape), whereas the difference is smaller for fraud-related offences (2.2 times).

The separate analysis by age group also shows that from age 21 upwards, crime levels fall off not rapidly but gradually. The number of suspects per 100,000 is of the same order for the 21 to 24 age group (and for men even up to age 29) as for the 14 to 15 age group. The 14 to 24 age group should therefore merit special attention on the basis of the police-reported statistics.

This assessment does not apply equally for all types of offence, however, as Figure 2.8 shows. For theft and damage to property, the largest number of suspects per 100,000 relates to the 14 to 17 age group. For violent crime, the 14 to 20 age group stands out with an especially large number of suspects per 100,000. For fraud, suspects are on average somewhat older again, with the largest number of suspects per 100,000 being found for individuals aged 18 to 29.

Fig. 2.7 Suspects per 100,000 for various age groups, all offences, by gender, 2010

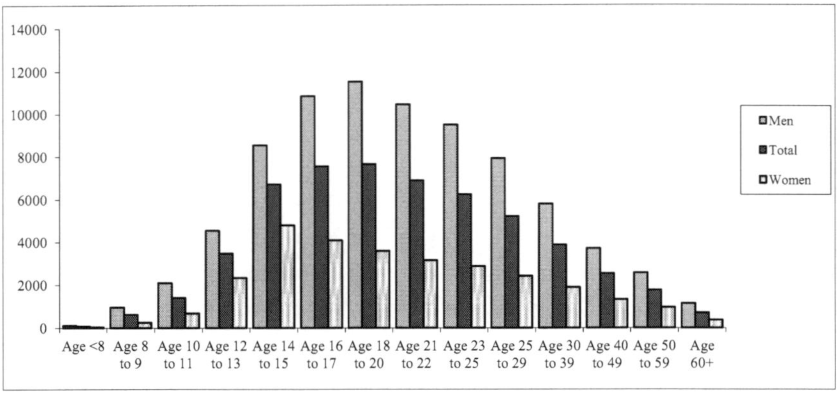

Fig. 2.8 Number of suspects per 100,000 for various age groups and various crimes in 2010

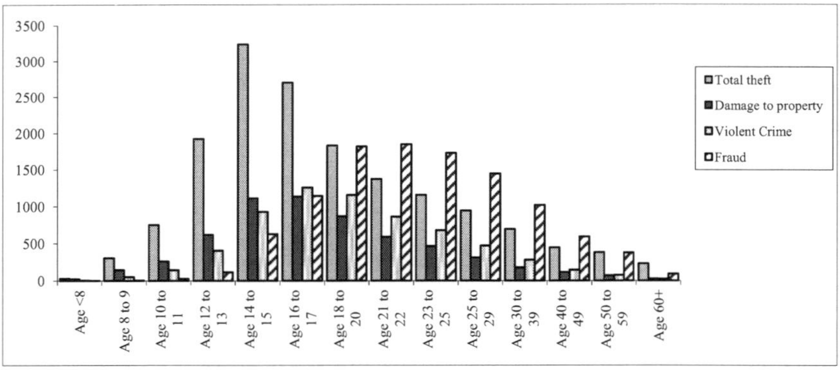

Younger age groups are disproportionally involved in crime. At the same time, crime levels in these age groups are not constant, as shown by a comparison of the numbers of suspects per 100,000 for 1995 and 2010 for the age groups between 14 and 25 in Table 2.2. Across all offences, the number of suspects per 100,000 decreased for adolescents (ages 14 to 17) and older youths (ages 18 to 20), but increased for young adults (ages 21 to 24). All three age groups show a decrease in the number of suspects per 100,000 for theft, and sharp increases in fraud and violent crime.

Table 2.2 Number of suspects per 100,000 population for various age groups and various offences, 1995 and 2010 in comparison

	14 to 17			18 to 20			21 to 24		
	1995	2010	Change (%)	1995	2010	Change (%)	1995	2010	Change (%)
All offences	7286.0	7149.7	–1.9	8155.5	7652.8	–6.2	6111.0	6569.8	7.5
Total theft	4347.3	2964.5	–31.8	3333.0	1834.1	–45.0	1923.8	1264.6	–34.3
Fraud	481.4	893.0	85.5	1119.3	1820.3	62.6	1041.1	1791.2	72.0
Damage to property	999.5	1124.2	12.5	731.0	868.2	18.8	372.4	528.0	41.8
Violent crime	798.6	1097.4	37.4	848.3	1155.4	36.2	498.1	770.3	54.6

Since with the exception of the 'all offences' omnibus category the three age groups under analysis and ultimately also the age groups not included in Table 2.2 show similar changes in the number of suspects per 100,000, the characteristic picture of crime where younger age groups account for a disproportionate share of criminal activity is maintained over time (Figure 2.9). Adolescents, for example, accounted for 12 percent of all offences in 1995 and still no less than 11 percent in 2010. Adolescents were responsible for 19 percent of all violent crime in 1995 and 18 percent in 2010. Based on the stability in the age distribution, which ultimately implies stability in the age-crime rate curve, it is possible to project a specific crime trend under different demographic conditions in the future, a point which will be briefly addressed in the last section of this paper.

Fig. 2.9 Percentage of perpetrators from various age groups for various offences, 1995 and 2010

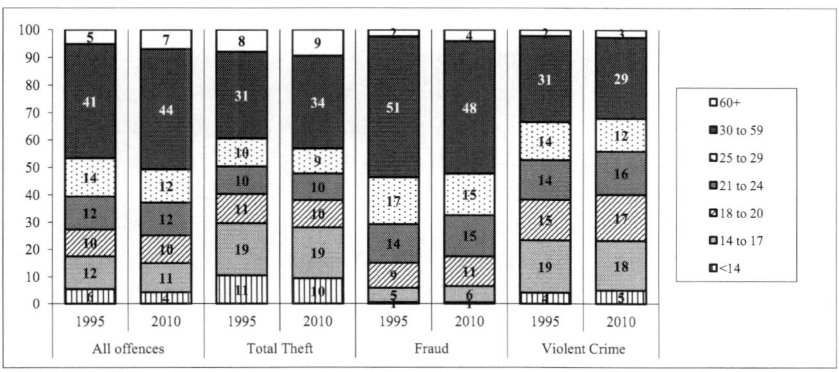

2.5 Crime in times of demographic change

Germany's population is rapidly ageing. Whereas only 20.7 percent of German residents were 60 or older in 1995, according to the 12th Coordinated Population Projection by the Federal Statistical Office this figure will rise to 36.4 percent by as soon as 2030 (Figure 2.10). The percentage of children and adolescents will shrink from 27.7 percent to 21.3 percent. Additional immigration will not be enough to halt this trend.

Fig. 2.10 Composition of the German population by age group in various years (in percent)

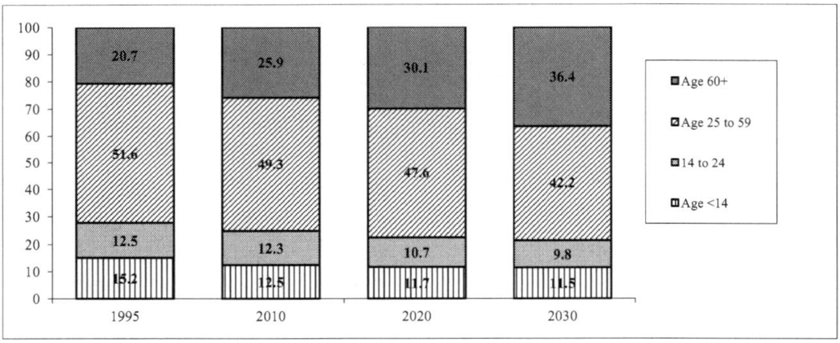

This population trend can be taken as the starting point for a projection. The size and structure of the population in 2030 are known from the projected population figures. In 2030, the German population will be down from 81.8 million to 77.7 million – a decrease of 5.1 percent. It remains to make an assumption about the trend in the number of suspects per 100,000. The simplest assumption is for this statistic to show no change and remain at the same level as in 2010. Based on the numbers for the different age groups in Figure 9, that would mean a fall in the number of police-recorded suspects from 2.2 million to only 1.8 million in 2030, representing a decrease of 16.5 percent – far more than the decline in the population. There would be a particularly large fall in the number of suspects in the 14 to 24 age group (a decrease of 23.8 percent), while the number of suspects aged 60-plus would rise (an increase of 33.3 percent). As this increase would be from a low base (because of the small number of suspects per 100,000 among the over-60s), the decrease in the younger age cohort would be the main determinant of the overall crime trend. Similar changes would be seen in specific offences and offence categories, although violent crime would go down more than fraud in line with the differing prevalence in different age cohorts.

This sort of modelling, however, only gives a first indication of actual future crime trends. A major point of criticism is the assumption of a constant number of suspects per 100,000 population. Experience shows that this number cannot be expected to stay constant. Retrograde extrapolations for specific offences for the period 1995 to 2008 have shown that the actual trend in suspect numbers can diverge significantly from that expected from the population age structure with a constant number of suspects per 100,000 (Kemme et al. 2011). To assume that suspects per 100,000 remain constant for each age group is to presuppose that the relevant determinants stay unchanged or at least that any change in them cancels out. This applies both for factors like unemployment, poverty, social cohesion, etc., and for factors like police density, investigation strategies, reporting behaviour and laws. An assumption of zero net change in these factors is likely to be unrealistic.

By the same token, changes in age structure remain an important determinant of future crime rates. Analyses at the level of individual German Federal States, for example, show change in the number of recorded suspects to be partly explained by change in the size of the different age groups (Kemme/Hanslmaier 2011). Other studies find that the percentage of young men has an effect on crime rates, young men being a group with greater crime affinity, (cf. e.g. Carrington 2001, Cohen/Land 1987, Entorf/Spengler 2000, LKA-NRW 2006, Lee 1984). Demographic change must therefore be a component in any projection of crime rates in a situation where the future age structure of a population is subject to major change.

All told, a projection of crime rates needs a more elaborate approach that takes in more than just the demographic component. For this reason, a research project in progress at the Criminological Research Institute of Lower Saxony uses panel analyses to make projections. The analyses pool time series of crime statistics and relevant economic, demographic and social variables for the years 1995 to 2010. Analysis is conducted both at the level of the Federal States and of administrative districts.[7] The aim of the analyses is to develop a model explaining crime for the years 1995 to

7 The analysis at administrative district level was performed for the States of Bavaria, Brandenburg, Lower Saxony and Saxony-Anhalt.

2010. The model quantifies the influence of demographic change and can be used as the basis for projections into the future.

Two problems arise with this approach, however. Firstly, little or no data are available for a number of important factors such as reporting behaviour and police density. This rules out such factors for use in a multivariate model. Secondly, ex-ante projection using a multivariate model requires the values of the independent variables to be known. Except for the population projections, there are no nationwide long-term projections for figures such as unemployment rates and socio-structural variables.

Generally speaking it is far harder to make reliable projections for crime rates than it is for population size, the determinants of which are well understood and largely known. It nonetheless appears important to work at projecting crime rates so that security policy can be placed on an empirical basis and is no longer reliant on public opinion alone.

References

Aebi, M. F., Cavarlay, B. A. de, Barclay, G., Gruszczyńska, B., Harrendorf, S., Heiskanen, M., Hysi, V., Jaquier, V., Jehle, J., Killias, M., Shostko, O., Smit, P., Þórisdóttir, R. (2010). European Sourcebook of Crime and Criminal Justice Statistics – 2010 (4th ed.). Den Haag: Boom Juridische uitgevers.

Baier, D., Kemme, S., Hanslmaier, M., Doering, B., Rehbein, F., Pfeiffer, C. (2011). Kriminalitätsfurcht, Strafbedürfnisse und wahrgenommene Kriminalitätsentwicklung. Ergebnisse von bevölkerungsrepräsentativen Befragungen aus den Jahren 2004, 2006 und 2010. KFN: Forschungsbericht Nr. 117.

Baier, D., Pfeiffer, C. (2007). Gewalttätigkeit bei deutschen und nichtdeutschen Jugendlichen - Befunde der Schülerbefragung 2005 und Folgerungen für die Prävention. KFN: Forschungsbericht Nr. 100.

Baier, D., Pfeiffer, C., Simonson, J., Rabold, S. (2009). Jugendliche in Deutschland als Opfer und Täter von Gewalt. Erster Forschungsbericht zum gemeinsamen Forschungsprojekt des Bundesministeriums des Innern und des KFN. KFN: Forschungsbericht Nr. 107.

Brings, S. (2005). Die amtlichen Rechtspflegestatistiken - Teil 2. Die Strafverfolgungsstatistik. Bewährungshilfe, 52, 67-87.

Bundeskriminalamt (2011). Polizeiliche Kriminalstatistik 2010. Bundesrepublik Deutschland. Wiesbaden: Bundeskriminalamt.

Bundesministerium des Innern/Bundesministerium der Justiz. (2006). Zweiter Periodischer Sicherheitsbericht. Berlin.

Carrington, P. J. (2001). Population Aging and Crime in Canada 2000-2041. Canadian Journal of Criminology, 43, 331-356.

Clarke, S. (2013). Trends in crime and criminal justice, 2010. Eurostat Statisics in Focus, 18/2013, 1–15.

Cohen, L. E., Felson, M. (1979). Social Change and Crime Rate Trends: A Routine Activity Approach. American Sociological Review, 44, 588–608.

Cohen, L., Land, K. (1987). Age Structure and Crime: Symmetry versus Asymmetry and the Projection of Crime Rates Through the 1990s. American Sociological Review, 52, 170-183.

Durkheim, E. (1966). Über die Anomie. In C. Mills (Ed.), Klassiker der Soziologie (pp. 394-436). Frankfurt am Main: S. Fischer.

Entorf, H., Spengler, H. (2000). Socioeconomic and Demographic Factors of Crime in Germany. Evidence from Panel Data of the German States. International Review of Law and Economics, 20, 75-106.

Entorf, H., Spengler, H. (2005). Die Abschreckungswirkung der deutschen Strafverfolgung – neue Evidenz durch Verknüpfung amtlicher Statistiken. Berlin: Deutsches Institut für Wirtschaftsforschung.

Gesis-ZUMA. (2007). System Sozialer Indikatoren für die Bundesrepublik Deutschland: Schlüsselindikatoren 1950-2005. System. Mannheim.

Heinz, W. (2012). Das Strafrechtliche Sanktionensystem und die Sanktionierungspraxis in Deutschland 1882 - 2010.

Kemme, S., Hanslmaier, M. (2011). Lassen sich Auswirkungen demografischer Veränderungen bereits in den Kriminal- und Rechtspflegestatistiken feststellen? Bewährungshilfe, 58, 5-23.

Kemme, S., Hanslmaier, M., Stoll, K. (2011). Kriminalitätsentwicklung 1995 bis 2008: Ergebnisse einer Expertenbefragung. KFN: Forschungsbericht Nr. 112.

LKA-NRW (2006). Trends in der Kriminalität in NRW. Eine Zeitreihenanalyse unter Berücksichtigung demographischer und ökonomischer Entwicklungen. 2006. Düsseldorf.

Lee, W. G. (1984). Are Crime Rates Increasing? A Study of the Impact of Demographic Shifts on Crime Rates in Canada. Canadian Journal of Criminology, 26, 29-41.

Merton, R. K. (1968). Sozialstruktur und Anomie. In F. Sack, R. König (Eds.), Kriminalsoziologie (S. 283-313). Frankfurt a.M.: Akademische Verlagsgesellschaft.

Pfeiffer, C., Wetzels, P. (1994). Die Explosion des Verbrechens? Zu Mißbrauch und Fehlinterpretation der polizeilichen Kriminalstatistik. Neue Kriminalpolitik, 2, 32-39.

Rat für Sozial- und Wirtschaftsdaten. (2009). Optimierung des bestehenden kriminalstatistischen Systems in Deutschland. Baden-Baden: Nomos.

Sampson, R. J., Groves, W. B. (1989). Community Structure and Crime: Testing Social-Disorganization Theory. American Journal of Sociology, 94, 774-802.

Schwind, H.-D. (2010). Kriminologie. Eine praxisorientierte Einführung mit Beispielen (20. Aufl.). Heidelberg: Kriminalistik Verlag.

Schwind, H.-D., Fechtenhauer, D., Ahlborn, W., Weiß, R. (2001). Kriminalitätsphänomene im Langzeitvergleich am Beispiel einer deutschen Großstadt. Bochum 1975-1986-1998. Neuwied: Luchterhand.

Shaw, C. R., McKay, H. D. (1969). Juvenile Delinquency in Urban Areas (Revised Ed.). Chicago: University of Chicago Press.

South, S. J., Messner, S. F. (2000). Crime and Demographie: Multiple Linkages, Reciprocal Relations. Annual Review of Sociology, 26, 83-106.

Part II:
What People Think about Crime and What They Really Experience

3. Public Perceptions of Crime

Dirk Baier, Michael Hanslmaier, Stefanie Kemme

3.1 Theoretical considerations and past research findings

Crime can be measured objectively using a range of crime statistics.[1] These have various disadvantages, the most important being that they only relate to reported crime. In addition crime also has a subjective side. At least two areas must be considered in this respect: fear of crime, and opinions on crime prevalence and past crime trends. In the following, such opinions are looked at more closely under the heading of 'perceptions of crime'.[2]

Unlike fear of crime, perceptions of crime are rarely the focus of empirical research about the subjective side of crime. This can perhaps be explained by the idea that perceptions may have fewer consequences and are thus less burdensome to the individual. On the other side, fear of crime may have more serious impact on behaviour (such as by triggering avoidance) and thus have greater impact on individual wellbeing. Whether the actual prevalence of or real trends in crime are over-estimated or under-estimated could be seen as of far little relevance. However, this paper will go on to contradict this view.

Based on the findings of Windzio et al. (2007), it can be assumed that over-estimation of crime prevalence and trends goes hand in hand with increased punitivity. Those who believe there is a constant rise in crime tend to call more frequently for policymakers to tackle the problem with stricter sentencing. If, at the same time, it is assumed that policy in general, and especially crime policy, is increasingly shaped according to the results of opinion surveys (cf. Albrecht 2004), then an over-estimation of crime shared by the majority would provide the basis for more punitive policies (including stricter sentencing, and criminalisation of certain behaviours and social groups). This in turn would be negative on two counts: On the

1 See Baier and Hanslmaier in this volume.

2 Fear of crime is addressed in the contribution by Hanslmaier, Kemme and Baier in this volume.

one hand, funding would be concentrated on one area (such as prosecution) and withdrawn from others (such as social and education policy); on the other it would support stricter sentencing whose crime-reducing effect is questionable. Looking to the example of juvenile crime, it has been repeatedly shown that rather than reducing crime, stricter sentencing actually promotes it (Heinz 2006).

The relationship between perceptions of crime and crime policy is not always a one-way street where policy responds to perception. Many national and international examples show that policymakers repeatedly push the issue of crime into the spotlight during election campaigns in order to win votes. In most cases, individual offences are used to establish general diagnoses for negative social trends that must be countered with harsh and determined action.[3] Crime perception within society can thus be shaped in this way, especially in the absence of prior realistic perceptions. Preventing this form of manipulation is another reason to give greater attention to the subjective side of crime.

As with other crime-related attitudes and assumptions, perceptions of crime are likely to be influenced not only by individual events of social relevance, but also by a range of other influencing factors. Baier et al. (2011, p. 9f) differentiate here between two key factors. The first of these is knowledge of the subject of crime, while the second involves character traits that match specific standpoints (and thus also standpoints on crime). The knowledge is shaped in turn by at least three factors. Of primary importance among these is personal experience as a victim of crime. People who have personally been a victim of crime have physical experience of the existence of crime and of what it means for those involved. Assumptions on how widespread crime is and on trends in crime are then co-shaped by such personal experience (cf. Lüdemann 2006) so that people exposed to crime tend to believe that crime is very wide-spread and constantly on the rise. Secondly, educational level is also likely to play a role in crime-related knowledge. A high level of education can be assumed to go hand in hand with a greater need to be well informed about social phenomena. This can lead to more realistic perceptions of crime. Windzio et al. (2007, p. 53 ff) confirmed this in their study. They also cite age (older respondents perceive a greater rise in crime) and gender (women perceive

3 For an example, see the 2008 election campaign in the German State of Hesse (Pfeiffer/Baier 2008).

a stronger rise in crime) as influencing factors. One explanation for both of these findings can be sought in the vulnerability hypothesis (cf. Kreuter 2002, Pantazis 2000). Certain social groups have greater vulnerability, meaning they are less able to defend themselves, incur more serious injuries when assaulted, and are less able to recover. Anticipation of this vulnerability results in a more negative standpoint.

Thirdly, knowledge of the subject of crime is largely tied to the media people use to obtain information. Communication of crime-related knowledge via the media can be both explicit and implicit. Explicit means that, for example, news programmes and other formats report precise numbers of crimes, the objective trends revealed in crime statistics, and also scientific findings on causes of crime. Implicit means that certain fictional formats allow conclusions to be drawn on crime trends, causes, prevention and intervention. In all of this, it can be assumed that in different ways, commercial and public service media and the tabloid and broadsheet press use explicit and implicit methods to report on crime, thus communicating different types of knowledge which in turn leads to differing perceptions, emotions and attitudes.

The media are the main channel through which people receive information about crime. However, this information, especially when it does not involve explicit information, is filtered in a special way or pre-prepared. In media logic, crime is a key issue that promises rare and exciting content. Crime is thus given wide media coverage. A small slice of reality is placed under the magnifying glass. Both in non-fictional and fictional formats, crime is frequently presented in a dramatic, emotive form, among other things by focusing on victims of crime or by demonising offenders (cf. Hestermann 2010, p. 198ff). As Pfeiffer et al. (2005) show, the establishment of commercial television in Germany, which largely targets public taste (meaning audience share), brought an increase in the number of programmes that focus on crime. Lehnert (2010) also reported that the volume of daily programming with crime-related content rose from 15.4 hours in 1985 to 239.2 hours in 2009. The share of crime-related programming in television as a whole increased across all television broadcasters analysed by Lehnert (2010). The increase is less prominent among public service broadcasters than with commercial broadcasters, and the share of such programming in public service television overall is significantly lower.

Explicit analysis of news programmes reveals significant differences between commercial and public service broadcasters, as seen in the findings of Krüger (2010). Crime-related topics take up more airtime in major news programmes on commercial television than they do in Germany's two public service broadcasters, ARD and ZDF. The commercial broadcasters "focus more on criteria such as emotionalisation, personal involvement and the entertainment value of news" (Krüger 2010, p. 55). When it comes to the different types of newspaper, Schwacker (1983) and Schneider (1991) report that tabloids tend towards sensation and drama, while the broadsheets write incidental, short, objective pieces about crime (cf. Hanslmaier and Kemme 2011).

These analyses are confirmed by findings on how media consumption influences perceptions of crime. For example, Pfeiffer et al. (2005) and Windzio et al. (2007) show that frequent consumption of news programmes broadcast by commercial television results in people perceiving a sharp increase in crime that has not in fact taken place in Germany. Reading supra-regional newspapers (the broadsheet press) has the opposite effect. However, watching public service news along with early-evening magazine shows and documentaries, which are mostly shown on commercial television, has no link whatsoever with perceptions of crime.

Aside from the factors already cited as influencing knowledge of crime (victimhood, education and other demographics, the media), it can also be assumed that differing personality traits shape perceptions of crime. Anxious people, for example, are more likely to perceive crime rates (along with with other fear-inducing phenomena) as being on the rise than are less anxious people. General anxiety is likely to result in the specific anxiety involved in the fear of crime. People who demonstrate heightened fear of crime can thus be expected to perceive crime as being on the rise.

One particularly noteworthy trait is authoritarianism (cf. Adorno et al. 1950, Altemeyer 1981). Authoritarian individuals tend to stick to established norms and place social conformity above personal autonomy (Feldman 2003). Butler (2009) assumes that authoritarians are especially sensitive to threats to social order and to the status quo. Such a threat can occur through criminal behaviour. Authoritarians are thus likely to be more concerned about trends in crime and have a heightened perception of crime than less authoritarian individuals. Other personality traits are, of course, also likely to be relevant. Nonetheless, given the available data, the empirical section of this paper focuses on the traits of fear of crime and authoritarianism.

The aim of this paper is firstly to use representative survey studies conducted throughout Germany to provide an insight into how people in Germany perceive the frequency of and trends in crime, and whether they tend to under-estimate or over-estimate frequency and trends. Secondly, in line with the findings presented, it focuses on the influencing factors of perceptions of crime. Thirdly and finally, the relationship between perceptions and punitivity is central to the analysis. In looking at that relationship, the authors draw on a longitudinal study which allows analysis of cause and effect relationships.

3.2 Samples

The Criminological Research Institute of Lower Saxony (CRLS) conducted similar surveys of representative groups of the German population in 2004, 2006 and 2010. Respondents were asked about their perceptions of crime, the influencing factors and possible consequences (Table 3.1). In each of the selected years, a postal survey was conducted, i.e. respondents received a personally addressed questionnaire which they were asked to complete and return. Sampling was based on an access panel. This involves a pool of households and individuals whose addresses and key socio-demographic data are stored by an opinion research institute and who have declared their willingness to participate in such surveys at regular intervals. Because access panel members are generally willing to take part in surveys and attention is paid to ensure that the panel reflects the overall population in Germany, these panels guarantee both a high response rate (over 60 percent in all three years) and a high level of reliability concerning the survey results.

The surveys in 2004 and 2010 were cross-sectional surveys. This was only partly the case for the 2006 survey: One half consisted of people surveyed for the first time, while the other half had been surveyed before. This was done in attempt to reach respondents from 2004. This approach has the advantage to draw causal conclusions because the causes are documented before the consequences. The basis of the longitudinal sub-study thus consisted of respondents from the 2004 survey. Unfortunately, it was only possible to write to around three-quarters of those respondents because some had left the access panel (cf. Windzio et al. 2007).

The cross-sectional surveys targeted people aged 16 and above who live in Germany. They were conducted at the beginning of the years in question, with most people being questioned in January. This period was chosen to prevent respondents checking the Police Crime Statistics in order to inform themselves about the number of crimes committed in the year prior to the survey. These statistics are published every spring to report the figures for the previous year.

Table 3.1 Survey and sampling (weighted data)

	2004	2006		2010
		Cross Section	Longitudinal	
Targeted age group	16 and over	16 and over	18 and over	16 and over
Survey period	8.1.-6.2.2004	5.1.-2.2.2006		7.1.-1.2.2010
Response rate (%)	64	70	81	86
Respondents for analyses	**2,017**	**1,110**	**1,206**	**3,245**
Male respondents (%)	48.0	48.1	42.0[a]	48.6
Education: low (%)	53.1	46.5	35.7[a]	44.8
Education: medium (%)	27.8	29.6	33.1[a]	27.9
Education: high (%)	19.1	23.9	31.2[a]	27.4
Average age	47.91	48.91	51.84[a]	49.25

[a] Figures based on non-weighted data.

A total of 2,017 people were questioned in the cross-sectional survey in 2004, 1,110 in 2006 and 3,245 in 2010. However, respondents were, at least in part, a selective group (cf. Baier et al. 2011, p. 26ff). In all three survey years, too few low educated people (no school leaving qualification or *Hauptschule* leaving qualification) took part in the survey compared with the overall population (Germany), as did too many high educated people (*Fachabitur*, *Abitur*, degree). This discrepancy was corrected with weightings. In the case of educational qualifications, this means that low educated respondents were weighted not with one but with a value greater than one, while high-educated respondents were weighted less than one. By using these weightings, the samples are adjusted to match the known distribution within the overall population. A large portion of the results presented in the following sections are based on weighted data. Only in the analysis of the longitudinal survey data were not weighted because the focus here was on the direction of the causal relationship.

At the time of all the surveys, around half the respondents were male (also Table 3.1). The average age was 48, although a comparison of the three surveys shows a slight increase in average age over time. This is not surprising given demographic trends in Germany. There is also a rise in the average education level: In 2004, only 19.1 percent of respondents had a high education level, while in 2010 this figure had risen to 27.4 percent.

Compared with the cross-sectional and longitudinal surveys conducted in 2006, noticeably fewer male, low educated, younger respondents were questioned. Because the longitudinal analysis was only used to verify the direction of the relationship between crime perception and punitivity, the discrepancies relative to the overall population appear unproblematic.

3.3 Perceptions of prevalence of and trends in crime

To ascertain how widespread people in Germany perceive crime to be, respondents were asked to look at a list of offences and then enter the number of offences recorded by the police in the year prior to the survey. In the 2010 survey, for example, respondents were asked to estimate the number of offences recorded by the police for 2009. Because such estimation questions are difficult to answer, respondents were given guidance in the form of the number of offences recorded eleven years prior to the survey – meaning they were given the data for 1999 with the 2010 survey. Thus, 2010 respondents could see that 6,302,000 crimes were committed in Germany in 1999. They were asked to enter their estimate for 2009 alongside the figures for 1999. The questionnaires cited the offences listed in Table 3.2. In contrast with the chapter on the Police Crime Statistics,[4] respondents were not asked about total theft, damage to property, violent crime (including robbery and rape), or drug-related crime. In the case of assaults, no distinction was made between assault and aggravated assault because, at least in terms of the trends, no differences exist between the two types of crime.

Because the respondents were able to freely estimate the number of crimes, some of the input produced very high figures. These would have a large impact when calculating means. Where such a distribution is encountered, two analysis approaches are available: Either outliers can be excluded from the analysis or the median can be used rather than the mean. Because the median is a value whose informational content is limited, it is wise to keep to presenting the mean. For this reason, the strategy of excluding outliers was applied. Outliers were defined as data in the upper and lower one percent of the distribution. Respondents with values in

4 Baier and Hanslmaier in this volume.

the upper and lower one percent of the distribution were not included in the analysis of mean values.

Table 3.2 shows that in all three years and for almost all types of offences listed, respondents' average estimates are higher, in some cases significantly higher, than the figures in the Police Crime Statistics. Respondents who took part in the 2010 survey estimated the number of crimes committed in Germany at over eight million – one third more than the actual figure. In 2006, the estimate (for 2005) was one quarter higher than the actual figure. The discrepancies are particularly big in respect of sexual murder, car theft, murder and domestic burglary. For sexual murder, for example, respondents in 2010 cited five-times as many crimes as actually occurred. Only in the case of fraud and assault did people's perceptions largely match actual trends. Where assault was concerned, estimates even assumed a slightly lower rise than shown in the Police Crime Statistics. Two findings can be construed from the data: Firstly, people in Germany appear to be inadequately informed about crimes whose frequency is on the decline; crimes that increase over the years are, however, correctly estimated. Secondly, compared with the three survey years, it appears that perceptions become more realistic over time. The relative deviations decrease in relation to domestic burglary, car theft and murder. People appear to be more realistically informed about these crimes as time goes by.

Table 3.2 Crime rates according to the Police Crime Statistics, survey responses and relative deviations (weighted data)

	Police Crime Statistics 2009	**2010 survey estimates**	**Relative deviation 2010 (%)**	**Relative deviation 2006 (%)**	**Relative deviation 2004 (%)**
total crimes committed	6,054,330	8,128,624	34.3	23.1	-[a]
fraud	735,058	752,768	2.4	2.9	-2.6
assault	544,853	518,613	-4.8	-10.2	1.9
domestic burglary	113,800	212,483	86.7	184.4	174.6
car theft	40,375	125,626	211.1	474.0	423.8
murder	299	572	91.2	104.7	136.6
sexual murder	8	41	408.9	239.2	549.1

[a] No difference is shown for 2004 because an erroneous comparison value was cited in the questionnaire.

What is interesting is not only the comparison with the year prior to the survey, because the number of crimes committed was unknown at the time of the survey; comparison with same time eleven years earlier, which respondents used as a reference in the questionnaire, clearly brings out the same misconception (Table 3.3). While the number of crimes is generally on the decline (down 3.9 percent between 1999 and 2009), respondents perceive a strong increase: They perceive a 29.0 percent rise in the number of crimes committed. By way of contrast, in the case of fraud and assault, trends in the Police Crime Statistics and perceived crime are close together, while with all other crimes the differences are very large. Although sexual murder dropped by 55.6 percent, respondents assume a rise of 126.2 percent. If the differences between the Police Crime Statistics and respondents' estimates are analysed, it becomes even more evident that the figures from both sources tend to converge over time. There is also evidence of ongoing decline in the difference as regards sexual murder.

Table 3.3 Trends in crime according to the Police Crime Statistics and respondents' replies (weighted data)

	Police Crime Statistics: Change 1999 to 2009 (%)	**2010 Survey: Change 1999 to 2009 (%)**	**Difference between survey and Police Crime Statistics 2010**	**Difference between survey and Police Crime Statistics 2006**	**Difference between survey and Police Crime Statistics 2004**
total crimes committed	-3.9	29.0	32.9	22.1	-[a]
fraud	28.7	31.8	3.1	4.2	-4.3
assault	40.3	33.5	-6.8	-16.7	3.0
domestic burglary	-23.6	42.6	66.2	95.8	94.8
car theft	-56.9	34.0	90.9	118.5	124.8
murder	-38.0	18.6	56.6	67.0	80.8
sexual murder	-55.6	126.2	181.7	257.6	343.2

[a] No difference is shown for 2004 because an erroneous comparison value was cited in the questionnaire.

Using an open-ended answer format to ask for perceptions of crime has the disadvantage that people who have difficulty in estimating large numbers shy away from giving an answer. This can be seen in the data in that (not adjusting for outliers) between 6.3 and 9.0 percent of respondents entered no figures for the individual items. For this reason, estimated crime trends are surveyed again using a closed-ended answer format. Respondents are asked to state whether they believe that over the past ten years, various crimes have '1 – become much rarer' to '7 – become far more frequent' ('4 – remained unchanged'). A detailed comparison with the Police Crime Statistics is then no longer possible. Instead, the trend analysis shown in Figure 3.1 for the years 2004 to 2010 is of interest.[5] Here it becomes evident that in the case of fraud and assault, once again the means are higher than for other types of crime; this means that respondents often perceive a rise in such crimes. Over time, the mean for both types of crime show the least decline. The lowest mean can be seen for murder, meaning that few respondents perceive an increase. Looking at crime overall, and four specific types of crime (car theft, domestic burglary, murder and sexual murder), the averages drop significantly over the years. Thus, the findings of the analysis of open-ended answers are confirmed: While respondents tend to perceive most crimes far differently to the actual trends, the positive trends shown in the Police Crime Statistics appear to be gradually taken into account by the general public.

*Fig. 3.1 Estimated trends in various types of crime (means shown; weighted data; * differences significant at $p < .05$)*

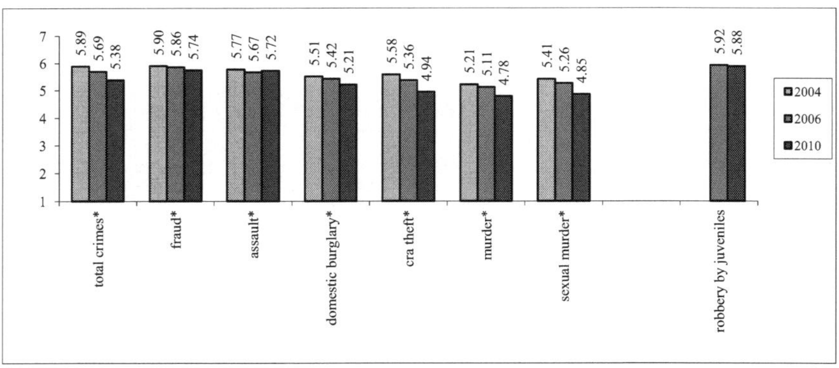

In the 2006 and 2010 surveys, respondents were also asked about the trend in acts of robbery performed by juveniles. The mean for these item changed only marginally over the period in question. In 2006, 70.1 percent of respondents said that juvenile robbery had become more frequent or much more frequent (answer categories 6 and 7). In 2010, 66.5 percent

5 The share of missing values varies for the associated items between 0.4 and 7.2 percent.

still thought so. In actual fact, robbery in Germany overall and that committed by juveniles has seen an ongoing decline since 1997 (cf. Baier 2011, p. 39). This positive trend appears to go unnoticed by the general public. It is possible that a particular pessimism exists when it comes to criminal behaviour among juveniles, who are viewed with great scepticism by the adult population. Interestingly in 2010, 92.3 percent of all respondents said that juvenile robbery was slightly on the increase or strongly on the increase. In respect of murder, for instance, only just over half the respondents (51.7 percent) in 2010 said there had been a rise over the past ten years.

The estimates for individual crimes correlate relatively closely in both the open-ended and closed-ended answers, allowing for them to be combined into a single scale.[6] For a six-item scale (omitting 'total crimes committed' and 'juvenile robbery and theft'), the open-ended answers produce Cronbach's alpha values of at least 0.65, while the closed-ended answer format produces at least 0.83 for all three survey years. However, the correlations between the scale values for the open-ended and closed-ended answers are only mid-scale, varying between 0.27 (2004) and 0.34 (2006; Pearson's r). Because the portion of missing values for the closed-ended answers is smaller, this six-item scale is used when analysing the influencing factors.

3.4 Influencing factors of perceived trends in crime

Only the 2010 survey is used for the analysis of influencing factors, because this is the most comprehensive survey of all with regard to such factors. In addition, as already mentioned, focus is placed on explaining perceived trends in crime using the closed-ended answer format. The mean of the six-item scale thus provides the variable to be explained.

As independent variables, demographic factors such as gender, age and education are used. These have already been shown in Table 3.1 above. Education is not, however, presented in grouped form, but as a continuous

6 Given the differing answer formats, the items were z-standardised prior to calculating reliabilities and correlations.

variable, meaning that educational qualifications were translated into years of education.[7]

Experience of victimisation was surveyed in respect of two types of crime: theft and assault. Respondents were asked about the frequency of experience in the past five years; a delineation was only made, however, between individuals with and without experience of victimisation. Some 10 percent of respondents said they had experienced at least one episode of theft, at least three percent had experienced assault (Table 3.4).

Media consumption was surveyed in slightly more detail. Traditional media consumption via daily newspapers and television was asked about separately from online media use. Answers were combined based on the maximum value. This is illustrated in the example of tabloid newspapers: If a respondent said they read a printed tabloid daily 'once a month or less', but read an online version of a tabloid 'several times a week', the value for the online media goes in the index value 'daily tabloid newspapers'. Because this involves an index, which theoretically combines different items (in this case genre), a strong correlation between items is not a precondition for combining them. However, the proven correlations and reliabilities for the media consumption variables show a positive relationship between use of traditional media and use of online media. Because the answer choices are identical for all four media variables, it was possible to compare the means. This showed that public service news programmes are the most frequently consumed format both on television and online; national daily newspapers, by way of contrast, are read least frequently.

Authoritarian attitudes were surveyed using four statements which borrow from Hübner et al. (2008). Two of the three dimensions of the authoritarianism construct were covered (authoritarian submissiveness and authoritarian aggression), as operationalised by Altemeyer (1981). Given the high level of reliability, all four items were combined into a mean scale. The answers provided with the individual statements ranged from '1 – does not apply' to '6 – fully applies'. At 3.22, the empirical mean lies slightly below the theoretical mean of 3.5: Most respondents can thus be classified as marginally authoritarian.

7 No qualifications translated into eight years of education, Hauptschule in nine years, and so on (Abitur: 13 years, University: 18 years).

To document personal fear of crime, respondents were first asked to estimate how often they feared becoming victim of six different types of offences. Secondly, they were asked how likely they thought they might fall victim to such offences in the next twelve months. In respect of the following types of offences, the fear of and the likelihood of their occurring were estimated: domestic burglary, being stolen from in some other way, being hit or injured, being attacked and robbed, being sexually abused, coerced or raped, or being killed in a violent assault. The answer categories regarding fear ranged from '1 – never', to '5 – very often', and those for the likelihood of occurrence from '1 – highly unlikely' to '5 – very likely'. In the survey, there was a correlation of at least .53 (Pearson's r) between the scores for fear and for likelihood in regard to specific offences. A high level of fear in relation to domestic burglary thus goes hand in hand with high expectations of the likelihood of them occurring. To establish a measure for fear of crime, the two estimates (fear and likelihood) were multiplied together for each type of offence. As a result, the estimated fear for each offence can vary between 1 and 25. The mean is very low, at 4.88, allowing the assumption that strong fear of crime is only characteristic of a small percentage of respondents.

Table 3.4 Items and descriptive statistics for the model variables (weighted data; 2010 survey)

	items	**answer categories**	**mean**	**standard deviations**
perceived trends in crime	6 items (Cronbach's alpha = .83)	1 – far less frequent, 7 – far more frequent	5.21	0.85
victim of theft in the past five years	'Items, money or other forms of payment or other important documents stolen'	0 – not experienced, 1 – experienced	0.10	0.30
victim of assault in the past five years	'Intentionally hit, beaten, pushed, strangled or injured with a weapons'	0 – not experienced, 1 – experienced	0.03	0.17
daily tabloid newspapers	2 items; *Bild*/other tabloid newspapers as daily newspapers or online (r = .19)	1 – never, 6 – (almost) daily	2.29	1.72
national newspapers	2 items; nationwide newspapers as daily newspapers or online (r = .34)	1 – never, 6 – (almost) daily	2.03	1.49

	items	**answer categories**	**mean**	**standard deviations**
commercial television	4 items; *RTL Aktuell, 18.30/Sat 1 news* or *Pro 7 news* as television news programme or online (Cronbach's alpha = .73)	1 – never, 6 – (almost) daily	3.44	1.87
public service television	3 items; *Tagesschau* or *heute* as television news programme or online (Cronbach's alpha = .58)	1 – never, 6 – (almost) daily	4.76	1.66
authoritarian attitudes	4 items; among others – 'We should be grateful for leaders who can tell us what we shall do' (Cronbach's alpha = .78)	1 – does not apply, 6 – fully applies	3.22	1.11
fear of crime	6 items; fear of crime multiplied by likelihood estimate (victim in next 12 months) for six offences (Cronbach's alpha = .89)	1 – never and highly unlikely, 25 – very often and highly probable	4.88	2.98
subjective status	2 items; among others – 'How much of what you want can you afford to buy' (r = .54)	1 – severely disadvantaged, 4 – privileged	2.57	0.69

The last variable used in the analysis is subjective status. This can serve both as a demographic status variable and as a personal evaluation of that status. Subjective status proved to correlate with objective status, which is reflected among other things in people's income (Baier et al. 2001, p. 81). People with low incomes tend to feel more disadvantaged. At the same time, prejudice and right-wing extremism research shows that it is less the objective factors themselves and more people's subjective estimates of the factors that are of importance in the development of prejudices and stereotypes. Focus is thus placed on relative deprivation (cf. Rippl/Baier 2005, Wagern/Zick 1998). These findings have not previously been applied in the explanation of crime perceptions. It is possible that people who subjectively feel disadvantaged are also more sceptical regarding social trends. To a certain extent, they make negative social trends responsible for their own negative situation.

The findings of the OLS regressions confirm a significant relationship between subjective status and perceived trends in crime (Table 3.5): People of higher status assume a lower rise in crime rates. Other demographic factors, however, show a stronger relationship. In particular, the influence of the subjective status lessens considerably if personality factors used in Model IV are applied, meaning that it is less people's estimated status and more the personal character traits determining that status influence perceptions of crime.

A similarly somewhat stronger mediation process can be seen in regard to education: Low educated respondents more frequently state that crime is on the rise. This is, however, partly a result of their media consumption and personality: Because these individuals tend to watch more news on commercial television, read few national daily newspapers and are more authoritarian by nature, they perceive crime trends in a more negative light.[8] Nevertheless, when controlled for these factors, the level of education (like subjective status) continues to exert an influence, indicating that these variables do also operate independently.

The mediation processes just mentioned can be made visible by integrating the variables stepwise in the Models. Most important, however, is Model IV, which includes all factors at once. Firstly, this allows the conclusion that experience as a victim of crime is irrelevant when it comes to perceptions of crime. Thus, victims are neither more frequently (nor less frequently) of the opinion that crime is on the increase in Germany. Experiences of crime may be too far in the past to still have an effect. It might be necessary to consider the frequency of victimisation, given that Skogan (1987) has already shown that the fear of crime rises with repeated experience as a victim of crime. Also, other forms of victimisation may be studied. According to Quann and Hung (2002), domestic burglary has, for example, a stronger influence on fear compared with personal assaults.

A second finding is that perceptions of crime are most strongly influenced by fear of crime. Those who fear becoming a victim of crime tend to believe that crime is on the increase. A question is whether the relationship only runs in this direction or also in reverse. No longitudinal studies exist on this topic to date.

Apart from fear of crime, perceptions of crime also appear to be influenced by authoritarianism. However, authoritarianism ranks behind the influence of the media and demographic factors. This shows that media consumption plays an important role. Of great importance is consumption of news programmes broadcast by commercial television. These appear to present crime in such a way that viewers often conclude that crime is con-

8 The years-of-education variable correlates (Pearson r) .32 with reading national newspapers, -.09 with watching news on commercial television channels, and -.15 with authoritarianism. With the exception of fear of crime (-.08), no notable relationships exist with other variables in the model.

stantly on the increase. Balanced, subjective reporting of crime would thus be desirable.

Regarding the demographic factors, there is evidence that gender is a key influencing factor in perceptions of crime. Women are more frequently of the opinion that crime is on the increase. Older respondents share the same view. This confirms the assumptions of the vulnerability theory.

In sum, it can be concluded that perceptions of crime are influenced by multiple factors. The factors used in the survey, however, can only marginally explain the variance in perceptions. The knowledge and personality factors must thus be supplemented with further influencing factors. It would be interesting to analyse how social and political discourse on specific crime cases influence people's perceptions. This discourse is likely to vary at both local and regional level, and could thus serve as an explanatory factor for individually different perceptions.

Table 3.5 Influencing factors on perceptions of trends in crime; beta coefficients from OLS regressions shown (weighted data; number of cases = 3,123)

	Model I	**Model II**	**Model III**	**Model IV**
gender: female	.15 ***	.15 ***	.14 ***	.12 ***
years of education	-.14 ***	-.14 ***	-.11 ***	-.09 ***
age in years	.10 ***	.11 ***	.12 ***	.08 ***
subjective status	-.09 ***	-.09 ***	-.08 ***	-.05 **
victim of crime in past five years: theft		-.01	-.01	-.03
victim of crime in past five years: assault		.03	.03	.01
daily tabloid newspapers			.07 ***	.05 **
national newspapers			-.06 **	-.06 **
commercial television			.13 ***	.12 ***
public service television			.02	.02
authoritarian attitudes				.08 ***
fear of crime				.19 ***
Corr. R^2	**.073**	**.073**	**.098**	**.142**

* $p < .05$, ** $p < .01$, *** $p < .001$

3.5 Perceived trends in crime and punitivity

In the introduction, it was mentioned that Windzio et al. (2007) and others see a relationship between perceptions of crime and punitivity. A study by Streng (2000, p. 429) also links an increased need for punishment with a "significantly greater sense of threat of bodily injury, and in particular greater uncertainty due to the general crime situation". Here, the survey data are used to analyse whether such a link is reconfirmed empirically and to identify the type of causal relationship that exists between perceptions and punitivity.

Attitudes towards punishment were measured in two ways in the survey. Firstly, a scale with four items was used whose reliability can be classified as satisfactory in all three survey years (Cronbach's alpha at least . 80). The wording used in the four items is as follows: 'For many offenders, stricter sentencing is the only way to stop them repeating offences', 'Many offences should receive stricter sentences than has been the case to date', 'Stricter sentences are necessary to prevent others from committing crime,' and 'Prisons should treat prisoners more harshly.' (Answer categories: '1 – does not apply', to '6 – fully applies'). The mean was calculated from the answers to the four items; for better analysis, respondents were divided into three groups.[9] The second measure for punitivity illustrates attitudes towards the death penalty. Here, respondents were asked whether they were generally in favour of or against the death penalty, with the answer choices 'for', 'against' and 'undecided'.

Different findings resulted for both the level of and the trends in punitivity depending on the method of measurement punitivity (Figure 3.2). Based on the answers to the four items, around two-thirds of respondents have to be classified as being in favour of very strict sentencing, with this number remaining more or less constant across all three surveys.[10] Less than a third are explicitly in favour of the death penalty in 2006; this is significantly lower than in 2010. A comparison with 2004 is not possible because attitudes to the death penalty were not part of that survey. Nonetheless, there is a positive correlation between the two punitivity

9 Respondents scoring a mean of 1.0 to 2.67 are classified as least punitive, those ranging from 2.67 to 4.34 as moderately punitive, and those scoring between 4.34 and 6.00 as highly punitive.

10 Looking at the averages rather than the percentages, no decline in punitivity is evident (2004; 4.77; 2006: 4.62; 2010: 4.74).

scores, with the 'undecided' and 'against' groups combined when calculating the correlation. The correlation (Pearson's r) was .33 in 2006 and . 31 in 2010.

Fig. 3.2 Punitivity over time (in percent; weighted data)

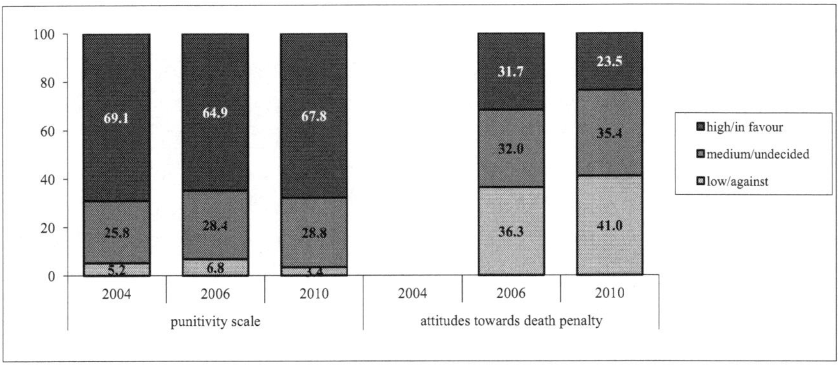

The correlations with the six items on the scale for perceived crime trends (closed answer format) are very similar, as shown in Table 3.6. This applies both when comparing the two attitude scores and when comparing the estimated trends in the different offences. The correlations with attitudes to the death penalty are somewhat lower than those for the punitivity scale; they are, however, all in the same direction as on the scale and are also significant. Assumed trends in fraud correlate slightly less well with punitivity levels than for other offences; the differences are not significant, however.

Table 3.6 Correlations (Pearson's r) between perceived trends in crime and punitivity (2010 survey; weighted data; all correlations significant at p < .05)

	punitivity scale	attitudes towards death penalty
fraud	.19	.10
assault	.25	.16
domestic burglary	.24	.12
car theft	.21	.13
murder	.25	.15
sexual murder	.23	.16

Given the observed correlations, it can be assumed that a significant relationship exists between perceived trends in crime and punitivity. Those who believe that crime is on the rise (regardless of which type of crime is involved), would like to see harsher treatment of offenders. Because the type of crime appears to be largely irrelevant, the relationship can be verified using the overall scale (see Table 3.7). The correlation is then .31, meaning that almost 10 percent of the variance in punitivity can be explained by perceived trends in crime. Controlling for other factors, this relationship is hardly weakened at all.[11] That a relationship exists cannot, therefore, be apportioned to personality traits or experiences as a victim of crime. Model II in Table 3.7 also shows that authoritarian attitudes are almost an equally strong predictor of punitive attitudes as perceived trends in crime. Media consumption continues to play an important role: People who frequently read tabloid newspapers or watch news programmes on commercial television call for stricter sentencing than those who inform themselves by reading national newspapers. Experience as a victim of crime has again no significant influence. Experience of assault actually reduces punitivity slightly. Higher education levels protect against punitive attitudes, while age and subjective status are irrelevant. Of particular interest is that women are less punitive. When it comes to gender, contradictory relationships are evident: Women tend to perceive a higher rate of crime, which leads to greater punitivity; at the same time, women are generally less punitive. Women's perceptions and attitudes are thus less balanced.

The findings underline that there is a stable relationship between perceived crime trends and punitivity which is not mediated by other factors. Nonetheless, the cause-effect relationship in the previous analyses remains unexplained because it was based on a cross-sectional survey conducted in 2010. The causal relationship between the two factors can additionally be investigated using the longitudinal studies from 2004 and 2006. For this purpose, a cross-lagged panel model is calculated for the 1,206 longitudinal cases in the two years using the Mplus 6.11 program as shown in Figure 3.3.

11 Looking at attitudes to the death penalty rather than the punitivity scale, the results do not change: The beta coefficient is .18 in Model I and .17 in Model II.

Table 3.7 Influencing factors for punitivity (scale); beta coefficients from OLS regressions shown (2010 survey; weighted data; number of cases = 3,114)

	Model I	Model II
perceived trends in crime	.31 ***	.24 ***
gender: female		-.05 **
years of education		-.08 ***
age in years		-.03
subjective status		-.02
victim of crime in past five years: theft		-.00
victim of crime in past five years: assault		-.03 *
daily tabloid newspapers		.09 ***
national newspapers		-.07 ***
commercial television		.06 *
public service television		-.03
authoritarian attitudes		.23 ***
fear of crime		.05 **
Corr. R^2	**.098**	**.193**

* p < .05, ** p < .01, *** p < .001

The models incorporate the constructs of perceived crime trends (closed-ended answer format) and punitivity (scale) for the two survey periods as latent variables. The factor loadings for the individual items can be classified as satisfactory across the board ($\lambda \geq .59$). Between the same items, error correlations are permitted over the years when they were significant (cf. Geiser 2010, p. 99ff). Also, for both survey periods a further significant error correlation was accepted per construct (between murder and sexual murder, and between the items 'For many offenders, stricter sentencing is the only way to stop them repeating offences' and 'Many offences should receive stricter sentences than has been the case to date.' The cause of the error correlation in the first instance may be that on both occasions, the issue is murder and when answering, respondents cognitively activate certain concepts of murder that has no relation to trends in crime.

Fig. 3.3 Cross-lagged panel model for estimated trends in crime and punitivity (number of cases = 1206; all paths/correlations significant at p < .01)

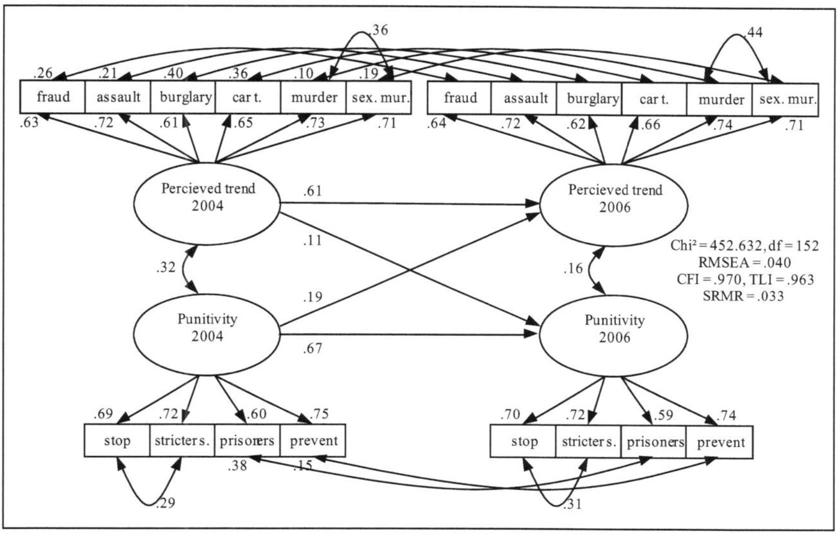

Both the perceived trends in crime and punitivity are stable over time. The coefficients (γ) varying between 0 and 1 or -1 attain a value of .61 or .67. More important, however, are the cross paths. It can be shown that at .19, the path from punitivity in 2004 to perceived trends in crime in 2006 is stronger than the reverse path (.11). Punitivity therefore appears to determine perceptions more than the other way around. A significance test shows, however, that the two paths do not significantly differ.[12] There is thus no reason to assume a clear causal relationship. The two factors determine each other to a rather same extent: Perceived trends in crime lead to greater punitivity and people who are more punitive perceive stronger trends in crime. Such perceptions can thus indeed be influential in the way proposed by Windzio et al. (2007), underscoring the need to focus on those perceptions and their influencing factors in social science research.

12 The significance test is performed by comparing two models. In the original model, the parameters are freely estimated, while in the restrictive model it is assumed that paths which cross adopt the same value. Because the more restrictive model shows no worser fit (Chi² = 453.482, df = 153), it can be assumed that the cross paths do not differ significantly.

3.6 Conclusion and discussion

The findings presented in this paper can be consolidated into three key results. Firstly, people over-estimate both the prevalence of and trends in crime. Negative perceptions dominate with regard to this topic, and they are particularly negative when it comes to estimate violent offences committed by juveniles.

Secondly, that such negative perceptions of crime are sustained is partly due to the media. News reporting in commercial television is especially worthy of criticism. Personal experience as a victim on the other side does not influence crime perceptions. Instead of direct experience of crime, it is indirect experience gained from the media that shapes people's perceptions of crime.

These perceptions have consequences. To an extent, the media create a reality that forms the basis for their reporting. If a rise in crime is perceived, this can lead to calls for stricter sentencing. If this becomes realty, then rather than a decline, a rise in crime may well be expected, which is then suitably reported in the media. The achieved results show, however, that it would seem not appropriate to demonise the media (cf. Pfeiffer 2004). Media consumption is only one influencing factor in perceptions of crime; and perceptions of crime are only one influencing factor in punitivity. Punitivity in turn influences perceptions of crime, as shown in the longitudinal studies.

Some findings from the analyses presented here have been insufficiently discussed to date. The evaluations of perceptions of crime have shown that, when it comes to the most observed offences, since 2004 perceptions have gradually adjusted to match actual trends in crime –especially for offences that are on the decline in Germany. The question which factors are responsible for that that trend is addressed by Baier at al. (2011 p. 147ff), who show that the percentage of people who were a victim of crime offences is dropping significantly. But because experience as a victim of crime has no relevance as an influencing factor of perceptions of crime, this trend fails to provide an adequate explanation. The situation is different regarding the findings on media consumption: The number of people who watch news programmes on commercial television or who read tabloid newspapers has almost halved over the six-year period. Also, there has been a rise in average education levels and a drop in the fear of crime. These trends provide an – albeit non-exhaustive – explanation for the changes in perceptions of crime.

One contradiction remains: The factors cited also influence punitivity which, at least as measured using the four-item scale, has remained high in recent years. Trends in punitivity have thus become decoupled from trends in other crime-related perceptions and attitudes. One possible hypothesis is that these trends reflect changes in media reporting. It is now the norm for certain criminal cases to be covered in all newspapers and programmes – even quality programmes and the broadsheet press are unable to ignore such cases. In such reporting, the public is told that the case in question is an isolated event, yet the focus on both the victims' suffering and that of their families helps keep punitivity levels high because people conclude that harsh sentencing is the only way to deal with the offenders. Victims are idealised as "likeable, weak and innocent", and "children make ideal victims" (Hestermann 2010, p. 199). When the media are 43 times more likely to report about children becoming victims of violence compared with older victims of violence, and when sexual murder (especially involving children) is ten times more likely to be reported than other types of murder (Hestermann 2010, p. 196 ff), it should be clear to the general public that such offences occur only rarely. But the offences are so monstrous that those who have committed them are not permitted a second chance – or any opportunity for resocialisation. Isolated cases thus heavily influence perceptions of offenders in general, and thus of how they should be punished.

References

Adorno, T.W., Frenkel-Brunswik, E., Levinson, D.J., Sanford, R.N. (1950). The Authoritarian Personality. New York: Science Editions.

Altemeyer, B. (1981). Right-Wing Authoritarianism. Winnipeg, Manitoba: The University of Manitoba Press.

Albrecht, H.-J. (2004): Öffentliche Meinung, Kriminalpolitik und Kriminaljustiz. In: M. Walter, H. Kania, H.-J. Albrecht (Eds.), Alltagsvorstellungen von Kriminalität. Individuelle und gesellschaftliche Bedeutung von Kriminalitätsbildern für die Lebensgestaltung. Münster: Lit.

Baier, D. (2011). Jugendgewalt in Deutschland – Eine Bestandsaufnahme. In: G. Deegener, W. Körner (Eds.), Gewalt und Aggression im Kindes- und Jugendalter (pp. 35-53). Ursachen, Formen, Intervention. Weinheim: Beltz.

Baier, D., Kemme, S., Hanslmaier, M., Doering, B., Rehbein, F., Pfeiffer, C. (2011). Kriminalitätsfurcht, Strafbedürfnisse und wahrgenommene Kriminalitätsentwicklung. Ergebnisse von bevölkerungsrepräsentativen Befragungen aus den Jahren 2004, 2006 und 2010. KFN: Forschungsbericht Nr. 117.

Butler, J.C. (2009). Authoritarianism and Fear of Deviance. North American Journal of Psychology, 11, 49-64.

Feldman, S. (2003). Enforcing Social Conformity: A Theory of Authoritarianism. Political Psychology, 24, 41-74.

Geiser, C. (2010). Datenanalyse mit Mplus. Eine anwendungsorientierte Einführung. Wiesbaden: VS Verlag.

Heinz , W. (2006). Kriminelle Jugendliche – gefährlich oder gefährdet? Konstanz: UVK Universitätsverlag.

Hestermann, T. (2010). Fernsehgewalt und die Einschaltquote. Welches Publikumsbild Fernsehschaffende leitet, wenn sie über Gewaltkriminalität berichten. Baden-Baden: Nomos-Verlag.

Hübner, M., Schmidt, P., Schürhoff, R., Schwarzer, S. (2008). Allgemeine Autoritarismus-Kurzform. In: A. Göchner-Rist (Ed.), Zusammenstellung sozialwissenschaftlicher Items und Skalen. ZIS Version 12.00. Bonn: GESIS.

Kreuter, F. (2002). Kriminalitätsfurcht: Messung und methodische Probleme. Opladen: Leske+Budrich.

Krüger, U.M. (2010). InfoMonitor: 2009. Fernsehnachrichten bei ARD, ZDF, RTL und Sat.1. Media Perspektiven 2/2010, 50-72.

Lehnert, S. (2010). Forschungsbericht. Fortsetzung der Inhaltsanalyse über Kriminalität im Fernsehangebot mit Auswertungen des Jahres 2007 und 2009. Hamburg.

Lüdemann, C. (2006). Kriminalitätsfurcht im urbanen Raum – Eine Mehrebenenanalyse zu individuellen und sozialräumlichen Determinanten verschiedener Dimensionen von Kriminalitätsfurcht. Kölner Zeitschrift für Soziologie und Sozialpsychologie, 58, 285-306.

Pantazis, C. (2000). Fear of Crime, Vulnerability and Poverty: Evidence from the British Crime Survey. British Journal of Criminology, 40, 414-436.

Pfeiffer, C. (2004). Dämonisierung des Bösen. Frankurter Allgemeine Zeitung vom 5.3.2004.

Pfeiffer, C., M. Windzio, M. Kleimann (2005). Media Use and its Impacts on Crime Perception, Sentencing Attitudes and Crime Policy. European Journal of Criminology, 2, 259-285.

Quann, N., Hung, K. (2002). Victimization Experience and the Fear of Crime. A Cross-National Study. In: P. Nieuwbeerta (Ed.), Crime Victimization in Comparative Perspective. Results from the International Crime Victims Survey, 1989–2000 (pp. 301–316). The Hague: NSCR, BJU.

Rippl, S., Baier, D. (2005). Das Deprivationskonzept in der Rechtsextremismusforschung. Eine vergleichende Analyse. Kölner Zeitschrift für Soziologie und Sozialpsychologie, 57, 644-666.

Schneider, H.J. (1991). Massenmedien. In: R. Sieverts, H.J. Schneider (Eds.), Handwörterbuch der Kriminologie (pp. 301.324). Band 5. Berlin: De Gruyter,.

Schwacke, B. (1983). Kriminalitätsdarstellung in der Presse. Frankfurt am Main: Peter Lang Verlag.

Skogan, W.G. (1987). The Impact of Victimization on Fear. Crime and Delinquency, 33, 135-154.

Streng, F. (2000): Die heranwachsende Juristengeneration und die Aufgabe des Strafrechts. Die Bewährungshilfe, 47, 422-435.

Wagner, U., Zick, A. (1998). Ausländerfeindlichkeit, Vorurteile und diskriminierendes Verhalten. In: H.W. Bierhoff, U. Wagner (Eds.), Aggression und Gewalt: Phänomene, Ursachen und Interventionen (pp. 145-164). Stuttgart: Kohlhammer.

Windzio, M., Simonson, J., Pfeiffer, C., Kleimann, M. (2007). Kriminalitätswahrnehmung und Punitivität in der Bevölkerung – Welche Rolle spielen die Massenmedien? Ergebnisse der Befragungen zu Kriminalitätswahrnehmung und Strafeinstellungen 2004 und 2006. KFN: Forschungsbericht Nr. 103.

4. Adolescents as Victims of Violence

Dirk Baier, Susann Prätor

4.1 Introduction and purpose of the study

According to the German Police Crime Statistics, adolescents and older youths – individuals aged 14 to 20 – have the greatest prevalence of violent crime both as victims and perpetrators. Therefore various studies in Germany have addressed violence in this age group with special focus on prevalence and determinants of perpetratorship. These studies on violent behaviour as well as on victimisation have one limitation in common: They are not representative[1] for Germany, but only for specific regions (mostly cities or federal states) or types of school. In 2007 and 2008, the Criminological Research Institute of Lower Saxony conducted the first nationally representative self-report study among juveniles. Presenting the results of that study is the purpose of this paper.

The focus in the present study is on forms of physical violence that are prosecuted under criminal law and can therefore be compared with Police Crime Statistics. These violent acts are robbery, extortion, sexual violence and (aggravated) assault. In the survey we asked for committing such violent acts as perpetrator as well experiencing these acts as victims. Experience of victimisation in school context, which was already a subject of earlier studies (cf. e.g. Fuchs et al. 2005, Holtappels et al. 1997) is likewise included; assaults of this kind mostly take place in largely controlled surroundings, however, and are therefore likely to be of minor severity.

Three past studies shed initial light on violent behaviour of adolesencts in Germany. In 1998, Wetzels et al. (2001) surveyed over 16,000 mostly ninth-grade adolescents in nine cities about their experience of violence. At least a fifth of adolescents reported that they experienced at least one of the above-mentioned forms of violence in the preceding year, but only a

---

1 Representative means that elements of a population (here: pupils in Germany) have been randomly selected (cf. Schnell et al. 2005, p. 304). With regard to past self-report studies, pupils were randomly selected only on the level of cities, regions or federal states but not for Germany in total.

small proportion of those offences were reported to the police. The risk of an offence being reported to the police was especially high for non-German perpetrators whose victims were of German origin. As this is a relatively common perpetrator-victim combination, rising crime rates in the Police Crime Statistics may be "seen as a phenomenon of violent delinquency becoming more visible because of an increase in the one perpetrator-victim combination that has the greatest likelihood of being reported" (Wetzels et al. 2001, p. 169).

Baier et al. (2006) confirmed this finding in a survey among over 14,000 adolescents carried out in nine cities and administrative districts. In this survey, victim rates in these areas ranged from 16.4 to 21.9 percent. About one in 25 adolescents also said they had experienced at least five violent acts. The most common form of violence was assault; the lowest rate was found for extortion. With the exception of sexual offences, victimization rates of boys are significantly higher in comparison to girls.

In 2006, Enzmann (2010) conducted a survey among 3,400 seventh to ninth grades adolescents (i.e. pupils aged 13 to 15) in seven German cities as part of the Second International Self-Report Delinquency Study (Junger-Tas et al. 2010). Enzmann (2010) reports that a third of all adolescents experienced at least one victimisation in the year before the survey, with theft being included in the survey alongside violence. Victimisation rates in cities were much higher than in towns. Once again, incidents were rarely reported to the police (robbery: 15.4 percent, assault: 10.4 percent).

The findings from these studies, which are relatively similar with regard to prevalence rates of victimisation and violent behaviour, support the assumption that a nationally representative survey would produce similar results. The present study, however, extends the focus of previous studies in several ways and, by taking various aspects into account, provides a more comprehensive picture of victimisation experienced by adolescents in Germany. The central research issues addressed in this paper can be summarised in four points:

1. Based on extensive data, the paper starts with a detailed description of different kinds of violence experienced. The analysis is more detailed because it combines different groups (for example by gender and ethnic origin), covers different types of violent offence and also looks at various contexts in which victimisation takes place (victimisation at home, in school, etc.). With regard to criminal forms of victimisation,

the paper also aims to provide a comparison with the Police Crime Statistics.

2. The paper also addresses the question how violence has developed in the last decade on the basis of self-report survey data. This development shall be compared with Police Crime Statistics in order to investigate if violence has actually increased or has merely become more visible (in Police Crime Statistics). This can be answered by looking at a small number of cities where repeated surveys have been conducted. Although these repeated surveys are not sufficient to draw conclusions at national level, they allow inferring certain trends.
3. Due to the meaning of reporting behaviour for the ratio between reported and unreported crime, we further analyse the willingness to report violent acts to the police. The paper aims to determine the reporting propensity for various types of offence and trends in reporting behaviour in the four cities in which repeat surveys have been carried out. Additionally, we try to explain reporting behaviour by offence, perpetrator and victim variables.
4. In order to identify factors influencing violent offending, cross-sectional data is often used. This approach is legitimated by well-developed theories and numerous sets of empirical findings that provide longitudinal or experimental evidence of a directional relationship. With regard to violent victimisation theoretical explanatory approaches or empirically supported findings are almost completely missing. Nonetheless, this paper subjects a number of potential influencing factors related to violent victimisation to bivariate and multivariate analysis. Furthermore we will also investigate consequences of violent victimisation; this includes both short-term consequences (injury and material loss) and long-term consequences (well-being).

4.2 The samples

The empirical analysis in this paper is based on written standardised surveys among ninth grade pupils[2] conducted by the Criminological Research Institute of Lower Saxony in various regions of Germany at irregular intervals since 1998. Questionnaires were completed in the classroom in the

2 In Germany ninth-grade pupils are ususally aged between 14 and 16 years.

presence of a test leader and usually the teacher. Ninth-grade pupils are chosen because a representative survey can be achieved with lower effort and this is an age group with particularly high exposure to violence both as perpetrators and victims. After ninth grade, educational careers diverge rapidly: Some leave school and enter vocational training, others leave school without a training place, and some stay at school to achieve a higher secondary school leaving qualification. With some exceptions (i.e. truants, those who are ill at the day of the survey), nearly all adolescents can be achieved in such a survey. Ninth-grade surveys are designed to be representative for the survey region – usually towns and cities or administrative districts. Representativeness is achieved either by including all ninth-grade classes in the survey or selecting classes to survey at random from a list of all classes. The survey always aims to cover a large number of pupils to produce reliable findings about offences that occur rather seldom. As entire classes are included in the survey, very high response rates are achieved of at least 50-60 percent.

Two samples are selected for the analysis (Table 4.1): A nationally representative survey of school students in Germany and a repeated survey in four German towns and cities. With regard to the repeated survey the same age cohort (ninth grade pupils) but not the same pupils were interviewed twice, i.e. this is a trend and not a longitudinal sample. The national schools survey took place in 2007 and 2008 in a total of 61 randomly selected administrative districts, towns and cities in Germany (cf. Baier et al. 2009 for further details on the study). The survey reached 44,610 adolescents. The trend study was conducted in 1998 and 2005/2006 in three major cities and one town.[3] The first survey covered 7,205 pupils and the second survey 8,490 pupils (cf. Baier 2008).The composition of both samples does not perfectly match that of the statistical population in terms of school type. Thus a weighting factor was constructed to correct any imbalance (i.e. if too many grammar schools were surveyed in a given area). If not explicitly mentioned the following analyses are based on weighted data.

3 Only in Hannover the repeated survey was conducted in 2006.

Table 4.1 Sample description

	Schools survey 2007/2008	Trend survey	
		1998	2005/2006
Representativeness	Nationwide	4 towns and cities (Munich, Stuttgart, Hannover, Schwäbisch Gmünd)	
Number of respondents	44,610	7,205	8,490
Percentage male	51.3	51.9	51.2
Average age	15.28	15.07	15.16
Percentage with migrant background	27.4	32.2	31.7
Percentage from major city	13.5	96.1	95.8
Percentage attending grammar school (*Gymnasium*)	29.8	38.9	41.0

In the various samples, about half of respondents were male and the average age is slightly more than 15. The samples differ substantially in some cases with regard to other socio-demographic characteristics. The trend survey almost exclusively comprises pupils from major cities with a population of at least 500,000; in the representative survey, only 13.5 percent of the pupils come from such cities. Grammar schools account for 29.8 percent of schools nationwide but approximately 40 percent of schools in the trend survey. In the representative survey, 27.4 percent of pupils have a migration background, i.e. at least one biological parent does not have German citizenship or was not born in Germany. The percentage reported for the trend survey is somewhat higher but is comparable to that for the nationwide survey as nationality is determined solely by reference to the respondent's current nationality or nationality at birth. This solution had to be taken out of necessity on account of migrant background being recorded differently in different years. In other surveys among pupils in major German cities, migrant background was recorded the same as in the representative survey, resulting in proportions of migrants around 40 percent or more (e.g. Baier/Pfeiffer 2011 for Berlin, Rabold et al. 2008 for Hannover).

4.3 Findings

4.3.1 Prevalence of violent victimisation

Violent victimisation was measured by three different questions: First, pupils were asked about criminal victimisation, second about victimisation in school and third about parental violence. The focus always was on physical assault; verbal or relational forms of aggression[4] were only asked with regard to the school context. The findings on criminal violent victimisation will be presented first; this form of victimisation can be compared with Police Crime Statistics. The following analyses are based on the national representative survey.

Adolescents were asked about their experience of victimisation with the question "Has anyone ever been violent towards you, have you ever been a victim of violence?" and, by way of explanation, "We do not mean situations where you have fought with others for fun." This was followed by questions on five offences:

- Robbery: "Something was violently snatched from you or taken from you with the threat of violence such as your bag or money."
- Extortion: "Someone demanded that you hand over money or things (such as a jacket or a watch) and threatened you with violence if you did not hand them over."
- Sexual assault: "You were forced with violence or under threat of violence to perform sexual acts or to tolerate sexual acts."
- Aggravated assault: "You were intentionally injured with a weapon or an object or several others intentionally hit you so hard that you were injured."
- Assault: "A single person intentionally hit you so hard that you were injured (e.g. with a bleeding wound or a black eye). No weapon or object was used."

With regard to these offences, respondents were asked about lifetime prevalence (whether or not they had ever experienced these offences), the number of attacks in the last twelve months (twelve-month prevalence/ twelve-month incidence) and the age in years at which they first experi-

4 Relational aggression means behaviour intended to harm others through damage of their peer relationships, for example by spreading rumours or exclusion from common activities (cf. Crick 1995).

enced the offences. The results are presented in Table 4.2. In addition to the individual offences, a catch-all 'violence' category is also reported. This indicates whether someone experienced at least one of the five offences and at what age any one of the offences was experienced for the first time.

With regard to sexual assault, 2.2 percent of students said they had experienced at least one act in their life; assault was significantly more frequent (20.1 percent). Almost a third of respondents experienced criminal victimisation at least once (30.5 percent) in their life so far. The twelve-month prevalence is about half of these figures. No less than 16.8 percent of pupils experienced at least one violent offence in the past year. Pupils victimised in the past twelve months were assaulted on average between 2.60 times (robbery) and 4.59 times (sexual assault). This does not mean that a majority experienced repeated victimisation; between 49.2 and 61.0 percent of victims (according to the offence) were victimised only once in the preceding year; the higher means are due to respondents who were victimised on a large number of occasions.[5] The fact that it is mostly sexual assaults that tend to be repeated is shown by the percentage of pupils who were victims of offences on at least five occasions: For sexual assault this figure is 26.5 percent, while for robbery and extortion it is only 12.6 percent; i.e. one in four respondents who experienced sexual assault did so at least five times in the past year. Such victims only account for 0.3 percent of all students, however, sexual assaults are the least common form of offence. Of all respondents, 3.9 percent stated that they had experienced violent assaults five times or more in the past twelve months.

On average, violent victimisation is first experienced around the age of twelve. Notably, the stated ages at first victimisation are somewhat lower than in surveys that are representative of the entire population and include older age groups. The adolescents surveyed have an average age of 15; those who have had no experience of violence so far may yet do so at some point in the future, which would increase the average age at first victimisation. The age at first victimisation is lowest for robbery (11.53 years) and highest for aggravated asault (12.76 years). The survey also records the average age at which the various crimes are perpetrated. Perpetration was recorded elsewhere on the questionnaire analogously to vic-

5 The reported incidence figures are an underestimate because respondents were only able to state up to 20 incidents of victimisation. Answer categories were 0, 1, 2,... to '20 or more times'.

timisation. The prevalence rates for perpetration are somewhat lower (cf. Baier et al. 2009, p. 64); for example, only 13.5 percent of respondents have perpetrated at least one violent offence. The average ages at first offence are significantly higher; only for assault the difference is about six months. This does not necessarily mean that victimisation is a causal factor of later offending. Firstly, any such relationship would have to be examined with longitudinal data. A number of studies are able to confirm a directional relationship of this kind (cf. Baier 2013, Schwartz et al. 1998). Secondly, the victims and perpetrators group in cross-sectional surveys are not usually identical. The comparison of age at first victimisation and first offence would at least have to be restricted to respondents who are both victims and perpetrators. Applying this to the sample used here shows that for the various forms of offences, victimisation preceded perpetration in at least 40 percent of cases; it is rarer for the two to come in the opposite order or at the same age. Thus, experience of victimisation seems to precede offending rather than the other way round.

Table 4.2 Prevalence rates and age at first victimisation for various offences (percent or means)

	Lifetime prevalence	**12-month prevalence**	**Incidence in past 12 months**	**Victims: at least 5 offences in past 12 months**	**Overall: at least 5 offences in past 12 months**	**Age at first victimisation**	**Age at first offence**
robbery	10.6	4.8	2.60	12.6	0.6	11.53	13.30
extortion	5.9	2.6	3.46	21.5	0.6	11.68	13.57
sexual assault	2.2	1.0	4.59	26.2	0.3	11.98	13.55
aggravated assault	5.4	3.2	3.31	19.3	0.6	12.76	13.71
assault	20.1	11.1	3.08	18.1	2.0	12.23	12.85
violence	30.5	16.8	4.21	23.3	3.9	11.74	12.81

There is a marked gender gap with regard to both prevalence rates and the age at first victimisation, as shown in Figure 4.1. With the exception of sexual assault, male respondents experienced the various forms of violent offences significantly more frequently than girls in the past twelve months. At least one violent offence in the past twelve months was reported by 20.2 percent of boys compared with 13.0 percent of girls. However, the first experience of violence tends to come at a somewhat earlier age for girls than for boys, at least with regard to extortion, aggravated assault and assault. This could be a milieu effect: Girls who experience violence may grow up more frequently in social milieus where physical violence is more widespread. Confrontation with violence then tends to come at an earlier age. With boys, in contrast, experience of violence is not concentrated on such milieus, but is an experience that belongs to the world of male children and adolescents across all groups. Where boys and girls become victims of violence, there is scarcely any difference with regard to frequency: 23.8 percent of male victims and 22.4 percent of female victims reported having experienced five or more violent offences. An exception is experience of sexual assault, where substantially more male victims than female victims stated they had been assaulted on repeated occasions (65.0 percent versus 17.8 percent). Boys are thus significantly less frequently exposed to sexual assault; when they are, however, in most cases it is on multiple occasions.

*Fig. 4.1 Prevalence rates and age at first victimisation for various offences, by gender (percent or means; *differences significant at p < .05)*

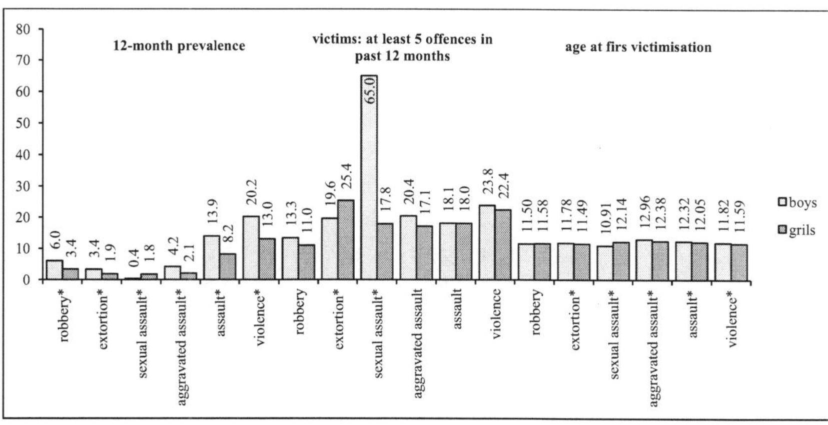

The differences in victimisation rates between the various ethnic groups are not as pronounced as the gender differences (Figure 4.2). Comparing German respondents against respondents with a migrant background, the percentages who have experienced at least one violent offence are 16.2 percent versus 17.6 percent. The rates are also similar if sexual assault is looked at separately (1.0 percent versus 1.1 percent). Looking at the data for specific ethnic groups, more differences in violence rates can be found. Migrants from Asian countries have the lowest prevalence rate for assault (including sexual assault) in the past year, and migrants from countries of the former Yugoslavia the highest; sexual assault is experienced most frequently by African adolescents. Prevalence rates for the two largest migrant groups living in Germany – Turkish students and students from countries of the former Soviet Union (SU) – are equal to those for their German schoolmates. Figure 4.2 additionally shows the percentage of migrants who have experienced racially motivated assaults (hate crimes) at least once in their life.[6] This type of offence was included in a questionnaire module addressed solely to migrants (cf. Baier et al. 2010, p. 41ff). Of all migrants, 2.2 percent said they had been injured this way in their lifetime to date. Once again adolescents from countries of the former Yugoslavia have the highest prevalence rates while Polish adolescents rarely experienced this kind of violent behaviour.

Fig. 4.2 Prevalence rates of various offences by migrant background (in percent)

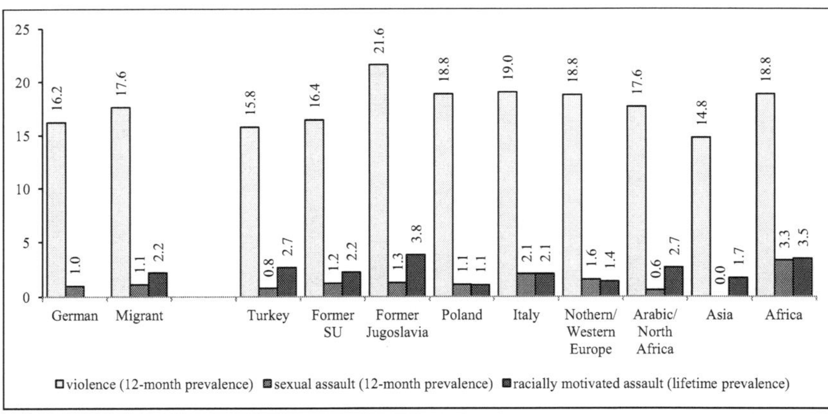

The offences were described in the questionnaire in such a way that comparison is possible with data on offences in the Police Crime Statistics. Among other information, the Police Crime Statistics state the number of adolescent (age 14 to 17) victims of criminal offences and in particular violent offences. The way the data are collected is nonetheless not fully compatible: In self-report studies, respondents ultimately decide how they

6 The question in the questionnaire was "I was hit and injured because I am not a native German.".

classify a given experience; the classification of criminal acts in the Police Crime Statistics is the responsibility of police officers largely working to objective criteria. The Police Crime Statistics do not have a standardised classification for extortion; hence no comparison is made with regard to this form of offence.[7] Comparison of reported crime and self-report data shows that prevalence rates are at least four times higher in self-report data. Aggravated assault is reported to police by only 0.77 percent of adolescents, whereas in the survey, 3.2 percent said they had experienced such an injury. The discrepancy is particularly large for rape, which is stated 20 times as often in the self-report survey as it is reported to the police. For robbery, too, there is a considerable difference between the two sources. The key factor in the discrepancy between reported and unreported crime is reporting behaviour. Not all offences committed are reported to or discovered by the police. People appear to be least inclined to report offences in the case of violent sexual offences. As victims' reporting behaviour was asked about in the survey, these assumptions can be empirically investigated (see below).

Fig. 4.3 Prevalence rates for various offences in the Police Crime Statistics and in the 2007/2008 schools survey (in percent)[8]

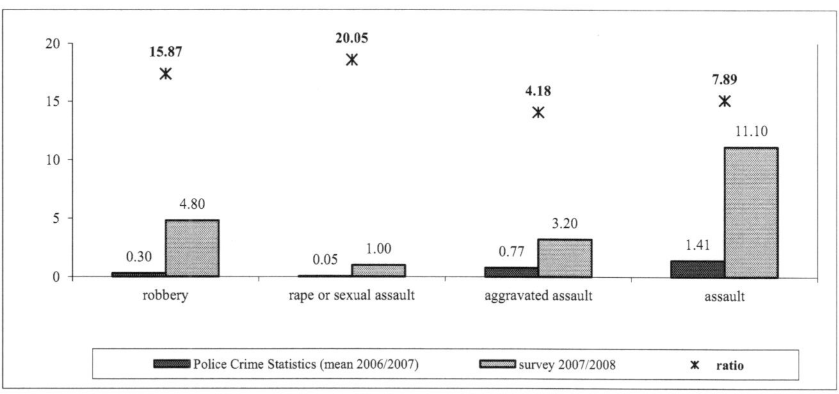

7 Extortion is recorded in the Police Crime Statistics under both category 6100 (extortion) and category 2100 (robbery, extortion accompanied by violence, and assault on motorists with intent to rob).

8 As respondents were asked in the questionnaire to state victimisation experienced in the past twelve months (i.e. in 2006 and 2007), the figures were taken from the Police Crime Statistics for 2006 and 2007.

Spotlight 1: School violence

The school is a special social space for adolescents. They spend a substantial part of their day there, are mostly together with others of their own age but are almost constantly under adult supervision. On the one hand it should therefore come as no surprise that when peers of the same age are frequently together, conflicts can arise that may be played out with violence. On the other hand, the adult supervision ought to prevent such conflicts from taking a serious course. Physical assault represents only one part of the potential forms of escalation. Damage to property, theft and more subtle types of aggression (such as relational aggression) also play a part. To take in the full range of aggressive acts, five school-related forms of victimisation were asked about, including victimisation by teachers as well as by schoolmates:

- Physical violence: This was covered by answers relating to two items: "I was intentionally hit or kicked by schoolmates" and "Schoolmates blackmailed me or forced me to hand over money or things."
- Damage to property: Pupils were asked here to answer how frequently "schoolmates deliberately damaged their things."
- Relational aggression: Three items in the questionnaire relate to this form of aggression ("Schoolmates teased me or said bad things about me", "I was excluded from common activities because schoolmates wanted it that way" and "Schoolmates acted as if I was not there and deliberately ignored me").
- Mental violence by teachers: Pupils were asked if they were made a laughing stock in front of schoolmates or if a teacher had been really mean to them.
- Physical violence by teachers: Pupils were asked here if they had been "hit by a teacher".

The answers were intended to relate to the past half school year and could be given on a scale from 'never' to 'more than once a week'. If a form of aggression was measured across several items, the maximum was recorded.[9] Figure 4.4 shows the proportion of adolescents who experienced the various forms of violence at most several times a month and the proportion of adolescents who experienced that at least once a week. An overall

9 For example, if a pupil was teased but not excluded, the answer for teasing was recorded in the relational aggression index.

bullying index is also shown, stating how many adolescents experienced at least one form of violence (from peers, not from teachers).

A total of 21.3 percent of respondents said that they were exposed to physical violence, with about one in 80 pupils (1.2 percent) saying that they had such experiences more frequently (at least once a week). Damage to property was less frequently and relational forms of aggression were significantly more frequent. Over half of all pupils were subjected to at least one form of violence in the past half school year, with 5.8 percent exposed to frequent bullying. At an average class size of 20, this means that on average there is one bullying victim per class. Attacks by teachers are likewise no exception, although they mostly take verbal form: 37.6 percent of pupils said they had experienced verbal denigration (mental violence), while 2.4 percent reported physical violence.

Fig. 4.4 Prevalence rates for school violence (in percent)

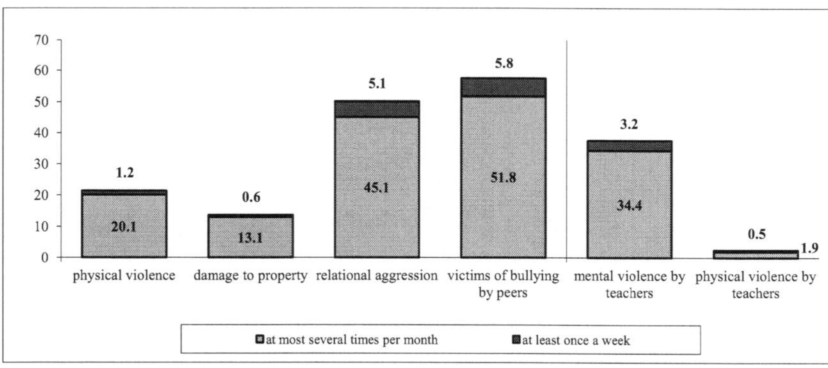

Physical forms of violence occur more frequently at lower school types (*Hauptschule*) than higher school types (grammar school/*Gymnasium*). However, pupils at higher school types more frequently reported having been victims of relational aggression (by schoolmates or teachers). A similar effect can be observed for gender: Girls experience physical violence significantly less frequently than boys but show a higher prevalence of relational aggression by schoolmates.

Spotlight 2: Parental violence

In addition to victimisation in school, the survey also provides information on experiences of violence in the family, dealt out by the parents. Pupils were asked to say if their father or mother showed any of the behaviours in Figure 4.5 before they reached the age of twelve; the items are based on the conflict-tactic scale according to Strauss (1979). The various forms of violence are asked about separately for the father and the mother; in the following, however, the two items are combined by taking the maximum response, i.e. if a pupil experienced violence from the father but not from the mother, the answer for the father is included.[10] The frequency was scored on a scale from 1 (never) to 6 (several times a week). As choices upwards of 4 (several times a month) were selected very rarely, Figure 4.5 only distinguishes between sporadic (once or twice) and recurring (three times or more) experience of violence. The various forms of violence are compiled into two index values. The 'minor violence' index comprises the first three items and the 'severe violence' index the remaining three. Once again, the maximum value was coded in each case. In other words, if a pupil only received a clip around the ear but not rough grappling or throwing of an object, the value for the clip around the ear was included in the index.

Fig. 4.5 Childhood experience of various forms of parental violence (in percent)

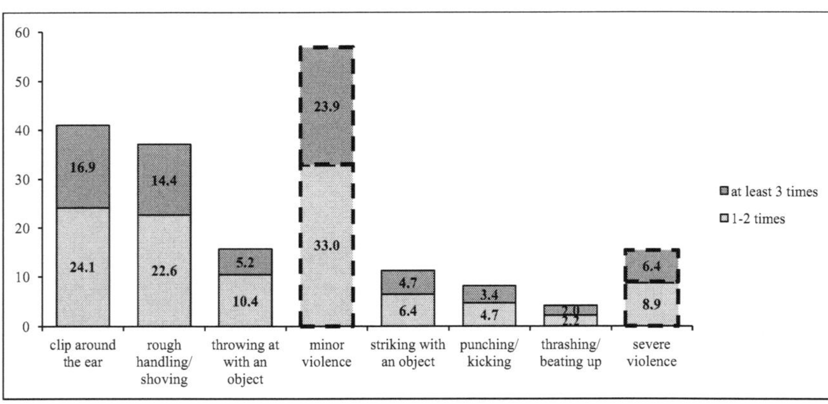

10 The correlations between the answers in relation to respondents' mothers and those in relation to their fathers are at least .40 (Person's r). Separate analysis by parent gender also show that mothers and fathers display violence towards children in almost identical ways (Baier et al. 2009, p. 53).

As Figure 4.5 shows, the majority of respondents reported at least minor violence in childrearing, with 56.9 percent of adolescents saying they had experienced such violence, mostly in the form of a clip around the ear or being roughly handled. Somewhat more adolescents reported one or two acts than more frequent incidents. No less than one in seven adolescents (15.3 percent) experienced severe violence in childhood, with 6.4 percent experiencing such violence at least three times.

Male and female respondents do not differ concerning intrafamilial experience of violence. Both sexes reported both minor and severe parental violence with equal frequency. There are pronounced differences, however, between ethnic groups: While only 11.4 percent of native Germans reported having experienced severe parental violence at least once, the equivalent figure for students with migrant backgrounds is more than twice as high at 25.2 percent. The lowest rates can be found for Northern and Western European adolescents (15.9 percent) while Asiatic, African and Turkish adolescents have particularly frequent experience of such violence (above 27 percent).

There is a close correspondence between being a victim of violence in the family and being subject to violent victimisation elsewhere. This connection is even stronger for female respondents than for male respondents, confirming findings that the experience of parental violence generally appears to have more serious consequences for girls (for example with regard to the risk of becoming perpetrators of violence themselves; cf. Baier 2011). Girls with more frequent (at least 3 times) experience of severe parental violence in childhood have a higher violent victimisation rate in terms of criminal offences than boys (38.6 versus 34.2 percent); these rates are also at least twice as high as for respondents without experience of parental violence (10.2 percent for girls, 18.4 percent for boys). The connection is likewise confirmed for school violence, although in this case girls subjected to intrafamilial violence do not attain the same level as boys. Various reasons can be put forward why victims of violence tend to become repeat victims. One possible explanation is that adolescents who experience violence at home seek out friends and free time activities with a certain affinity to violence. It is also possible that the experience of violence shapes the personality in such a way (with low self-esteem and timidity) that perpetrators preferentially seek out such individuals as victims.

4.3.2 Trends in violent victimisation

According to the Police Crime Statistics, the number of adolescents who became victims of violent crime increased significantly between 1997 and 2005, from 32,423 to 39,432, but then decreased again to 30,953 in 2010.[11] As the number of adolescents in Germany decreased between 2005 and 2010, it is not accurate to compare absolute victim numbers. Instead, these must be placed in relation to the number of adolescents, which is done by stating the number of victims per 100,000 population – in this case the number of adolescents becoming victims of a criminal offence per 100,000 of the same age group. The number of victims per 100,000 rose from 886.5 (1997) to 1,019.3 (2005) and then decreased only slightly up to 2010 (955.8). Victimisation risk thus increased between 1997 and 2005 for adolescents in Germany regardless of how the figures are looked at. These two years have been chosen for analysis because the trend sample surveys were carried out in 1998 and 2005/2006 to collate twelve-month prevalence figures that consequently related to the years 1997 and 2004/2005. Looking at individual violent offences, however, the conclusion that there has been a general rise in victimisation risk cannot be maintained: For robbery-related offences, the number of victims per 100,000 decreased over the period in question (from 381.8 to 291.0); there has only been an increase in the number of victims per 100,000 for rape (from 41.5 to 51.9) and aggravated assault (from 457.3 to 673.2).[12]

The self-report survey findings (which only relate to four towns and cities) contradict the trends in the Police Crime Statistics in several ways (Figure 4.6). Firstly, the percentage of adolescents who have experienced at least one violent offence in the past year has decreased from 21.4 percent to 19.1 percent. Secondly, both for sexual assault and aggravated assault, victimisation rates prove to be broadly constant with no perceptible increase. Thirdly, prevalence rate for assaults shows only a slight increase from 11.8 percent to 12.9 percent. Fourthly, prevalence rates for robbery fell even more steeply on the basis of the self-report survey data than in the reported statistics (from 6.5 percent to 4.1 percent). Generally speak-

11 In the Police Crime Statistics, the violent crime category covers murder and manslaughter, rape, robbery, and aggravated assault; this only partly corresponds with the violent offences covered in the survey of students.

12 Assaults, which are not classified as violent crime in the Police Crime Statistics, likewise shows an increase (from 811.0 to 1,275.7).

ing, the self-report survey findings allow a less dramatic picture to be painted than do the Police Crime Statistics. Youth violence remains broadly constant or is on a slight decreasing trend; there is no sign of any sharp increases. These discrepancies between official crime statistics and self-report survey data can largely be explained by trends in reporting behaviour (see below).

*Fig. 4.6 Prevalence rates for various offences, by survey year in percent; LP: lifetime prevalence; 12-MP: 12-month prevalence; * differences significant at p < .05)*

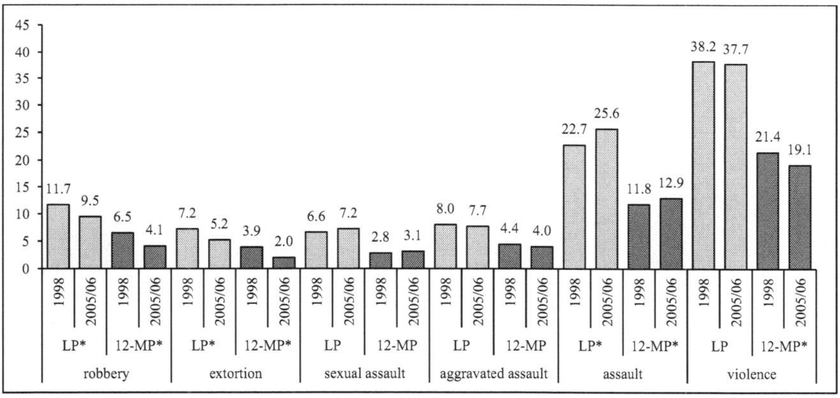

With regard to school violence, comparison of the survey years shows only a slight decrease in relational forms of aggression (cf. Baier 2008, p. 29ff). Experience of parental violence, on the other hand, shows a significant decrease: In 1998, 59.1 percent of adolescents said they had experienced minor or severe parental violence in childhood, in 2005/2006 the figure was down to 48.2 percent (Baier 2008, p. 50). Both German and migrant families display declining trends. The improvement is largely restricted to minor forms of violence, however; there are only small (insignificantly) differences between severe forms of violence reported in 2005/2006 and in 1998 respectively. The finding that there has been a decrease in parental violence (and especially minor forms of violence) is in line with surveys among other age groups. For example, comparison of two victim surveys representative of the German population (age 16 to 40) in 1992 and 2011 shows nonviolent childrearing to have increased from 26.4 percent to 52.1 percent (minor violence down from 58.4 percent to

36.0 percent; severe violence from 15.2 percent to 11.9 percent).[13] A decrease in the experience of parental violence also emerges on analysis of the various age groups from the 2011 victimisation survey (Pfeiffer 2012).

Analysis of the trend sample can also rebut two further assumptions about changes in youth violence: Firstly, there are no indications that adolescents are showing greater brutality today when they exercise violence. In fact, the opposite trend applies. In cases of assault, the number of victims who have to seek medical attention for their injuries is decreasing (cf. Baier 2008, p. 24). The second assumption is that girls are now more frequently involved in violence, not only as victims but also as perpetrators. The data show on this point that both the victimisation and offense rates are falling both for boys and for girls, with the gender gap remaining largely constant (see Baier 2008, p. 22 and 29).

4.3.3 Phenomenological description of assaults and of reporting behaviour

In order to describe characteristics and circumstances of youth violence in detail, adolescents who had become victims of violence were asked to report various details on the most recent victimisation. This was done solely with regard to violent criminal offences.

As Table 4.3 shows, only up to a quarter of such violent crime takes place at school or on the way to school; with sexual assault this is very rare indeed. Almost half of all sexual assault takes place at home/at relatives and at friends, i.e. in places which should actually be sheltered surroundings. This is in line with findings of a victimisation survey on sexual abuse among children and adolescents conducted by the Criminological Research Institute of Lower Saxony in 2011: Of all victims of sexual abuse with physical contact, over three quarters of respondents reported the perpetrator to be a (male) relative or acquaintance (Stadler et al. 2012, p. 36).

A relatively large proportion of youth violence takes place elsewhere. It is not possible to give detailed information on where such violence took place because respondents were not given an opportunity to provide this information. It can be inferred from another survey that the locations in-

---

13 Identical items were used for parental violence in the two survey years.

volved include public spaces such as roads, squares, playgrounds and parks (see Baier et al. 2010a, p. 44).

Table 4.3 Selected characteristics of the most recently experienced offence (in percent)

		robbery (N=957)	**extortion (N=438)**	**sexual assault (N=211)**	**aggravated assauls (N=527)**	**assault (N=3579)**
Location of assault	School/on way to school	21.8	24.9	7.5	14.3	25.4
	At home/relatives	8.1	5.6	21.0	3.8	9.5
	Friends	3.3	2.8	24.5	1.8	3.9
	Public transport	14.3	18.4	4.0	15.9	9.5
	Elsewhere	52.5	48.2	43.0	64.1	51.7
Male perpetrator(s)		90.6	88.1	94.7	90.3	85.0
Individual perpetrator		44.1	41.2	76.8	20.3	59.8
Age of perpetrator(s) between 14 and 18		70.6	66.3	41.3	61.1	70.6
Familiarity of perpetrator(s)	Unknown	60.8	46.1	27.5	52.4	37.7
	Known, first offence	31.9	43.5	52.7	36.3	46.4
	Known, repeat offence	7.4	10.4	19.8	11.3	15.9
Origin of perpetrator(s)	German	44.4	42.6	59.3	38.3	55.6
	Turkey	26.3	27.8	14.9	30.4	20.4
	Former SU	8.8	8.8	2.6	11.7	8.7
	Other	20.6	20.8	23.2	19.6	15.4
Offence photographed/ videoed		2.9	1.1	9.1	9.1	4.1
Monetary loss	No loss	16.2	44.7	92.3	83.1	92.2
	Small loss (up to €25)	29.2	35.5	2.9	6.2	4.1
	Medium loss (up to €100)	26.4	11.4	3.3	6.6	2.6
	Large loss (€100 or more)	28.2	8.4	1.4	4.1	1.2
Bodily injury	No injury	76.5	77.4	45.6	5.3	6.3
	Slight injury (no medical attention)	18.4	15.6	40.3	32.8	66.6
	Medium injury (medical attention)	4.4	5.6	11.2	43.7	23.5
	Severe injury (hospitalised)	0.7	1.4	2.9	18.2	3.6
Told someone else	Yes	91.2	82.8	84.8	90.2	88.3
	Of which: parents	73.8	56.0	34.1	57.6	56.5
	Of which: friends	75.7	76.2	88.8	82.8	81.4
	Of which: teachers	15.5	10.6	17.3	18.4	17.6
Reported to police		40.2	18.8	18.0	36.8	18.9

The majority of perpetrators are male. Regardless of the form of violence, about nine out of ten perpetrators were of male gender. Individual perpetrators are most frequent in the case of violent sexual offences and least frequent in the case of aggravated assault. A majority of perpetrators were in the adolescent age group (between the ages of 14 and 18) at the time of the offence; a higher proportion of older perpetrators is only seen for violent sexual offences.

There are likewise major differences between the different forms of offence with regard to the familiarity and origin of perpetrators. With the majority of sexual assaults the perpetrator is known and in a particularly large number of cases will already have assaulted the victim in the past. The majority of robberies, on the other hand, are carried out by unknown perpetrators. Compared with the percentage of the sample accounted for by migrants (27.4 percent), the responses on the presumed origin of perpetrators indicate disproportionate involvement by migrants, with the proportion of perpetrators with a presumed migrant background ranging from 40.7 percent to 61.7 percent. Analysing the self-report data on violence, the offender rates are consistently higher for almost all migrant groups, and in some cases substantially higher than for native Germans (cf. Baier et al. 2009, p. 70), hence it can be inferred from victims' responses that migrants in Germany are more readily inclined to violence than Germans; at the same time, however, this greater inclination is not in evidence for all offences (cf. Baier/Pfeiffer 2009, Rabold/Baier 2011).

There are major differences between the various forms of offence with regard to their direct financial and physical consequences. In the case of assaults the monetary loss tends to be small, whereas with robberies more than one in four offences results in a loss of at least €100. At the same time, robbery or extortion tend more rarely to have major physical consequences. It is mostly assaults involving that necessitate hospitalisation. The impacts of assaults on well-being were not asked about; such impacts can be explored indirectly in the section of this paper addressing further consequences of victimisation. One possible consequence is that victims become re-victimised when pictures or videos of the assault are distributed. However, this appears to be relatively rare. Only sexual assault and aggravated assault, a substantial fraction of victims (9.1 percent) reported the assault being photographed or videoed.

A majority of victims subsequently turn to trusted individuals; almost nine out of ten report having done this, regardless of the type of offence. Reasons for not doing so were not asked in the survey. Findings from another schools survey show that adolescents who do not speak to someone often do not consider the victimisation to have been serious (Baier et al. 2009a, p. 89). The first port of call for victims comprises friends, especially where experience of sexual assault is involved. Victims turn to parents especially infrequently when it comes to sexual assault and especially frequently in cases of robbery. Teachers can be rated as trusted individuals only for a small fraction of adolescents. On average, one in six or one in seven victims of violence turn to teachers in order to tell someone what they have experienced.

The last topic covered in Table 4.3 is reporting behaviour. Adolescents who were victims of a violent assault were asked to say if the most recent offence was reported to the police. The purpose of choosing the most recent offence is because details are likely to be relatively fresh in the victim's memory. For all types of offence, the number of unreported incidents is higher than the number of reported incidents. Reporting rates are especially high for robbery (40.2 percent) and aggravated assault (36.8 percent) and only half as high for sexual assault (18.0 percent), extortion (18.8 percent) and assault (18.9 percent). Discrepancies between reported and self-report victimisation rates in Figure 4.3 can be partly explained by these findings on reporting behaviour. The discrepancy between the two sources is only disproportionate for robbery. It is possible that there is a heightened tendency for incidents to be classified as robbery in the school pupils survey that would not be so classified on legal examination, for example because of the minor nature of the incident. Interestingly, sexual assault has the largest discrepancy between the two data sources but the lowest reporting rate. The opposite is true for aggravated assault.

Based on the repeated survey it is also possible to draw conclusions on trends in reporting behaviour. Four of the five offences show an increase in reporting rates (not: extortion), with the strongest rise for violent sexual offences (from 9.8 to 17.3 percent) and robberies (from 34.3 to 49.4 percent; aggravated assault: from 21.6 to 23.5 percent, assault: from 14.8 to 19.7 percent). Across all violent offences, no less than nearly 12 percent more offences were brought to the attention of the police in 2005/2006 (an increase from 19.4 percent to 21.7 percent). From a constant or decreasing number of unreported offences, then, an increasing proportion of offences is being reported, and by definition this means a rise in reported crime in the official statistics. The increases in violent crime identified in the Police Crime Statistics thus at least partly reflect previously unreported crime being reported (as a result of a greater inclination to go to the police). The schools survey data thus provide an important example of how changes in reported crime statistics may relate to reporting rates and conceal true trends.

As reporting behaviour is central to the assessment of the Police Crime Statistics, determinants of reporting were additionally subjected to multivariate logistic regression analysis (cf. Backhaus et al. 2003). Results of this analysis are presented in Table 4.4. The coefficients indicate whether a factor is associated with enhanced (values greater than 1) or reduced inclination to report an incident to the police (values less than 1). The first model includes only the type of offence and confirms that extortion, sexual assault and assault are reported significantly less frequently than robberies. These differences do not disappear in Model II, where other characteristics of an offence are controlled for; i.e. the greater inclination to report robbery is not solely a result of the greater monetary loss. Why robbery is more frequently reported cannot therefore ultimately be answered from the data; the reporting rates for the remaining types of offence, on the other hand, are bunched together, as can be seen from the similar coefficients in Model II. The greater inclination to report aggravated assault is thus attributable to the more severe harm inflicted.

Incidents at home or at relatives or friends are significantly less frequently reported than assaults at school, on public transport or elsewhere. Male and known offenders run a lesser risk of being reported, as do individual offenders and adolescent offenders. Offenders with a migrant background are more frequently reported, and most of all those with an 'other' origin. Additional analyses shows that the combination of ethnicities involved is also crucial: The highest reporting rate is seen where non-German offenders come up against a German victim (cf. Baier et al. 2009, p. 45f). Reasons for the greater risk of being reported faced by non-German offenders could be that victims see less opportunities for reaching agreement on informal terms; possibly, they desire that individuals who are 'guests' in Germany be sanctioned for their delinquent behaviour.

Assaults resulting in greater material loss or physical injury are significantly more frequently reported. Incidents that are photographed or videoed are likewise more likely to be reported. It is possible that victims do not want pictures to be circulated.

The final model (Model III) additionally included socio-demographic variables of the victim. The coefficients show that different groups of pupils differ significantly in their reporting behaviour. Male victims and victims with migrant backgrounds less frequently report incidents to the police. This could be because these groups have less confidence in the police (cf. Baier et al. 2010, p. 141) and expect to achieve little by pressing charges, or that their victimisation occurred in the context of violence in which they were also involved as perpetrators, causing them to refrain from reporting the incident to the police. It also emerges that reporting rates are lower in southern Germany and in rural areas. The overall reporting rate for violent crime is about a fifth lower in southern Germany and in rural administrative districts than in northern, western and eastern Germany or in urban areas (Baier et al. 2009, p. 42). This puts a different perspective on the north-south and urban-rural differences seen in the Police Crime Statistics.[14]

Table 4.4 Factors determining whether an offence is reported to the police (logistic regression; coefficient: Exp(B))

		Model I	**Model II**	**Model III**
Violent assault	Robbery	*Reference*	*Reference*	*Reference*
	Extortion	0.343 ***	0.413 ***	0.413 ***
	Sexual assault	0.330 ***	0.468 **	0.419 ***
	Aggravated assault	0.867	0.450 ***	0.473 ***
	Assault	0.346 ***	0.366 ***	0.311 ***
Location of assault	At home/relatives		*Reference*	*Reference*
	School/on way to school		2.234 ***	2.260 ***
	Friends		1.020	0.974
	Public transport		2.034 ***	2.020 ***
	Elsewhere		1.703 **	1.739 **
Male perpetrator(s)			0.641 ***	0.741 *
Individual perpetrator			0.851 *	0.859
Age of perpetrator(s)	18 or older		*Reference*	*Reference*
	Between 14 and 18		0.653 ***	0.660 ***
	Under 14		0.705	0.710
Familiarity of perpetrator(s)	Unknown		*Reference*	*Reference*
	Known, first assault		0.593 ***	0.591 ***
	Known, repeat assault		0.571 ***	0.550 ***

14 See Baier and Hanslmaier in this volume.

		Model I	Model II	Model III
Origin of perpetrator(s)	German		*Reference*	*Reference*
	Turkey		1.136	1.154
	Former SU		1.065	1.167
	Other		1.497 ***	1.545 ***
Offence photographed/ videoed			1.775 ***	1.761 **
Monetary loss	No loss		*Reference*	*Reference*
	Small loss (up to €25)		0.597 ***	0.616 **
	Medium loss (up to €100)		1.285	1.308 *
	Large loss (€100 or more)		3.322 ***	3.292 ***
Bodily injury	No injury		*Reference*	*Reference*
	Slight injury (no medical attention)		0.841	0.852
	Medium injury (medical attention)		3.506 ***	3.508 ***
	Severe injury (hospitalised)		5.118 ***	5.198 ***
Gender: Male				0.792 *
Origin: Migrant				0.800 **
Home surroundings: Rural				0.795 **
Home region: Southern Germany				0.841 *
Number of cases		**5566**	**5566**	**5566**
Nagelkerk's R^2		**.059**	**.226**	**.233**

* p < .05, ** p < .01, *** p < .001

4.3.4 Regional differences in violent victimisation

Analysis of the 2007/2008 schools survey not only reveals regional variation in reporting rates; victimisation rates in general likewise show a broad range across the 61 areas included. The total violent victimisation rate was only 9.6 percent in at least one area and 25.2 percent in at least one other (Table 4.5). For sexual assault, there was at least one area where not one respondent reported being a victim, whereas at least one other area showed a rate of 2.3 percent. A very wide range also emerges for extortion. The victimisation rates for the various offences correlate across the 61 areas. Where assault is more frequent, there are also more robberies, and so on. Only correlations with sexual assault are low, meaning this form of violence is less dependent on the prevalence of other violent crime.

Table 4.5 Victimisation rates by area and correlation between victimisation rates across 61 areas (in percent resp. Pearson's r)

	Lowest prevalence area	Highest prevalence area	Extortion	Sexual assault	Aggravated assault	Assault
Robbery	1.3	9.4	.66***	.17	.45***	.66***
Extortion	0.3	6.2	-	.28*	.59***	.50***
Sexual assault	0.0	2.3	-	-	.33*	.22
Aggravated assault	0.7	5.3	-	-	-	.56***
Assault	7.5	16.6	-	-	-	-
Violence	9.6	25.2	-	-	-	-

* $p < .05$, ** $p < .01$, *** $p < .001$

It is not yet possible conclusively to identify the factors behind these area to area differences due to insufficient data. It would doubtless be necessary to systematically survey the work of the police, social workers and others involved in violence prevention and to link the results to victimisation rates. Another point open to discussion is the suitability of analysis at the level of administrative districts. Can administrative districts or towns and cities really influence their citizens' behaviour as regards violence? This appears a legitimate question because administrative districts are unlikely to be internally heterogeneous. Towns and communities within a mixed urban-rural administrative division are likely to differ with regard to violence rates just like districts and neighbourhoods within a city. It is not without reason that the investigation of macrosocial units has focused in recent years on urban districts and neighbourhoods (cf. e.g. Sampson et al. 1997, Oberwittler 2004, Rabold/Baier 2009). Neighbourhoods are places where children and adolescents spend their time and which can thus have a socialising influence; the greater the regional unit, the weaker their socialising influence is likely to be (cf. Nonnenmacher 2007).

Table 4.6 nonetheless shows the aggregate correlations between various indicators describing the social and economic structure of the 61 areas and the victimisation rates in those areas. Data relating to the economic environment are seen to be only weakly related to violence: While a high unemployment rate correlates with higher rates of robbery and extortion, there are no further relationships to be found either for unemployment rates or for average income. A large share of migrants[15] is related with higher rates of aggravated assault but, once again, further relationships are not evident for this indicator. The largest number of relationships all pointing in the same direction is for the proportion of single parents and for social cohesion. Both of these indicators are aggregated out of the schools survey data. The adolescents were asked if they currently live with one parent (father alone, mother alone or alternately with the mother or father) or with both parents together. With regard to cohesion, the pupils were presented five statements such as 'People in my neighbourhood help each other'[16]; higher values stand for greater perceived social cohesion. It can be seen that higher victimisation rates are observed where there is a large proportion of single parents and low social cohesion. This speaks in favour of control theory considerations: Where social control is weak on account of structural constraints (less frequently two parents performing childrearing and supervision) or sociocultural circumstances (little mutual interest due to low cohesion), there are more opportunities for offenders to be violent. Although these findings require confirmation from multivariate analysis including other potential explanatory factors, they indicate that it is possible for relationships with individual behaviour to be meaningfully interpreted for larger units; somewhat greater attention should therefore be paid in future to investigating the influence of regional characteristics both on victimisation and offender rates.[17]

Table 4.6 Correlations between victimisation rates and various area indicators (Pearson's r)

	Unemployment rate (2006/2007)	Average income (2006)	Proportion of single parents	Proportion of migrants	Cohesion
Robbery	.30*	-.19	.40**	-.01	-.37**
Extortion	.37**	-.15	.54***	.08	-.54***
Sexual assault	-.03	.16	.19	.20	-.11

15 The share of migrants relates to ninth-graders and is aggregated from the survey data.

16 Cronbach's alpha for the scale is .78 (cf. Baier 2011a, p. 56 for exact wording of all items).

17 The same incidentally also applies to the influence of other contexts such as school and school class. As school violence is not the focus of this paper, potential school-related factors in violent victimisation are not presented here.

	Unemployment rate (2006/2007)	Average income (2006)	Proportion of single parents	Proportion of migrants	Cohesion
Aggravated assault	.10	.04	.39**	.43**	-.39**
Assault	.23	-.19	.34**	-.03	-.23

* p < .05, ** p < .01, *** p < .001

4.3.5. Determinants of violent victimisation

Investigation of the factors influencing violent victimisation using a cross-sectional survey faces a central problem: Victimisation and offending are reported in some cases by the same population. The investigation of the factors influencing victimisation is thus simultaneously an investigation of the factors influencing offending. Using data from the 2007/2008 schools survey, the overlap between victims and offenders with regard to criminal offences can be illustrated. In the twelve months before the survey, 24.7 percent of all students perpetrated or fell victim to some form of violent offence. 11.2 percent of respondents were exclusively victims and 8.0 percent were exclusively offenders; 5.5 percent of adolescents were both victims and offenders. The ratio between both groups varies from offence to offence, but for all offences there is a group of adolescents, of varying size (between 0.1 percent and 3.8 percent), who were both victims and offenders. While it is not necessary to exclude this group when analysing the factors influencing victimisation, it does need to be analysed separately.

Including adolescents who were both victims and offenders adds a further problem: To the extent that physical violence is a domain of male adolescents, this group includes a disproportionate number of male respondents. Looking at violent behaviour as a whole, the number of boys in the group of school pupils who were neither victims nor offenders is 45.8 percent; in the victims only group it is 54.6 percent, whereas in the victims and offenders group it is 76.5 percent. For sexual assault, on the other hand, the victims only group contains scarcely any male adolescents (12.3 percent), while the victims and offenders group consists almost entirely of boys (80.8 percent); at the same time, this group is so small in number (21 pupils) that detailed analysis does not appear meaningful. For this reason, the focus in the descriptive analysis that follows is on boys when looking at violent behaviour as a whole and on girls when dealing with sexual assault (excluding those respondents who were both victims and offenders).

There is far less agreement among criminological researchers regarding the factors relating to violent victimisation than regarding the factors relating to violent offending. One of the few criminological approaches to supply possible explanations for victimisation is routine activities theory (Cohen/Felson 1979). This directs attention simultaneously at offenders, victims and the situations in which they encounter each other. Three factors are needed for an assault to be committed: Firstly, a motivated offender, secondly, a suitable target or opportunity and, thirdly, the lack of a guardian or preventing circumstances. Cohen and Felson (1979) set out their thoughts in further detail by the example of violent offences: A combination of greater prosperity and shorter working hours means that more and more people go out in their free time (most of all in the evening). This includes spending time in places such as bars and discos where potential offenders are more likely to be encountered and there is less social control. By going to such places, victims expose themselves to a greater risk of assault and so take an 'active' part in the victimisation process. People for whom it is less important to go to such places or do not frequent them for other reasons have a lesser victimisation risk.

Engagement with a range of free time activities should therefore be looked at when investigating influencing factors of victiimsation. In addition, as the analysis presented further above already indicated, earlier victimisation influences later victimisation. For these reasons, the factors shown in Table 4.7 are to be investigated with regard to their relationship with victimisation.

Factors included with regard to family make-up consist of growing up with only one parent (15 percent of respondents) and experience of severe parental violence in childhood (likewise 15 percent of respondents). These variables as well as cohesion have already been presented. It should be noted that the cohesion variable is recoded for the analysis; as risk factors for victimisation are under investigation here and it is assumed that a low level of cohesion in the neighbourhood raises the risk of assault.

Responses are collected for four variables relating to leisure time activities and lifestyle. The adolescents were first asked if they spend time going to bars, discos, etc.; 73 percent said yes. Secondly, they were asked about their affiliation with delinquent groups of friends; 65 percent of the adolescents said they knew at least one such friend. Contact with such groups of friends ought to increase the risk of involvement in violent encounters. Thirdly, respondents were asked if they had played truant for at least one day in the last half school year (27 percent of respondents). As truants usually avoid home and spend their time instead at places where there is less adult supervision, they are likely to face greater risk of violent victimisation. Fourthly, the survey asked about binge drinking, which 54 percent of the school students said they had engaged in at least once in the preceding 30 days. Excess alcohol intake releases inhibitions, which in turn goes hand in hand with greater exposure to violence.

The effect of two personality factors also requires investigation. According to self-control theory (Gottfredson/Hirschi 1990), low self-control ought to go with heightened risk not only of offending but also of victimisation. Risk seeking was asked about as a dimension of low self-control. People who advocate violence more than others are also likely to be more frequently involved in violent encounters in the context of which they also become subject to victimisation.

Table 4.7 Items and descriptive statistics for influencing variables

	Items	**Response categories**	**Mean**	**Standard deviation**
Growing up with single parent	Individuals currently lived with	0: With both biological parents, with mother and partner or with father and partner; 1:With mother alone, with father alone or alternately with mother and father	0.15	0.36
Childhood experience of severe parental violence	Struck with object, punched/kicked, thrashed/beaten up at least once by mother or father before age 12	0: No; 1: Yes	0.15	0.36
Low neighbourhood cohesion	Five items, e.g. "There is often conflict between neighbours where I live" (Cronbach's alpha = .78)	1: Not true; 4: Exactly true	2.04	0.68
Time spent every day going to bar, disco etc.	Time spent on school day or at weekend going to bar, disco, cinema or other event	0: No; 1: Yes	0.73	0.44
Contact with at least one delinquent friend	Number of friends who have committed shoplifting, robbery, assault, damage to property or drugs dealing	0: No delinquent friends 1: At least one delinquent friend	0.65	0.48
At least one day's truancy in last half school year	Number of whole school days truancy in last half school year	0: No days; 1: At least one day	0.27	0.44
Binge drinking at least once in last month	Drunk five or more glasses of alcohol in succession on at least once occasion in past 30 days	0: No; 1: Yes	0.54	0.50

	Items	Response categories	Mean	Standard deviation
High degree of risk seeking	Four items, e.g. "I like to test my limits by doing something dangerous" (Cronbach's alpha = .85)	1: Not true; 4: Exactly true	2.11	0.80
High acceptance of violence	Four items, e.g. "A bit of violence is part of having fun" (Cronbach's alpha = .87)	1: Not true; 4: Exactly true	1.54	0.72

Table 4.8 shows the various factors by group affiliation. The proportion of male adolescents who have been neither victims nor perpetrators of violence in general and grow up with a single parent is 14.2 percent; significantly higher percentages are found for male adolescents who have been victims of violence (17.0 percent for victims only; 19.0 percent for victim-offenders). For sexual assault, on the other hand, family composition appears to be irrelevant. For all other factors analysed, significant differences are found between the groups, and all in the direction that is to be expected (greater prevalence among victim groups). One striking point is that the victim-offender group has greater prevalence figures still than the victim group, underscoring that the factors included can also affect the likelihood of offending.

Table 4.8 Influencing factors, by group affiliation (percent or means)

	Violence: Male respondents			Sexual assault: Female respondents	
	Neither victim nor offender	Victim only, not offender	Both victim and offender	Neither victim nor offender	Victim only, not offender
Growing up with single parent	**14.2**	**17.0**	**19.0**	15.4	18.7
Childhood experience of severe parental violence	**11.3**	**18.0**	**28.0**	**14.5**	**39.9**
Low neighbourhood cohesion	**1.95**	**2.03**	**2.16**	**2.07**	**2.30**
Time spent every day going to bar, disco etc.	**62.8**	**71.5**	**87.0**	**77.6**	**89.4**
Contact with at least one delinquent friend	**61.5**	**75.9**	**95.1**	**58.6**	**83.2**
At least one day's truancy in last half school year	**19.2**	**29.0**	**52.6**	**26.2**	**51.8**
Binge drinking at least once in last month	**51.4**	**64.8**	**84.6**	**47.9**	**71.1**
High degree of risk seeking	**2.13**	**2.36**	**2.83**	**1.90**	**2.34**
High acceptance of violence	**1.56**	**1.66**	**2.33**	**1.32**	**1.73**

Bold: Differences significant at $p < .05$

To assess which factors are especially closely related to victimisation with the other factors taken into account, multivariate logistic regression models have been calculated, the results are presented in Table 4.9. Gender and offending were controlled for. All independent variables were also z-standardised to make the coefficients directly comparable. The three most important factors influencing violent victimisation are seen to be violent delinquency, contact with delinquent friends and childhood experience of severe parental violence. The composition of the family and whether adolescents frequent certain kinds of location in their free time (bars, discos, etc.) are only weakly related to the risk of assault. The influence of acceptance of violence is ultimately reversed: Adolescents with strong affinity to violence are less frequently victims. This could be connected with such adolescents appearing particularly self-confident and thus deterring potential attackers. It also cannot be ruled out that being the target of an assault contradicts their self-image, as a result they do not perceive assaults as victimisation or fail to disclose them in surveys.

Table 4.9 Factors influencing victimisation (binary logistic regression; coefficient: Exp(B))

	Model: Violence	**Model: Sexual assault**
Gender: Male	1.154 ***	0.311 ***
Offender	1.403 ***	1.142 ***
Growing up with single parent	1.047 *	1.015
Childhood experience of severe parental violence	1.254 ***	1.370 ***
Low neighbourhood cohesion	1.075 ***	1.103
Time spent every day going to bar, disco etc.	1.043 *	1.185 *
Contact with at least one delinquent friend	1.316 ***	1.259 **
At least one day's truancy in last half school year	1.115 ***	1.245 ***
Binge drinking at least once in last month	1.203 ***	1.205 **
High degree of risk seeking	1.178 ***	1.301 ***
High acceptance of violence	0.948 **	1.302 ***
Number of Cases	**37416**	**36938**
Nagelkerke's R^2	**.146**	**.147**

* $p < .05$, ** $p < .01$, *** $p < .001$

The findings on sexual assault differ in part from those on violent victimisation in general. The three most important influencing factors are gender, childhood experience of parental violence and personality traits such as risk seeking and affinity to violence (this time in the expected direction). Family composition and neighbourhood cohesion are not relevant. This latter finding can be explained by the fact that sexual assault tends to take place not in the public but in the private arena, where the controlling effect of neighbourhood reaches its limits. The analysis speaks in favour of a multi-causal explanation of victimisation, with particular importance being attached to intrafamilial violence. Victims within the family have a certain likelihood of becoming victims of violent crime at a later date. At the same time, the small size of the explained variances indicates that the included variables only explain violent victimisation to a small degree. Rather than speculate about further influencing factors here, it may be more useful to highlight another point: It may not be possible to attain the same levels of explained variance for victimisation as for delinquency for the fundamental reason that victimisation is partly random and random events cannot be predicted. Whereas delinquency requires a conscious act and hence a decision by an individual to behave one way or another, victimisation is something that is experienced. The victim experiences an assault and is sought out by the offender possibly for the sole reason that he or she is in the wrong place at the wrong time.

4.3.6 Consequences of violent victimisation

The direct financial and physical effects of victimisation have already been addressed. The 2007/2008 schools survey also allows various other consequences of victimisation to be investigated. Using a cross-sectional survey, however, it cannot be said with finality that the proposed effects are not also part of the cause. This can at least be ruled out for one aspect because of the way the question is worded. That aspect is well-being. The adolescents were asked to say how they felt in the last week. For the great majority, the violent victimisation took place before the last week before the survey (sometime in their lifetime or in the last twelve months), and to this extent the cross-sectional data are open to causal analysis. For this reason, the focus in the following is on mental state as a potential (longer-term) effect of victimisation.

Well-being was measured using three sub-dimensions of the KINDL scale for adolescents (cf. Ravens-Sieberer et al. 2007). The three dimensions are physical distress, emotional distress and low self-esteem (Table

4.10). Respondents were asked to make responses to various questions for the last week on a scale from 1 (never) to 5 (all the time).[18] The items in the various scales correlate closely enough to be combined into a mean scale. The highest mean is for low self-esteem. An overall measure for poor well-being was also constructed from all three scales; the reliability of this measure constructed from the three subscales can be considered adequate (Cronbach's alpha = .68).

Table 4.10 Survey items for mental state

	Items	Answer categories	Mean	Standard deviation
Physical distress	Four items, e.g. 'During the past week I felt ill' (Cronbach's alpha = .65)	1: Never; 5: All the time	2.54	0.79
Emotional distress	Four items, e.g. 'During the past week I felt alone' (Cronbach's alpha = .56)	1: Never; 5: All the time	2.08	0.68
Low self-esteem	Four items, e.g. 'During the past week I was proud of myself' (reverse item; Cronbach's alpha = .62)	1: Never; 5: All the time	2.78	0.78
Poor well-being	Three scales: Poor physical well-being, poor emotional well-being and low self-esteem (Cronbach's alpha = .68)	1 to 5	2.47	0.59

There are significant gender differences for all three subscales and for the aggregate scale, with girls reporting poorer well-being than boys. The connection between victimisation and mental state should therefore be analysed separately for boys and girls as there are gender differences with regard to the independent variable (victimisation).

Table 4.11 looks at four groups of victimised adolescents with regard to overall experience of violence (i.e. without distinguishing separate offences): Adolescents with no lifetime experience of victimisation; adolescents with experience of victimisation, but more than twelve months in the past; adolescents with infrequent experience of victimisation (a maximum of four times) in the last twelve months; and adolescents with frequent experience of victimisation (four times or more) in the last twelve months.

18 The exact wording of the questionnaire can be seen at kindl.org/cms/fragebogen. An explorative factor analysis with all twelve items only partly confirms the theoretically expected factor structure. The scale is nonetheless used here as proposed by Ravens-Sieberer et al. (2007), as this is replicated in various other studies.

The findings are almost identical for the various subscales and for both sexes. The poorest well-being is found for adolescents with multiple victimisation experience. Significantly better well-being values are found for the two middle groups, where no significant differences can be found. The best well-being values are seen for adolescents without experience of victimisation. Victimisation experience thus goes along with more negative well-being on several counts (physical, emotional and in terms of self-esteem); adolescents subjected to repeat victimisation are particularly affected. The connection is also somewhat stronger for girls than for boys, as shown by higher F-values across the board.

Table 4.11 Well-being, by victimisation experience (means)

		No violence in lifetime to date (1)	Violence in lifetime to date but not in last 12 months (2)	Violence in last 12 months: Maximum 4 incidents (3)	Violence in last 12 months: At least 5 incidents (4)	F-value	Significant differences (p < .05)
Boys	Physical distress	2.27	2.37	2.41	2.52	75.077 ***	1 vs. 2, 3, 4; 2 vs. 4; 3 vs. 4
	Emotional distress	1.97	2.05	2.07	2.19	61.528 ***	1 vs. 2, 3, 4; 2 vs. 4; 3 vs. 4
	Low self-esteem	2.64	2.66	2.66	2.77	9.732 ***	1 vs. 4; 2 vs. 4; 3 vs. 4
	Poor well-being	2.29	2.36	2.38	2.49	67.962 ***	1 vs. 2, 3, 4; 2 vs. 4; 3 vs. 4
Girls	Physical distress	2.71	2.88	2.92	3.13	112.636 ***	1 vs. 2, 3, 4; 2 vs. 4; 3 vs. 4
	Emotional distress	2.11	2.27	2.28	2.56	132.821 ***	1 vs. 2, 3, 4; 2 vs. 4; 3 vs. 4
	Low self-esteem	2.89	2.98	2.98	3.13	30.973 ***	1 vs. 2, 3, 4; 2 vs. 4; 3 vs. 4
	Poor well-being	2.57	2.71	2.72	2.94	136.562 ***	1 vs. 2, 3, 4; 2 vs. 4; 3 vs. 4

* p < .05, ** p < .01, *** p < .001

The results for the various subscales are similar – with the low self-esteem dimension showing the smallest differences – the analysis in the following can concentrate on the overall scale. Two questions remain to be addressed here: Do the effects of victimisation experience persist when other factors affecting well-being are taken into account? And do the different types of offence have different effects on well-being?

The findings from Table 4.12 answer the first question with the help of multivariate OLS regressions. As the coefficients shown are standardised, they can be compared with each other and are to be interpreted as correlation coefficients (ranges between 0 and 1 or –1). The first model confirms that girls have significantly worse well-being values than boys. Experience of violence is also seen to have a significant effect.[19] Interaction variables between gender and the victimisation groups were also specified. The findings confirm that victimisation has a significantly stronger impact on well-being for female than for male respondents; the differential effect is relatively minor, however, and only partly persists after controlling for other factors. This does not apply for the main effect of victimisation itself; i.e. victimisation can continue to be considered as significant factor in well-being after controlling for other variables that affect well-being. Model II includes various factors from the central socialisation domains of family, friends and school. As the survey was not primarily designed as a study dedicated to the explanation of well-being, no other factors are available for analysis. Separation of parents, death of a parent or moving home[20] are associated with poorer well-being; here again, however, the effects are not very pronounced. Childhood experience of severe parental violence, lack of contact with friends and poor school grades, on the other hand, have a significantly stronger impact on well-being.[21] The impact of victimisation is only slightly weaker than the impact of these variables. Also, there is no longer any difference to be seen between the two groups comprising adolescents subject to infrequent and frequent victimisation.[22]

---

19 The two middle groups were combined into one group for this analysis.

20 Respondents were asked only about moves in which they lost friends.

21 With regard to friends, respondents were asked if they have a group of friends whom they spend time with outside school. The school performance variable combined the most recent report grades in German, mathematics and history.

22 Model II once again included violent delinquency as a control variable. This proves to have a negative effect: Offenders have slightly better well-being. Exercising power over others may boost the individual's own self-esteem, with adolescents thus experiencing self-effectiveness.

Table 4.12 Factors influencing well-being (OLS regressions; coefficients: beta coefficients)

	Model I	Model II
Gender: Female	.26 ***	.26 ***
No violence in lifetime to date	*Reference*	*Reference*
Violence in lifetime to date (maximum 4 incidents) (1)	.08 ***	.06 ***
Violence in last 12 months (at least 5 incidents) (2)	.09 ***	.07 ***
Interaction between gender and (1)	.03 ***	.01 *
Interaction between gender and (2)	.03 ***	.02 ***
Violent delinquency in lifetime to date		-.03 ***
Parental separation/divorce experienced		.04 ***
Death of parent experienced		.02 ***
Moving home experienced		.02 ***
Childhood experience of severe parental violence		.10 ***
No group of friends		.07 ***
Poor school performance		.11 ***
Number of cases	**40624**	**40624**
R^2	**.073**	**.105**

* $p < .05$, ** $p < .01$, *** $p < .001$

The second question, regarding potential differences in the impact of individual offences, is addressed by the OLS regressions shown in Table 4.13. In models Ia to Ie the lifetime prevalence of each crime is analysed together with gender. Lifetime prevalence figures are used because as the multivariate analysis in Table 4.12 confirmed, the crucial distinction is between victims and non-victims and the number of victimisation experiences is not ultimately the deciding factor. The coefficients for the various offences are almost equal; a somewhat higher coefficient is only found for assault. This is also confirmed when all forms of victimisation are included in model II. That the strongest impact should be for assault appears somewhat surprising, this being per se the slightest form of offence compared with all offences. An explanation may be that assault is the most widespread form of victimisation. It is experienced across a range of population groups, including groups which generally have little experience of violence. For these groups, any such experience will have a greater impact. Other forms of violence may be more restricted to specific social milieus. Early experience of violence (e.g. in the family) in such milieus has the effect that later experiences have a lesser impact on well-being, possibly because the individual has become accustomed to adverse experiences over time.

Table 4.13 Victimisation as a factor influencing well-being (OLS regressions; coefficients: beta)

	Model Ia	Model Ib	Model Ic	Model Id	Model Ie	Model II
Gender: Female	.25 ***	.25 ***	.24 ***	.25 ***	.25 ***	.25 ***
Robbery (over lifetime)	.06 ***					.04 ***
Extortion (over lifetime)		.05 ***				.03 ***
Sexual assault (over lifetime)			.06 ***			.05 ***
Aggravated assault (over lifetime)				.06 ***		.02 ***
Assault (over lifetime)					.08 ***	.06 ***
Number of cases	**42628**	**42628**	**42628**	**42628**	**42628**	**42628**
R^2	**.063**	**.062**	**.062**	**.062**	**.065**	**.072**

* p < .05, ** p < .01, *** p < .001

4.4 Summary and outlook

The analysis has shown that violent victimisation in adolescence is very common. No less than one in six adolescents report falling victim to assault, robbery or extortion. The majority of assaults are relatively slight; only in cases of aggravated assault did nearly one in five victims have to be hospitalised. It is important to reiterate that the respondents were ninth-graders, i.e. individuals with an average age of 15. On the age-crime curve, this is an age group with one of the highest levels of crime risk (from both a victim and an offender perspective). Other age groups can be expected to face lower risk of victimisation; however, representative self-report studies that investigate violent victimisation at such a detail level for other age groups are not yet available for Germany. A comparison of findings from surveys carried out in different years in four towns and cities clearly shows that the violent victimisation rate for adolescents is slightly falling. The background to this trend has not yet been conclusively investigated. Firstly, however, there is a demonstrable decline in intrafamilial violence. Secondly, an attitude of aversion to violence is becoming increasingly widespread among adolescent groups of friends (cf. Baier

2008, p. 55ff). Thirdly, schools are also likely to have a hand in the positive trend. Most of all, the recently stepped up prevention programmes in schools (cf. Baier et al. 2010, p. 228ff) may be one explanation for the decline in violence.

The greater risk to offenders of charges being pressed and hence of police pursuit and apprehension is not to be ignored. Heightened risk of this kind is a stronger deterrent than the level of sanctions that potential offenders expect to face (cf. Hawkins/Zimring 1976). Change in reporting rates also helps explain the trend discrepancy between reported and unreported crime: Whereas the victim numbers rose in the analysis period according to the Police Crime Statistics, victim numbers according to self-report surveys declined or held constant. If there is a doubling of reporting rates, as has happened in the case of sexual assault, then significantly more offences will be reported in the official statistics while the self-report figures stay the same. Reporting behaviour is consequently very important in the interpretation of the Police Crime Statistics. The explanatory model on reporting behaviour has shown that the inclination to report an offence depends on the severity of loss or injury (the greater the severity, the more likely an offence is to be reported), on the perpetrator (e.g., charges are less frequently brought if the offender is of the same age as or is known to the victim) and on the victim (e.g., male adolescents and migrants are less likely to report an offence).

Of those violent offences investigated, sexual assault differs notably from the other forms of violence. The proportion of offences that are unreported is still expected to be largest for sexual assault despite the increased reporting rate. The age at first victimisation is lowest for male adolescents, while a very high proportion of boys are subject to repeat victimisation. In many cases, this form of violence does not take place between individuals of the same age, the majority of offenders being older individuals, in almost half of all cases relatives or acquaintances. It therefore comes as no surprise that victims relatively rarely go to their parents for help. The determinants and impacts of experience of sexual assault, on the other hand, resemble those of other violent offences. A crucial influencing factor is childhood experience of parental violence: Adolescents who report severe violence from their parents are two to three times as likely to be victims of violence in adolescence – in the form of sexual assault just as much as other violent offences. Contact with delinquent peers and personality traits such as low self-control likewise help explain violent victimisation.

With regard to potential long-term consequences, well-being was selected for analysis. It emerges very clearly that violence and victimisation adversely affected physical and emotional well-being and, to a somewhat lesser degree, self-esteem. The connection is closer for girls than for boys. The recency of victimisation experience and its recurrence ultimately appear to have less of an impact on well-being. Merely the fact of experiencing violence once in one's lifetime so far is enough to significantly lower well-being. The various types of offence show hardly any difference in this regard: Assault reduces well-being somewhat more than other offences, which may be due to assault being experienced by a larger number of adolescents, including those with no prior experience of violence (and for whom such an experience is then particularly salient).

Alongside these findings, the analysis also points to various issues that should be given attention in future. Four research questions deserve brief mention here. Firstly, a variance in victimisation rates is evident for the 61 survey areas. The rates vary with external factors that can be interpreted with reference to control theory. It is questionable whether these findings would hold up to multilevel analysis. This was found not to be the case either for delinquency or right-wing extremism (cf. Baier et al. 2010, p. 190ff; Baier/Pfeiffer 2010). Therefore the question is which area-related factors truly affect individual victimisation risk. This is also a key question with regard to another context: The school classes and schools included in the survey likewise differ significantly in victimisation rates; to date, however, little attention has been paid to the potential influencing variables at aggregate level.

A second future research topic is under what conditions crimes make the transition from unreported to reported crime data. Various factors were included in the present analysis, but the explained variance is remarkably small. It may be necessary to look closer at whether victims are encouraged to press charges by people around them (friends, parents, etc.), whether they had prior contact to the police, and what confidence they have in the police. Indications that police contact and confidence in the police can affect reporting behaviour are found by Baier et al. (2010, p. 135ff). The question of how crimes become reported can only be partly answered by analysing reporting behaviour. It would be interesting, for example, to carry out research on police work targeting adolescents. In what urban districts and at what schools are the police present and can contribute in catching violent offenders? How are suspects treated once charges have been pressed? Are they actually recorded in the Police Crime

Statistics or does some police diversion take place that results in victim and offender not being included in the statistics?

A third research topic gone into at various points in this paper is the double vicious circle of victimisation. Earlier victimisation experience (for example in the family) is related to later violent victimisation; however it also increases the risk of becoming a violent offender. Victims become victims and victims become offenders. These vicious circles, which is only analysed on a cross-sectional basis here, needs to be subjected to more longitudinal analysis, and especially the link between delinquency and victimisation. Additionally, the specific mechanisms responsible for these linkages are not yet conclusively understood. Learning theory, personality theory, milieu-specific and other explanations are conceivable and would have to be subjected to comparative testing. It is also particularly important to include factors – known as resilience factors – that prevent such a vicious circle from developing in the first place. While the findings show that nearly twice as many (18.0 percent) of male victims of violence have experienced violence from their parents than adolescents without experience of victimisation, the equivalent figure for the latter group is still 11.3 percent; i.e., there is a group of victims for whom intrafamilial experience of violence is not reflected in further victimisation. It is possible that these adolescents receive special encouragement and control in their surroundings (for example at school). Genetic characteristics could also provide an possible explanation for such resilience. It will probably be revealing to shift the focus away from cases who fail to escape the vicious circle and towards those who do succeed in escaping it.

Fourthly, this paper focused on offences that involve physical violence. A similarly detailed analysis of victimisation experience for other types of offences is likely to be highly informative. This includes other types of criminal offences such as theft and damage to property. Given the growing public debate on cases of school bullying (and especially cyber-bullying), investigation of these forms of aggression would also appear important for Germany. As cyber-bullying especially represents an ongoing experience of aggressive behaviour no longer restricted to the school context, it is likely to have a particularly severe impact on well-being. There are as yet no representative studies on this topic for Germany so far.

References

Backhaus, K., Erichson, B., Plinke, W., Weiber, R. (2003). Multivariate Analysemethoden. Eine anwendungsorientierte Einführung (10. Auflage). Berlin: Springer.

Baier, D. (2008). Entwicklung der Jugenddelinquenz und ausgewählter Bedingungsfaktoren seit 1998 in den Städten Hannover, München, Stuttgart und Schwäbisch Gmünd. KFN: Forschungsberichte Nr. 104.

Baier, D. (2011). Jugendgewalt und Geschlecht – Erkenntnisse aus Kriminalstatistik und Dunkelfelduntersuchungen. Zeitschrift für Jugendkriminalrecht und Jugendhilfe, 22, 356-364.

Baier, D. (2011a). Jugendliche als Opfer und Täter von Gewalt in Wolfsburg. KFN: Forschungsbericht.

Baier, D. (2013). Entwicklung und Bedingungsfaktoren des Gewaltverhaltens. Ergebnisse wiederholt durchgeführter Schülerbefragungen. Manuskript im Druck.

Baier, D., Pfeiffer, C. (2009). Turkish Children and Teenagers as Perpetrators and Victims of Violence. In: M. Coester, E. Marks (Eds.), International Perspectives of Crime Prevention 2 (pp. 5-32). Mönchengladbach: Forum Verlag.

Baier, D., Pfeiffer, C. (2010). Regionale Unterschiede im Rechtsextremismus Jugendlicher. Zeitschrift für Jugendkriminalrecht und Jugendhilfe, 21, 135-145.

Baier, D., Pfeiffer, C. (2011). Jugendliche als Opfer und Täter von Gewalt in Berlin. KFN: Forschungsbericht Nr. 114.

Baier, D., Pfeiffer, C., Rabold, S., Simonson, J., Kappes, C. (2010). Kinder und Jugendliche in Deutschland. Gewalterfahrungen, Integration, Medienkonsum. KFN: Forschungsbericht Nr. 109.

Baier, D., Pfeiffer, C., Simonson, J., Rabold, S. (2009). Jugendliche in Deutschland als Opfer und Täter von Gewalt. KFN: Forschungsbericht Nr. 107.

Baier, D., Pfeiffer, C., Windzio, M., Rabold, S. (2006). Schülerbefragung 2005: Gewalterfahrungen, Schulabsentismus und Medienkonsum von Kindern und Jugendlichen. Abschlussbericht über eine repräsentative Befragung von Schülerinnen und Schülern der 4. und 9. Jahrgangsstufe. KFN: Forschungsbericht.

Baier, D., Rabold, S., Pfeiffer, C. (2010a). Jugendliche als Opfer und Täter von Gewalt im Bundesland Sachsen-Anhalt. KFN: Forschungsbericht Nr. 110.

Cohen, L., Felson, M. (1979). Social Change and Crime Rate Trends. A Routine Activity Approach. American Sociological Review, 44, 588-608.

Crick, N.R. (1995). Relational Aggression: The Role of Intent Attributes, Feelings of Distress, and Provocation Type. Development and Psychopathology, 7, 313-322.

Enzmann, D. (2010). Germany. In: J. Junger-Tas, I.H. Marshall, D. Enzmann, M. Killias, M. Steketee, B. Gruszczynska (Eds.), Juvenile Delinquency in Europe and Beyond. Results of the Second International Self-Report Delinquency Study (pp. 47-64). Dordrecht: Springer.

Fuchs, M., Lamnek, S., Luedtke, J., Baur, N. (2005). Gewalt an Schulen. 1994-1999-2004. Wiesbaden: VS Verlag für Sozialwissenschaften.

Gottfredson, M.R., Hirschi, T. (1990). A General Theory of Crime. Stanford: University Press.

Hawkins, G.J., Zimring, F.E. (1976). Deterrence. The Legal Threat in Crime Control. Chicago: University Press.

Holtappels, H.G., Heitmeyer, W., Melzer, W., Tillmann, K.-J. (Hrsg.). Forschung über Gewalt an Schulen. Erscheinungsformen und Ursachen, Konzepte und Prävention. Weinheim: Juventa.

Junger-Tas, J., Marshall, I.H., Enzmann, D., Killias, M., Steketee, M., Gruszczynska, B. (2010) (Eds.). Juvenile Delinquency in Europe and Beyond. Results of the Second International Self-Report Delinquency Study. Dordrecht: Springer.

Nonnenmacher, A. (2007). Eignen sich Stadtteile für den Nachweis von Kontexteffekten? Kölner Zeitschrift für Soziologie und Sozialpsychologie, 59, 493-511.

Oberwittler, D. (2004). A Multilevel Analysis of Neighbourhood Contextual Effects on Serious Juvenile Offending. The Role of Subcultural Values and Social Disorganization. European Journal of Criminology, 1, 201-236.

Pfeiffer, C. (2012). Weniger Hiebe, mehr Liebe. Der Wandel familiärer Erziehung in Deutschland. Centaur, 2/11, 14-17.

Rabold, S., Baier, D. (2009). Stadtteile als Bedingungsfaktoren von Jugendgewalt. Stadtforschung und Statistik, 1/2009, 24-28.

Rabold, S., Baier, D. (2011). Why Are Some Ethnic Groups More Violent Than Others? The Role of Friendship Network´s Ethnic Composition. Journal of Interpersonal Violence, 26, 3127-3156.

Rabold, S., Baier, D., Pfeiffer, C. (2008). Jugendgewalt und Jugenddelinquenz in Hannover. Aktuelle Befunde und Entwicklungen seit 1998. KFN: Forschungsberichte Nr. 105.

Ravens-Sieberer, U., Ellert, U., Erhart, M. (2007). Gesundheitsbezogene Lebensqualität von Kindern und Jugendlichen in Deutschland: Eine Normstichprobe für Deutschland aus dem Kinder- und Jugendgesundheitssurvey (KIGSS). Bundesgesundheitsblatt – Gesundheitsforschung – Gesundheitsschutz, 50, 810-818.

Sampson, R. J., Raudenbush, S. W., Earls, F. (1997). Neighborhoods and Violent Crime: A Multilevel Study of Collective Efficacy. Science, 277, 918-924.

Schwartz, D., McFadyen-Ketchum, S.A., Dodge, K.A., Pettit, G.P., Bates, J.E. (1998). Peer Victimization as a Predictor of Behavior Problems at Home and in School. Development and Psychopathology, 10, 87-100.

Stadler, L., Bieneck, S., Pfeiffer, C. (2012). Repräsentativbefragung Sexueller Missbrauch 2011. KFN: Forschungsberichte Nr. 118.

Straus, M. A. (1979). Measuring Intrafamily Conflict and Violence: The Conflict Tactic (TC) Scales. Journal of Marriage and The Family, 41, 75-88.

Wetzels, P., Enzmann, D., Mecklenburg, E., Pfeiffer, C. (2001). Jugend und Gewalt. Eine repräsentative Dunkelfeldanalyse in München und acht anderen deutschen Städten. Baden-Baden: Nomos.

5. Sexual Abuse of Children and Adolescents: Prevalence and Trends

Lena Posch, Steffen Bieneck

5.1 Introduction

The widely debated cases of institutional sexual abuse that have come to light in increasing numbers since early 2010 have once more brought the issue to general notice and highlighted the need for up-to-date figures on the prevalence and experience of abuse in childhood and adolescence. Alongside absolute prevalence rates, a major focus of current debate is on changes in prevalence over time.

Internationally, statistics from various institutions show decreasing rates of reported child sexual abuse since the early 1990s (cf. Finkelhor et al. 2010). For Germany, too, the data for reported cases in the Police Crime Statistics show a declining trend for child sexual abuse. The number of victims in relation to the population of this age group for child sexual abuse dropped by a total of 4.8 percent between 1994 and 2010 (children and adolescents under the age of 14; offences under sections 176, 176a and 176b of the German Criminal Code). Little is so far known, however, about how the prevalence of child sexual abuse has developed in the last two decades on the basis of self-report survey data. Also, there is a lack of knowledge about whether any impact has been made by prevention and intervention strategies implemented to an increased extent during the same period or by public relations and awareness campaigns against child victimisation in particular and intrafamilial violence in general.

Funded by the German Federal Ministry of Education and Research, the present study was carried out to obtain up-to-date, reliable figures on the prevalence of child sexual abuse in Germany and on specific high-risk circumstances, perpetrator-victim relationships, forms of abuse and the behaviours leading up to it, and how abuse is dealt with. The study also focuses on other victimisation experiences (for example in the form of polyvictimisation or revictimisation) in childhood, adolescence and adulthood that may be associated with experiences of sexual abuse. In addition to childhood sexual abuse, the study therefore also covers intrafamilial violence and emotional and physical neglect in childhood and adolescence, physical violence in relationships, rape (inside and outside of an intimate relationship or marriage) and stalking.

The study replicates and expands on a much-cited German epidemiological study on child sexual abuse (Wetzels 1997), which was likewise carried out at the Criminological Research Institute of Lower Saxony in 1992 based on a representative German national sample of 16-to-59-year-olds (3,289 respondents); this was the only previous representative survey for Germany and is now two decades old.

Because the study design and survey instrument are largely replicated, it is possible to make comparisons, for example to show how the prevalence and severity of sexual abuse and various forms of intrafamilial violence have changed over the last years.

This paper presents up-to-date findings on the prevalence of and trends in the experience of sexual abuse and various perpetrator-victim relationships together with reporting rates from a sample of 16-to-40-year-old men and women (9,175 respondents) of German descent. Both differences between age-cohorts and comparisons with the prior 1992 survey will be reported.

5.2 Object of investigation and epidemiology

Child sexual abuse is defined in social science research as a range of acts and behaviours of varying scope. There is currently no standard or generally accepted definition. Instead, many attempts have been made at defining child sexual abuse, each including different aspects (such as physical proximity [with/without physical contact], victim age, victim-perpetrator age gap, intensity of abuse, possible consequences of abuse, and perpetrator intent), in some cases with little overlap and each with different limitations (cf. Wipplinger/Amann 2005). A central feature of child sexual abuse is exploitation of power and control over the child or of a position of authority/dependency (Barnett et al. 2011, Deegener 2005, Engfer 2005) independent of the infliction of physical violence on the child (Deegener 2005).

One important factor in identifying sexual abuse is the age limit taken as the age of consent. Epidemiological research usually uses age limits based on legal definitions and hence relates to sexual contact with children and adolescents under 14, 16 or 18 years of age (cf. Deegener 2006).

Under German law, any (attempted or actual) sexual activity with a child under 14 years is a punishable offence (section 176 of the German Criminal Code). This includes exhibitionism/sexual activity in the presence of a child (section 176 (4) 1). Sexual activity with a 14 or 15-year-old is a punishable offence in certain circumstances (such as when taking advantage of an exploitative situation or for financial reward – section 182 (1) and (2) – or if the adolescent is a minor entrusted to the adult for education or care – section 174). Sexual activity with a 16 or 17-year-old is likewise a punishable offence if it is in abuse of an exploitative situation or for financial reward (section 182 (1) and (2)) or in abuse of dependence on account of the minor being entrusted to the adult for education or care or subordinate to the adult in a training or employment context (section 174).

A rough behavioural classification of sexual abuse distinguishes acts with and without physical contact (Barnett et al. 2011). Sexual abuse with physical contact includes acts such as anal, oral or vaginal penetration or sexual/genital touching between the child/adolescent and an adult, while non-contact abuse includes sexual acts in the presence of children, exhibiting the genitals for sexual stimulation, and showing pornography (Deegener/Koerner 2005).

Viewed overall, cultural factors also play an important part when it comes to the perception and judgement of sexual behaviour and interactions between children and adults. What is regarded as completely inappropriate sexualised behaviour in one culture may be considered a perfectly normal everyday interaction in another (e.g., parental nudity in the presence of children; Barnett et al. 2011).

The different definitions and inclusion criteria and their differing methodological implementation result in wide variation in reported prevalence rates in social science research. Retrospective identification of sexual abuse experience also differs according to sample type and selection, such as whether the sample is a selective group such as undergraduate students (Elliger/Schoetensack 1991, Bange 1992), school students or vocational school trainees (e.g., Raupp/Eggers 1993) or a representative population sample (Wetzels 1997, Haeuser et al. 2011). The range of prevalence rates found thus varies between about 6 and 25 percent for women and between about 2 and 8 percent for men (Engfer 2005). Finkelhor (2005), in a comparison of epidemiological studies from 20 countries, similarly reports large variation in prevalence rates, ranging between 7 and 36 percent for women and between 3 and 29 percent for men. He ascribes this heterogeneity primarily to methodological and definitional differences and less to real country-to-country prevalence differences of the extent suggested by the data. In his own studies, for example, Finkelhor uses his own Juvenile Victimization Questionnaire (JVC; Finkelhor et al. 2011a), in which sexual abuse is measured as lifetime prevalence using seven screening questions (sexual touching, involvement in sexual acts, attempted or completed sexual intercourse, indecent exposure and verbal sexual comments) and a number of follow-up-questions if applicable. Other studies are based on approaches in which sexual abuse is identified using a number of interval-scaled items (such as the Childhood Trauma Questionnaire, Bernstein et al. 2003).

In a recent German study, Haeuser et al. (2011) investigated the prevalence of child sexual abuse (emotional and physical abuse alongside emotional and physical neglect) using the German version of the Childhood Trauma Questionnaire (CTQ; Bernstein et al. 2003) with a representative German sample aged between 14 and 90 (2,504 respondents). Sexual abuse is identified in the CTQ with five items on a five-point scale (1 = never to 5 = very often). The CTQ is based on a very broad definition of sexual abuse with very nonspecific wording (cf. Kappis/Hardt 2005) such as "Someone threatened me unless I did something sexual", "Somebody molested me" or "I believe I was sexually abused". The prevalence rates found in this way were 1.9 percent for 'severe to extreme' sexual abuse (scale values 13 to 25), 4.3 percent for 'moderate to severe' sexual abuse (scale values 8 to 12), and 6.3 percent for 'low to moderate' sexual abuse (scale values 6 to 7). In total, 12.5 percent of respondents experienced some form of sexual abuse. Consistent with current international research, the risk of becoming a victim of sexual abuse was significantly greater for women than for men.

In another recent study (Bebbington et al. 2010) with a random English national sample ranging in age from 16 to over 75, sexual abuse was identified with references to acts of varying degrees of severity from unpleasant sexual language directed at the victim to sexual touching and sexual intercourse. In total, 8.3 percent of respondents (11.1 percent of female and 5.3 percent of male respondents) reported having experienced sexual abuse with physical contact (sexual touching or sexual intercourse) before the age of 16.

These findings are limited in comparability, however, due to the differing methodology for identifying sexual abuse. A recent meta-analysis (Pereda et al. 2009) covering 65 publications (37 studies with male samples and 63 studies with female samples) from 22 countries attempted to control for the various definitional and methodological problems and make generalisable conclusions on the prevalence of child sexual abuse. The authors report an average prevalence rate of sexual abuse before the age of 18 of 19.7percent for women and 7.9 percent for men (19.2 and 7.4 percent with outliers excluded). The studies reported very diverse prevalence rates, varying between 0.2 and 66.9 percent for women and between 0.1 and 87.1 percent for men. Once again, consistent with the research findings to date (with the exception of one study), the prevalence rate for women was greater than that for men by an average across all studies of 2.5:1. In an analysis of the potential influence of various moderator variables on the large identified differences in prevalence, however, the authors were unable to find evidence for the explanations usually given (such as differences in methodological access and sample type, or different ages of consent) (cf. Wynkoop et al. 1995).

A direct comparison of the prevalence of sexual abuse at different points in time (and thus a quasi-longitudinal analysis) is presented by Finkelhor et al. (2010). The researchers compared the answers of two groups of subjects questioned by telephone interview in 2003 and 2008 on their individual sexual abuse experiences up to the age of 17. Both studies used the items from the Juvenile Victimization Questionnaire (JVQ; Finkelhor et al. 2011a) and are therefore directly comparable in methodological approach. Analysis of sexual victimisation prevalence rates showed a significant decrease from 8.0 (2003) to 6.7 percent (2008), which the authors attributed among other things to intensive violence-prevention and intervention programmes (most of all in schools).

5.3 Methodology

5.3.1 Material

Taking into account the above-mentioned limitations regarding the comparability of epidemiological studies, a proven survey instrument was selected for the present study in order to trace changes in childhood and adolescent abuse experience in Germany over the last 20 years. The survey material is therefore largely based on the 1992 study by Wetzels (1997) subject only to modifications or additions to the wording in a few places. In regards to child sexual abuse, a question complex was added among other things in which respondents are asked if any experiences stated in answer to previous questions were recorded and reproduced/distributed (for example by the perpetrator or someone else) and if so, which experiences, and whether the respondent came to know the perpetrator via the Internet (for example in a social network or chat). This was done to make allowance for recent developments in the use of media for "child grooming" (i.e., approaching and befriending children by using social networks to prepare them gradually for sexual activities).

The survey was carried out using a drop-off questionnaire in combination with a brief prior face-to-face interview. While the brief interview merely covered sociodemographic data (age, gender, educational background, etc.) and two forms of victimisation outside of the family (assault and burglary), the drop-off questionnaire, which respondents completed independently and anonymously in the absence of the interviewer, contained question complexes covering very personal topics relating to victimisation with physical and sexual violence in childhood and adulthood.

It is not possible to tell whether a questionnaire was completed alone or in presence of other people (and whether the fact may have affected the answers) because this was not asked in the questionnaire. Only in the face-to-face interview did the interviewer note if other individuals were present or interrupted the interview.

5.3.2 Survey conduct and sample recruitment

While in the 1992 study a random-route sampling design (random selection of starting points of the surveying interviewers, e.g. each 3rd household) was used, for economic reasons the current study is based on a quota sample as also used in other victimisation studies (e.g., Painter/Farrington 1998). The sample is a quota sample that is representative of the private-household (i.e., non-institutionalised) population of Germany with regard to the set of characteristics comprising population distribution among German federal states, urban-rural distribution, age, gender, highest level of education and size of household. The survey was conducted by a field research institute in Nuremberg (Germany) with profound experience in drawing national representative quota samples. Interviewees/study participants were selected and recruited by interviewers in accordance with quota distributions stipulated by the field research institute. Interviewers were advised and trained to select potential participants randomly in order to ensure quality of data and representativity as much as possible in a quota sample (Bechhofer/Paterson 2000). Interviewers were asked to send a list with eligible study participants to the field research institute where a central check of quota distributions was conducted and continuously updated. After having obtained the feedback of the field research institute, interviewers could start surveying the respective eligible participants. The survey was carried out between January and May 2011. Out of 12,357 interviews conducted in total, following initial quality control by the field research institute, 11,667 questionnaires were sent to the Criminological Research Institute of Lower Saxony for analysis. After internal checking and elimination, a total of 11,428 data sets remained (taking together the sub-samples for respondents of German descent and respondents of Turkish or Russian migration background). A refusal rate cannot be stated as interviewers did not note how many individuals declined to take part in the study when asked.

5.3.3 Sample description

The full sample includes 11,428 individuals, of whom 48.1 percent are male and 51.9 percent are female. This paper relates solely to the sub-sample of German descent (9,175 respondents). The age range for respondents was set in advance at 16 to 40 years of age, the mean age of the sample was 27.0 (*SD* = 7.7 years).

The 41-to-60-year-olds included in the 1992 study were left out of the present study because a sample of this age group was already surveyed as 22-to-41-year-olds in 1992. The youngest, 16-to-20 age group was oversampled to allow the finest possible level of analysis for abuse experienced most recently. With regard to the following analyses, this oversampling is offset by weighting. Other key demographic data for the sample are presented in Table 5.1.

Table 5.1 Key demographic data for the sample (in percent, unweighted data)

Gender	Female	52.1
	Male	47.9
Age (mean)		27.04
Age group	16 to 20 years	28.2
	21 to 30 years	36.2
	31 to 40 years	35.6
Marital status	Single	72.7
	Married	21.4
	Widowed/divorced	5.4
Level of education	No qualification (or none yet)	11.7
	Secondary modern school certificate (*Hauptschule*)	18.3
	secondary school leaving certificate/O-level (*Realschule*)	34.1
	A-Levels (higher education entrance qualification) or Advanced Vocational Certificate of Education	22.5
	University or University of Applied Sciences degree	11.0
	Others	2.3
Occupational status	At school/in training	35.1
	Employed	50.0
	Not employed	11.8
	Other	2.5

5.3.4 Definition and measures of child sexual abuse (CSA)

To allow for the fact that child sexual abuse is not a clearly defined behaviour pattern and to identify the various forms of sexual abuse as accurately as possible while reflecting different degrees of severity, child sexual abuse was surveyed in the present study with six different specifically described behaviours plus a catch-all 'other sexual activities' category. The wording was taken over in full from the 1992 survey (Wetzels 1997).

The questions relating to each of the seven behaviours constituting sexual abuse were followed by a question complex on the perpetrator-victim relationship, the age of the victim and of the perpetrator on the first and last occurrence, where the abuse took place, and if and when the victim reported the abuse to the police, thus permitting these aspects to be distinguished in the analysis.

As the instructions (see Figure 5.1) on the question complex show, child sexual abuse is identified in this study as follows:

- Occurrence of at least one of the seven sexual behaviours,
- between a child or adolescent under the age of 16,
- and a person at least five years older (in each case at the time of the first incident).

Fig. 5.1 Description of the scenarios used to measure child sexual abuse (English translation of German original used for the study)

Many children experience, even at a very early age, adults performing sexual acts on them or demanding such acts from them. Such acts can include a broad range of behaviours. In the following you will see listed a range of sexual acts and experiences. Please state how often you experienced any such act in your childhood or adolescence (up to the age of 16) with a person at least five years older than yourself.

How often did it occur in your childhood/adolescence (up to the age of 16) that:
(1) ... a man exposed his genitals in your presence for his own sexual stimulation? (CSA1)
(2) ... a person at least five years older than yourself asked you to touch their genitals or otherwise to sexually stimulate them manually or orally? (CSA2)
(3) ... a person at least five years older than yourself touched your genitals, your breasts or your anus for their own or for your sexual stimulation? (CSA3)
(4) ... a person at least five years older than yourself inserted their finger, their tongue or an object into your vagina or anus for their own or for your sexual stimulation? (CSA4)
(5) ... a man at least five years older than yourself inserted or attempted to insert his penis into your vagina or anus? (CSA5)
(6) ... a man at least five years older than yourself inserted or attempted to insert his penis into your mouth? (CSA6)
(7) In your childhood/adolescence (up to the age of 16) did a person at least five years older than yourself perform other sexual acts (other than those already mentioned) with you or in your presence? (CSA7)

To better take into account differences in the legal definition and judgement of sexual acts by an adult towards a child/adolescent, a number of analyses relate to different ages of consent (14 or 16). Responses are classified by age of consent based on the age of respondents at the first reported incident.

In the presentation of the results in the following, the first form of behaviour (CSA1) is discussed as indecent exposure by the perpetrator (for the purpose of sexual manipulation) or exhibitionism and represents one form of child sexual abuse without physical contact. It is not possible to tell in such cases whether the genital exposure took place in the context of further sexual activities (such as touching or penetration) or as a singular act (exhibitionism in the usual sense of the word). Responses to the second to sixth behaviours (CSA2, CSA3, CSA4, CSA5 and CSA6) are collapsed into the category of contact child sexual abuse (contact CSA). This category thus comprises being asked to touch the perpetrator sexually, the perpetrator touching the victim's genitals, vaginal or anal penetration of the victim by finger, tongue, object or penis, or oral penetration with the penis. Acts not otherwise specified come under the other sexual activities category, which is shown in all cases as a separate category as it can include sexual acts both with and without physical contact.

5.4 Findings

5.4.1 Prevalence rates

To identify the prevalence of sexual abuse and the frequency of abuse per victim, subjects were invited to state how frequently they experienced the six specific sexual behaviours on a six-point scale (1 = Never to 6 = Several times per week). Incidents taking place more than once (answer options 'Twice' to 'Several times a week') were classified as multiple occurrences of abuse. The question relating to experience of 'other sexual acts' had a dichotomous (Yes/No) answer choice; hence no frequency data are available for this category.

Among female respondents, a total of 6.7 percent experienced contact CSA before the age of 16. While for 2.1 percent of female respondents this was a once-only occurrence, more than twice as many (4.7 percent) were exposed to sexual abuse with physical contact on multiple occasions. A further 5.6 percent of women (additionally[1]) experienced exhibitionistic acts (with roughly equal frequencies for single and multiple occurrences) by an adult male and 1.5 percent experienced 'other' sexual activities (see Table 5.2). Among male respondents, 1.4 percent experienced sexual abuse with physical contact before the age of 16. For male respondents too, sexual abuse with physical contact tended to involve multiple occurrences rather than being a singular event (0.5 versus 0.9 percent). Among

1 The three abuse categories are not mutually exclusive and a single individual can have experienced multiple types of abuse and come under more than one category as a result. It is also impossible to tell whether reported experiences of individual abuse scenarios relate to different incidents or a single incident. For example, it cannot be ruled out that a reported experience of exposure by the perpetrator took place in the context of or prior to other sexual abuse behaviours (such as penetration).

men, 1.4 percent (additionally) experienced exhibitionistic acts before the age of 16 and a further 0.4 percent experienced 'other' sexual activities.

Looking separately at each of the behaviours in the sexual abuse with physical contact category, it becomes clear that the most frequent behaviour was sexual touching, most of all touching of the victim's genitals by the perpetrator (a total of 5.6 percent among women and 1.0 percent among men) or the victim being asked to orally or manually stimulate the perpetrator's genitals (3.4 percent of women and 0.9 percent of men). The least frequently experienced behaviour was oral penetration (0.9 percent of women and 0.2 percent of men), but if experienced at all, this tended not to be a once-only but a repeated occurrence, both for women and for men. Overall, women significantly more frequently report being victim to acts of penetration than men, by between 4.5 and 10 times (see Table 5.2). In total, 0.5 percent of male respondents and 2.7 percent of female respondents experienced at least one act of penetration (oral, anal or vaginal) before the age of 16.

Table 5.2 Prevalence rates of sexual abuse before the age of 16, by single and multiple incidents of abuse, for individual acts and the composite category of abuse with physical contact (in percent, weighted data)

		Male (N = 4391)			Female (N = 4784)			Total (N = 9175)		
		Single	Mult.	Total	Single	Mult.	Total	Single	Mult.	Total
CSA 1	Indecent exposure by the perpetrator/ exhibitionism	0.8	0.6	**1.4**	2.6	3.0	**5.6**	1.7	1.8	**3.5**
CSA 2	Touching of the perpetrator	0.3	0.6	**0.9**	1.2	2.2	**3.4**	0.7	1.4	**2.1**
CSA 3	Touching of the victim	0.4	0.6	**1.0**	2.2	3.4	**5.6**	1.3	2.0	**3.3**
CSA 4	Penetration with finger/tongue/object	-	0.2	**0.2**	0.6	1.3	**1.9**	0.3	0.8	**1.1**
CSA 5	Anal/vaginal penetration	0.1	0.1	**0.2**	0.4	1.0	**1.4**	0.3	0.5	**0.8**
CSA 6	Oral penetration	-	0.2	**0.2**	0.2	0.7	**0.9**	0.1	0.5	**0.6**
CSA 7	Other sexual acts			**0.4**			**1.5**			**0.9**
Abuse with physical contact[1] (CSA2-CSA6)		0.5	0.9	**1.4**	2.1	4.7	**6.7**	1.3	2.8	**4.1**

Mult. = multiple; totals may contain rounding differences; [1] The prevalence analysis for abuse with physical contact includes all study participants who experienced at least one of the behaviours CSA2 to CSA6; the prevalence rates cannot therefore be taken additively for the five individual behaviours.

The dependence of prevalence rates on underlying definition criteria (such as ages of consent) is once again evident in this sample: Depending on the form of abuse and the respective age of consent, prevalence rates range between 4.6 and 9.4 percent for women and between 1.1 and 2.2 percent for men (see Table 5.3). Taking the legal definition of child sexual abuse in Germany (i.e., based on a consensual age of 14), 1.1 percent of men and 5.2 percent of women experience sexual abuse with physical contact. Including 14 and 15-year-old adolescents (taking an age of consent of 16), 1.4 percent of men and 6.7 percent of women experience sexual acts with physical contact. Just 9.4 percent of women and 2.2 percent of men experienced sexual abuse at least once (including exhibitionism and 'other' sexual activities) before the age of 16. The gender differences in prevalence rates are statistically highly significant both for the individual behaviours and for the composite categories of sexual abuse with physical contact and sexual abuse overall (at least one experience of abuse out of all seven individual behaviours) (chi square test, $p < .001$).

Table 5.3 Prevalence rates of child sexual abuse, by age of consent (N resp. in percent; weighted data)

Categories of sexual abuse		Male (N = 4391)	Female (N = 4784)
Indecent exposure/exhibitionism			
Age of consent:	under 16	68 (1.5%)	248 (5.5%)
	under 14	62 (1.3%)	206 (4.6%)
Contact CSA			
(excluding other sexual activities and indecent exposure/exhibitionism)			
Age of consent:	under 16	67 (1.4%)	301 (6.7%)
	under 14	52 (1.1%)	234 (5.2%)
At least one experience of CSA (under 16) (including indecent exposure/exhibitionism, other sexual activities and contact CSA)		104 (2.2%)	424 (9.4%)

Despite the diverging prevalence rates depending on definition criteria, the gender ratio among respondents proves to be highly uniform across all abuse categories. Women thus are four times more likely to fall victim to sexual abuse before the age of 16 as men (proportion of female victims:

78.4 percent indecent exposure, 81.9 percent abuse with physical contact, 79.3 percent other sexual activities). Wetzels (1997) in his study reported a ratio of about 1:3.

In just under two-fifths (38.4 percent) of cases of contact CSA before the age of 16, the abuse consisted of acts involving penetration (anal, vaginal or oral); i.e., the majority of cases of sexual abuse with physical contact take the form of sexual touching without any kind of penetration of the victim. There is no significant gender difference regarding penetrative acts (anal, vaginal or oral penetration) as a percentage of all incidents of sexual abuse with physical contact (women: 40.0 percent; men: 31.3 percent; χ^2 (1, N = 367) = 1.74, p =.19).

The age at first victimisation with child sexual abuse (under 16) is between 2 and 15 years (M = 10.4 years; SD = 3.2) and is relatively homogeneous across all individual categories with the average ranging from 9.6 to 10.7 years. There is no difference here between female (M = 10.4 years, SD = 3.2) and male (M = 10.3 years, SD = 3.2) respondents.

5.4.2 Trends in prevalence rates of sexual abuse over the past two decades

A first indication regarding the trend in the risk of sexual abuse in the past two decades can be obtained by comparing the prevalence rates for the different age groups.[2] As can be seen from Figure 5.2, the prevalence rates vary considerably between the three age groups. In all three abuse categories, the prevalence of sexual abuse is roughly three times as great in the oldest age group comprising respondents aged 31 to 40 than in the youngest age group comprising respondents aged 16 to 20. Among men, this finding was limited to exhibitionism (indecent exposure) and sexual abuse with physical contact. The 'decline' in the prevalence rates for men is also somewhat less pronounced than for women, with prevalence rates being in the oldest age group about twice as high as in the youngest age group.

2 Because of the oversampling for this age group (before weighting), the youngest age group covers a smaller age range (five years) than the two older age cohorts (10 years each).

Fig. 5.2 Prevalence rates of child and adolescent sexual abuse (before the age of 16; in percent; weighted data)

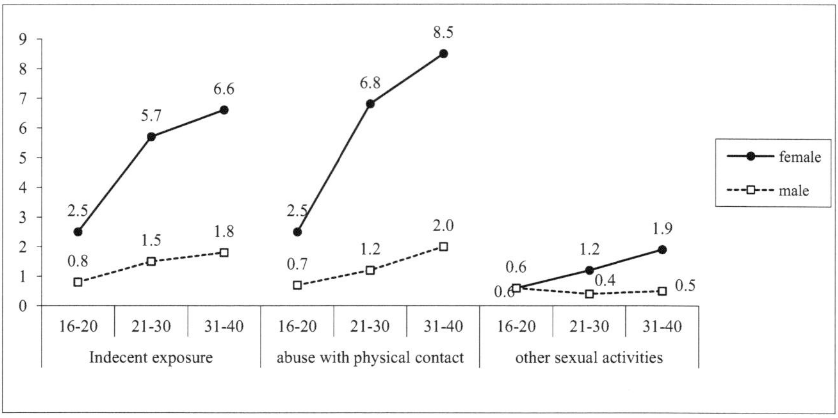

The differences in prevalence rates between age cohorts with regard to contact CSA are significant for male respondents (χ^2 (2, N = 4.663) = 9.32, p < .01) and highly significant for female respondents (χ^2 (2, N = 4.475) = 32.11, p < .001). With regard to indecent exposure, the differences between age groups are likewise highly significant for female respondents (χ^2 (2, N = 4.470) = 18.44, p < .001) but not significant for male respondents (χ^2 (2, N = 4.660) = 4.16, p = .13). With regard to 'other' sexual activities, statistically significant differences between age groups are once again found only for women (χ^2 (2, N = 4.464) = 7.23, p < .05).

To learn more about potential changes in the prevalence of child sexual abuse, a comparison was made with the original study dating from 1992.[3]

3 As the published prevalence rates from the 1992 survey (Wetzels 1997) relate to a sample with a wider age range (16 to 59) than the present survey, the 1992 sample was restricted to the 16-to-40 age range (N = 2,162) for better comparability. The 1992 data set was also restricted to German respondents (in 1992, origin was identified with nationality – German citizenship: yes/no – and not additionally by reference to migration background as in 2011). The very small group of respondents with other nationalities in 1992 – 2.4 percent of the total – was excluded for the presented analysis. The comparisons presented here thus relate for the 1992 survey solely to individuals aged 16 to 40 with German citizenship (N = 2,098, of which n = 1,020 male and n = 1.078 female). Although migration background was not additionally recorded in the 1992 survey, it may be assumed that limiting the sample to respondents with German citizenship for 1992 and to German respondents without

Fig. 5.3 Prevalence of sexual abuse before the age of 16 – KFN survey 1992 and 2011 (excluding 'other sexual activities'; in percent; weighted data)

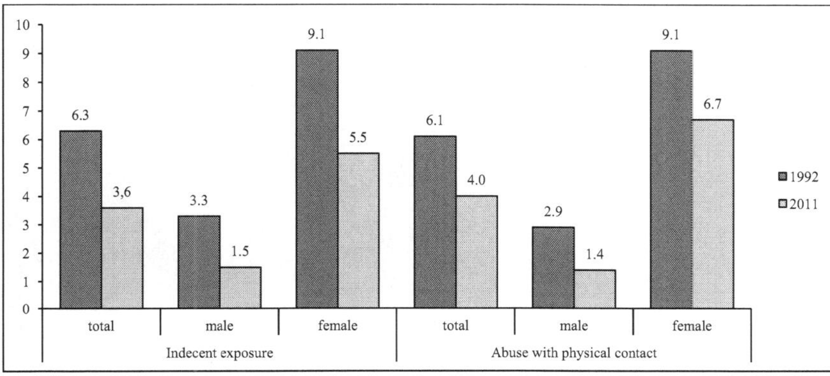

Comparing the prevalence figures from the two studies for contact CSA before the age of 16 supports the trend towards a decline in child sexual abuse discussed above (see Figure 5.3), as the recent prevalence rates for both sexes show a statistically significant difference from the 1992 figures (χ^2_{men} (1, N = 5.669) = 10.39, p ≤ .001; χ^2_{women} (1, N = 5.538) = 7.35, p < .01). In 1992, 9.1 percent of female respondents and 2.9 percent of male respondents were victims of child sexual abuse with physical contact before the age of 16; in the present study, the figures are 6.7 percent for female respondents and 1.4 percent for male respondents. The proportional decrease in the prevalence of sexual abuse is therefore larger for boys than for girls. With regard to indecent exposure, the prevalence rate fell from 9.1 (1992) to 5.5 percent (2011) for female respondents and from 3.3

---

migration background for 2011 yields the best possible degree of comparability in view of the changes and developments in migration and naturalisation that have taken place in the intervening years. As naturalisations have increased in the last 10 to 15 years (i.e., essentially since the 1992 survey; see Statistisches Bundesamt, 2011), the percentage of individuals with migration background left over after excluding individuals with non-German citizenship ought to be relatively small. It may also be assumed that only a small percentage of respondents with German citizenship will simultaneously have 'Aussiedler' status (individuals of German descent, primarily from former Eastern Bloc countries, who have claimed German nationality) as few of this group are likely to have been reached by the survey due to language difficulties.

(1992) to 1.5 percent (2011) for male respondents. This difference (decrease) is once again statistically significant, with χ^2_{men} (1, N = 5.665) = 15.62, $p < .001$; χ^2_{women} (1, N = 5.533) = 18.88, $p < .001$.

The statistically significant differences between the two studies (1992 and 2011) are spread equally across the different ages of consent (age < 14: male 2.2 vs. 1.1 percent, female 6.8 vs. 5.2 percent; age < 16: male 2.9 vs. 1.4 percent, female 9.1 vs. 6.7 percent). Statistical comparison by age of consent (chi square test) yields significant differences between the genders ($p \leq .001$ and $p < .01$ respectively).

5.4.3 Reporting rates

Victims were asked for each of the seven abuse behaviours whether the incident(s) were reported to the police. Overall, victims showed relatively little readiness to report occurrences of sexual abuse, for example with a figure of 14.0 percent for sexual abuse with physical contact (Figure 5.4).[4] The most frequently reported behaviour was exhibitionism (indecent exposure) with 18.7 percent – as also reported by Wetzels (1997).

No significant gender differences with regard to reporting are found for indecent exposure (χ^2 (1, N = 315) = 1.72, p = .19), sexual abuse with physical contact (χ^2 (1, N = 365) = 0.68, p = .41) or for other sexual activities (χ^2 (1, N = 77) = 0.5, p = .82). In all instances, however, female victims show a higher reporting rate than male victims (indecent exposure: female 20.2 percent, male 13.2 percent; sexual abuse with physical contact: female 14.7 percent, male 10.8 percent; other sexual activities: female 14.8 percent, male 12.5 percent).

---

4 Calculated for respondents who had experienced at least one of the five individual behaviours in the contact CSA category and at least one valid value for the 'Reported' item across all five grouped variables. To count towards the reporting rate for the combined abuse with physical contact variable, a case must feature experience of at least one of the five abuse behaviours with physical violence and having reported at least one of them. No account is given here to how many of any multiple number of sexual abuse behaviours were reported (i.e., for the purposes of the reporting rate, someone who has experienced a single act of abuse and reported it is treated the same as someone who experienced four such acts and reported only two of them).

Fig. 5.4 Reporting of indecent exposure, contact CSA and other sexual activities, by gender (in percent; weighted data)

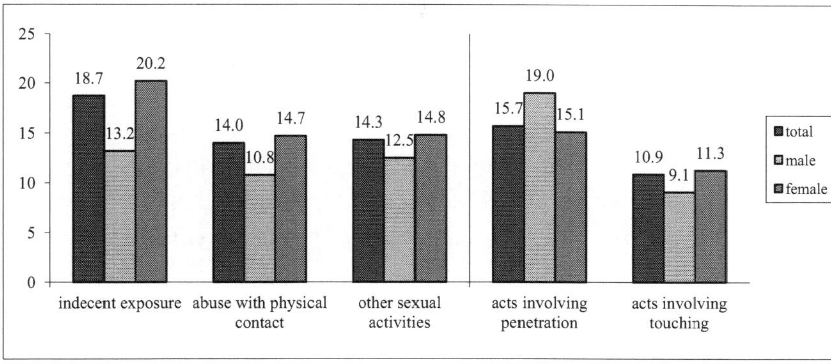

For a closer look at the reporting rates for differing severities of abuse behaviour within the sexual abuse with physical contact variable, an approach similar to Engfer's (2005) categorisation of sexual abuse by intensity was applied, with cases assigned to subcategories separating acts involving touching ('intensive abuse', Engfer 2005) from acts involving oral, anal or vaginal penetration (classified as the most intensive form of abuse, see Engfer 2005). The touching subcategory was strictly limited to cases where no acts involving anal, vaginal or oral penetration were reported. This was to make allowance for the inability to tell whether different acts took place in combination (for example whether a reported offence involving touching took place in combination with a penetration offence such that it was not so much the touching as the penetration that was reported). This could result in the reporting rate for more 'minor' acts of abuse (sexual touching) being overstated. Cases in which at least one act of anal, vaginal or oral penetration (if applicable in combination with touching) are assigned to the penetration category.

If sexual abuse with physical contact is divided as described into acts involving penetration and acts solely involving touching (without the victim additionally experiencing penetration), it emerges that penetration offences are reported significantly more frequently, with a reporting rate of 15.7 percent, than acts solely involving touching of the victim or of the perpetrator by the victim (10.9 percent). There are no significant gender differences in the reporting rates (acts involving touching: female 11.3 percent, male 9.1 percent; acts involving penetration: female 15.1 percent, male 19.0 percent); $\chi^2_{touching}$ (1, N = 221) = 0.18, p = .67); $\chi^2_{penetration}$ (1, N = 140) = 0.21, p = .65.

An analysis of reporting rates by age group (see Figure 5.5) provides indications of a change in the tendency to report child sexual abuse in recent decades. Both indecent exposure (χ^2 (2, N = 315) = 11.96, p = .001) and sexual abuse with physical contact (χ^2 (2, N = 366) = 14.86, p ≤ .001) show (highly) significant differences in reporting rates between age groups. This takes the form of increasing propensity to report, with reporting rates at their lowest in the oldest age groups and at their highest in the youngest (e.g., abuse with physical contact: 16-to-20-year-olds 34.6 percent versus 9.0 percent in 31-to-40-year-olds). No significant differences emerge on the other hand for other sexual activities (χ^2 (2, N = 78) = 1.11, p = .57), for which there is also no identifiable trend across age groups.

Fig. 5.5 Reporting rates for indecent exposure, sexual abuse with physical contact and other sexual activities, by age group (in percent; weighted data)

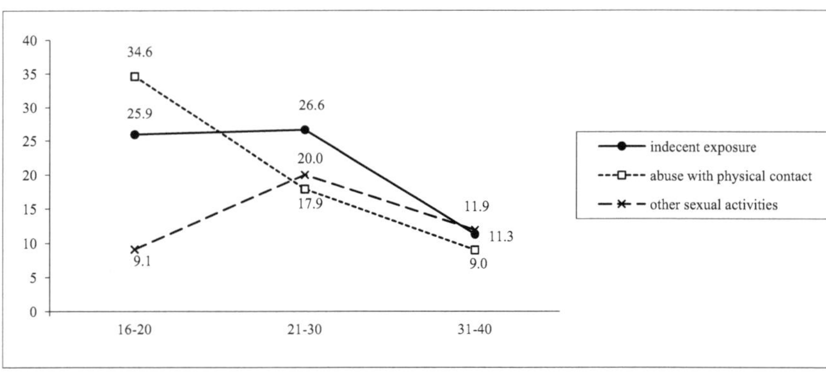

According to the Police Crime Statistics (Bundesministerium des Inneren, 2010; Figure 5.6), reported cases of child sexual abuse (offences under sections 176, 176a and 176b of the German Criminal Code) declined by 27.4 percent among female and 24.4 percent among male victims between 1994 and 2010. In light of the increasing propensity to report just described, this can be taken as further evidence of the declining trend in child sexual abuse shown by the self-report survey data. The combination of findings from reported cases and self-report surveys also shows the decline in cases of child sexual abuse to be even more pronounced than is evident from the Police Crime Statistics time series.

Fig. 5.6 Trend in reported cases of child sexual abuse (offences under sections 176, 176a and 176b of the German Criminal Code) as shown in the Police Crime Statistics, 1994 to 2010[5]

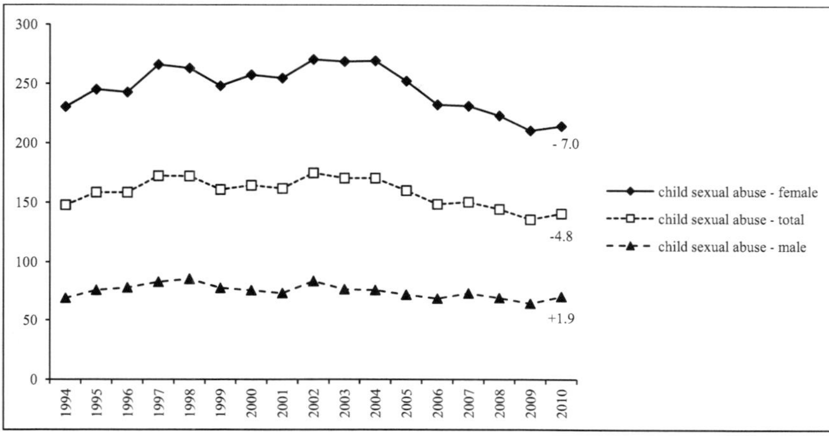

5.4.4 Perpetrators of child and adolescent sexual abuse

The question concerning the perpetrators of sexual abuse contained an extensive list of items from which respondents were asked to select all that applied. One fact that stands out with regard to the overall sample of 16-to-40-year-olds is that for indecent exposure, in by far the largest number of cases (39.9 percent) the perpetrator was identified as an unknown male individual. These unknown perpetrators can probably be assumed to be 'conventional' exhibitionists who gain sexual simulation by displaying their genitals to a male or female victim, usually in a public place, without any further sexual act being involved (such as acts involving physical contact with the victim). With other perpetrators – those known or related to their victims – acts of exhibitionism are less likely to be singular acts and more likely to be accompanied by or precede other forms of sexual abuse. In the case of exhibitionism by unknown perpetrators, too, however, it

5 The figures shown are the number of victims of child sexual abuse (children/adolescents under 14; offences under sections 176, 176a and 176b of the German Criminal Code) per 100,000 inhabitants adjusted for the size of each group as a percentage of the population.

cannot be ruled out that the indecent exposure may take place in conjunction with other acts of abuse (with physical contact). Female perpetrators were not cited as a result of the question on this offence being asked solely in relation to male perpetrators.

With regard to contact CSA (Figure 5.7), the perpetrators as cited by both female and male respondents are predominantly male relatives[6] (female respondents: 32.4 percent; male respondents: 27.0 percent) and male acquaintances[7] (female respondents: 29.8 percent; male respondents: 19.1 percent). Among female respondents, the perpetrator was identified in 9.2 percent of cases as the natural father and in 9.7 percent as the stepfather; among male respondents, the equivalent figures were 7.4 percent and 12.3 percent. For both sexes, the perpetrator was thus identified in just under 20 percent of cases as the father or the stepfather. Uncles were cited most frequently when it came to male relatives (female respondents: 9.1 percent; male respondents: 15.4 percent). Taking male relatives and the separate figures for fathers and stepfathers together, about half of all perpetrators are identified by both sexes as members of the family.

Overall, female perpetrators are cited very rarely, but when they are it is primarily by male victims (15.1 percent). The latter finding is most evident for other sexual activities. More male respondents than female respondents cite female perpetrators in this category (38.5 versus 1.7 percent). Female perpetrators of child and adolescent sexual abuse thus appear to display a clearer preference for victims of the opposite sex than do male perpetrators, who account for a very large proportion of perpetrators for male victims. It should be taken into account in this connection, however, that victim gender preference among perpetrators, who are predominantly male in any case, is already reflected in the roughly four-fold higher incidence of female victims. Engfer (2005) additionally notes that the proportion of female perpetrators generally tends to be underestimated, as physical contact with children is more a part of everyday life for women

---

6 The male relatives category does not include fathers and stepfathers. These are reported separately. The male relatives category comprises relatives such as grandfathers, uncles, brothers and male cousins.

7 With regard to the male acquaintances category, respondents were able to provide specific information on the perpetrator in response to an open question. The category includes acquaintances such as neighbours, friends and acquaintances of the victim or of his or her parents, brothers and sisters or friends, and perpetrators from the school/leisure activities context.

and is less readily perceived as overstepping a limit; plus, male victims of sexual abuse by older women less frequently perceive themselves as victims.

Fig. 5.7 Distribution of combined groups of perpetrators of sexual abuse with physical contact before the age of 16, by gender (Multiple responses possible; in percent; weighted data)

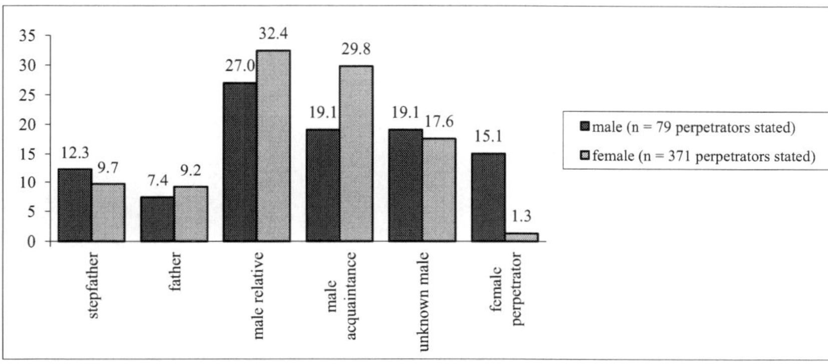

An analysis of perpetrators by age cohort (Table 5.4) shows that the described decrease in sexual abuse in the last three decades appears to relate primarily to sexual abuse in the family. Thus, in parallel with the continuous decline in cases, male relatives accounted for a significantly smaller percentage of all perpetrators for 16-to-20-year-old respondents (26.7 percent) than for 31-to-40-year-old respondents (51.7 percent). It should be noted here that although there has indeed been a shift in the relative share of unknown male perpetrators when it comes to abuse with physical contact (from 15.8 percent for 31-to-40-year-old respondents to 33.6 percent for 16-to-20-year-old respondents), this does not imply a heightened risk of abuse from such perpetrators. With the prevalence of abuse declining overall, the percentage increase merely means that the number of offences committed by unknown perpetrators has tended to remain unchanged (rather than decreasing with the number committed by perpetrators in the family). The relative share of male acquaintances among perpetrators of abuse with physical contact has held near-constant over the three decades. When interpreting these figures, however, it is necessary to take into account the limitations imposed by the large difference in the number of perpetrators cited by each age cohort (n = 27 for 16-to-20-year-olds versus n = 255 for 31-to-40-year-olds).

Table 5.4 Distribution of combined groups of perpetrators by age cohort (in percent; weighted data)

	Indecent exposure			Abuse with physical contact			Other sexual activities		
	16-20	21-30	31-40	16-20	21-30	31-40	16-20	21-30	31-40
Perpetrators stated	28	142	186	27	168	255	9	26	51
Male relatives	24.3	42.2	44.5	26.7	51.4	51.7	32.4	46.2	51.6
Male acquaintances	15.5	19.1	17.7	37.2	26.7	27.8	8.5	14.6	31.2
Unknown males	60.2	38.7	37.8	33.6	18.4	15.8	30.4	33.5	10.1
Female perpetrators	--	--	--	2.5	2.5	4.7	28.7	5.7	7.1

Multiple responses possible

5.5 Discussion

The prevalence rates for sexual abuse determined in the present study – 6.7 percent among women and 1.4 percent among men for abuse with physical contact before the age of 16 – are at the lower end of the spectrum compared with the range found across different studies (cf. Pereda et al. 2009). The prevalence rates are also lower than the German study by Haeuser et al. (2011) carried out in the same year. Given the large differences in definitions (the CTQ covers a broader and less specific range of behaviours than the specific sexual behaviours surveyed in the present study) and the substantially larger age range sampled in Haeuser et al. (2011), it is scarcely possible to compare with the present study (or for that matter with the study by Wetzels (1997), as Haeuser et al. (2011) themselves note). It is conceivable for example – looking at the lower prevalence rates in younger age groups – that the lower prevalence rates partly reflect the young age structure of the sample in the present study relative to that used by Haeuser et al. (2011).

The indications of declining prevalence rates of sexual abuse with regard to the forms of abuse surveyed here are also supported by findings from international studies (cf. Bebbington et al. 2010, Finkelhor et al. 2010, Laaksonen et al. 2011). Bringing together various US studies, for example, Finkelhor et al. (2010) likewise report decreases in sexual abuse between 1993 or 1995 and 2005. The authors additionally report from studies of their own (telephone surveys of 2-to-17-year-old children and adolescents or their closest caregivers) significantly lower prevalence rates for sexual abuse in 2008 compared with 2003.

Bebbington et al. (2010), in their study based on a random sample of English households (7,353 respondents) featuring an age-group-specific analysis of three age cohorts between the ages of 16 and 44, similarly identified a decline in prevalence rates through the age groups from 35-to-44-year-olds down to 16-to-24-year-olds (with prevalence rates of 10.7, 8.0 and 6.6 percent). Interestingly, although the prevalence rates held broadly constant around 10 percent for the three age groups between the ages of 35 and 64, prevalence rates were significantly lower again in the two oldest age groups (ages 65 to 74 and over 75, at 6.1 and 2.7 percent). This effect can be interpreted by drawing on cognitive psychology, as events tend to be recalled less readily (i.e., less frequently) the further removed they are from the present (cf. Solso 2005), hence if the incidence rate stays constant, retrospective recall of events from childhood or adolescence would be expected to result in the lowest prevalence rate in the oldest age group. The differences between cohorts in the study presented in this paper, on the other hand, run contrary to these expectations and may therefore speak in favour of a real decrease. This conclusion is also supported when comparing the present data with findings from Wetzels (1997), where for three age cohorts closely equivalent to the present study – ages 16 to 20, 21 to 29 and 30 to 39 – only minor differences were found regarding sexual abuse with physical contact (male respondents: 2.9, 2.8 and 2.9 percent; female respondents: 9, 9.6 and 10 percent). With regard to the lower prevalence rates found for each of the oldest age cohorts in his study, Wetzels (1997) notes as additional factors to be taken into account when interpreting age cohort comparisons the possibly lesser readiness of older age groups to talk about sexual topics (cf. Casey/Nurius 2006) and the greater sensitisation of younger age groups to sexuality-related topics that has largely come about through increased public airing of such topics. In light of the young age structure of the sample in the present study, such factors may be assumed to play a lesser part here; if that is the case, however, it would speak even more strongly in favour of the decrease in prevalence rates being real.

It must also be noted at this point, however, that mechanisms such as memory repression or suppression in connection with traumatic experiences may continue to operate with effects whose persistence is hard to estimate. For example, it is conceivable that repression of traumatic abuse experiences might be more pronounced in the youngest age group (for whom the abuse is most recent) than in older age groups, with the result of the abuse not (yet) being accessible to conscious memory, thus providing one explanation for the lower prevalence rates in younger age groups. In a prospective study Williams (1994) was able to show that of 129 women with documented experiences of sexual abuse between the age of 10 months and 12 years, 38 percent were unable to recall the experience when surveyed about their childhood 17 years later. This applied most of all for those whose abuse took place at a very young age or for whom the perpetrator was someone they knew. A more recent study by Goodman et al. (2003), on the other hand, found that of 175 surveyed individuals with documented sexual experiences of abuse, 81 percent were able to say in interview that they had been abused. Factors identified by the authors as relevant to whether the abuse was reported in interview included being older when the abuse ceased, maternal support after the abuse came out, and severity of the abuse experience. The authors conclude that if people do not report a recollection of abuse, the cause is not necessarily memory inaccessibility, and that such inaccessibility applies in only a small number of cases. Viewed from the opposite direction, there were still 20 percent who did not state/recall having been abused, hence it may be assumed that epidemiological studies based on retrospective self-reporting such as the present study tend if anything to underestimate the actual incidence of abuse. Whether this underestimation is spread systematically across age cohorts is something that cannot be judged due to the many different influencing factors (see above). It must be noted with regard to the studies targeting the recall validity of traumatised individuals, however, that the samples used are very specific (comprising respondents whose abuse is documented and are surveyed in a follow-up to treatment or intervention; cf. Hardt/Rutter 2004).

The supplementary analysis of perpetrators by age cohorts showed that the identified decline in sexual abuse primarily relates to abuse in the family. This trend is also reported by Casey and Nurius (2006) in a study of a household sample of 18-to-96-year-old women (1,325 respondents) from the State of Washington. This is an indication that the increased efforts since the early 1990s to raise awareness of (sexually) transgressive acts towards and their effects on children, together with the resulting prevention efforts, have been particularly effective in this context. Another potential explanation is that is has become easier in the last 20 years to impose (spatial) separation in cases of violence and problem relationships (for example under Germany's Protection from Violence Act 2002). Apart from that, various legislative changes in Germany have had an overall effect on intrafamilial violence, including marital rape being made punishable

(1997) and abolition of the parental right to administer corporal punishment (2000). Taking into account the fact that children who experience sexual abuse frequently face violence on multiple fronts within the family (such as interparental violence and physical maltreatment; cf. Wetzels 1997), effective intervention in domestic physical and sexual violence may be expected to lower the risk of intrafamilial sexual abuse for any children. It can also be concluded from the empirically proven correlation between the various forms of child maltreatment and abuse (cf. Haeuser et al. 2011, Wetzels 1997) that the decline in sexual abuse – and notably sexual abuse in the family – is partly an indirect consequence of abolition of the parental right of corporal punishment (2000) and, hand in hand with that, increasing awareness in favour of non-violent child-rearing. Whether the decline in sexual abuse is accompanied by declining prevalence rates for other forms of victimisation in childhood and adolescence (such as neglect or physical maltreatment) and by a general decline in violence in the family (including interparental physical and sexual violence) is something that remains to be examined in further analysis of the data. A number of studies already provide empirical evidence of parental physical violence in particular having declined in Germany since the 1990s (Baier 2008, Brettfeld/Wetzels 2004, Bussmann 2005).

The rising reporting rates in the last 20 years may be seen as an expression of social change in which child sexual abuse has come under increasingly explicit condemnation and victims have been increasingly enabled in consequence both to perceive abuse for what it is and to make it public. This conclusion is corroborated by findings from other studies (cf. Casey/Nurius 2006, Finkelhor et al. 2011b). From the perpetrator perspective, the resulting heightened risk of discovery may act as a deterrent and thus represent a further explanatory factor for the decline in the forms of child sexual abuse (notably those with physical contact) reported in the present study. To what extent this leads, however, to more anonymous forms of child and adolescent sexual abuse (for example via Internet forums) is something that cannot be answered here.

In summary, the findings of the present study may first of all give reason to conclude that in terms of prevention, public relations work, the establishment of intervention and support for victims and the committed work of victim counselling services, the efforts already underway are going in the right direction. At the same time, the finding that 6.7 percent of surveyed 16-to-40-year-old women of German descent and 1.4 percent of men experienced sexual abuse with physical contact before the age of 16 shows that much remains to be done. Additionally, while reporting rates for sexual abuse have increased, it must not be forgotten that sexual abuse – including in its severe forms abuse featuring penetration – is still a crime that is rarely reported overall (14.0 percent of cases of sexual abuse with physical contact before the age of 14). In other words, the majority of sexual abuse still goes unreported. It must therefore be assumed that many sexually abused children still do not (and cannot) receive the support they need.

There are some additional methodological limitations that must be taken into consideration when interpreting the findings and with regard to their suitability for generalisation. Thus due to the sample type and recruitment method – a quota sample recruited by commissioned interviewers according to stipulated quota characteristics – certain groups were not reached, some of which may display heightened prevalence of sexual victimisation (such as patients in psychiatric clinics, prison inmates, residents of care homes for people with mental and/or physical disabilities, homeless people, prostitutes, and people in the drug scene). Reference is made in this regard to a study just completed on the living situation of and pressures faced by women with impairments and disabilities in Germany (Schroettle et al. 2011), the first study of its kind in Germany to collate representative data on violence and abuse experienced by women with disabilities. The study shows that women with disabilities and impairments are between two and three times more likely to have been victims of sexual abuse in childhood and adolescence than the average for women in the German population as a whole, and represent a particularly vulnerable group with regard to sexual violence and abuse. This should be taken into account when interpreting the findings to the extent that the figures reported here must be considered a bottom limit and relate to unreported cases in a population segment that excludes groups such as those just mentioned. All population-based self-report surveys of this kind are subject to the same problem, however (including, for example, telephone surveys as in Finkelhor et al. 2010). To this extent it is indeed possible – while allowing for differences in methodology and definition – to compare the findings with those of other representative surveys. This applies in particular to the 1992 study in which Wetzels (1997) noted similar limitations.

Besides the systematic inability to reach certain groups of the population, another potential and unquantifiable limitation to the representativeness of the data is lack of knowledge about any selection effects regarding individuals' propensity to participate. For example it is possible that individuals with experiences corresponding to the nature of the survey may take part precisely because they have something to report. On the other hand, the opposite could also be the case, with a greater refusal rate among victims explicitly wanting to avoid giving details about their victimisation (cf. Hardt 2005). Edwards et al. (2001), however, found no significant differences in abuse experience between respondents who participated and those who refused. The slight differences that they did identify went in the direction of people who have experienced abuse tending more to take part in surveys than to refuse. Another limitation in this context is that a refusal rate cannot be stated as interviewers did not note how many potential study participants they contacted and how many of these finally refused their participation.

Finally, regarding interpretation of the declining rates of sexual abuse in the last two decades, it is expressly pointed out that these relate solely to 'conventional' forms of sexual abuse specifically included in the survey. The study is unable to answer whether there has been a shift within or diversification of forms of abuse. For example, with the huge growth in new media (such as mobile Internet, texting and picture messaging, ubiquitous camera phones, chat rooms, social networks and video telephony) compounded by children and adolescents having early access to such media and the resulting proliferation of opportunities (easier access to pornography, means of recording sexual contacts with children and sharing the recorded content, and the ability to enter into contact with children and adolescents anonymously in social networks), abuse with physical contact may now have made way for other forms of child sexual abuse that are not explicitly covered by the study (although they may be included in the not further specified category 'other sexual activities').

References

Baier, D. (2008). Entwicklung der Jugenddelinquenz und ausgewählter Bedingungsfaktoren seit 1998 in den Städten Hannover, München, Stuttgart und Schwäbisch Gmünd. Kriminologisches Forschungsinstitut Niedersachsen: KFN: Forschungsbericht Nr. 104.

Bange, D. (1992). Die dunkle Seite der Kindheit. Köln: Volksblatt Verlag.

Barnett, O. W., Miller-Perrin, C. L., Perrin, R. D. (2011). Family Violence Across the Lifespan: An Introduction. Thousand Oaks: Sage Publications.

Bebbington, P. E., Jonas, S., Brugha, T., Meltzer, H., Jenkins, R., Cooper, C., King, M., McManus, S. (2010). Child Sexual Abuse Reported by an English National Sample: Characteristics and Demography. Social Psychiatry and Psychiatric Epidemiology, 46, 255-262.

Bechhofer, F., Paterson, L. (2000). Principles of Research Design in the Social Sciences. London: Routledge.

Bernstein, D.P., Stein J. A., Newcomb M.D., Walker, E., Pogge, D., Ahluvalia, T., Stokes, J., Handelsman, L., Medrano, M., Desmond, D., Zule, W. (2003). Development and Validation of a Brief Screening Version of the Childhood Trauma Questionnaire. Child Abuse & Neglect, 27, 169–190.

Brettfeld, K., Wetzels, P. (2004). Über die präventive Kraft des Wissens. Zum gesellschaftskritischen Potential und kriminalpolitischem Nutzen kriminologischer Dunkelfeldforschung. In: K.-M. Karliczek (Ed.), Kriminologische Erkundungen. Wissenschaftliches Symposium aus Anlass des 65. Geburtstages von Klaus Sessar (p. 226-265). Münster: Lit.

Bundesministerium des Inneren (Eds.) (2010). Polizeiliche Kriminalstatistik: Deliktarten Zeitreihe 1993-2010. Berlin: Bundesministerium des Inneren.

Bussmann, K.-D. (2005). Report über die Auswirkungen des Gesetzes zur Ächtung der Gewalt in der Erziehung. Bundesministerium der Justiz. Verfügbar unter: http://bussmann.jura.uni-halle.de/publikationen/ [19.12.2011].

Casey, E. A., Nurius, P.S. (2006). Trends in the Prevalence and Characteristics of Sexual Violence: A Cohort Analysis. Violence & Victims, 21, 629-644.

Deegener, G. (2005). Kindesmissbrauch. Erkennen, Helfen, Vorbeugen. Weinheim und Basel: Beltz.

Deegener, G. (2006). Erscheinungsformen und Ausmaße von Kindesmisshandlung. In: W. Heitmeyer, M. Schroettle (Eds.), Gewalt. Beschreibung, Analysen, Prävention (p. 26-44). Bonn: Bundeszentrale für politische Bildung.

Deegener, G., Körner, W. (2005). Kindesmisshandlung und Vernachlässigung. Ein Handbuch. Göttingen: Hogrefe.

Edwards, V. J., Anda, R. F., Nordenberg , D. F., Felitti, V. J., Williamson, D. F., Howard, N., Wright, J. A. (2001). Bias Assessment for Child Abuse Survey: Factors Affecting Probability of Response to a Survey About Child Abuse. Child Abuse & Neglect, 25, 307–312.

Engfer, A. (2005). Formen der Misshandlung von Kindern – Definitionen, Häufigkeiten, Erklärungsansätze. In: U. T. Egle, S. O. Hoffmann, P. Joraschky, (Eds.), Sexueller Missbrauch, Misshandlung, Vernachlässigung (p. 3-19). Stuttgart: Schattauer.

Elliger, T. J, Schoetensack, K. (1991). Sexueller Missbrauch von Kindern – eine kritische Bestandsaufnahme. In: G. Nissen (Ed.), Psychogene Psychosyndrome und ihre Therapie im Kindes- und Jugendalter (p. 143-154). Bern: Huber.

Finkelhor, D. (2005). Zur internationalen Epidemiologie von sexuellem Missbrauch an Kindern. In: G. Amman, R. Wipplinger (Eds.), Sexueller Missbrauch – Überblick zu Forschung, Beratung und Therapie. Ein Handbuch. (3rd Ed.) (p. 81-94). Tübingen: dgvt-Verlag.

Finkelhor, D., Hamby, S., Turner, H., Ormrod, R. (2011a). The Juvenile Victimization Questionnaire: 2nd Revision (JVC-R2). Durham, NH: Crimes Against Children Research Center.

Finkelhor, D., Ormrod, R., Turner, H., Hamby, S. (2011b). School, Police, and Medical Authority Involvement With Children Who Have Experienced Victimization. Archives of Pediatrics & Adolescent Medicine, 165, 9-15.

Finkelhor, D., Turner, H., Ormrod, R., Hamby, S. L. (2010). Trends in Childhood Violence and Abuse Exposure. Evidence From 2 National Surveys. Archives of Pediatrics & Adolescent Medicine, 164, 238-242.

Goodman, G. S., Ghetti, S., Quas, J. A., Edelstein, R. S., Alexander, K. W., Redlich, A. D., Cordon, I. M., Jones, D. P. (2003). A Prospective Study of Memory for Child Sexual Abuse: New Findings Relevant to the Repressed-Memory Controversy. Psychological Science, 14, 113-118.

Hardt, J., Rutter, M. (2004). Validity of Adult Retrospective Reports of Adverse Childhood Experiences: Review of the Evidence. Journal of Child Psychology and Psychiatry, 45, 260–273.

Haeuser, W., Braehler, E., Schmutzer, G., Glaesmer, H. (2011). Misshandlungen in Kindheit und Jugend - Ergebnisse einer Umfrage in einer repräsentativen Stichprobe der deutschen Bevölkerung. Deutsches Ärzteblatt, 108, 287-94.

Kappis, B., Hardt, J. (2005). Standardisierte Verfahren zur retrospektiven Erfassung von Kindheitsbelastungen. In: P. Joraschky, U.T. Egle, S.O. Hoffman (Eds.). Sexueller Missbrauch, Misshandlung, Vernachlässigung – Erkennung, Therapie und Prävention der Folgen früher Stresserfahrungen. (3rd Ed.). Stuttgart: Schattauer.

Laaksonen, T., Sariola, H., Johansson, A., Jerna, P., Varjonen, M., von der Pahlen, B., Sandnabba, N.K., Santtila, P. (2011). Changes in the Prevalence of Child Sexual Abuse, Its Risk Factors, and Their Associations as a Function of Age Cohort in a Finnish Population Sample. Child Abuse & Neglect, 35, 480 – 490.

Painter, K., Farrington, D.P. (1998). Marital Violence in Great Britain and its Relationship to Marital and Non-marital Rape. International Review of Victimology, 5, 257-276.

Pereda, N., Guilera, G., Forns, M., Gómez-Benito, J. (2009). The Prevalence of Child Sexual Abuse in Community and Student Samples: A Meta-Analysis. Clinical Psychology Review, 29, 328–338.

Raupp, U., Eggers, C. (1993). Sexueller Missbrauch von Kindern. Eine regionale Studie über Prävalenz und Charakteristik. Monatsschrift für Kinderheilkunde, 141, 316-322

Schroettle, M., Hornberg, C., Glammeier, S., Sellach, B., Kavemann, B., Puhe, H., Zinsmeister, J. (2011). Lebenssituation und Belastungen von Frauen mit Beeinträchtigungen und Behinderungen in Deutschland. Kurzzusammenfassung der zentralen Ergebnisse. Verfügbar unter: http://www.uni-bielefeld.de/IFF/for/for-gewf-fmb.html [19.12.2011].

Solso, R. L. (2005). Kognitive Psychologie. Heidelberg: Springer Medizin Verlag.

Statistisches Bundesamt (2007). Bevölkerung und Erwerbstätigkeit – Bevölkerung mit Migrationshintergrund. Ergebnisse des Mikrozensus 2005 (Fachserie 1 Reihe 2.2). Wiesbaden: Statistisches Bundesamt.

Wetzels, P. (1997). Gewalterfahrungen in der Kindheit. Sexueller Missbrauch, körperliche Mißhandlung und deren langfristige Konsequenzen – Interdisziplinäre Beiträge zur kriminologischen Forschung. Baden-Baden: Nomos Verlagsgesellschaft.

Williams, L. M. (1994). Recall of Childhood Trauma: A Prospective Study of Women's Memories. Journal of Consulting and Clinical Psychology, 62, 1167-1176.

Wipplinger, R., Amann, G. (2005). Sexueller Missbrauch – Überblick zu Forschung, Beratung und Therapie. Ein Handbuch (3rd. Ed.). Tübingen: dgvt-Verlag.

Wynkoop, T. F., Capps, S. C., Priest, B. J. (1995). Incidence and Prevalence of Child Sexual Abuse: A Critical Review of Data Collection Procedures. Journal of Child Sexual Abuse, 4, 49–67.

Part III:
Findings on Special Groups

6. Police Officers as Victims of Violence: Findings of a Germany-wide Survey

Karoline Ellrich, Dirk Baier

6.1 Introduction and research questions

In the line of duty police officers are confronted with a wide range of difficult and dangerous situations. Although most police-public interactions are without conflict, sometimes a situation escalates and police officers are subject to violent assault. In a study conducted by Klemisch et al. (2005), 64 percent of the police officers surveyed had been physically injured while on duty; 55 percent had been in life-threatening situations. Various studies confirmed that such events are a source of severe stress in police officers (cf. Hallenberger et al. 2003, Neugebauer and Latscha 2009).

For Germany, no official statistics on the prevalence of violent assaults on police officers exist. Thus the number of reported cases of resistance to state authorities as published in the Police Crime Statistics is often used as a proxy. Over the period 2000 to 2008 this statistic shows an almost constant increase of such offences, adding up to a three-fold (35 percent).[1] This trend is often seen as an indication of a growing readiness to use violence against the police. But based on these figures, conclusions regarding the prevalence and trends in police exposure to violence cannot be easily drawn: Firstly, up to the year 2008, the reported number of resistance offences related to persons in law enforcement in general. This does not permit separate analysis of cases involving solely police officers. Secondly, the Police Crime Statistic documents only the most severe offence in each case. If a resistance offence is accompanied by an assault, only the latter is counted in the statistics. The registered cases of resistance therefore underrepresent serious assaults on police officers. Thirdly, no conclusion can be drawn from the Police Crime Statistics about the circumstances leading to assaults on police officers, what groups of police officers are especially

1 From 2009, a decline in the number of cases of resistance against state authorities can be stated in the Police Crime Statistics.

vulnerable to violence, or the consequences that can arise from such assaults. This information is, however, necessary for use in vocational and further training to better prepare police officers for such dangerous situations and to provide them with appropriate support if they experience assault.

Both national and international studies have focused on a phenomenological description of typical situations in which police officers are assaulted (cf. Bragason 2006, Brown 2004, Falk 2000, FBI 2010, Jäger 1988, Ohlemacher et al. 2003).[2] In German research, the topic has been addressed from a range of different perspectives, which among other things restricts the possibility to compare findings. Apart from studies on murder and attempted murder of police officers (Ohlemacher et al. 2003, Sessar et al. 1980), others exist which focus on police officers being rendered unfit for work for periods of several days following an assault (Jäger 1988, Ohlemacher et al. 2003). Other studies address resistance offences against police officers (such as Falk 2000) which, although they need not necessarily result in violent assaults and injury, still involve confrontational situations in police-public interaction.

The most recent comprehensive study on violence against police officers was conducted in 2000 (Ohlemacher et al. 2003). The study focused on serious violence against police officers who were subject to either an attempted murder or at minimum needed seven days' absence from work as a result of a violent assault. Since then, available information on the extent of violence against police officers on duty is restricted to the before mentioned registered cases of resistance against state authorities reported in the Police Crime Statistics. To gain current data at the start of 2010 an online survey on violence against police officers was conducted. Ten of 16 German federal states decided to take part in this study. The sample consists of 20,938 police officers, making for a response rate of 25.1 percent (Ellrich et al. 2012, p. 36). Around one in five officers was female. The age of the respondents varied between 19 and 62, with an average of 41.3

---

2 In general these studies are based on an analysis of those cases in which assaults occur (Johnson 2011, Ohlemacher et al. 2003). This allows conclusions to be drawn as to the circumstances in which the violence occurred and the assailants involved. It is not, therefore, possible to conduct risk analyses, meaning to evaluate which situations and which individuals are particularly dangerous. To do so, information is needed regarding the frequency with which police officers are confronted with certain situations and individuals during their day-to-day work.

years. Mostly the participants were out on the beat or on vehicle patrol (44.3 percent), or conducting investigations (23.2 percent). Just under one-twelfth (8.4 percent) served in special units (other types of duty: 23.9 percent). In addition, most of them (72.8 percent) operated in areas, which had fewer than 250,000 inhabitants. Compared with overall police numbers in the ten German federal states surveyed, female officers, young police officers and police officers from regions in western Germany (including Berlin) were overrepresented in the sample (Ellrich et al. 2012, p. 42).

The aim of the survey was to gain a comprehensive overview of police officers' experience of violence in the course of their duties. In this regard, answers were sought to the following questions, which also shape the structure of this paper:

- To what extent are police officers exposed to different forms of violence during the course of their duties?
- What characterises share a) officers affected by violence, b) assailants who carried out assaults, and c) the situations in which violence against police officers occurred?
- How have trends developed in respect of violence against police officers in the period 2005 to 2009?
- How do violent assaults affect the officers involved?

6.2 Findings

6.2.1 To what extent are police officers exposed to different forms of violence in the course of their duties?

Violence can take many forms, and not just in physical assaults or the use of weapons. Threats and insults can also be defined as violence. The frequency with which police officers were exposed to violence while on duty in 2009 is shown in Figure 6.1.

It can be stated that 80.9 percent of police officers had been insulted or called names while on duty, with one in five experiencing this at least once a month. The rate is somewhat lower as regards threats, at 65.4 percent, although here, too, the majority of respondents had rarely been exposed to this form of violence (once/a few times). Taking together police officers are relatively frequently confronted with verbal violence in the line of duty. All other forms of violence listed in figure 6.1 were experienced significantly less frequently. That the number of officers affected decreases relative to the increasing degree of violence is also shown in other studies (cf. Bosold 2006, Manzoni 2003). Slightly more than a third of all respondents reported mild physical violence in the form of pushing, shoving, being held or manhandled, while one in five or one in six police officers had been kicked and/or hit by a citizen at least once in 2009. More serious forms of violence, such as threatening with or the use of weapons/ dangerous objects are rarer in comparison. Nonetheless, almost one in eleven officers said they had been assaulted with a weapon or a dangerous object at least once in a given year.

Fig. 6.1 Frequencies of different experiences of violence while on duty in 2009 (in percent)

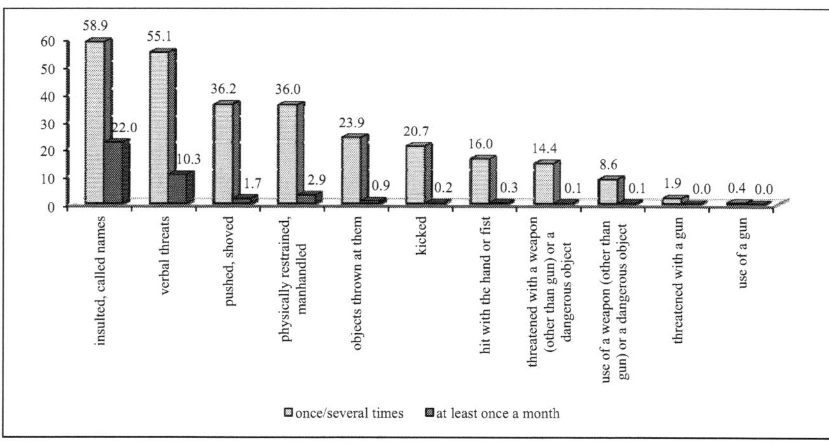

6.2.2 *What characterises share officers affected by violence?*

From a preventive standpoint, it is important to know whether there is a link between characteristics of the officers and the likelihood of an assault. According to Schmalzl (2005, p. 10), for example, negligent behaviour, mistakes in ensuring personal safety, and lack of coordination with fellow officers on the beat or patrol can act as an accelerator of violence, making it more likely for an officer to be assaulted while on duty.

In general a distinction can be made between visible and non-visible characteristics of police officers (Baier/Ellrich 2012). Visible traits include gender, physical stature and age, all of which citizens can readily recognize. Non-visible traits manifest themselves when the two sides interact. Factors that play a role are attitudes and abilities, both of which affect the behaviour of police officers and of citizens. Because the survey provides no information on the non-visible traits of police officers, the analyses presented in this paper are based on the visible factors only. These include the usual demographic factors such as gender, age, body height, body weight and ethnic origin of the police officers surveyed. For analysis, victims of violence were operationalized as all officers who reported at least one physical assault (pushing, restraining, kicked, and hit) in 2009. This applies to just over half of the respondents surveyed (50.7 percent). The selection was based on two criteria: firstly, when compared with the use of dangerous objects/weapons, these forms of violence are experienced relatively frequently. Secondly, the physical integrity of a police officer is damaged by their experience of violence, so assaults have serious consequences. To identify which factors influence an officer's risk of victimisation, logistic regression analysis was used (cf. Backhaus et al. 2003). This highlights the impact of a variable (such as gender) given the influence of other variables (such as age). As shown in Table 6.1, two models were run. The first focuses solely on the named characteristics of the affected police officers, while the second model considered the additional influence of duty-related factors (type of duty, area of operation). These factors describe the police officers' everyday working situation and thus determine to a certain extent the kind of situations they are generally exposed to. To interpret the influence of individual variables, reference is made to the exponential coefficient B (Exp(B)). If this has a value of over 1, the concerning variable raises the risk of an officer being physically attacked. Values below 1 state that the concerning variable has a reducing effect on the risk.

As the analysis shows, male officers have a significantly higher risk of being subject to physical assault compared to their female colleagues. So 52.1 percent of all male officers were assaulted at least once in 2009, but only 45.2 percent of female officers. There is also evidence that age influences the likelihood of experiencing violence. While around two-thirds of all officers under 30 (69.6 percent) had been victims of an assault while on duty, this applies to only around one third of all those over 50 (31.8 percent; and 52.4 percent of officers aged 30 to 49). There are also indications that the officers' body height increases their risk, while their weight plays no role at all. Where the officers have an immigrant background, i.e. at least one of their biological parents is not of German origin, their risk of falling victim to violence is greater compared with their German colleagues who have no immigrant background. As the second model shows, apart from the personal factors stated, the type of duty they perform also plays a significant role. Those out on the beat or patrol are more than five times (69.6 percent) as likely to be physically assaulted compared with those performing other duties such as criminal investigations (22.3 percent). For officers belonging to special units, the risk is more then six times as high (73.3 percent). By way of contrast, the area of operation – measured in terms of inhabitants – has, according to the analyses, no direct influence on their risk of being exposed to violence.

Table 6.1 Officer-related influencing factors of physical attacks in 2009 (logistic regression; coefficient: Exp(B))

	Model 1	**Model II**
Gender: Male	1.826***	1.655***
Age: Under 30	*Reference*	*Reference*
Age: 30 to 49	0.408***	0.583***
Age: 50+	0.156***	0.300***
Height: Small (under 1.76 m)	*Reference*	*Reference*
Height: Medium (1.76 m to 1.83 m)	1.098*	1.109*
Height: Large (1.83 m and over)	1.145*	1.177**
Weight: Light (under 78 kg)	*Reference*	*Reference*
Weight: Average (78 kg to 90 kg)	0.959	0.943
Weight: Heavy (91 kg and over)	0.955	0.904
Immigrant Background	1.280*	1.313*
Type of Duty: Other		*Reference*
Type of Duty: Special unit		6.460***
Type of Duty: Regular beat (including on foot)		5.247***
Area of operation: Rural/urban (less than 250,000 inhabitants)		*Reference*
Area of operation: Town/city (250,000+ inhabitants)		0.929
Number of cases **Nagelkerke's R^2**	**18.101** **.085**	**18.101** **.243**

*** $p < .001$, ** $p < .01$, * $p < .05$

Looking at Nagelkerke's R^2 it becomes clear that demographic characteristics only explain a small portion of the variance (Model I, 8.5 percent). The percentage rises almost three-fold (24.7 percent) when the type of duty is also taken into account. As a result, visible characteristics appear to have only a small influence on the risk of being physically assaulted. Of more importance are structural factors like the type of duty and the associated activities. That police officers on the beat or patrol are frequently exposed to violence is also confirmed by earlier studies (cf. Falk 2000, Griffiths/McDanie 1993, Manzoni 2003). Given that they interact daily with citizens who are emotionally upset, drunk, aggressive and helpless, it is not surprising that they have a higher risk of being victimized. The same applies for officers assigned to special units where the duties involved expose them to a greater risk of violence (such as demonstrations). It is much more difficult to explain the victim-related differences found as regards gender, age, immigrant background, and body height. The following offers a number of possible explanations for these findings, which should be analysed in future studies.

Evidence that female police officers are rarely exposed to violence while on duty can be found in the works of Bosold (2006), Bragason (2006), and Burke and Mikkelsen (2005). One possible explanation could be that assailants, who are mostly male, are more reluctant to assault a woman officer than a male officer. It might also be possible that female officers are assigned to less violence-related tasks than their male colleagues. Evidence of a gender stereotype in the assignment of duties, where female officers especially deal with situations involving children and women, can be found in Rustemeyer and Tank (2001). In addition, male officers could have a natural 'protector' instinct why they place themselves in front of their female colleagues as a protective barrier especially in dangerous situations (Manzoni 2003). Further, it has been suggested that female officers due to their socialisation are more communicative, empathetic, supportive, and less aggressive in police-citizen interactions than their male peers (Rabe-Hemp 2008). Hence female officers could have a calming effect on conflict situations, which in turn lessens their risk of being assaulted. However, the assumption that female officers are more supportive towards citizens is only partly confirmed by empirical evidence (Rabe-Hemp 2008). Rather, when compared with their male colleagues, they are less likely to use extreme controlling behaviours such as threats and violence in interactions with citizens (Garner et al. 1996, Manzoni 2003, Rabe-Hemp 2008, Schuck/Rabe-Hemp 2005). So the fact that the use of violence by citizens and by the police are mutually dependent (cf. Garner et al. 1996, Mazoni 2003), could be the reason why female police officers report fewer assaults.

The finding that younger officers are more frequently exposed to violence than older officers while on duty can be assumed to be relatively reliable based on the findings of other studies (cf. Bosold 2006, Bragason 2006, Griffiths/McDaniel1993, Manzoni 2003). It would appear that older officers are more familiar with other types of activities than their younger colleagues, so that the latter have a greater risk of experiencing an assault. A comparison of the two models (see Table 6.1) provides evidence, at least in part, to support this because the coefficients are weakened by the inclusion of the type of duty performed. Another reason for the differences observed could lie in the fact that, due to their experience, older officers are better able to assess the level of danger in a given situation or with a certain type of citizen (e. g. drunken person), and can take the necessary action to prevent possible escalation. It is also possible that younger officers in particular are under pressure to prove themselves. They may respond less calmly to provocation, issues threats far faster, and thus foster conflict.

Although by determining a minimum body height for police officers it can be implicitly suggested that physical stature plays a role in the profession, little empirical study has been conducted to confirm this assumption. The few studies that have taken account of the height and weight of officers who have suffered assaults provide inconsistent results (cf. Garner et al. 1996, Griffiths/McDaniel 1993, Rabe-Hemp/Schuck 2007). Thus, the findings of this study are to be interpreted with caution. Some of the explanations discussed in connection with the gender effect revealed could also be true in this case. For example, selection effects could be responsible for the fact that officers of bigger stature are more frequently assaulted by virtue of their larger size, and are frequently assigned to attend dangerous situations or place themselves in front of their colleagues in such situations. But it could also be possible that an assailant deliberately targets a bigger officer because they see them as the greatest threat. A further explanation could be that the officers themselves, on account of their knowledge of their physical strength, are less likely to shy away from confrontation.

Another issue to be treated with caution is the risk-increasing effect of an immigrant background, due to the low number of such cases.[3] The dif-

3 Only 2.5 percent of the officers surveyed had an immigrant background. They also came from various countries, meaning that the existence of an immigrant background was not necessarily evident.

ferences shown could be explained at least in two ways: First, it may be possible that, due to a lack of acceptance, officers with an immigrant background have a greater need to win the public's respect. They thus react harshly when confronted with an obvious lack of respect. Second, it could also happen that a citizen demonstrates a racist attitude towards a migrant officer, thus escalating the situation.

6.2.3 How have trends developed in respect of violence against police officers in the period 2005 to 2009?

To obtain detailed information on trends in violence against police officers, all participants were asked how often they had been experienced an assault in the period 2005 and 2009 which resulted in being unfit for work for at least one day. The reference period of five years was chosen in line with the retrospective focus of the survey. It can be assumed that violent events and its circumstances (such as the location of the assault, and the number of assailants) which occurred in the past five years are easier to recall than those experienced far earlier. For this reason, also the criterion of being unfit for work following an assault was chosen which highlights particularly serious, consequential attacks.

Of all 20.938 police officers in the survey, about one in eight (12.9 percent) had suffered at least one assault that had rendered them unfit for work for at least one day between 2005 and 2009. Over the five-year period, the number of victimized officers rose steadily from 2.6 percent to 4.5 percent (Figure 6.2), while the average number of assaults per victim remains relatively constant (1.09 in 2005, 1.16 in 2009). A differentiated analysis of assaults according to the length of time an officer is unfit for work shows various trends. Extremely serious assaults leading to officers being unfit for work for periods of over two months remain at a constantly low level over the reporting time. The rate of assaults resulting in officers being away from work for at least one week and at most eight weeks is relatively stable over the first four years. The only significant increase is between 2008 (0.9 percent) and 2009 (1.3 percent). Thus, the increase in assaults with a maximum of six days' sick leave is responsible for the rise observed between 2005 and 2009. However, the problems involved in retrospective surveys must be taken into account (distorted recall, for example).

Fig. 6.2 Police officers assaulted and made unfit for Work (in percent)

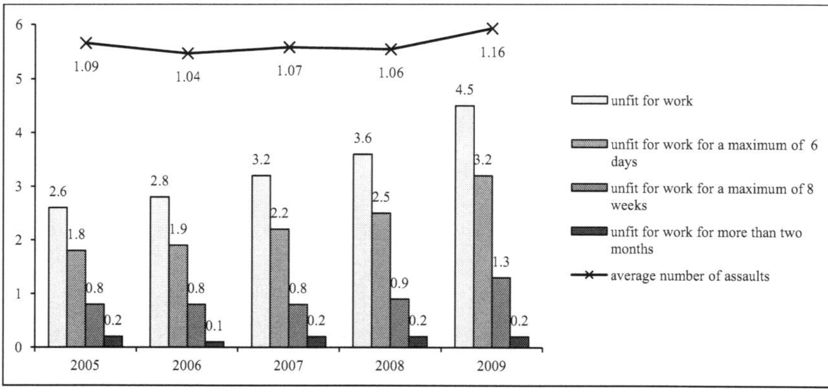

One key question that must be answered is how to explain the evident rise in violent assaults that render officers unfit for work. In many instances, reference is made to a general increase in the lack of respect shown towards police officers, especially by teenagers and young adults. This is contradicted by studies that show that most school children and adults have a positive attitude towards the police (Baier et al. 2010, Baier et al. 2011). The assumption that the increase is due to a greater willingness in society to use violence does not hold up given the decline in violent crime recorded by German Police Crime Statistics since 2007, and which was previously shown in self-report studies (Baier et al.2009). As a possible cause of the rise in violence against police officers, Ellrich et al. (2012, p. 49) point to an increasing polarising trend in society. This sees a greater divide between societal groups. Polarisation is evident in various areas, such as a polarisation between low-income and high-income families, and between nationals and immigrants. In recent years, greater polarisation has occurred regarding political views (left and right-wing tendencies) in society. Such gaps cannot in themselves explain the phenomenon of the rise in violence against the police. The increased polarisation can, however, be seen in connection with the fact that today, more and more communities are emerging which do not share the same standards and values as the rest of Germany. Within these communities, no-one fears the thought of exercising violence against police officers. Violent assaults are seen as a way to gain recognition within the community; they also serve to underpin political ideologies, as is the case among left-wing groups. Over the past few years, reports by Germany's Ministry of the Interior show a correlation with rising violence among left-wing extremists, especially against police officers (BMI 2011). Because this hypothesis has yet to be supported by empirical evidence, other explanations must also be thought of (for example, an increasing tendency for teenagers and young adults to spend their free time on the street and in public places).

6.2.4 What characterises share assailants who carried out assaults, and the situations in which violence against police officers occurred?

As part of the survey, officers who had suffered an assault between 2005 and 2009 that rendered them unfit for work were asked to describe such a case in detail.[4] Data collected on 2,603 cases comprises not only statements regarding the assailants, but also on the circumstances and the outcomes of the assaults.

The following conclusions can be drawn regarding the assailants involved in violent assaults:

- Almost three out of four assaults were carried out by one assailant (74.8 percent)
- The assailants were almost exclusively male (92.9 percent)
- Younger individuals are over-represented among the assailants when compared with their numbers among the overall German population. A total of 59.3 percent of assailants were under 25 at the time of the assault.
- In six out of ten cases (59.4 percent), officers stated the assailants to be German, 36.1 percent were non-German, with the most frequent countries named being the former Soviet Union (e.g. Russia and Kazakhstan), Turkey and other Muslim countries (such as Iran and Iraq).
- In almost three-quarters of cases, the assailants were alcohol affected at the time of the assault (71.7 percent). There is also a rise in the percentage of drunken assailants in the past five years.
- In two out of three assaults (64.8 percent), individuals were involved who were already known to the police.

4 The choice of assault for the detailed description was made based on two criteria: the most serious assault experienced by an officer which was operationalised via the length of sick leave days, or the most recent assault (Ellrich et al. 2012, p. 51).

- The assailants mostly used physical violence in the form of jostling with, hitting or kicking a police officer (84.0 percent). The use of weapons or other dangerous objects (such as fence planks) was reported for one in five assaults (19.3 percent). Therefore violent attacks against police officers seem to occur in the course of the interactions rather than be planned.

Similar findings on assailants are reported in various national and international studies (cf. Brown 1994, Falk 2000, FBI 2010, Griffiths/McDaniel 1993, Ohlemacher et al. 2003). However, based on this description, no conclusion can be drawn regarding which assailants pose a greater risk of the officers being assaulted. Because police officers are often confronted with drunken people, it is not really surprising that many of those drunken people are among their assailants. To conduct a risk analysis, it is necessary to compare police-citizen interactions that result in a violent assault with those that proceed peacefully. Few studies have performed such analyses so far (Johnson 2011). As part of a supplemental survey module, in which respondents are asked about their most recent incident involving domestic violence, the question of which factors might increase officers' risk of being injured on duty can be analysed (Ellrich et al. 2012, p. 163 ff). Apart from the composition of the police team, respondents were also asked about origin and gender of the offender of domestic violence, and whether they were affected by alcohol. Further, the officers should answer if they or their colleagues had been injured in this most recent incident. As such, the injury of an officer serves as a measure with which to assess the degree of danger involved in certain types of situation. The analysis was restricted to incidents in which only two officers were present. It can be stated that one in seventeen incidents involving domestic violence ends with at least one officer being injured (6.0 percent). The variables influencing this risk are listed in Table 6.2, which also presents findings of logistic regression analysis.

As can be seen, in cases of domestic violence, the offender's gender plays no role in terms of a police officer's risk of being injured. Incidents of domestic violence in which women were the offender ended just as frequently with an officer being hurt as with male offenders. Where other offender constellations are involved (e.g. both women and men as joint offenders), there is evidence of a slightly greater risk that officers will be hurt. It is possible that the parties join forces against the police and launch an assault together.

Table 6.2 Influencing factors in the injury of at least one officer in the most recent incident of domestic violence (only two-person teams, logistic regression; coefficient: Exp(B))

	Model I
offender: only woman	*Reference*
offender: only man	0.924
offender: Other	2.097
offender drunk	5.546***
Family with immigrant background	1.439*
Woman officer on team	0.786†
Officer with immigrant background on team	1.749
Number of cases **Nagelkerke's R^2**	**3.819** **.067**

*** $p < .001$, ** $p < .01$, * $p < .05$, † $p < .10$

The greatest influencing factor as regards injury involves alcohol consumption on the part of the offender of the domestic violence. Police who are confronted with drunken offenders have a 5.5 times greater risk of being injured when compared with non-alcohol situations. That alcohol is a key risk factor for assaults on police officers attending incidents of domestic violence has been shown in other studies (Johnson 2001, Rabe-Hemp/Schuck 2007). A lack of self-control resulting from alcohol consumption, along with increased emotional responses in the form of anger, bitterness, frustration and fear could all be responsible for this effect (Johnson 2011, Schmalzl 2005).

In addition, there is evidence that officers are injured slightly more frequently in incidents involving families with immigrant backgrounds. One explanation is that police 'interference' in the private affairs of people with other cultural backgrounds is far less accepted than by families of German origin. It is also possible that failure to observe certain behavioural norms (e.g. if a male officer speaks alone with the woman of the household) can lead more easily to escalation.

If there is at least one woman officer in the team, the risk of injury lessens when compared with exclusively male teams. The assumption that when dealing with such incidents, female officers mainly focus on the victims, and thus the likelihood of injury for them is less, provides no explanation here: Supplementary analyses show that the presence of a woman officer reduces the risk of both officers being injured (Ellrich et al. 2012, p. 179). These indicate that female officers have a de-escalating effect in such conflict situations. Whether this is due to particular skills that female officers possess or to greater reluctance on the part of the offenders to attack a mixed-gender team remains unclear. The extent to which the findings on domestic violence situations can be transferred to other incidents attended by the police must be subjected to future analysis.

Fig. 6.3 Situations resulting in assaults where officers are made unfit for work (in percent)

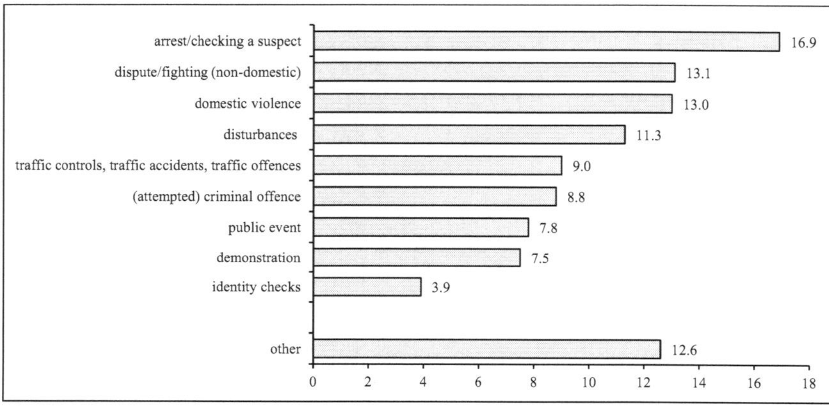

The situations with the most frequent occurrence of assaults which render officers unfit for work involve arrests and checking suspects (16.9 percent, see Figure 6.3). Arrests in particular can be perceived by the people involved as a massive intrusion and a severe restriction of their personal freedom which they try to escape (Haller et al. 1999, Schmalzl 2005). About the same frequency is reported by officers attending disputes/fighting and domestic violence (13.1 percent and 13.0 percent resp.). Also, one in nine respondents stated that the attack had occurred while they were attending a disturbance (e.g. unruly behaviour by drunkards; 11.3 percent). Similar findings are shown in other studies (Bragason 2006, Brown 1994, Falk 2000, FBI 2010, Griffiths/McDaniel 1993, Manzoni 2003, Ohlemacher et al. 2003). Publicly debated police activities such as demonstrations and soccer matches are named relatively rarely. But this does not allow the assumption that officers are confronted with less violence when performing such duties compared with before mentioned incidents. Rather, it can be suggested that demonstrations for example result in fewer attacks that lead to an officer being unfit for work because the officers are better equipped (particularly with protective gear), and are trained to deal with such dangerous situations.

With regard to timing and locality, the following was found:

- At weekends in particular, there is an increased concentration of assaults. Almost two-thirds of all assaults (63.1 percent) occurred between Friday and Sunday.
- The assaults occurred largely in the evening and during the night (between 8 pm and 4 am: 53.2 percent).
- With regard to the nature of the area, it can be said that the assaults occurred in largely residential areas (44.0 percent), while more socially problematic areas were rarely cited (27.4 percent). On the one hand, that problematic areas are not the prime location for assaults can be explained by their small share in a town. On the other, it can be assumed that the officers expect these areas to be more dangerous and are thus more observant and respond more cautiously than in more residential areas.
- Almost one in two assaults (47.0 percent) occurred in a public space (street, square, or park), while 23.6 percent of officers were attacked in private homes or gardens. In most cases the place where the assault occurred is not deemed to be dangerous for the police (80.3 percent).

Similar findings regarding timing and locality can also be seen in other studies (cf. Bragason 2006, Falk 2000).

Data was also collected on the information available to the police officers, how they assessed the situation prior to the assault, and how they behaved towards the offenders. Analysis showed that:

- The officers rarely had detailed information regarding the individuals involved in the incident (e.g. if they were armed or had a police record), or the level of escalation (12.4 and 21.5 percent respectively, Ellrich et al. 2012, p. 67ff). Perhaps compared with officers with no information better informed officers are more able to prepare themselves to deal with the situation and the assailants, and can adopt a situation-specific strategy.
- Only two out of five officers (39.8 percent) assessed the situation as (fairly) dangerous prior to the assault.
- In 74.4 percent of cases, the subsequent assailant was deemed (fairly) aggressive prior to the attack.

- The officers in three out of four cases (75.4 percent) had communicated with the subsequent assailant before the assault occured.
- The officers themselves frequently used physical restraining measures when dealing with offenders (84.0 percent). Significantly rarer was their use of a pepper spray or a baton to fend off an assault (26.2 and 29.9 percent respectively). Only in 35 assaults (1.5 percent) it was necessary for them to use their firearms.

Against the backdrop that in most cases, the assault was preceded by communication with the subsequent assailant (who had been assessed as aggressive), the question arises as to why the assaults could not be prevented given that there were signs that the situation could escalate. In other studies, assaults mostly came to the officers as a surprise, although most assaults did not occur immediately the officers arrived on the scene, but rather in the course of interaction with the individuals concerned (Ohlemacher et al. 2003, Sessar et al. 1980). In reference to this, Schmalzl (2005) questions whether there might not have been an indication or warning signs for the apparent sudden assault which were not sufficiently recognised or assessed. He points to the development of a psychological early warning system or risk radar (also Füllgrabe 2002) which would enable better awareness and risk assessment.

6.2.5 How do violent attacks affect the officers involved?

Exposure to violence can be a life-changing experience. One's previously assumed 'invunerability' and perceived ability to deal with situations (even difficult ones) can be shattered by such events, inducing fear and anxiety (Reiser/Geiger 1984). This is confirmed by the findings of the survey.

With regard to physical consequences resulting from a violent assault, the officers surveyed cited injuries to the hand and arm as the most frequent incurred (46.6 percent, Ellrich et al. 2012, p. 120 f). Significantly less frequent were injuries to the face/head (29.6 percent), and to the neck, throat, shoulder and back area (22.6 percent). However, the latter type of injury appears to be the most serious. Officers with neck, throat, shoulder and back injuries not only were unfit for work for longer periods, but they were often deployed to other duties after an assault or were declared unfit for active duty and assigned to a desk job.

Problems in other areas of life also play an important role. More than one quarter of those affected said they had difficulties sleeping after the assault (27.7 percent), and one in seven officers (14.9 percent) said their relationships had been affected, i.e. interaction with their partner or others in their social environment. Additional analyses found, that the longer an officer is unfit for work, the more they are affected by such problems. Because police officers are confronted in the line of duty with a wide range of extreme, stressful and potentially traumatic events, including their own experience with violence, many studies have addressed the issue of post-traumatic stress disorder (cf. Gasch 2000, Schneider/Latscha 2010). This psychological syndrome takes in nightmares, withdrawal, avoidance behaviour, and psychosomatic complaints such as anxiety and disturbed sleep patterns following a traumatic experience (Saß et al. 2003). In the sample, a total of 4.9 percent of officers who had been assaulted showed signs of post-traumatic stress disorder four weeks after the attack (Ellrich et al. 2012, p. 124 f). There were no significant differences regarding gender, age or type of duty performed. However, there is evidence of a link between the length of time an officer is unfit for work and a diagnosis of suspected post-traumatic stress disorder. Officers who were unfit for work for more than two months were nine times more likely to be suspected of suffering from the disorder than those with a maximum two days away from work (18.6 versus 2.1 percent respectively). In addition, a number of other assault-related characteristics were linked to the psychological disorder. These include the officers' perceived reasons for the attack. Those who claimed the assailant was anti-police/state, or had personal differences or a desire to kill were far more likely to be suspected of suffering from post-traumatic stress disorder. If the assault involved weapons or other dangerous objects, the number of cases of officers suspected to have the disorder doubled.

Up to now, little attention has been paid to the potential psychological effects of facing legal consequences in the form of a complaint, charges being pressed or a disciplinary hearing after the assault. While this is rarely the case – only about two out of ten officers (17.7 percent) faced any legal charges – the effect on the police officers involved should not be underestimated (Ellrich et al. 2012, p. 134 ff). As can be seen, the greater the legal measures, the greater the stress an officer is exposed to. Disciplinary hearings are shown to be particularly stressful. Around one in five officers (19.6 percent) who faced a criminal investigation or a disciplinary hearing showed symptoms of post-traumatic stress disorder, while only

4.1 percent of officers who faced no legal consequences did so. Available data allows no conclusions to be drawn regarding the underlying reasons. It is possible that some officers are aware that they made mistakes during an assault and are afraid of the consequences. Others, by way of contrast, may feel they have been wrongly accused, and cannot understand that the assailant-victim relationship has been reversed. In addition, legal consequences spark existential fears, which also result in severe mental stress. Against this backdrop, the provision of support for the officers concerned would be of help, especially in such situations.

Apart from physical and mental problems, experience as a victim of violence can also cause changes in attitudes and perceptions. This is supported, for example, for the concept of fear of crime (Skogan 1987). One component of this construct is cognitive fear, and the expectation of falling victim to crime in the near future. In the context of this survey, this included the likelihood of experience an assault in the next twelve months. The analysis shows that officers who experienced such attacks in the five years between 2005 and 2009 were eight times more likely to believe they would be a victim of a further assault within the next year than their colleagues who had not been assaulted (31.7 versus 4.1 percent).[5] As a result, the officers who had had been attacked were accompanied by greater fear while on duty. It can be assumed that such fear manifests itself in precisely those situations that follow a similar pattern to the one in which the officer suffered a violent assault. The associated strong emotional stress can in turn have a negative effect on the officer's ability to make a decision and to act, thus increasing their risk of re-victimization.

What also can be shown is that exposure to violence can be linked to a police officer's self-image on the job. Those who had been victimized agreed more frequently with the statement that they were emotional dustbins or scapegoats. It can be suggested that officers who feel they are society's scapegoats tend to take a harder line when dealing with citizens. This in turn can lead more easily to escalation when attending an incident, and to a repeated violent assault.

5 Given the cross-sectional design of the survey, a reversed causal relationship cannot be ruled out where greater fear of crime might have resulted in officers experiencing a violent attack.

6.3 Summary

The aim of this paper was to provide an insight into the subject of violence against police officers in Germany. Findings were taken from a survey of police officers concerning their exposure to violence. Conducted in early 2010, the study showed that police officers are often exposed to various types of violence, with verbal and mild physical assaults the dominant forms. They also experience serious assaults that lead to them being unfit for work: About one in eight officers had experienced at least one such assault in the five-year period covered by the survey. Regarding the latter mentioned cases an increase especially in assaults with less serious outcomes could be stated between 2005 and 2009. In line with the findings of previous research studies, the assaults (causing officers to be unfit for work) mostly followed an arrest or a dispute where the assailant acted alone, was male and young, had a police record, and was affected by alcohol. Further, it can also be concluded that apart from physical and mental problems, exposure to violence can result in a heightened fear of repeated assaults, and to a negative self-image.

One area of focus in the survey was to identify factors which are linked to the risk of an assault on a police officer. Only a few studies have so far attempted to conduct this type of risk assessment (Johnson 2001, Rabe-Hemp/Schuck 2007). As was shown using the data collected in the survey, young male officers of large height, and officers with an immigrant background have a greater risk of being assaulted. Also, officers out on the beat or on patrol in a vehicle, and those belonging to special units, are more likely to fall victim to violence compared with colleagues who perform other duties. Looking at the assailants, the influence of alcohol and an immigrant background increase the risk of an officer being assaulted while attending an incident in which domestic violence is involved.

The specific processes responsible for certain officers being assaulted more frequently than others cannot be sufficiently illustrated with available data. In general, however, it can be assumed that several factors play a role. Explanations for the gender differences involved can be apportioned to structural effects (e.g. differing tasks), an assailant's hesitance in attacking a woman, and the de-escalating skills of female officers on account of their social skills. Looking at the development of suitable vocational and further training measures for police officers in respect of violence prevention, a study of non-visible characteristics, meaning certain attitudes and abilities in which male and female officers differ, appears useful. If female officers experience less violence because they are less frequently exposed to dangerous situations or because the assailants are hesitant to assault them because of their gender, special training would not be necessary. But if female officers were less at risk of a violent assault because they have better social skills than their male colleagues, use fewer threats, exercise less force and are generally more cautious in their interaction with citizens indeed, these findings could be used to develop special programmes (such as communication skills training).

What needs to be analysed also is the extent to which certain constellations raise the risk of a violent confrontation. Different people will react differently in different situations and in interaction with different police officers. Indications of such differing effects can be seen, for example, in the study by Rabe-Hemp and Schuck (2007). They report that for female police officers, the greatest risk of assault occurs when they are confronted with drunken individuals while attending incidents of domestic violence. In other words, the combination of alcohol, gender and situation play a key role in their victimisation risk. To reveal such complex causal structures, additional studies are needed which use a range of different methodological approaches (such as questioning and observation, and quasi-experimental design).

References

Backhaus, K., Erichson, B., Plinke, W., Weiber, R. (2003). Multivariate Analysemethoden. Eine Anwendungsorientierte Einführung (10th Edition). Berlin: Springer.

Baier, D., Ellrich, K. (2012). Welche Einsätze sind für Polizeibeamte besonders gefährlich? In: T. Ohlemacher, J-T. Werner (Eds.), Empirische Polizeiforschung XIV: Polizei und Gewalt. Interdisziplinäre Analysen zu Gewalt gegen und durch Polizeibeamte (pp. 23-46). Frankfurt: Verlag für Polizeiwissenschaft.

Baier, D., Peiffer, C., Simonson, J., Rabold, S. (2009). Jugendliche in Deutschland als Opfer und Täter von Gewalt. KFN: Forschungsbericht Nr. 107.

Baier, D., Pfeiffer C., Rabold, S., Simonson, J., Kappes, C. (2010). Kinder und Jugendliche in Deutschland: Gewalterfahrungen, Integration, Medienkonsum. KFN: Forschungsbericht Nr. 109.

Baier, D., Kemme, S., Hanslmaier, M., Doering, B., Rehbein, F., Pfeiffer, C. (2011). Kriminalitätsfurcht, Strafbedürfnisse und wahrgenommene Kriminalitätsentwicklung. Ergebnisse von bevölkerungsrepräsentativen Befragungen aus den Jahren 2004, 2006 und 2010. KFN: Forschungsbericht Nr. 117.

Bosold, C. (2006). Polizeiliche Übergriffe. Aspekte der Identität als Erklärungsfaktoren polizeilicher Übergriffsintentionen. Baden-Baden: Nomos.

Bragason, O. O. (2006). Assaults Against Police Officers: A Self-report Study Among Icelandic Police Officers. Reykjavik: The Office of the National Police Commissioner.

Brown, B. (1994). Assaults on Police Officers: An Examination of the Circumstances in Which Such Incidents Occur. London: Home Office Research Group.

Bundesministerium des Innern (BMI, 2011). Entwicklung politisch motivierter Kriminalität. Pressemitteilung vom 15.04.2011. Available at: http://www.bmi.bund.de/SharedDocs/Pressemitteilungen/DE/2011/04/pmk.html.

Burke, R. J., Mikkelsen, A. (2005). Gender Differences in Policing: Signs of Progress? Employee Relations, 27, 425-436.

Ellrich, K., Baier, D., Pfeiffer, C. (2012). Polizeibeamte als Opfer von Gewalt. Ergebnisse einer Befragung von Polizeibeamten aus zehn Bundesländern. Baden-Baden: Nomos.

Falk, E. (2000). Widerstand gegen Vollstreckungsbeamte. Ein praxisbezogenes Forschungsprojekt (Texte Nr. 25). Villingen-Schwenningen: Hochschule für Polizei.

Federal Bureau of Investigation (FBI, 2010). Law Enforcement Officers Killed and Assaulted 2009. Available at: http://www.fbi.gov/about-us/cjis/ucr/leoka/2009/leoka-2009 [15.11.2010].

Füllgrabe, U. (2002). Psychologie der Eigensicherung. Stuttgart: Booberg.

Garner, J., Buchanan, J., Schade, T., Hepburn, J. (1996). Understanding the Use of Force by and Against the Police. National Institute of Justice.

Gasch, U. (2000). Traumaspezifische Diagnostik von Extremsituationen im Polizeidienst. Polizisten als Opfer von Belastungsstörungen. dissertation.de

Griffiths, R., McDaniel, Q. P. (1993). Predictors of Police Assaults. Journal of Police and Criminal Psychology, 9, 5-9.

Hallenberger, F., Heiderich, M., Rieger, S. (2003). Stress und Stressbewältigung im Polizeiberuf. Polizei & Wissenschaft, 3, 36-49.

Haller, B., König, I., Pelinka, A. (1999). Die zwei Seiten der Gewalt. Konflikte zwischen Sicherheitsexekutive und BürgerInnen. In: J. Fehervary, W. Stangl (Eds.), Gewalt und Frieden. Verständigungen über die Sicherheitsexekutive (pp. 15-34). Wien: Universitätsverlag.

Jäger, J. (1988). Gewalt und Polizei. Beiträge zur gesellschafts-wissenschaftlichen Forschung (Bd. 6). Pfaffenweiler: Centaurus-Verlagsgesellschaft.

Johnson, R. R. (2011). Predicting Officer Physical Assaults at Domestic Assault Calls. Journal of Familiy Violence, 26, 163-169.

Klemisch, D., Kepplinger, J., Muthny, F. A. (2005). Stressfaktoren und Positiva im Polizeiberuf - Selbsteinschätzungen durch Polizeibeamte. Polizei & Wissenschaft, 2, 10-20.

Manzoni, P. (2003). Gewalt zwischen Polizei und Bevölkerung. Einflüsse von Arbeitsbelastungen, Arbeitszufriedenheit und Burnout auf polizeiliche Gewaltausübung und Opfererfahrungen. Zürich: Rüegger.

Neugebauer, U., Latscha, K. (2009). Bewältigung belastender Ereignisse bei Polizeibeamten. Polizei & Wissenschaft, 3, 55-61.

Ohlemacher, T., Rüger, A., Schacht, G., Feldkötter, U. (2003). Gewalt gegen Polizeibeamtinnen und -beamte 1985-2000. Baden-Baden: Nomos.

Rabe-Hemp, C. E., Schuck, A. M. (2007). Violence Against Police Officers. Are Female Officers at Greater Risk? Police Quarterly, 10, 411-428.

Rabe-Hemp, C. E. (2008). Female Officers and the Ethic of Care: Does Officer Gender Impact Police Behaviors? Journal of Criminal Justice, 36, 426-434.

Reiser, M., Geiger, S. P. (1984). Police Officer as a Victim. Professional Psychology: Research and Practice, 15, 315-323.

Rustemeyer, R., Tank, C. (2001). Akzeptanz von Frauen im Polizeiberuf. Polizei & Wissenschaft, 3, 3-14.

Saß, H., Wittchen, U.-H., Zaudig, M. (2003). Diagnostisches und statistisches Manual psychischer Störungen - Textrevision - DSM-IV-TR. Göttingen: Hogrefe.

Schmalzl, H. P. (2005). Das Problem des "plötzlichen" Angriffs auf Polizeibeamte. Polizei & Wissenschaft, 3, 8-18.

Schneider, D., Latscha, K. (2010). Polizeikultur als Schutzfaktor bei traumatischen Belastungen. Polizei & Wissenschaft, 4, 30-40.

Schuck, A. M., Rabe-Hemp, C. (2005). Women Police: The Use of Force by and Against Female Officers. Women & Criminal Justice, 16, 91-117.

Sessar, K., Baumann, U., Müller, J. (1980). Polizeibeamte als Opfer vorsätzlicher Tötung. BKA-Forschungsreihe, Bd. 12. Wiesbaden: Bundeskriminalamt.

Skogan, W. G. (1987). The Impact of Victimization on Fear. Crime and Delinquency, 33, 135-154.

7. Violence Against Police Officers: The Victims' Perspective

Bettina Zietlow

7.1 Introduction

Violent assaults are part and parcel of a police officer's working world. How various forms of violence are perceived and experienced, and how the experience is dealt with in the context of additional (job-related) stress, is the focus of a study in which 35 police officers (men and women) provided input on their personal experience. The aim of this qualitative study, funded and promoted by the German Police Union (GdP), is to provide a detailed insight into personal experience with violence and how the experience is processed. It thus concentrates on factors which help officers dealing with potentially stressful situations.

The findings can be used to address factors which can be influenced by the police authorities – supervisors and colleagues, and altered structures – in their dealings with victims of violence and (job-related) stress.

7.2 Conceptual reflections

In the everyday lives of police officers, stressful situations can arise that have no direct relation to police activities. These include interpersonal conflict, dissatisfaction with supervisors or exposure to bullying. There are, however, other stressful situations that are directly linked to police work, such as changing shifts, and confrontation with extreme situations (Reinecke et al. 2006). The level of stress involved can be categorised into two groups (Nörenberg et al. 2006, Sennekamp/Martin 2003). There is the stress that arises in the performance of normal duties, often resulting from the type of incidents officers are called upon to attend (operative stressors). These include confrontation with the death or injury of others, especially children, and confrontation with danger to one's own life. Secondly, there is the stress experienced in connection with police force structures (administrative stressors). These involve the pressure of work, staffing shortages, dissatisfaction with police leadership, an imbalance between work and family life, and shift work (cf. Hallenberger/Mueller 2000, Sennekamp/Martin 2003). Assaults on one's own person are an operative stress factor for the police officers involved.

Not every potentially stressful event is perceived as stressful and not every potentially stress-inducing situation sparks a stress response in all individuals. Perception and evaluation processes play a role in the development of stress. This underlying notion matches the transactional model used by Lazarus (1966). In a primary evaluation, it is assessed whether a situation is irrelevant, positive or stressful. In a next step, situations perceived as highly stressful are assessed as to whether they involve loss or damage, or pose a threat or a challenge. The secondary evaluation serves in verifying the stress management options and a person's ability to cope with the situation. This information is then used to re-evaluate the situation. If the stress management options and ability to cope are perceived as inadequate, a stress reaction occurs (Wittchen/Hoyer 2006, Klemisch 2006).

Stress factors can be divided into three categories: daily hassles, critical life events, and traumatic events. Daily hassles – everyday pressures – are not as intense as crisis or traumatic events but, due to their frequency, they have a high risk of becoming chronic and thus heighten the risk of a person developing physical and mental ailments. In everyday police work, these can take the form of verbal attacks or behaviour perceived as disrespectful to one's own person.

Critical life events have a clear time span. The person affected must adjust accordingly and may have to reorganise their life (Filipp 1990). Examples of critical life events include the death of a dependant, divorce, and job loss, and also events that are not necessarily negative in nature, such as promotion or getting married. Even positive critical events can often be perceived as stressful.

Traumatic events are characterised by great intensity and the lack of adequate coping mechanisms. The affected individual is unable to adapt to the situation. Traumatic events are "undesired, unpredictable, extremely negative, […] and are difficult to control if at all", (Klemisch 2006, p. 6). Such events heighten the risk of acute stress-related disorders, adjustment disorders, and post-traumatic stress disorders.

Apart from (general) interpersonal conflict arising from dissatisfaction with supervisors and colleagues, police work can also give rise to duty-specific stress (shift work, and confrontation with extreme situations)

(Reinecke et al. 2006). Among the situations perceived as the most stressful are exposure to bullying, the death of a personal acquaintance, the death or injury of a child, and exposure to a life-threatening situation. Police officers perceive critical events as particularly stressful when they cannot be prevented or controlled (Wagner 1986). This corresponds with the general finding that such an event is experienced as especially aversive, as uncontrollable or unpredictable (cf. Barlow 1988, Ehlers et al. 1997, Mineka/Kihlstrom 1978).

What is known as 'perceived self-efficacy' could thus, by way of contrast, be a protective factor in traumatic situations. Bandura's concept is based on an individual's belief that their abilities can help them influence a situation to reach a successful outcome (Bandura 1997, Benight/Bandura 2004). Internal convictions of being able to deal with a situation also have a positive influence on stress management (Lefcourt 1983).

By nature of the type of duties performed and the associated frequent confrontation with critical and stressful events, police officers are at greater risk of developing a psychological disorder (such as post-traumatic stress disorder, depression, alcohol abuse, and alcoholism) (Klemisch 2006). However, it is not only single dramatic events that can trigger psychological and physical illness. Less intense, but ongoing exposure to stress can deplete an officer's ability to cope because they are nonetheless constantly in a state of alarm. If this feeling of heightened alert, fear and danger collides with an officer's need to appear and actually be in control, their stress levels rise again (McCafferty et al. 1992). Especially for officers working nights and shifts, the adjustment needed in such situations leads to psychosomatic complaints such as anxiety, disturbed sleep patterns, and gastro-intestinal problems (GdP 1988). Efforts to cope with stress can also result in aggressiveness, impulsiveness, bad temperedness, and an increased need to take control (Klemisch 2006), which in turn can result in further stress. However, compared with work-related stress, job satisfaction and the degree of job dissatisfaction appear to be the better indicators of physical well-being. Klemisch (2006) showed that job satisfaction has a negative correlation with fear, depression and psychosomatic disorder. The experience of violence can be both stressful and traumatic.

Post-traumatic stress disorder (PTBS)

A trauma is defined as a "potential or real threat of death, serious injury or bodily harm to one's own person or to another which triggers a reaction of intense fear, helplessness or shock" (DSM-IV, APA 1996, p. 487). This includes accidents with injuries and/or deaths, natural disaster, hostage-taking, rape/sexual abuse and torture (Hallenberger 1998, 2001, Maercker 2003).

After being confronted with such an event, those affected often show immediate reactions that fade away within a matter of hours or days. In colloquial terms, these reactions are known as 'shock'. If the symptoms (constant flashbacks, e.g. dreams or intrusive thoughts, avoidance behaviour relative to thoughts about the trauma or places and situations associated with it, and a heightened state of anxiety in the form of sleeplessness, hyper-vigilance, bad temper and startled responses) last for a minimum of two days (but no more than four weeks), they are defined as an acute stress response. If the disturbances last for more than a month and the symptoms cause clinically significant impairments to key functions, then post-traumatic stress disorder (PTSD) can be diagnosed (Wittchen/Hoyer 2006). Most police officers experience at least one potentially traumatic event during their police career (Gasch 1998, Klemisch et al. 2005, Sennekamp/Martin 2001, Teegen 2003). The lifetime prevalence for a post-traumatic stress disorder is said to be eight percent for the general public. For police officers, statistics range between seven and 21 percent (Klemisch et al. 2005).

Among the factors that influence the likelihood of an individual developing PTSD after experiencing a violence assault are variables that exist before the traumatic event occurred. Such 'pre-traumatic' factors include previous stressful events, gender, educational level and age. A further group of variables describes what are known as peri-traumatic factors – states displayed by an individual at the time of the traumatic event (such as intoxication), and characteristics of the trauma itself. Yet another group of post-traumatic factors involves psychological and social processes in coping with the trauma. Research findings on this group have been so far inconsistent. None of the groups of factors studied so far provided an adequate explanation as to how post-traumatic stress disorder evolves (Wittchen/Hoyer 2006, p. 828). It is possible that cumulated, stressful events at work and in private life are a risk factor for the occurrence of post-traumatic stress disorder (Myrtek et al. 1994). Job routine does not, therefore, provide a stronger psychological shield, but rather the experiences encountered on the job lead to greater sensitivity.

The question of protective factors is addressed by Schneider and Latscha (2010) in their study of police culture. They assume that police officers have access to a good social network which serves as a protective factor. In duty situations, collegiality and team spirit among police officers has a preventive effect (cf. Engel 1995). They also assume that police officers possess personal traits that allow them to cope with their experiences, thus preventing the development of post-traumatic stress disorder (Schneider/Latscha 2010). This personality structure is shaped by police work and being part of police culture. For police officers, standing up to the threat of physical assault is an everyday occurrence (Waddington 1999). The risk of falling victim to a violent assault is seen as part of the job. The personality structure of police officers should be characterised by a high degree of assertiveness, strong self-confidence, good communications and problem-solving skills, heightened self-efficacy belief, and resilience (Schneider/Latscha 2010). In the study conducted by Schneider and Latscha (2010), the police officers surveyed demonstrated significantly greater resilience and self-efficacy belief when compared to members of the general public. Within the group of police respondents, those who did not become ill after a stressful experience achieved higher scores on the resilience scale and demonstrated a stronger perception of social support. Both resilience and perceived social support (especially within the police community) can be seen as protective factors in relation to post-traumatic stress disorder. This is in line with findings from earlier research (Schützwohl/Maercker 1997, Solomon/Horn 1986,). "A lack of respect and recognition can contribute or lead to advanced re-traumatisation" (Maercker 2003, p. 27).

Further, through various forms of prevention, the impacts of work-related stress can be reduced and self-efficacy and assertiveness can be heightened. Primary prevention – prior to the occurrence of a stressful event – in the form of vocational and further training serves to supplement both skills and resources. Better preparation for specific events and their potential consequences should ensure that those affected perceive their feelings as normal and do not hide themselves behind a tough façade (Hallenberger 2006, p. 33,). Behavioural training is a form of prevention. Having received such training, officers retain their assertiveness in extreme situations regardless of disrupting factors (stressful cognitions). This is achieved by means of highly automated processes, which must be practiced more intensively the more complex the required behaviour (Hallenberger 2006). The idea is to be able to withstand the "laming effect of shock" (Hallenberger 2006, p. 39). This involves regular practice at interactive shooting ranges, which enjoy great acceptance among police officers on account of the near-reality experience. During the training, stress levels should be higher than those expected in the real-life situation in order to build up stress resistance (Ungerer 1999). When decision-making processes are practiced for dealing with critical situations, they become automatic and require less conscious attention (Hallenberger 1995, Schmidt 1982). To select the best approach in these decision-making processes, specialist skill is needed to avoid the selection process being exacerbated by an excess of information and knowledge, and acute time pressure. Standardised rules and checklists can be used for the purpose (Eckert 1996, Lasogga/Gasch 2000, Ungerer 1999). Secondary prevention – immediately following a stressful event – is primarily defined in terms of crisis intervention. Tertiary prevention, in the form of psychotherapy and supervision, is more of a long-term measure (Nörenberg et al. 2006).

Coping

People respond differently to stress situations. They have their own way of coping with stress. Some use problem-orientated approaches, while others apply emotion-orientated coping strategies (Lazarus/Launier 1981). When applying problem-orientated coping strategies, individuals try to change either the situation or their own attitude to it. With emotion-orientated coping mechanisms, they try to alter negative feelings such as fear and anger in order to reduce tension (e.g. by means of denial or avoidance behaviour). Efforts to cope are influenced by personality traits, stressor characteristics and available social resources (Klemisch 2006).

According to Teegen (2003), constructive strategies in dealing with stressful situations of a police nature include good collegiality, the feeling of being able to rely on colleagues, the belief in one's own strength, and recognition of the purposefulness of the activity in question. Dysfunctional strategies include a grim sense of humour, and thoughts of one's own family. Important in processing traumatic situations are the perception and expression of emotions. If in everyday working life it is expected that officers are professional, neutral and have their emotions under control, this can result in dysfunctional coping behaviour, as shown by Schütte et al. (2009). They also show that when compared with non-traumatised colleagues, traumatised police officers achieve significantly high scores for coping criteria such as depressive processing, regressive tendencies, mistrust and pessimism. Scores for controlled emotions and social withdrawal were, however, only significantly high in some traumatised police officers. If critical events are interpreted and evaluated as purposeful, this tends to result in reduced stress levels (Antonovsky 1987, Frankl 1999).

Problem-solving coping strategies are also of benefit, such as taking a positive attitude and seeing the situation as a challenge. A selective perception of positive factors of the crisis event is helpful. Constructive expression and communication of emotion is also seen as effective. In the case of especially stressful situations, intellectualisation and distance are useful coping mechanisms. Less of benefit in processing the experience are self-blame and self-deprecation (Laux/Weber 1990). Many of these coping strategies (intellectualisation, distancing, re-assessment) can be grouped under the heading of cognitive control (Averill 1973). This also includes self-instruction such as 'I can deal with this', and 'I have to help' (Hermanutz/Buchmann 1994), and the attempt to regulate one's emotions (Eckert 1996). Police officers often use talking with close friends and relatives as a means of coping with stressful situations (Steinbauer 2001). The way in which colleagues and supervisors react to the problems of fellow officers plays a decisive role in how the officers cope with a situation (Mittendorff 1996, quote from Steinbauer 2001). According to Hallenberger (2001), the inhibition threshold in accepting help from others can have a negative effect on any subsequent performance evaluation by an officer's supervisor or can give the supervisor a false impression: "... the boss thinks I'm mad!" (Ziehme/Müller-Cyran 2011).

When it comes to how police officers perceive, evaluate and process a violent experience, it is less a matter of looking at isolated events, and more about events which are embedded in a professional and social context, and which can bring their own set of problems and conflicts (Ziehme/Müller-Cyran 2011), while also providing useful resources. To identify these complex events, it appears necessary to take a qualitative research approach. This is the only way to obtain an insight into why, despite apparently beneficial objective circumstances, a violent experience is processed in a less than beneficial way.

7.3 The study

The survey on violence against police officers conducted by the Criminological Research Institute of Lower Saxony in ten German federal states[1] was supplemented with a qualitative section. The aim was to illustrate isolated cases in their entirety independent of the known objective factors, and to use the knowledge gained to develop preventive measures. A qualitative research approach was chosen with problem-focused, semi-structured interviews which allowed comparison of the survey findings while still being open enough to illustrate the characteristics of the cases in question. The research question to be answered on the basis of the interviews is: How are violent assaults on one's own person perceived and what factors foster positive processing of the experience? To obtain answers to these question, the survey looked at factors which make it possible to analyse similarities and differences separately from the findings arrived at with the main study. The analysis of the interviews allows inclusion of the subjective assessment of the affected officers, and identification of helpful intervention and influencing factors in addition to the traditional measures used.

7.3.1 Sample

The participants questioned in the quantitative study provide the basis for the sample. The 1,289 respondents who stated that, following a violent assault, they had been unfit for work for a period of five days or more between 2005 and 2009, all received a questionnaire with the following invitation:

> "Before we present a range of questions on further training measures, personal assessments and demographic factors, we would like to offer you the opportunity to take part in a personal interview about the violent assault. From this, we hope to obtain a detailed insight into what you experienced and how you coped with the situation. Violent assaults cannot be adequately documented on the basis of pre-formulated questions alone. A member of our team will conduct interviews with 30 randomly chosen officers. The interviews will be held on your premises. If you are interested in participating in a personal interview, please let us know by sending us a brief message."

1 See Ellrich and Baier in this volume.

Some 78 police officers (four women and seventy-four men) responded to the invitation. The benefit of this self-activation sampling methodology is that it guarantees voluntary participation coupled with increased motivation, although there is an element of automatic selection in favour of individuals who show heightened initiative (Reinders 2005). Of these 78 responses, a sample of 32 individuals was chosen. All responses from women polices officers were taken into account, as were those from the six German states which were under-represented in terms of their share in the overall sample. For the remaining places, a (proportionate) random selection was made for three German states with the aim of maximum diversity. Because the purpose of qualitative research is not necessarily to reach general conclusions on the individuals questioned in the survey, but rather to analyse and describe complex environments and interactions, no attempt was made to achieve a sample representative of the population. The aim of the sample was instead to achieve a heterogeneous group of people who contrasted in the relevant traits, thus providing the information needed for the survey (Patton 2002). In the course of the survey, the sample was expanded to include an additional woman police officer who had responded to the interview invitation at the recommendation of a colleague. Two male police officers who had been assaulted while on duty but had not been rendered unfit for work had also responded to the online questionnaire. Both had stated that it had been a 'lucky break' that they had avoided serious or fatal injury, and that the assault had a lasting effect. Because it cannot be ruled out that the criterion of being rendered unfit for work does not necessarily reflect the degree of assault or the extent of its impact on those involved, interviews were also held with these police officers. The 35 interviews held were conducted in the period March 2010 to February 2011.

To save interviewees time and to spare them the need to travel, the interviews were conducted in their immediate vicinity – at their duty police station or another location. Some 29 officers were interviewed at their duty police stations, four at the institute in Hanover, and two in their homes. The interview were mostly held during officers' working hours and were arranged in such a way that they could not be interrupted by a third party. The interviews held in police stations were made easier in that all respondents said that their colleagues and supervisors had been told about the survey and the interviews, making it possible for the interviewees to speak openly and frankly. For the most part, the officers said they had wanted to take part in an interview because "it was important for them to tell their stories, to bring the phenomenon of violence against police officers to the public's attention, to help researchers study it more closely, and to assist in developing preventive and supportive measures for those affected" (Zietlow 2011).

Most respondents were on the beat or on vehicle patrol at the time of the assault (29 respondents). One of these officers was driving an unmarked vehicle, while another was off duty and attending personal business. Four officers were members of special deployment units, while two were assigned to other duties (one as a scout in a federal police team, the other on traffic control).

Ten of the police officers questioned (including three women) are midgrade civil servants, and 25 (including two women) were higher-intermediate grade. None were in higher grades. The average age of respondents was 39.4 years. The youngest was 25 and the oldest 56. Splitting the officers into three age groups (under 30, 30 to 50, and 50 plus), the majority (30) fall in the middle category. The respondents' length of police service ranged from six to 39 years, making for an average 20.1 years of service. Ten respondents policed rural areas, eight urban, and 17 were on duty in large cities (500,000+ inhabitants) at the time they experienced the assault.

7.3.2 Method

The interviews were transcribed in full and anonymised. The evaluation of the data collected focused on qualitative content analysis according to Mayring (2008). Content analysis serves the purpose of systematic processing of communicative material (in verbal, picture or musical form). This must not necessarily be limited to the content of the material to be processed – the analysis can also take in formal aspects and underlying meaning. Three different approaches can be taken in qualitative analysis: summary, explication and structuring (Mayring 2008). For the purposes of this survey, a summarising content analysis was used. This methodology aims to "reduce the material to such an extent that the key content remains intact and, by means of abstraction, create a manageable corpus which still reflects the original material" (Mayring 2008). Repeated patterns of meaning were revealed – based on the interview guidelines – which were coded using the MAXQDA software program and then transferred to evaluation categories. The key statement patterns were then summarised using representative quotes to provide a result. The interview evaluation focused in terms of content on similarities and differences in police officers' standpoints.

7.4 Findings

7.4.1 The assault and its impact

Interviewees repeatedly spoke of an 'assault out of the blue' (Schmalzl 2008, p. 21). The assaults on the respondents arose from routine incidents which had so far gone smoothly and calmly. The police officers involved had not expected the situation to escalate.

> "I don't know, I mean I just wasn't prepared. Not even mentally. No, I certainly wasn't prepared mentally. We were really relaxed. Even when the guy started to get a bit out of hand, I thought, uh oh, but even then I didn't really think any more about it. I just, well, I wouldn't say I went in completely clueless, but well, yeah naïve. Based on all my, let's say the years of positive experience I've had up to now." (Interview No. 3).

When asked why assaults often come as such a surprise, one officer offered an explanation:

> "Because when nothing's happened for such a long time, you get sort of complacent. That's just the way it is. And then it's often the case, that, well, I can imagine that in many incidents a sort of carelessness creeps in, where, if it hadn't, lots of situations just wouldn't arise." (No. 12).

This corresponds with respondents' statements about the conclusions they drew from the assault or what advice they would give to younger colleagues. Issues named here include avoiding routine, being more alert and being more aware that something unexpected could happen at any minute.

7.4.2 Thoughts and feelings during the assault

Some of the police officers questioned talked about their thoughts and feelings during both the incidents they attended and the assaults they experienced. One of the most common statements involved the feeling of helplessness – having the impression that one's own behaviour ('measures taken') had no effect.

> "… you just can't respond any other way, you can't, well, just pull your gun, that's just not an option. That would be a complete over-reaction, and, well,

> you just can't react, all you can do is just sort of stand there and let it all happen [...]. I mean, you just, well, there are situations and moments when, you, erm, just have to deal with things." (No. 10).

> "... like helpless when some goes berserk, how helpless you are right then, [...] it's like they get a rush of adrenaline and have super-human strength, it doesn't matter what you do, you just can't stop them..." (No. 12).

Another officer went into the issue of the availability/lack of support and the influence of over-arching police strategies:

> "... and when you're out there on your own, especially when you're sitting in a vehicle monitoring a radar trap, when there's no-one else around and you know it'll take about half an hour for colleagues to reach you, then you have to tussle and fight for half an hour, and it might not be just one assailant, there could be a few of them, until you get some assistance and support. That's all still at the back of my mind..." (No. 30).

The extent of the responsibility involved is also perceived as stressful.

> "...what really put me under pressure was, well, the tension, the responsibility of dealing with the incident. You've just called for the SWAT team and they'll get hold of this person at some point and, there's the risk that they'll be seriously hurt, and there's also the risk that a colleague will be seriously hurt, and in the end, well, the first thing anyone will ask you is how it all came about, isn't it?" (No. 9).

A woman police officer described in some detail how helpless she had felt and how she feared for her life during an assault in which both she and colleagues were involved:

> "... he was like a robot, felt no pain, I've never seen anything like it. It was just horrible. It was just like being in a film, fighting against a machine. I lost all hope, I thought, we'll never get this under control [...] it was just the worst because I just knew I could die any minute. If he gets hold of my baton, he's already beaten me half dead just with his fists, he'll hit me twice on the head and I'll be dead." (No. 3).

The situation described here and the helplessness and fear of being killed underscore that an assault on one's own person can meet the criteria to indicate a trauma.

7.4.3 Impact on future behaviour

The respondents stated that their own behaviour changed after the assault. They are more cautious, more alert and keep a safer distance from others.

> "... well, I approach people really cautiously, and as soon as I start talking to them, as soon as I have the slightest indication [...] that they're, well, reacting a bit strangely, even if it's just someone on the street, I take a step back. I keep a safe distance between us so I can react straight away."

Some officers became more aggressive after the assault and placed higher priority on their personal safety.

> "... I don't care, if he raises his hand or tries to hit me, then I make sure I get him down on the floor and get the handcuffs on, I don't think, oh my God, the poor guy, that's bound to hurt. No. That's all over. I used to think like that, but, erm, no. Who knows what he's got in the other hand, maybe he's got a knife..." (No. 16).

Other respondents said the assault had made them afraid of future physical confrontations, and that their colleagues noticed their insecurity.

> "... I couldn't be out on the street. The mere thought of any resistance and I'd start to shake. [...] I was immediately filled with fear. [...] And, erm, my patrol mate, who really knew me well, he noticed that I've changed. He said I'm becoming more insecure and that he didn't want to go out on the street with me any more because he knew I can't look out for him like I used to." (No. 3).

7.4.4 Impact on private lives

In many instances, officers described the impact of the assaults on their private lives.

> "... of course it's affected my private life, because when you're unable to sleep and you can't concentrate any more, when you're restless, when there's somehow [...] a kind of listlessness about you, both in, well, in your sexual relations and in other activities, then it [...] really puts a burden on your private life..." (No. 22)

One respondent feared he had been infected with the HIV virus during the assault. Apart from the mental anguish this caused, it also affected his family life.

> "... the whole time no-one was able to tell me whether or not my assailant was HIV positive. That means, well, our son was much younger then, he was smaller, and, well, we can't very well explain to him now what the problem is. Back then, I kept my distance for preventive reasons, and my wife did, of course, we both had to change how we went about things because I didn't know if I'd been infected ..." (No. 20)

7.4.5 Psychological impact

The assaults cause psychological problems by many of the police officers questioned: disturbed sleep patterns, constant worrying, flashbacks to the assault, and heightened emotions in the form of uncontrollable bouts of crying.

> "…I kept thinking about it during the day, erm, and this restless sleep. […] it was more, this this constant nagging, asking myself if I'd handled it all properly. Could you, could you have prevented it, erm, it was like, like not being able to go to sleep and then waking up and then these thoughts kept coming through the night…" (No. 9)

Another policewoman was diagnosed with post-traumatic stress disorder following her assault.

> "… the guilt that remains […] and the feeling of fearing for your life, although, well, at first I was able to blot it all out, but my guilty conscience towards my colleague, I couldn't ignore that. […] after about three months I realised it was getting worse instead of better." (No. 3)

Another officer suffered post-shooting trauma following an incident in which his colleague fired a lethal shot:

> "Well, in the first few weeks after the shooting, it was awful. I had all the symptoms of trauma. I was restless, had problems concentrating, I couldn't sleep. I kept seeing these pictures before my eyes of the guy, who, erm, how he's […] hit by my colleague and then just collapses and dies. I'd keep hearing the the sound of the two shots in my head, I, well, well, when I'd go to bed at night, just when I'd settled down, that's when it was worst." (No. 20)

7.4.6 Support in the workplace and from colleagues

The officers made statements (sometimes upon request) about whether following the incident in which they were assaulted there had been any formal post-incident debriefing and processing in the workplace. Some said there had and assessed the measures taken as positive.

> "[Post-incident processing] really, with the whole group and, well, yeah our boss at the time had, erm, excuse the language, had the balls to stand up and say 'I really messed up'. 'I just did the wrong thing, and that can't happen again, we have to work that through', and, well, that's what he did, like." (No. 2)

Another group of respondents stated that there was no adequate or no post-incident debriefing and processing, which they perceived as negative.

> "Like I said, in the post-incident debriefing […] everything was presented very differently, it wasn't at all like, erm, like we all experienced it, and of course no-one argued because you just don't. […] That was it, there wasn't any debriefing and the gushing praise they all give out afterwards, well, I don't want any part of that because there isn't usually any open and honest debriefing. I mean, if anyone has anything to say, any criticism, it's generally not taken on board. You just take note and act as if you haven't heard it." (No. 8)

Nearly all officers addressed the issue of support from colleagues following the assault. Many interviewees reported that they had received support from colleagues and said they welcomed it.

> "… erm, at the court hearing I was lucky enough to have support from my duty station. Someone accompanied me so I didn't have to face it all alone. […] Outside the court, the press were naturally there with all kinds of questions, but my colleagues shielded me well from it all and […] well, for me personally, that was about the best thing they did for me… " (No. 16)

Support from supervisors following the assault was addressed by almost all officers questioned. Where they received such support, they said it had been helpful.

> "… my supervisor, he set a perfect example […] I was in contact with my team leader more or less the whole time, I mean he called me more than usual […] he basically made sure I was okay. I'm still in contact with him today… " (No. 7)

Where no support was received from supervisors, officers reported the situation as extremely negative and doubly stressful. Only few respondents received professional help.

> "… two women from social services, they'd been contacted by my family […] and, erm, were there to give me support […] I talked to them for about an hour, these two women from social services, and one of them still gives me support today…" (No. 22)

Other officers received no such support but would have welcomed it.

> "Whether from a psychological standpoint and no-one offered the family any support, none whatsoever. I had to, we had to, cope with it all by ourselves. I thought that was really poor show. […] something has to be done there, that, well, colleagues are helped when they experience something like that. And not just a quick 'Oh yeah, how're you feeling?" […] after-care is really important, and after-care for the family is especially important." (No. 20)

7.4.7 Coping

Almost all officers questioned stated that they had coped with the assault by talking to family and friends.

> "... it's clear that, I took the longest to deal with this story, with this, this group of people who assaulted me, because I was the one who talked about it most with friends and family, to anyone who would listen or even when they didn't want to hear it, I told them anyway [...] because I mean, it's, well, talking helps you get things off your chest, things that bother you and also things you didn't think were bothering you, but you talk about them and you rid yourself of them subconsciously... " (No. 10)

Some police officers reported that they had coped with the assault by taking convalescent leave or by going into therapy. Another coping strategy took the form of increased alcohol consumption.

> "Just to be able to sleep at night, I took to drinking alcohol, something I rarely do, a crate of beer usually lasts me a month, but suddenly it was gone in a week. [...] Like I said, I couldn't get to sleep at night. I'd sit in front of the television until two in the morning, no idea what was on, what I was watching, I couldn't say. Because I just can't remember. [...] Yeah, and then a beer, a stiffer drink, one after the other, until I couldn't stand up anymore, that I just needed to fall back on the sofa and then I'd fall asleep." (No. 30)

Some respondents said they tried to get back to everyday (working) life as soon as possible after the assault.

> "... but it's not as if, that I want to be sort of mollycoddled for the next six weeks or six months. There comes a point when you've had enough, that's when I just switch off. Erm, you know, being protected and wrapped up in cotton wool is okay at the start, it's really nice, but after a while, it gets to be too much." (No. 2)

> "... to be honest, I could have stayed home for three or four months, but I'd had enough after a week, I was thoroughly bored... " (No. 7)

Some (a few) officers chose a change of job as a way of coping with the stressful event.

> "... I wanted to get away from F, I couldn't stand it any more [...] I decided at some point to tell my station head 'you know, I think I need to get away from here for a while, I can't cope' [...] Yeah, that's how I ended up in R and I have to say that in the meantime, I really like it here, I've been well accepted [...] I was able to go out on the beat quite normally and that really helped me to feel whole again, a true policeman, I might not have been fit for work in the city, but I am here." (No. 3)

Almost all officers said that to cope with the assault, it was important for them to think (critically) about the event and sort things out in their minds.

> "... you know, you think a lot, and you reflect on things for yourself, what could I have done better, what did I do wrong, and somewhere along the line you tell yourself it would have happened no matter what [...] you couldn't have stopped it, that's just the way it is. But it's so important that you find closure at some point, that you say okay, some things just can't be explained, they just happen and you just have to get on with it." (No. 1).

> "My colleague thought the same, if we'd known that the [offender] was so aggressive, we'd have used the [riot stick] properly right from the outset [...] I wanted to arrest him, but [...] I don't really want to hurt anyone badly just in order to arrest them. If there's another way, I'll take it. But that was the wrong way to think at that moment. I should have just thought, yeah, I'll knock your head off, and that would've been it, maybe." (No. 3)

7.4.8 Legacy stress

A large number of officers reported that they had experienced other stressful situations prior the assault in question. These included other assaults and other negative events in the workplace or at home which had resulted in the officer seeking professional help.

> Stressfull experiences lots, lots. Well, a man died in my arms. I was in O on rotating shifts, and during that time, we knew right away there was nothing more we could do. He was trapped in his car I held his hand and I thought it was good, how he dealt with it and how I dealt with it at that moment, but it's something you never forget, you know. Erm, he even said 'yeah, I know, my time has come and give everyone my love' and he didn't even cry, not at all, only when suddenly, his his hand, it was lifeless, and it just slipped from mine. That was an awful moment. (No. 6)

7.5 Discussion

The interviews show that people react very differently to personal assaults. The duration and intensity of their feelings differ from person to person and depend on a variety of factors (Nörenberg et al. 2006). Apart from the physical severity of the assault, other influencing factors include the extent to which the individual concerned is otherwise affected (cf. Klemisch et al. 2005, Steinbauer 2001), the person's personality and the available personal and social resources (Schneider/Latscha 2011). Yet other influences arise from the effectiveness of the coping strategies used (Neugebauer/Latscha 2009, Reininger/Gorzka 2011), whereby the evaluation of whether the assault was severe or less severe need not necessarily be based on objective criteria. An individual's personal threshold plays a role, as does their previous experience with violence. Situations in which someone is repeatedly pushed, shoved and insulted can be just as stressful over time as being assaulted with a weapon. The experience of violence can also result in the development of post-traumatic stress disorder (Maercker 2009).

In the medium and longer term, the experience of a violence assault can have psychological effects such as burnout, exhaustion, listlessness, withdrawal from the workplace and inner resignation (cf. Bär et al. 2004, Nörenberg et al. 2006). But it can also lead to greater alertness, a more cautious attitude and more resolute action while on duty. Violent assaults change the way people act (at work). They are seen as a learning experience (as a source of professional and personal development), but they can also alter people's professional self-image to such an extent that it results in further negative experience. To deal constructively with such events, the police community and being part of police culture (Schneider/Latscha 2011) can be of help when they are experienced as part of a closed unit rather than out on the beat or during vehicle patrol. The predictability of the event, preparation for it and (direct) support from colleagues afterwards appear to be relevant factors. Here, it is important to identify the individual's personal needs as regards the type and level of support required.

Psychological after-care is provided at different levels directly following an assault. Firstly, in the case of 'typical incidents of overwhelming stress' (confrontation with injury, death, and the use of guns), officers can make use of emergency counselling (cf. Nörenberg et al. 2006) offered by a wide network of advisory organisations and services, and also pastoral resources. These services must be known and accessible at short notice. Secondly, supervisors and colleagues are assigned an important role (cf. Steinbauer 2001). It is seen as positive when they make themselves available as a point of contact, and when they are able to show empathy and create a protective atmosphere. The situation is less clear when it comes to dealing with events that are not understood as highly stressful. Anyone who suffers a violent assault that is seen as just 'part of the job' (Behr 2006, p. 134) is reliant on a supportive environment. To make sure communication becomes routine when dealing with difficult situations, systematic debriefing and after-care would appear helpful, although this does not appear to be the norm following violent assaults (Ellrich et al. 2011, p. 98).

In the context of everyday routine, the moment when an officer returns to work after a period of sick leave is also important. Indifferent attitudes and 'funny comments' from supervisors and colleagues are all perceived as stressful. Those police officers who have access to a stable network in the workplace and at home, and who also have a strong feeling of coherence (they perceive the world as understandable and manageable, and see a meaning in what they do), see work-related stress less negatively and tend to remain healthy and capable following extreme events (Fährmann et al. 2006).

The situation thus differs depending on the case involved. Experience of violence is part of police routine. Not all assaults are perceived as stressful or traumatising. Discourse on the issue of adopting a professional attitude when dealing with aggression appears necessary, as does discourse on how police culture can be shaped to allow a supportive environment to develop without doing away with specific (apparently) unalterable traditional patterns of thinking and acting.

References

Antonovsky, A. (1987). Unraveling the Mystery of Health. San Francisco: Jossey-Bass.

Averill, J.R. (1973). Personal Control Over Aversive Stimuli and its Relationship to Stress. Psychological Bulletin, 80, 286-303.

Bär, O., Pahlke, C., Dahm, P., Weiss, U., Heuft, G. (2004). Sekundärprävention bei Traumatisierung im Polizeidienst. Zeitschrift für Psychosomatische Medizin und Psychotherapie, 50, 190-202.

Bandura, A. (1997). Self-efficacy: The Exercise of Control. New York: Freeman.

Barlow, D.H. (1988). Anxiety and its Disorders: The Nature and Treatment of Anxiety and Panic. New York: Guilford Press.

Behr, R. (2006). Polizeikultur. Routinen-Rituale-Reflexionen. Bausteine zu einer Theorie der Praxis der Polizei. Wiesbaden: VS Verlag.

Benight, C.C., Bandura, A. (2004). Social Cognitive Theory of Posttraumatic Recovery: The Role of Perceived Self-efficacy. Behaviour Research and Therapy, 42, 1129-1148.

DSM-IV (1996). Diagnostisches und Statistisches Manual Psychischer Störungen der American Psychiatric Association. Göttingen: Hogrefe.

Eckert, F.J. (1996). Streß und Situationsbewältigung bei extremen Belastungen (I und II). Polizei heute, 5, 170-180 und 6, 224-228.

Ehlers, A., Clark, D.M., Winton, E. (1997). Predicting Response to Exposure Treatment in PTSD: The Role of Mental Defeat and Alienation. Journal of Traumatic Stress, 11, 457-471.

Ellrich, K., Baier, D., Pfeiffer, C. (2011). Gewalt gegen Polizeibeamte. Befunde zu Einsatzbeamten, Situationsmerkmalen und Folgen von Gewaltübergriffen. Forschungsbericht Nr. 3. Hannover: KFN.

Engel, H. (1995). Psychische Reaktionen und Verarbeitungsmechanismen am Beispiel der Identifizierungskommission des BKA. In: K.E Buchmann, M. Hermanutz, (Eds.), Trauma und Katastrophe. Villingen-Schwenningen.

Fährmann, A., Remke, S., Reschke, K. (2006). Der Einfluss des Kohärenzgefühls auf das subjektive Erleben berufsbedingter Belastungen bei Polizeibeamten. In: C. Lorei (Ed.), Polizei & Psychologie (pp. 107-124). Frankfurt: Verlag für Polizeiwissenschaft.

Filipp, S.-H. (1990). Subjektive Theorien als Forschungsgegenstand. In: R. Schwarzer (Ed.), Gesundheitspsychologie (pp. 247-262). Göttingen: Hogrefe.

Frankl, V.E. (1999). Theorie und Therapie der Neurosen. München: Reinhardt.

Gasch, U. (1998). Polizeidienst und psychische Traumen. Kriminalistik, 52, 819-823.

Gewerkschaft der Polizei (1988). Fachveranstaltung `88. Dienst für den Bürger rund um die Uhr – Wechselschichtdienst der Polizei. Polizei.

Hallenberger, F. (1998). Polizeiliche Beanspruchung – Ein Plädoyer für polizeiliche Supervision. Die Polizei, 150-156.

Hallenberger, F., Mueller, S. (2000). Was bedeutet für Polizistinnen und Polizisten Stress? Polizei & Wissenschaft, 1, 58-65.

Hallenberger, F. (2001). Polizeilicher Schusswaffengebrauch: Erleben und Folgen. Polizei & Wissenschaft, 2, 3-12.

Hallenberger, F. (2006). Primäre Prävention für kritische Ereignisse – Vorbereitung auf Hochstress. Polizei & Wissenschaft, 7, 29-51.

Hermanutz, M., Buchmann, K.E. (1994). Körperliche und psychische Belastungsreaktionen bei Einsatzkräften während und nach einer Unfallkatastrophe. Die Polizei, 294-302.

Klemisch, D. (2006). Psychosoziale Belastungen und Belastungsverarbeitung von Polizeibeamten. Dissertation, Westfälische Wilhelms-Universität Münster.

Klemisch, D., Kepplinger, J., Muthny, F. A. (2005). Belastungen, Belastungsstörungen und psychische Störungen von Polizeibeamten. Polizei & Wissenschaft, 6, 27-42.

Lasogga, F., Gasch, B. (2000). Psychische Erste Hilfe bei Unfällen: Kompensation eines Defizits. Wien: Stumpf und Kossendey.

Laux, L., Weber, H. (1990). Bewältigung von Emotionen. In: K.R. Scherer (Ed.), Psychologie der Emotion. Göttingen: Hogrefe.

Lazarus, R. S. (1966). Psychological Stress and the Coping Process. New York: McGraw Hill.

Lazarus, R. S., Launier, R. (1981). Stressbezogene Transaktionen zwischen Person und Umwelt. In: J. R. Nitsch (Ed.). Stress. Theorien, Untersuchungen, Maßnahmen (pp. 213-259). Bern: Huber.

Lefcourt, H.M. (1983). Research With the Locus of Control Construct (Vol. 2). New York: Academic Press.

Maercker, A. (2003). Erscheinungsbild, Erklärungsansätze und Therapieforschung. In: A. Maercker (Eds.): Therapie der posttraumatischen Belastungsstörungen. Berlin: Springer.

Maercker, A. (2009). Symptomatik, Klassifikation und Epidemiologie. In: A. Maercker (Eds.), Posttraumatische Belastungsstörungen (pp. 13-33). Heidelberg: Springer.

Mayring, P. (2008). Qualitative Inhaltsanalyse. Grundlagen und Techniken. 10. Auflage, Weinheim und Basel: Beltz.

McCafferty, F. L., McCafferty, E., McCafferty, M. A. (1992). Stress and Suicide in Police Officers: Paradigm of Occupational Stress. Southern Medical Journal, 85, 233-243.

Mineka, S., Kihlstrom, J.F. (1978). Unpredictable and Uncontrollable Events: A New Perspective on Experimental Neurosis. Journal of Abnormal Psychology, 87, 256-271.

Myrtek, M., Itte, H., Zimmermann, W., Brügner, G. (1994). Psychische Bewältigung von Unfällen bei Lokomotivführern: Die Relevanz von Copingfragebogen zu Erfassung von funktionalen und dysfunktionalen Copingprozessen. Zeitschrift für Klinische Psychologie, 23, 293-304.

Neugebauer, U., Latscha, K. (2009). Bewältigung belastender Ereignisse bei Polizeibeamten. Polizei & Wissenschaft, 10, 55-62.

Nörenberg, L., Hering, T., Arndt, D., Beerlage, I. (2006). Belastungen im Polizeiberuf, Belastungsfolgen. Polizei & Wissenschaft, 7, 28-42.

Patton, M.Q. (2002). Qualitative Research and Evaluation Methods. Thousand Oaks: Sage.

Reinders, H. (2005). Qualitative Interviews mit Jugendlichen führen. München: Oldenbourg.

Reinecke, S., Runde, B., Bastians, F., Bär, O., Weiss, U., Heuft, G. (2006). Qualität, Intensität und Quantität von psychischen Belastungen innerhalb der Polizeiarbeit. Bericht über ein Forschungsprojekt. Polizei & Wissenschaft, 7, 4-16.

Reininger, K. M., Gorzka, R. (2011). Copingmuster bei Polizistinnen und Polizisten. Polizei & Wissenschaft, 12, 48-56.

Schmalzl, H.P. (2008). Einsatzkompetenz. Frankfurt/a.M.: Verlag für Polizeiwissenschaft.

Schmidt, R.A. (1982). Motor Control and Learning. Champain, Ill.: Human Kinetics Publishers.

Schneider, D., Latscha, K. (2010). Polizeikultur als Schutzfaktor bei traumatischen Belastungen. Polizei & Wissenschaft, 11, 30-43.

Schneider, D., Latscha, K. (2011). Geschlechtsdifferenzierte polizeispezifische Schutzfaktoren bei traumatischen Belastungen. Polizei & Wissenschaft, 12, 2-14.

Schütte, N., Bär, O., Weiss, U., Heuft, G. (2009). Copingmechanismen von Polizeibeamten mit psychischen und psychosomatischen Symptomen nach einem potenziell psychotraumatischen Ereignis. Z Psychosom Med Psychother, 55, 70-83.

Schützwohl, M., Maercker, A. (1997). Social Support and Coping as Predictors of PTSD Thirty Years after Traumatization. In: A.Maercker, M. Schützwohl, Z. Solomon (Eds.), Posttraumatic Stress Disorder: A Lifespan Developmental Perspective. Seattle: Hogrefe & Huber.

Sennekamp, W., Martin, H. (2003). Psychosozialer Beratungsbedarf von Polizeibeamten bei dienstlichen Belastungssituationen. Polizei & Wissenschaft, 4, 29-36.

Solomon, R.M., Horn, J.M. (1986). Post-Shooting Trauma Reactions: A Pilot Study. In: J.T. Reese, H.A. Goldstein (Eds.), Psychological Services for Law Enforcement. Washington, D.C.: U.S. Government Printing Office.

Steinbauer, M. (2001). Stress im Polizeiberuf und die Verarbeitung von belastenden Ereignissen im Dienst. Polizei & Wissenschaft, 2, 46-59.

Teegen, F. (2003). Posttraumatische Belastungsstörungen bei gefährdeten Berufsgruppen. Bern: Huber.

Ungerer, D. (1999). Stress und Stressbewältigung im Einsatz. Stuttgart: Kohlhammer.

Waddington, P.A.J. (1999). Policing Citizens. London: Routledge.

Wagner, H. (1986). Belastungen im Polizeiberuf. Die Polizei, 80-84

Wittchen, H.-U., Hoyer, J. (2006). Klinische Psychologie & Psychotherapie. Springer.

Zieme, C., Müller-Cyran, A. (2011). „... Der Chef hält mich doch für verrückt!?“ In: C. Lorei (Eds.), Polizei & Psychologie 2009 (pp. 403-415). Frankfurt: Verlag für Polizeiwissenschaft.

Zietlow, B. (2011). Gewalt gegen Polizeibeamte. Zwischenbericht zum qualitativen Teil der Studie – Interviews mit von Gewalt betroffenen Polizeibeamten und Polizeibeamtinnen. Hannover: KFN.

8. Victimisation and perpetration among Prison Inmates

Steffen Bieneck, Dirk Baier

8.1 Introduction

The subject of violence in various contexts such as the school or the individual's social proximity (such as in partnerships) is thoroughly studied and documented in empirical research (cf. Baier et al. 2009, Krahé et al. 2005). Victimisation in prison, however, remains an underrepresented research area in German criminology (cf. Bieneck 2010). Yet empirical data from other countries underscore that this is a topical issue. Camp and Camp (1997), for example, report that in 1996 there were some 30,000 assaults among inmates in US prisons and just under 14,000 assaults by inmates against prison staff. In Germany, prisons occasionally compile internal statistics on incidents involving violence between inmates. These statistics are rarely aggregated, however, and systematic research approaches remain the exception.

The present study addresses this research gap. An exhaustive survey in prisons of five German federal states is used to gather comprehensive data on experiences of victimisation and perpetration in prison. The project's findings help in quantifying the problem and in the development of suitable intervention measures to significantly reduce violence inside prison.

8.2 Violence in prisons: research findings

Querying relevant psychological databases for studies dealing with violence in prison yields a large volume of data for the US and the UK. Power et al. (1997), for example, investigated victimisation among Scottish young offenders. The authors designed a questionnaire that 707 prisoners between the ages of 15 and 21 (M = 18.6 years) completed by marking boxes. The questions asked included how frequently respondents were victims of or witness to aggression and how frequently they themselves engaged in violence against other inmates. The analysis showed that 76 percent of respondents were witness to an assault at least once during their current sentence, 29 percent of inmates reported being victims and 16 percent said they themselves had bullied others. Victims stated verbal threats and physical assault as the most frequent form of violence experienced.

A study in British prisons by Ireland (1999) arrives at somewhat higher prevalence rates. The study included data on 74 female and 235 male young and adult offenders who had completed the Direct and Indirect Prison Behaviour Checklist (DIPC). The DIPC asks in some detail what forms of violence respondents have inflicted on others or experienced themselves. It also records demographic data on respondents (such as age, sentence length, and offence type) to enable more precise analysis of experienced victimisation. Just under 58 percent of respondents said they had maltreated another inmate at some time. Male bullies outnumbered female bullies (by 61.3 percent to 47.3 percent), although the differing sample sizes need to be taken into account when interpreting the data. Some 52 percent of respondents reported having been a victim of bullying at some time, with equal prevalence for males and females. With reference to the demographic data, younger offenders are significantly overrepresented among bullies. This group stands out both for more frequent verbal abuse and in terms of physical violence.

Figures for American prisons are provided by a comprehensive study by Wolff et al. (2007). The study analysed data on 7,221 men (with an average age of 34.2) and 564 women (average age 35.5) from various prisons in a single US state. Respondents were first asked in general about their experience as victims and perpetrators of violence in the preceding six months and during their entire prison term. They were then asked to state which specific listed forms of violence (such as hitting, kicking, biting or strangling) they were confronted with. The figures on physical victimisation were classified according to whether weapons (such as knives, screwdrivers or similar objects) were used. The overall prevalence rates for the preceding six months were the same for both men and women, with some 21 percent having experienced victimisation. However, women experienced violence without weapons substantially more frequently (14.9 percent) than violence with weapons (9.4 percent). The picture was reversed for the male sample, where 11.7 percent reported violence not involving weapons compared with 14.1 percent for violence involving weapons.

For German-speaking countries, very few publications have so far addressed the topic of violence in prison. The studies have additionally remained superficial and tend to be narrative in character. Heinrich (2002), for example, presented a paper on the development of violence in prisons in the state of Hesse. The analysis was based on inmates' prison files for the years 1989 to 1998. All files on incidents and charges were included where violence by inmates against other individuals was involved. A total of 1,229 incidents were found to meet the search criteria and were included in the subsequent analysis for the reporting period. As a result Heinrich (2002) points out that the perpetrators were mostly younger prisoners: The individuals involved in violence had an average age of 27, whereas the average age of the Hesse prison population as a whole was 34. Individuals born in countries other than Germany and without German citizenship comprised the largest group of perpetrators. The most frequent form of violence was assault (1,058 incidents), followed by threats with and without the use of weapons (110 incidents). The majority of incidents had causes relating to the individual (including mental disturbances, intoxication or aggressiveness). Subcultural structures (primarily violence as a means of enforcing interests or of gaining power or respect) within prison likewise played a significant part. These findings are meaningful only to an extent, however, because subcultural rules in prisons mean that not every assault among inmates is reported to prison staff. The reported prevalence rates therefore tend to understate the problem of violence in prison.

In a similar way to Heinrich (2002), Wirth (2007) presents the findings of an analysis of files on violent offences in prisons in North Rhine-Westphalia in 2005. The offence/offender-based analysis relates to 403 verifiable offences with 518 offenders. All reported incidents of note involving violence were surveyed, including sexual coercion/rape, murder and manslaughter, assault, participation in a brawl, threats, coercion, robbery or extortion. The core findings of the analysis underscore that violence among inmates that comes to official notice is predominantly a situational phenomenon that rarely features any identifiable background planning. The majority of cases did not result in bodily injuries requiring treatment (less than 10 percent of incidents had serious consequences). The offenders primarily showed indications of social marginalisation, more rarely had a fixed place of abode, more frequently had no school leaving qualification and more frequently were of foreign origin.

A broad-based, more comprehensive study of victimisation in prisons by Ernst (2008) draws on data relating to 2,215 adult males in 33 prisons in the states of Bavaria, Berlin, North Rhine-Westphalia, Saxony and Schleswig-Holstein. The response rate – the number of usable questionnaires as a percentage of questionnaires handed or laid out – came to 29.6

percent. Respondents were selected for the survey by cluster sampling. The survey took place over a long period from February 2005 to April 2006, largely because of differences in approval procedures from state to state. More than a third of respondents were young adults and the overall age range extended from 18 to 84. The questionnaire developed for the study was issued solely in German. Inmates with only limited command of the German language were consequently excluded from participating. This limitation may distort the results to the extent that inmates whose ability to communicate and make themselves understood and who are restricted by language difficulties are no less liable to become victims of assault.

The dependent variables in the study by Ernst (2008) comprise victimisation and perpetration of threats, extortion and assault in the preceding six months. 25.6 percent of respondents reported having suffered victimisation in the period concerned. Most instances related to threats and assaults. The analysis points to the conclusion that not all inmates are at equal risk of victimisation. The great majority suffer victimisation one to five times, whereas a small number exceed ten times. The question of whether the victim group with the greatest victimisation risk has certain recurring features is not answered by the study, however. No less than 17.6 percent of respondents report also being perpetrators of violence. There is a significant overlapping of victims and perpetrators. Moreover, it is reported that violence occurs less often in daytime release prisons than in secure prisons. Findings on the perpetrators are, among others, as follows: The perpetrator rate drops with increasing age; non-German prisoners are more often violent; drug users are more often seen to be perpetrators of violence; inmates condemned as violent offenders show violent behavior more frequently, the same is true for people who had already been in prison before their present sentence and who are seen to "basically condone violence" (Ernst 2008a, p. 370).

The aim of the following study was to supply current data on the extent of violence and aggression in prisons against the background of the state of research in Germany to date. The emphasis of the study was placed on adult prisons. In contrast to other studies in the past, unrecorded cases of violence were to be considered, not just reported crimes. It therefore seemed adequate to use an anonymous, standardized survey. Following enquiries to the Ministries of Justice in various states, five states finally agreed to participate: Brandenburg, Bremen, Lower Saxony, Saxony and Thuringia.

The study had two further aims: First, in contrast to earlier studies, the violent behavior of various immigrant groups was to be examined in detail. To this end, inmates were questioned on their ethnic backgrounds; furthermore, the questionnaire was translated into 18 languages in order to include those immigrants whose knowledge of German was not sufficient for a questioning in German. Second, attention was to be paid to possible factors influencing violent behavior, whereby limitations were necessary here in order not to make the questionnaire too extensive. A few individual features were selected. Prison features were also investigated because some studies point out that these features are relevant for violent behavior in prison, too. Among others, Hinz und Hartenstein (2010) state that the "climate of the institution" (p. 181) is an important environmental variable as regards aggressive behavior and one which can be influenced practically. The study of Ortmann (2002) also points to the role of prison features such as the staff-prisoner relationship or the relationships among prisoners.

8.3 The sample

In 2011 and 2012, the Criminological Research Institute of Lower Saxony carried out questionnaire surveys in a comparable manner in 48 prisons in five states. The states concerned are Brandenburg (survey carried out: January/February 2012), Bremen (March 2011), Lower Saxony (April/May 2011), Saxony (April to June 2012) und Thuringia (April/May 2012). At the time of questioning, 11,884 people were in the prisons, of whom 5,983 took part (response rate: 50.3 %). Surveys were not carried out in men's and women's prisons in all states; moreover, juvenile prisons were not included in all states. The following analyses therefore apply primarily to males in adult prisons. Data for 4,436 men are available. In addition, 460 women and 1,087 people in prisons for adolescents/young offenders were questioned.

The male persons in adult prisons are on average 35.9 years old.[1] Somewhat more than every fourth person questioned comes from an immigrant community (26.6 %). In order to determine a participant's origin,

1 In the questionnaire, ages were grouped together. In order to calculate an average age, the various categories were replaced by average values ("between 14 and 17 years" = 15.5 years, "between 18 and 21 years = 19.5 years, etc.). The last category

details of the origin of his natural mother and his natural father ("Which country does … come from") and of the participant's own nationality were used. Participants are considered to be German if both their parents are of German origin and they themselves are German citizens. If a non-German origin/nationality was reported, the person concerned is considered to be an immigrant, whereby in the case of contradicting details the origin of the mother was counted. The largest group of immigrants in the survey is from the former Soviet Union (5.5 %), the second-largest group from Poland (5.1 %); a Turkish origin is the third-most frequent (3.5 %). In the three East German states, the proportion of immigrants among the prisoners is only about half as high as in the two West German states (Brandenburg 18.2 %, Saxony 16.2 %, Thuringia 12.2 %; Bremen 40.0 %, Lower Saxony 35.2 %).

Of the men in adult prisons, 55.8 % have either no school qualification or a low school qualification (junior high school at the most). Two thirds of those questioned are in closed prisons, 13.6 % on daytime release, 16.4 % in custody; 4.8 % are in a different kind of prison (e.g. remand pending deportation). Almost a third of those questioned (32.5 %) is serving a sentence because they have committed, among other things, a crime of violence. A further 11 % are in prison because of, among other things, a sexual offence. The remaining prisoners are not in prison because of either a violent or sexual offence and have therefore, for example, committed theft or a drugs-related crime.[2]

Of the men questioned, 54.5 % had served at least one prison sentence before their present sentence. Correspondingly, the majority (76.7 %) has

("older than 55 years") was replaced conservatively by 56 years. The average age presented is therefore a slight underestimation in as far as those questioned in this category were certainly also older than 56 years. The proportion of over 55 year-olds the random sample is 6.3 %.

2 In the questionnaire, it was possible to give several answers concerning the crime for which one had been sentenced. With regard to the central question of the survey, that of victimization and aggression, multiple answers were combined in a variable as follows: If "sexual offence" was reported, this was recorded as the offence for imprisonment. If not "sexual offence" but "violent offence" was indicated, the latter was coded. If neither of these offences were named but a different offence instead, this was recorded in the group "other". It should be pointed out here that 1,302 participants gave no details of the crime for which they had been sentenced, the results for this variable are therefore to be interpreted with caution. In the case of the other survey variables, rates of missing data are normally half as high at the most.

at least one previous conviction (not counting the current sentence). Somewhat more than half of those questioned (54.8 %) are serving a sentence of three years at the most; 9.5 % report a sentence of more than ten years. Most of the men (76.7 %) filled out the questionnaire in their own cells, 19.1 % in the common room and 4.2 % in a different place.

8.4 Findings

8.4.1 Extent of victimization and aggression

Based on Ireland (1999), a number of behaviors from the perspective of both victims and perpetrators were recorded in the questionnaire, whereby it was to be estimated how often these behaviors had been experienced/ perpetrated during the last four weeks and the last calendar year. As the last four weeks are a reasonable timeframe in which to recollect details, only these prevalence rates are to be reported below. Furthermore, only behaviors which are classified as physical violence are included. Threats, verbal abuse or similar behaviors, which were also recorded in the questionnaire, are not reported here. Table 8.1 shows which statements in the questionnaire were combined to the indexes "sexual violence", "physical violence" and "extortion". The individual items were combined in the indexes via the maximum. The highest frequency for a behavior therefore determines the index value.[3] If, for example, a participant was seldom forced to satisfy other prisoners with his mouth but had, for example, never been forced to have sexual intercourse, the participant receives the value "seldom" on the index "sexual violence".

3 Possible answers were "never", "seldom", "sometimes" and "often". As a cross was only very rarely made beside the category "often" (at the most by 1.4 % of those questioned on the offences considered here), a distinction is made only between participants who have experienced/perpetrated something and those for whom this is not true. Therefore only prevalence rates - not incident rates - are reported and inasmuch the question answered as to what proportion of the participants has at least rarely experienced/perpetrated at least one offence of the relevant index.

Table 8.1 Victimization and perpetration indexes

Index	Victim items	Perpetrator items
Sexual violence	• I had to satisfy other prisoners with my mouth. • I was forced to have sexual intercourse/ anal intercourse.	• I forced other prisoners to satisfy me with their mouth. • I forced other prisoners to have sexual intercourse/anal intercourse.
Physical violence	• I was pushed deliberately. • I was beaten by hand/fist or kicked. • I was tormented/tortured. • I was beaten with an object.	• I pushed other prisoners deliberately. • I beat other prisoners with hand/fist or kicked them. • I tormented/tortured other prisoners. • I beat other prisoners with an object.
Extortion	• I had to pay for other prisoners' purchases. • I had to ask family/friends to send other prisoners money. • I was instructed to send other prisoners money when I left prison. • I had to give up some of my purchases. • I was forced to give other prisoners my telephone card/my PIN code.	• I forced other prisoners to pay for my purchases. • I forced other prisoners to have their family/friends send me money. • I asked other prisoners to send me money when they left prison. • I forced other prisoners to give me some of their purchases. • I forced other prisoners to give me their telephone card /their PIN code.

As Table 8.2 shows, experiences of violence in prisons are not unusual: 16.8 % of those questioned in men's prisons report having experienced physical violence in the last four weeks, 10.6 % to having carried it out. Extortion is somewhat rarer, sexual violence very rare: About every 50th person questioned reported having experienced sexual violence. The results coincide with those of Ernst (2008, 2008a). In women's prisons, the victim rates for physical and sexual violence are clearly lower; the rate for extortion is slightly higher. Seen from the point of view of the perpetrators, the differences between male and female prisons are smaller. This allows the interpretation that fewer perpetrators may have taken part in the survey in men's prisons than in women's prisons. When comparing the rates, it should be noted that prisons for women were not included in all states; the data between men and women are therefore not completely comparable. What is very clear is that in prisons for adolescents/young people the highest prevalence rates from the point of view of both victims and perpetrators are to be observed. Prison violence is therefore especially an issue in prisons for younger age groups.

Table 8.2 Violence prevalence rates per prison group (in percent)

	Victims			Perpetrators		
	physical violence	extortion	sexual violence	physical violence	extortion	sexual violence
Men's prisons	16.8	11.4	2.1	10.6	6.1	1.4
Women's prisons	11.4	12.7	1.1	9.6	4.0	1.4
Prisons for young offenders and young adults	32.4	19.6	3.3	31.2	17.9	3.2

Table 8.3 shows the prevalence rates for victims of both physical and sexual violence and for extortion for various groups of participants. Furthermore the rate for physical violence is presented. The older a participant in the survey is, the less likely he was to be a victim of violence (exception: sexual violence) and a perpetrator of violence. Clear distinctions are found for the different kinds of prison: Those questioned on daytime release report the least number of violent attacks; Ernst (2008, 2008a) und Wirth (2007) report comparable results. This would seem, on the one hand, to be a result of differing opportunity: If the prisoners are not in the prison during the day, they cannot experience or perpetrate violence – they are less exposed to those conditions of imprisonment which promote aggression. On the other hand, the composition of prisoners should also differ from the composition of prisoners in other prisons. This is confirmed if one looks at previous convictions: The percentage for people on daytime release is the lowest (44.2 %; regular prisons: 58.8 %).

Differing rates of violence are also noted with regard to the offence for which the prisoner was sentenced. The highest rate for victims of physical violence is found for people imprisoned for a sexual offence. The highest perpetrator rate is noted for violent delinquents, which also confirms the results of Ernst (2008, 2008a) und Wirth (2007); as regards victim prevalence for sexual violence there are no differences for the groups observed. Participants who have already been in prison once report experiences as a victim of violence more frequently; they are also more often perpetrators of violence. Here it is also to be assumed that this is a specific group of prisoners so that it is not ultimately a repeated sentence which is responsible for the differences but, for example, personality factors.

At the bottom of Table 8.3, the victim and perpetrator rates for German and immigrant prisoners are shown. According to these rates, immigrants are somewhat more often victims of sexual violence and also more often perpetrators of physical violence. The disadvantage of considering immigrants as a homogenous group is that the differences which exist between

Table 8.3 Violence prevalence rates for selected groups (only men's prisons, in percent, bold: significant at $p < .05$)

	Victims			Perpetrators
	physical violence	extortion	sexual violence	physical violence
Up to 30 years	**17.9**	**12.7**	1.7	**15.2**
Up to 50 years	**15.2**	**10.1**	1.5	**8.8**
Over 50 years	**12.8**	**5.7**	1.6	**3.2**
Custody	**16.6**	**14.0**	**1.8**	**12.4**
Closed prisons	**17.1**	**10.6**	**1.6**	**11.3**
Daytime release	**8.7**	**6.8**	**0.6**	**5.2**
Other	**19.4**	**13.4**	**5.6**	**10.0**
Sexual offence	**20.3**	**8.9**	1.5	**4.5**
Violent offence	**13.8**	**6.8**	0.7	**13.2**
Other offence	**16.1**	**12.0**	1.9	**9.6**
Previous conviction: no	14.9	9.9	**1.2**	**6.7**
Previous conviction: yes	16.8	11.0	**2.0**	**13.5**
German	15.7	10.1	**1.2**	**9.7**
Immigrant	15.6	11.2	**1.9**	**13.1**

the individual groups of immigrants do not become visible. For this reason, the victim and perpetrator rates for physical violence for the various groups are shown in Figure 8.1. Two groups are especially noticeable: Africans taking part in the survey show the highest victim prevalence and the lowest perpetrator prevalence. By contrast, prisoners of Russian origin report most rarely on being victims while their perpetrator prevalence is higher than average. Similarly high perpetrator rates are found for the Polish participants and for those questioned from former Yugoslavia. It is basically true that the larger a group of immigrants becomes, the more its perpetrator rates rise and its victim rates fall. This could be an indication that in prisons subcultures form along the line of ethnic backgrounds; the larger a subculture is, the more easily it can assert itself physically against others and does not have to fear attacks from other groups.

Fig. 8.1 Prevalence rates of physical violence for ethnic groups (in percent)

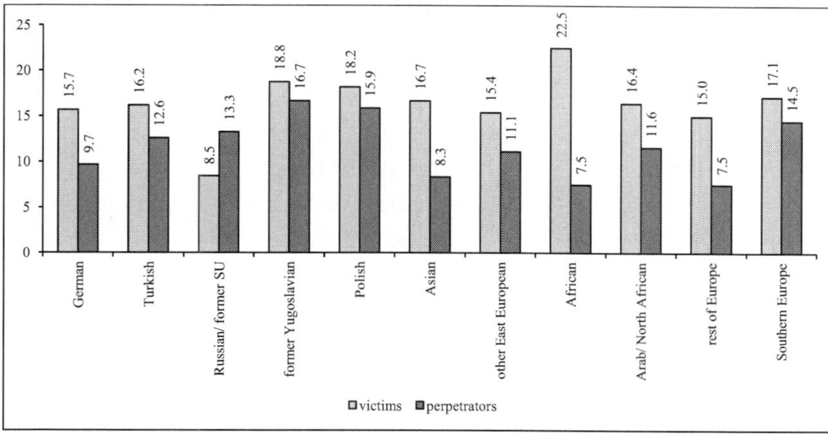

8.4.2. Analyses of the worst experience of violence

After reporting victimization, the participants of the survey were to describe their worst experience of violence with other inmates in the prison in which they currently were. They were to describe this experience in their own words; these freely written texts were then combined in categories. However, the majority of the participants (87.5 %) did not give any details of their worst experience at all. The rest reported mostly verbal attacks. Furthermore, the participants did not just report experiences as a victim but also experiences as a perpetrator or witness. For the following analyses, only those participants who gave details of an attack of physical violence were selected. This applied to 141 participants.

Those surveyed with a worst experience of physical violence indicated more frequently that the attack had been carried out by one perpetrator (47.5 %) and more rarely by two to three perpetrators (35.0 %) or by more than three perpetrators (17.5 %). As regards the place in which the attack took place, only 76 participants of the survey gave details. Their own cell or a different cell was cited most frequently (13 cases each). The corridor/the stairs or the work area were the areas which were mentioned second-most frequently (11 cases each).

A total of 74 participants informed someone of their experience, 51 kept the experience to themselves; 16 gave no details here. The inmates confided most frequently in department/prison staff (47 cases), followed by department managers (34 cases) und family/friends (28 cases). They also quite often spoke to other prisoners (25 cases) and doctors/medical staff (24 cases). A total of 32 of those surveyed stated that they had submitted an account of their experience in writing. These were mostly addressed to a department manager, a lawyer or the prison governor.

There were basically three reasons for not telling anyone about the experience: 26 of those surveyed stated that they did not want to be seen as a traitor: 23 were of the opinion that one does not do that in prison and 21 were afraid of further attacks. Furthermore, 12 prisoners stated that they had been threatened not to give anything away. All the same, nine victims of violence were of the opinion that they would not have been believed anyway.

All prisoners, i.e. not just those with a worst experience, were asked whether they avoided certain places in prison if possible in order to escape danger. This was confirmed by more than every fourth inmate (29.1 %). However, this percentage refers to only 2,410 of those questioned, i.e. almost half gave no details here.

With reference to those prisoners who stated that they avoid certain places and who made at least one valid reply to the answer options presented in the questionnaire (N= 676), it was found that other cells are avoided most often (50.4 %). Almost half of the participants who avoid places keep away from the prison yard in their free time (42.9 %). Other places which are often avoided are the washroom (33.7 %), sports rooms/ sports ground (28.1 %), the group living area/department (22.5 %) and leisure rooms (20.6 %).

8.4.3 Factors influencing aggression

Various factors which are considered to influence violent behavior were also recorded in the questionnaire. Table 8.4 shows some of the selected factors and the results of a multivariate explanatory model which contains these factors (binary logistic regression). The data of 3,525 participants are included in this model; the explained variance (Nagelkerkes R^2) is 33.5 %.[4]

Parental violence was recorded via the frequency of the experience of light violence (e.g. handled me rough/shoved me, gave me a clip around the ear) and severe violence (e.g. punched/kicked/bit me, thrashed me/beat me up) (cf. Straus 1979). Three groups of participants are distinguished: People without experiences of light or severe violence, people with rare experiences of light violence (at the most "sometimes") and people with frequent experiences of light or severe violence. Of the group of prisoners, 46.7 % stated that they had frequently experienced light or even severe violence in their childhood. Comparative data for the rest of the population are unfortunately not available here. However, in a survey of ninth-grade students carried out all over Germany in 2007/2008, only 17.4 % of the students stated that they had frequently experienced light or severe parental violence (Baier et al. 2013). Prisoners therefore seem to constitute a group of the population with especially negative experiences as far as their upbringing is concerned. For the prisoners in this survey, the experience of parental violence proves to be a significant factor which influences their own violent behavior; both groups with experiences of violence show a rate of violence which is approximately 1.5 times as high as the rate of violence for prisoners without experiences of violence.

A significant influence also arises from the three factors drug consumption, affinity for violence and victimization. That 16.8 % of those surveyed had experienced physical attacks in the last four weeks, has already been reported. 16.5 % report drug use, 22.7 % a high affinity for violence. In order to measure the affinity for violence, six items were used (e.g. "You sometimes have to hit someone who wants to run you down", "If someone picks a fight, then he deserves to be beaten"; cf. Mills et al. 2002). The statements could be agreed or disagreed with using comments from "1 – does not apply at all" to "4 – applies fully"; average values over 2.5 therefore indicate a high affinity for violence. With reference to drug consumption, it was asked whether cannabis had been smoked, drugs had been injected or whether other drugs apart from cannabis had been taken during the last four weeks.

4 Table 8.4 shows the correlations between the explanatory factors and aggression by means of the Exp(B)- coefficients. Values over 1 indicate that a factor increases the risk of aggression, values under 1 that a factor reduces this risk.

Table 8.4 Factors influencing aggression

	in %	Exp (B), binary logistic regression
Parental violence in childhood: never	29.6	*Reference*
Parental violence in childhood: seldom light	23.6	1.508 *
Parental violence in childhood: frequent light/severe	46.7	1.435 *
Drug use	16.5	4.926 ***
Affinity for violence	2.7	2.558 ***
Victim of physical violence	16.8	2.795 ***
Positive relationship between prisoners and staff	52.6	0.791 *
Positive relationship among prisoners	58.3	1.054
Adequate leisure activities	38.8	1.027
Negative prison climate	31.2	1.158

* $p < .05$, ** $p < .01$, *** $p < .001$

The participants of the survey were also to assess various dimensions of the prison in which they were (cf. Liebling 2004). Based on this, the following four scales can be constructed as below:

- Positive relationship between prisoners and staff: Those surveyed were to reply to a total of six comments ("1 - does not apply at all" to "4 – applies fully") such as "I feel that staff treat me with respect" or "The relationships between staff and prisoners are good". Somewhat more than half those surveyed considered this relationship to be good.[5]
- Positive relationship among prisoners: Three items such as "The prisoners look after one another here" or "It is relatively peaceful among the prisoners" were used; 58.3 % of the prisoners considered the relationship to be more or less good.
- Adequate leisure activities: Three comments such as "One has sufficient opportunities to do sports in this prison" or "One has sufficient opportunities to be creative in this prison" were to be assessed. Only somewhat more than a third of those surveyed agreed with these comments (38.8 %).
- Negative prison climate: The participants were asked to comment on three statements such as "There are a lot of threats / violent confronta-

5 Values over 2.5 are classified as agreement in the case of the four prison-related scales.

tions here" and "One is treated unjustly and unfairly here". A total of 31.2 % of the prisoners agreed with these statements.

As important as these assessments undoubtedly are in evaluating the quality of prisons, they are mostly irrelevant in terms of violent behavior. It is, for example, not the case that people who are more satisfied with the leisure facilities available resort less often to violence. There is, however, one exception: Prisoners who assess the staff-prisoner relationship as positive are significantly more rarely perpetrators of violence. Such inmates possibly feel more accepted and appreciated as a person when staff treat them in a positive way. This causes less frustration which finds expression in aggressive behavior towards other prisoners.

8.5 Discussion

The survey proves first that physical violence is not unusual in prisons: Every sixth adult male inmate reports attacks of violence, some of which are severe (e.g. beaten by hand/fist or kicked), every 50th sexual attacks. The quotas in women's prisons are somewhat lower, in juvenile prisons clearly higher. That there are attacks in such a context is not surprising; whether, however, quotas are high or low cannot be finally judged here as comparative data from earlier surveys or from other contexts (e.g. adolescents in schools) would be helpful. It should be pointed out that the quota is not equally high in all prisons: There is at least one prison in which the victim rate is 5.2 %, in another prison it is 34.8 %.[6] This proves that there are ways of reducing violence in prisons further.

Second, indications of which factors can be considered to this end can be taken from the analyses of the factors of influence. In particular, the result that a positive relationship between prisoners and staff helps reduce violence, should be of relevance for practical work in the prison system. Each prison could easily determine the current state of these relations itself using a short questionnaire. The prisoners could also be asked for their ideas on improving this relationship. As far as the other prison-related factors are concerned, the analyses show no significant correlations with physical aggression. However, it may prove worthwhile in future to exam-

6 Only prisons in which more than 20 inmates gave details of physical aggression were included in this comparison (N = 34).

ine the effect of other factors starting with the size of the prison through its facilities (state of the building, leisure rooms, video cameras) to other social-climatic conditions.

The finding that drug consumption is connected with higher rates of violence also points to an important area of prevention. Detecting and preventing drug use (and dealing) should be an issue for those who organize the penal system. That experiences of parental violence and an attitude which condones violence also encourage violence in prisons confirms findings for other populations. The results permit the conclusion that in initial talks more attention should be paid to the upbringing of prisoners and appropriate therapeutic help should be offered; furthermore, people who are more likely to use violence should be better identified and shown methods to improve their conflict-solving or self-control competences.

Third, the study showed interesting differences with regard to the various groups of prisoners. In this differentiated form, the findings on the ethnic groups are the first of their kind to date. Although there are initially hardly any differences between Germans and immigrants, a breakdown of the immigrant group shows differing results, e.g. that African prisoners are especially often victims of violence while Polish inmates or inmates from the former SU or Yugoslavia have an especially high perpetrator rate. The bigger an ethnic group is in prison, the more able it is to assert itself violently. Prisons must be sensitive to this formation of subcultures.

That older participants and participants from day release prison have lower victim and perpetrator prevalence rates is not surprising. What is interesting is that those prisoners surveyed who are serving a sentence for a sexual crime are more often the target of attacks from others. This apparently confirms that these prisoners are at the bottom of the prison hierarchy and are therefore more often targeted; on the other hand, these people become perpetrators very much more rarely than, for example, prisoners who have been sentenced for a crime of violence.

The various findings give an insight into the extent of violence in prisons. The method of standardized surveying does though reveal some disadvantages which should be mentioned here. It should be noted that in spite of a response rate of over 50 %, it cannot be ruled out that there is a disproportionally high number of victims and perpetrators of violence under the non-participants who did not want to tell anybody about their experiences. That at least four out of ten victims of violence stated that they had not confided in anybody and this mostly because they did not want to be seen as a traitor or similar shows that the willingness to give information, even when anonymity is guaranteed, is lower than for other groups of the population. Moreover, the ability of the prisoners to read and concentrate may well be lower than for other groups of the population, which limits the extent to which they can be questioned. Therefore more studies which look at the methodological possibilities and limitations of standardized surveys in prisons are required in future. On the other hand, doubts about this approach are not appropriate: The correlations alone which have been found between the factors of influence and the perpetration of violence and which were partly to be expected in this form, indicate that the results of the survey are valid.

References

Baier, D., Pfeiffer, C., Simonson, J., Rabold, S. (2009). Jugendliche in Deutschland als Opfer und Täter von Gewalt. KFN: Forschungsbericht Nr. 107.

Baier, D., Pfeiffer, C., Thoben, D.F. (2013). Elterliche Erziehung in Deutschland: Entwicklungstrends und Auswirkungen auf Einstellungen und Verhaltensweisen. Manuskript in Vorbereitung.

Bieneck, S. (2010). Viktimisierung im Justizvollzug: Forschungsstand und Notwendigkeiten. Praxis der Rechtpsychologie, 20, 279-289.

Camp, C. G., Camp, G. M. (1997). The Corrections Yearbook 1997. South Salem, NY: Criminal Justice Institute.

Ernst, S. (2008). Gewalt unter erwachsenen männlichen Inhaftierten in deutschen Justizvollzugsanstalten. Hamburg: Verlag Dr. Kovač.

Ernst, S. (2008a). Zum Ausmaß der Gewalt in deutschen Justizvollzugsanstalten. Kernbefunde einer Täter-Opfer-Befragung. Bewährungshilfe, 55, 357-372.

Heinrich, W. (2002). Gewalt im Gefängnis – eine Untersuchung der Entwicklung von Gewalt im hessischen Justizvollzug (1989-1998). Bewährungshilfe, 49, 369-383.

Hinz, S., Hartenstein, S. (2010). Jugendgewalt im Strafvollzug. Eine retrospektive Untersuchung im Sächsischen Jugendstrafvollzug. Zeitschrift für Jugendkriminalrecht und Jugendhilfe, 21, 176-182.

Ireland, J. L. (1999). Bullying behaviors among male and female prisoners: A study of adult and young offenders. Aggressive Behavior, 25, 161-178.

Krahé, B., Bieneck, S., Möller, I. (2005). Understanding gender and intimate partner violence from an international perspective. Sex Roles, 52, 807-827.

Liebling, A. (2004). Prisons and their Moral Performance. A Study of Values, Quality, and Prison Life. Oxford: University Press.

Ortmann, R. (2002). Sozialtherapie im Strafvollzug. Eine experimentelle Längsschnittstudie zu den Wirkungen von Strafvollzugsmaßnahmen auf Legal- und Sozialbewährung. Freiburg: edition iuscrim.

Power, K. G., Dyson, G. P., Wozniak, E. (1997). Bullying among Scottish young offenders: Inmates' self-reported attitudes and behavior. Journal of Community and Applied Social Psychology, 7, 209-218.

Straus, M.A. (1979). Measuring Intrafamily Conflict and Violence: The Conflict Tactics Scales. Journal of Marriage and the Family, 36, 13-29.

Wirth, W. (2007). Gewalt unter Gefangenen. Kernbefunde einer empirischen Studie im Strafvollzug des Landes Nordrhein-Westfalen. Bewährungshilfe, 54, 185-206.

Wolff, N., Blitz, C. L., Shi, J., Siegel, J., Bachman, R. (2007). Physical violence inside prisons. Rates of victimization. Criminal Justice and Behavior, 34, 588-599.

9. Homicide of Children

Theresia Höynck, Ulrike Zähringer

9.1 State of knowledge

The only official sources on the extent of homicidal crime in Germany are the Police Crime Statistics and cause of death statistics. Both have severe limitations with regard to information value and therefore do not lend themselves to systematic analysis even in respect of reported crime. Cause of death statistics are based on death certificates issued by doctors[1] stating diseases leading to death and any other causes of death. The age groups used for children are <1, 1 to <5, 5 to <10 and 10 to <15. Injury by another person with intent to harm or kill is given as 'assault'[2] regardless of how the injury is inflicted.

The Police Crime Statistics classify child and adolescent victims in even broader age groups: 0 to <6, 6 to <14 and 14 to <18. It is also impossible to connect different characteristics beyond the small amount of detail provided in the Police Crime Statistics, since they don't offer individual case information. For example, it is not possible to tell from the Police Crime Statistics if offender-victim relationships differ between age groups. Being compiled of a specific reporting date, the Police Crime Statistics also have the problem that they only include what the police stated at the end of their investigations and do not reflect whether a case is later dropped by the prosecution service or if the case is dismissed in court or the offender finally sentenced. For example, if at the end of their investigations the police suspect manslaughter, then the case will be recorded as manslaughter in the Police Crime Statistics, even if a court ultimately hands down a sentence for assault resulting in death or even lets the suspect go free. The Police Crime Statistics are not corrected after the final ruling of the court. Additionally, they also distort timing as crimes are included when detected, not when committed. In most cases this is unimpor-

1 Registry offices provide additional demographic data once a death notice is issued.
2 According to the ICD-10 categories X85-Y09.

tant as most crimes are detected quickly. Where there is a long time lag, however, it is easy to imagine that this can lead to major distortions, at least for rare crimes.[3]

The Police Crime Statistics can nonetheless be used to gain a general overview of the frequency of (reported) child homicide in Germany (see Figure 9.1). As the official data show, contradicting the picture often painted in public, the number of homicides involving children under six in Germany is, at least in terms of reported crime, on a downward trend with slight fluctuation since 1997.

Fig 9.1 Victims of intentional, completed homicide under 6 years of age in Germany, 1997-2010 (source: Police Crime Statistics; own calculation).[4]

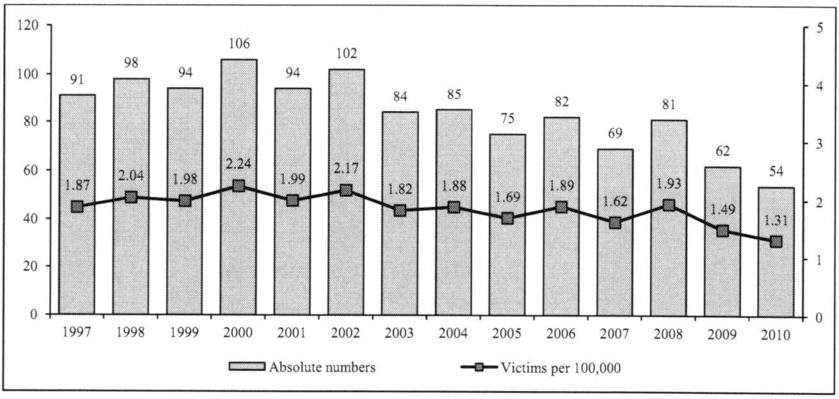

3 An example that attracted strong media interest is the Brieskow-Finkenheerd case in Germany where a woman had nine children between 1988 and 1998 and killed them all at birth. The crimes only came to light in 2005 and were not included in the Police Crime Statistics until 2006 (after the investigations were completed).

4 The following crimes are aggregated in the chart: Murder, § 211 German Criminal Code StGB; Manslaughter, §§ 212, 213 StGB; killing on demand, § 216 StGB; Infanticide, § 217 StGB (which existed until 1998, relating to the killing by the mother of an illegitimate child at birth; since the abolition of this offence, neonaticides come under the general provisions of the Criminal Code relating to crimes involving assault resulting in death, manslaughter or murder);assault resulting in death, § 227 StGB; Sexual assault and rape resulting in death, § 178 StGB; Sexual child abuse resulting in death, § 176b StGB.

Academic research on child homicide in Germany has so far been restricted to regional studies, studies relating to specific categories of crime, and studies mainly addressing selected aspects of crimes and their circumstances (Bozankaya 2010, Hömberg 2011, Hempel 2013, Schlang 2006, Schmidt et al. 1996, Schläfke et al. 2003, Trube-Becker 1982, Raic 1997, Vock 1999, Vock/Meinel 2000, Vock/Trauth 1999). Internationally, too, although there is abundant research, most of it merely sheds light on a subset of cases (e.g. Friedman et al. 2005, Resnick 1970), covers only a small number of cases (e.g. Bourget/Gagné 2002, Bourget/Gagné 2005) or relates to far older age groups, with the result that only isolated conclusions can be drawn about young child victims (e.g. Bijleveld/Smit 2006). Some reviews have been published which pointed out some general trends but also a included great number of inconsistent findings (Bourget/Grace/Whitehurst, Friedman/McCue/Resnick 2005, Friedman/Resnick, 2007 and 2009, Porter/Gavin 2010).

Concerning the victims age, the existing studies show consistent trends, apparent differences are based on age group variations, especially on whether or not the neonaticides are included. A child's risk of being killed is clearly highest during the first year of life (Mariano/Chan/Myers 2014; Paulozzi/Sells 2002; Vock/Trauth 1999; Raic 1997), then rapidly decreases and is only slightly rising from the early teens (Mariano/Chan/Myers 2014; Strang 1996). No major differences regarding the victim's sex were found in larger studies (Vogt/Block 2005), studies with smaller samples show a slightly higher rate of male victims (Vock 1999; Vanamo/Kauppi/Karkola et al. 2001).

Offenders of child homicide cases are most likely persons of the closest social environment of the children, usually parents or stepparents (Porter/Gavin 2010; Flynn/Windfuhr/Shaw 2009), although the proportion varies, probably again due to different sample compositions. When it comes to the offenders' sex, results are not that consistent, except for the neonaticide cases, which are mostly committed by the biological mothers alone (Beyer/McAuliffe Mack/Shelton 2008; Herman-Giddens/Smith/Carlson/Butts 2003; Vanamo/Kauppi/Karkola et al. 2001). A german study on intra-familial child homicide cases[5] for the years 1985-1989 showed a significantly higher rate of male offenders (Schlang 2006), just like Strang (1996) for Australian child homicide cases between 1989 and 1993 on

5 Victim's age: <18 years, without neonaticide cases.

children under 15 years of age. For the subsample of 58 lethal child maltreatment cases, Vock et al. (1999) also found a dominance of male offenders: In each about 30 % fathers and mothers were perpetrators, but in an additional group of 16 %, the biological mothers new partner had killed the child. About 25 % of the cases of this sample were committed by both parents together. In summary to this point it can be said that mothers as offenders of child homicide are overrepresented for newborns and very young children, whilst with increasing victim age, male perpetrators become more important.

In the existing studies, results concerning a higher risk for children with stepparents ("cinderella effect") are also inconsistent: Daly/Wilson (1988, 2001, 2005) as well as Harris/Hilton/Rice/Eke (2007) describe a higher risk for infanticide for children with stepparents in analyses of British and Canadian data and attribute their findings to evolutionary mechanisms. Weekes-Shakelford/Shakelford (2004) confirmed these findings for the USA regarding biological mothers and stepmothers, whereas Brookman/Nolan (2006)[6] could only show effects for stepfathers, but not for stepmothers. Stiffman/Schnitzer/Adam et al. (2002) analysed data from the Missouri Child Fatality Review Panel System[7] and could show a higher risk for children living in the same household with one or more non-relative male/s for lethal maltreatment compared to children living with both biological parents. These observations are contradictory to the ones of Schnitzer/Ewigman (2005), who also looked at data from Missouri[8] and could identify a dominance of male offenders (71 %), but not a considerably higher risk for children living with stepparents. Swedish studies[9] did also not find a connection between being a stepparent and an increased risk of child homicide.

Available information on the offender's socioeconomic backgrounds varies widely. For Germany, Raic (1997) could show a higher proportion of middle-/upper class- perpetrators for the subcategory of extended suicides. In a review from 2005, Hatters Friedman/McCue Horwitz/Resnick described a medium-low socioeconomic background for neonaticide of-

---

6 Investigation of 298 cases in England and Wales between 1995 and 2002.

7 1992-1992, age of victims < 5 years.

8 149 cases of lethal maltreatment cases committed by a parent or caregiver (1992-1999).

9 Termrin/Buchmayer/Enquis 2000 (1975-1999); Temrin/Nordlund/Sterner 2004 (1965-1999).

fenders, whereas perpetrators of homicides of elder children were found to being poor and socially isolated. Hässler/Bomke/Schäffler (2003), who analysed 56 psychiatric reports from the Psychiatric Department of the University of Rostock (Germany) for the years 1980-2000 on the other hand associate most offenders (59.6 %) to social middle class, 32.7 % to lower social class and 7.7 % to the upper class.

The majority of studies dealing with backgrounds and possible triggers for child homicide discuss psychiatric illness of the parents, which probably refers to the fact, that quite a number of authors have a psychological/ psychiatric background. For neonaticides the knowledge to these questions is inconsistent. Oberman (2003), who looked at cases from Chicago between 1870 and 1930, found that a large number of offenders suffered from psychiatric diseases. Resnick (1970) as well as Schläfke/Galleck/ Höppner/Hässler (2003) describe a rather low proportion of psychical problems for these perpetrators. For the age-group of 231 < 18 year-old victims, Schlang (2006) describes mental disorders for 52.7 % of the female and for 29.5 % of the male offenders, with personality and behaviour disorders being most frequently (34 %), followed by disorders caused by psychotropic substances, of schizophrenic or affective kind (each about 15 %).

Overall homicide of children in the age group 0-5 years is far from being fully understood. Some general lines have been detected but knowledge regarding the exact circumstances, risk factors and determinants of homicides is still quite limited. For this reason, the Child Homicide project has been conducted at the Criminological Research Institute of Lower Saxony since 2007.

9.2 The Child Homicide project[10]

The project involved an exhaustive survey of all homicides involving children under 6 years of age in Germany for the period 1997-2006 based on analysis of the relevant court files. The state bureaus of criminal investigation were first asked for a list of relevant reference numbers. These were then presented to the respective state prosecution services, who were asked to send the case files to the Criminological Research Institute of

10 The project received funding from the Fritz Thyssen Foundation.

Lower Saxony. The case files were analysed by trained coding staff using paper and pencil to compile comprehensive information for each victim on the biological and (if applicable) social parents and any other individuals accused. An approximately one-page case outline was additionally written out for each case, presenting the case history from when the case first came to police notice. These case outlines frequently proved useful during later analysis as they helped bringing each case to mind beyond the basic facts. Finally, the compiled data were entered in SPSS ready for further analysis.

As all further analysis is based on the criminal investigation files, it is important at this point to note the special characteristics and limitations that apply to the study. One problem was the fact that some files were visibly incomplete; relatively frequently, for example, psychological/psychiatric reports or records on the main court hearing were missing. In most cases the absence of individual parts of a file was not really a problem because the same information was referred to elsewhere in the file, for example in the court decision; in other cases, however, missing information could not be made up in this way and remained missing from the entered data. In any analysis of criminal investigation files, it is important to remember that the focus is on identifying the offender and criminal appraisal of their actions, and not on reconstructing the case to the last detail. Information only makes it into the file if the investigating authorities consider it important to the criminal prosecution. Also, the statements made by all parties come in the context of a given (procedural) role (e.g. as witness or accused) and may therefore be coloured by self-interest. All these aspects must be taken into account when going on to analyse information from criminal investigation files.

9.3 Findings: All Cases

A total of 627 files were analysed. These included 507 relevant cases[11] with 535 victims and 354 offenders. Most victims were killed in their first year (69.2 percent), which mainly reflects the large number of neonati-

11 The remaining files related, for example, to attempted homicides that children survived, other age groups or other crimes.

cides.[12] Even without this category, however, still no less than 30 percent of the victims were killed in their first year, 10.6 percent in their second, 6.8 percent in their third, 6.6 percent in their fourth, 3.3 percent in their fifth and 3.6 percent in their sixth year. The risk of children in the studied age group for becoming a victim of homicide is thus by far the highest in the first year, with a clear concentration in the first 24 hours after birth.

9.3.1 Necessity of classification into case groups

For adequate analysis of the great diversity of cases involved, different categories based on classifications used in the literature (Resnick 1969, d'Orbán 1979, Scott 1973) were developed. The classifications were adapted and modified several times in the course of the project. At the beginning, for example, there was a "revenge killing" category as found in the literature (Resnick 1969, d'Orbán 1979). On closer examination of our sample, however, there were no cases in this category and the category was therefore dropped. The classification ultimately chosen combines characteristics of the homicides, the delinquents and the victims.

Neonaticide

This case group comprises 199 victims (37.2 percent). Victims were almost exclusively killed by the biological mother during or immediately after birth; only in very exceptional cases assistance was provided by another person. 'Typical cases' are those in which the mother, immediately after giving birth without assistance, left the infant unprovided or killed it – mostly by suffocating – without conscious premeditation. Almost all such cases involved an unwanted pregnancy where labour commenced unexpectedly. There were very large differences as to whether and how a pregnancy was denied and/or concealed. With regard to concealing the killing, the spectrum ranges from no attempt at concealment and 'poor' hiding places for the body such as the mother's own wardrobe to elaborate elimination of traces.

---

12 Neonaticide is the killing of a child within 24 hours of birth, in the great majority of cases by the mother alone, usually after a concealed and/or denied pregnancy.

Maltreatment

The death by maltreatment case group (n=137 or 25.6 percent) combines various forms of maltreatment resulting in death: Blunt force (with/without an object), shaking, and in rare cases substance administration. The duration and intensity of maltreatment varied considerably, from one-off acts in the heat of the moment (often the case with fatal shaking of the infant) through to longer-term maltreatment only leading to the death of the infant after some time or in combination with other injuries.

Extended suicide

The extended suicide case group includes both suicides and attempted suicides. The category comprises 69 victims in total (12.9 percent). In cases of completed extended suicide there is usually very little information about the perpetrator as the criminal prosecution was closed immediately. Not infrequently, before both suicides and attempted suicides it was already known that the perpetrator had major psychological problems of a depressive nature, often in connection with a family crisis. In most cases of attempted extended suicides, the perpetrator's own suicide was not completed because of an extraneous disturbance or rescue; in other cases the offender abandoned the plan to commit suicide after killing the child. There are also variations with regard to the fatality risk of the suicide attempts. 'True' extended suicides predominated, where the offenders' usual motive was to take the child with them so that it would not be left behind alone. The remaining cases were suicide attempts where the child was more or less coincidentally present or the child disturbed a suicide attempt and was killed in that connection. In a few cases, other individuals were killed immediately before the suicide or attempted suicide, most frequently the other parent and/or other children.

Mental illness

In this group those cases were included (n=33; 6.2 percent) where severe mental illness such as postpartum depression, psychosis or an acute schizophrenic episode was the direct trigger of the killing, regardless of other case characteristics. Cases with a suicidal component on the other hand were always assigned to the extended suicide category regardless of any mental illness. The case group contains numerous variations at many different levels: The duration of the illness ranges from a few weeks to many years, some illnesses were treated, while others were not even known to people close to the perpetrator. In only very few cases, the treating physician or family had the idea that the illness could possibly be a danger to others; in most cases, the offender's direct environment had not the slightest suspicion of the actual risk potential.

Purposeful homicide

This group includes all cases (n=32; 6.0 percent) where the perpetrator purposefully carried out the homicide with clear intent to kill, by ways or means relatively certain of killing, that do not come into any of the other categories (such as extended suicide or mental illness). In some cases it was hard to distinguish cases in this group from maltreatment case group. Many of the cases were homicides committed in the context of separation problems and custody disputes, mostly with a range of motives such as not wanting to give up the child or begrudging it the partner compounded with altruistic components (such as saving the child from a presumed hard or sad future). This category also includes cases, however, where a child was killed because it was 'in the way' and the perpetrator wanted to 'get rid' of it.

Neglect

This category subsumes cases (n=20; 3.7 percent) where children died because they were not supplied with sufficient food and/or liquids or because they were denied necessary medical treatment. These are cases of pure neglect; the extremely rare cases in which neglect was accompanied by physical maltreatment of the child were classified as maltreatment.

Natural death/accident

With regard to victims in this category, investigations were initially carried out for suspected homicide, however in the course of investigations it emerged that the children died a natural[13] or accidental[14] death. This category consists of 29 victims (5.4 percent).

Unclear sudden infant death syndrome (SIDS)

With the cases in this group (n=8; 1.5 percent), there was suspicion of homicide but the cause of death could not be identified with certainty (unlike the natural death/accident category). Sudden infant death syndrome and, for example, intentional suffocating are both possible in such cases.

Other

A small number of cases (n=8; 1.5 percent) could not meaningfully be assigned to any of the other categories but did not have any salient common features and hence were grouped in an 'other' category. An example is cases where the child was a chance victim.[15]

In the last three case groups, the children did not (with certainty) die as a result of intentional homicide, but are retained as victims in the overall sample for analysis as the starting point of our study was the classification of cases at the end of police investigations. This circumstance is taken into account descriptively later on, however, when focusing on the various case groups.

9.3.2 Perpetrators

The term 'perpetrator/offender' is reserved in the project for persons who were issued with a final sentence, persons acquitted on account of exemption from criminal responsibility, and persons who killed a child in an extended suicide. Cases were included in the study when the police classifi-

13 Such as following myocarditis or undetected diabetes.

14 For example because the child fatally injured itself falling out of bed or died in a domestic fire it inadvertently started itself.

15 For example in a gas explosion or in a road accident deliberately caused by a driver travelling on the wrong side.

cation of the incident was intentional homicide.[16] Sometimes the conviction was for a less severe crime (usually because it was not possible to establish intent to kill). Such cases usually ended in a conviction for maltreatment of persons under the offender's care, assault, or homicide by negligence. The analysis included 354 persons who satisfied this definition of a perpetrator. The number of perpetrators is thus significantly smaller than the number of victims, mostly because of the large number of newborns found dead where the perpetrator could not be identified. In other cases, however, a suspicion was unable to be confirmed in a way that provided sufficient grounds for prosecution or conviction, resulting in dropping of charges or acquittal. From a victimological point of view, however, the circumstances in some such cases justify a classification as victims.[17]

Fig. 9.2 Relationship between delinquent and victim (in percent)

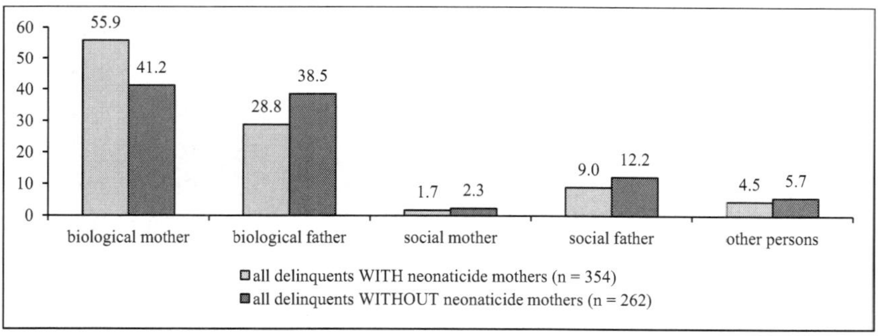

With rare exceptions, the perpetrators came from the children's immediate surroundings[18] and the great majority were the biological and/or social parents[19]; in rare cases, the perpetrators were 'other persons' such as

16 See footnote 4.

17 As in cases where it was clear that one of the parents must have committed the homicide but the court was unable to establish which one and had to acquit both as a result. There were also neonaticide cases where it was not possible to determine with certainty whether the child had been stillborn or killed by the mother.

18 One such exception was a driver travelling on the wrong side of the road who deliberately collided with an oncoming vehicle.

19 A social parent is partner to a natural parent, such as the mother's new boyfriend. To count as social 'parents' such individuals must at least contribute towards providing for the child and take responsibility in childcare.

grandparents and roommates. Looking at all perpetrators, biological mothers visibly dominate, but this effect almost disappears after deducting the large number of biological mothers who were perpetrators of neonaticides (see Figure 9.2).

9.4 Findings by case groups

In view of the large differences between the various case groups, selected findings of the study are presented separately by category in the following.

9.4.1 Neonaticide

The neonaticide case group is the group with the largest number of victims, including numerous newborns found dead for whom no perpetrator could be identified despite in some cases with very intensive investigations. As this case group included large differences despite its basic homogeneity, four subcategories were defined:

- 'Typical' neonaticide (n=96; 48.2 percent): In these cases, the biological mother killed the infant immediately at the time of birth, either actively or by not providing for it. In such cases the pregnancy was denied/concealed, birth and the homicide were unassisted.
- 'Atypical' neonaticide (n=13; 6.5 percent): These cases differ from typical neonaticides on at least one count. In some cases the victim was born in hospital and killed at home a few days later, or the mother had assistance with the birth. Despite these distinguishing features, the remaining circumstances, and particularly the denied/concealed pregnancy, justify classification in the neonaticides group.
- Unclear neonaticide (n=36; 18.1 percent): It was not possible to establish sufficient proof but classification as neonaticide was justified from a victimological standpoint.[20]
- Unknown dead newborn (n=54; 27.1 percent): In such cases, a newborn is found dead that is highly probable to be victim of a homicide but it was not possible to identify the perpetrator.

---

20 Examples include where it was not possible to prove a specific homicidal act with final certainty.

The perpetrators had an average age of 24 years at the time of the homicide; approximately 16 percent were under 18, just under 21 percent were between 18 and 20, and the largest group were women between 21 and 29. Over 50 percent of the perpetrators already had biological children at the time of the neonaticide, although only eight women lived with these children in a common household at that time. Eight women had put up one or more children for adoption before the neonaticide.[21] The case group included seven cases with two victims and three cases with three victims. As is to be expected, the victims showed no gender bias: 50 percent were female and 48 percent male.[22] None of the infants was disabled. Of the infants for which the pregnancy term could be determined, eight percent were premature.[23] This is not significantly higher than in the general population.[24]

Almost all women underwent psychological/psychiatric examination in the course of the investigations; mental health problems were found for 42 women at the time of the offense and for 29 in the past. The spectrum of findings was very broad, although acute stress reactions and fearful-avoidant personality traits were frequent. Only very rarely did the perpetrators engage in alcohol or in medical or narcotic drug abuse with rates of less than 5 percent for each. Almost all women had previously denied and/or concealed the pregnancy. In the cases analysed, it was not possible to observe the clear distinction often made in the literature between denial and concealment; instead there were a wide range of hybrid forms and blurred transitions. Pregnancy denial/concealment was always one of the key reasons for the neonaticide. In most cases the women were surprised by the birth and were unable to deal with the situation in a premeditated and appropriate manner, even in cases where they had given thought in advance to what they would do with the child once born. Other aspects, such as fear of being left by a partner or of being unable to cope with the new situation in life, as with the influence of alcohol or drugs, only acted in favour of the neonaticide in isolated cases. Interestingly, even women who

21 Three women had already put up two children for adoption and one women three children.

22 In the remaining 2 percent of cases, the gender could no longer be determined.

23 For the purposes of the project, premature births were defined as prior to the 37th week of pregnancy.

24 In 2007, for example, 7.1 percent of births in Germany were premature (European Foundation for the care of newborn infants 2010).

had chosen other courses of action in past unwanted pregnancies[25] were evidently unable to act this way again when it came to the victim infant, and were also unable to explain why they couldn't.

The dominant act of homicide, at about 23 percent, was suffocation, including both active forms such as smothering with a pillow and passive forms such as wrapping in a blanket. The second most frequent, at about 11 percent, was failure to provide for the newborn (which then died of hypothermia or lack of nutrition) or active violence (throttling/choking/strangulation). About 7 percent of infants drowned[26], and only low single digit percentages were found for stabbing, blunt force and throwing of the child out of the window. In about 37 percent of the cases the precise course of events remained unclear or could no longer be reconstructed more precisely, largely due to the discoveries of unknown dead newborns where the passage of time meant the cause of death could no longer be established with certainty.

In a sense it is possible to say that in most cases the denial of the pregnancy persisted beyond the birth, and that the women acted more in an attempt to "bring the situation to an end" without proceeding in a planned or premeditated way. This can be concluded especially in the cases where the dead body was later 'concealed' somewhere in the mothers home, even though this made a detection highly likely.

The very large majority of perpetrators in the neonaticides case group was convicted of manslaughter (§ 212 of the German Criminal Code StGB) or a less serious case of manslaughter (§ 213 StGB), with convictions being made significantly more frequently for action than for omission (see Figure 9.3).

Sentencing was dominated by unsuspended prison or juvenile prison sentences (43 resp.14 cases), followed in second play by suspended prison or juvenile prison sentences (18 resp.15 cases), meaning that in total 56 of 92 women, or some 60 percent, received an unsuspended sentence. The severity of the unsuspended sentences was mostly in the lower to middle range (2-6 years of prison), although no less than seven women were sentenced to six to ten years and another six to over ten years imprisonment.

25 Besides the eight women who put up children for adoption, it is known in respect of 20 women that they had one or more abortions behind them.

26 This included only very isolated cases of active drowning by the mother.

*Fig. 9.3 Neonaticide: Final judgement – Distinction by offenses (in percent; *Value is for action and omission).*[27]

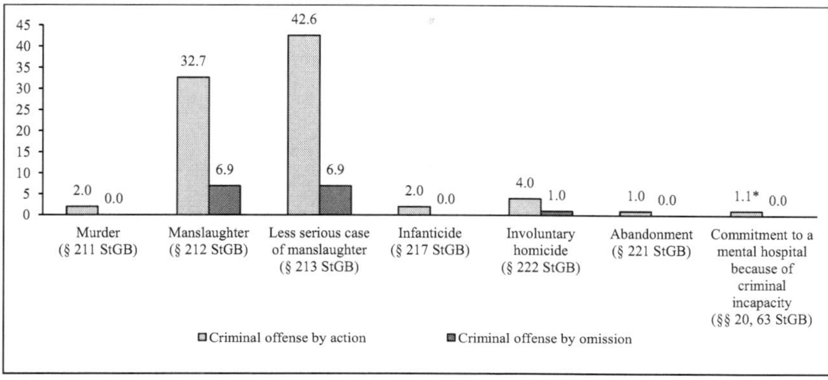

9.4.2 Maltreatment

Given the large differences within it, the death by maltreatment category was likewise subdivided, although in some cases it was hard to distinguish based on the files between, for example, cases of single and cases of multiple maltreatment. The figures can therefore only serve as guidance to the general size of the subcategories. Cases can be divided into single instances of maltreatment (n=37; 27 percent), multiple instances over a period of time (n=49; 35.8 percent), and cases where infants died following a shaking trauma (n=26; 19 percent), as the latter group of cases are particularly important from a forensic medicine point of view. There were also cases of maltreatment where it was not possible to establish with legal certainty whether, and most of all by whom, the children had been maltreated (n=17; 12.4 percent) or shaken (n=8; 5.8 percent) but where a victimological point of view justified a classification as victims.

Among the 126 perpetrators, the biological mothers and fathers were represented in roughly equal numbers, at 34.4 percent, resp. 35.2 percent. The proportion of social fathers as perpetrators was significantly higher

27 § 217 StGB existed until 1998, relating to the killing by the mother of an illegitimate child at birth. Since the abolition of this offence, neonaticides come under the general provisions of the Criminal Code relating to crimes involving assault resulting in death, manslaughter or murder.

than in any other case group, at 21.6 percent. Other perpetrators such as social mothers or friends/acquaintances of the parents were found only in very isolated cases. More than a quarter of perpetrators had themselves been victims of abuse in childhood and there were at least clear indications of this having been the case for a further 5.6 percent.[28] 78 percent of perpetrators in this case group underwent psychological/psychiatric assessment in the course of criminal prosecution, with just under 45 percent showing problems in the past and 36 percent at the time of the offense. The most frequent problems were substance abuse[29] (28 resp.10.4 percent) and personality disorders (5.6 resp. 11.2 percent). Only rarely were there additionally other or combined mental problems/disorders such as depression, adjustment disorders or Münchhausen-by-proxy syndrome.

This case group included a very wide range of acts of homicide, although the children most frequently died of blunt force/maltreatment[30] (44.5 percent) or shaking (26.3 percent). Other forms of homicide such as suffocating, poisoning, strangulation or drowning were found only in isolated cases. In 13.1 percent of cases the act of homicide remained unclear, with multiple possibilities coming into question and no way of being certain which was ultimately fatal. The homicide was usually triggered in this case group by a situation where the perpetrator was unable to cope with the child, usually coupled with a general inability to cope with their situation as a whole or with specific circumstances. In many cases the child screamed or cried before the incident for an unspecific reason and – in some cases despite serious and persistent attempts on the part of the perpetrator – was unable to be calmed. In such cases, the perpetrators lost their nerve and committed the homicide mostly in the heat of the moment so that the child would at last be 'quiet'. With just under a fifth of perpetrators, the homicide was presumably abetted by disinhibition and/or heightened aggression due to alcohol or drugs. In some cases, the fatal maltreatment was the expression of what the perpetrator considered to be 'teaching

---

28 Here especially, absence of information should not be equated with absence of maltreatment in the perpetrator's childhood. Instead, it is probable that such experience of maltreatment is not asked about in the course of investigations if the investigators consider it to have had no influence on the offense in question.

29 This subsumes abuse of various substances including alcohol, medical drugs and narcotic drugs, and long-term excessive as well as abusive consumption.

30 For example striking with the hand, slamming of the head against an object or against a wall, or scalding. This case group showed particularly large variation in the nature and intensity of the homicidal acts involved.

a lesson', often with pent-up aggression released against the child for some trivial reason. In some such cases the maltreatment was extreme.

With regard to the age of victims, the high risk period clearly is the first six months of a child's life, a period in which 54 percent of victims in this case group were killed. The risk level then decreases significantly and is subject to only minor variation thereafter. The maltreatment group is the only case group to show marked differences in victim gender, with 65 percent (n=89) of victims being male and 35 percent (n=48) female. The reasons for this heightened risk are unclear so far and deserver further attention.

Maltreatment perpetrators were most frequently (50 percent) convicted for assault resulting in death (§ 227 StGB), with significantly more accusations of criminal offense by action than by omission. In 17.5 percent of cases the final conviction was for manslaughter (§ 212 StGB) and in 2.4 percent for a less serious case of manslaughter (§ 213 StGB). 11.2 percent were convicted for murder (§ 211 StGB), 10.3 percent for involuntary homicide (§ 222 StGB), 6.4 percent for maltreatment of charges (§ 225 StGB) and 2.4 percent for (serious) assault (§ 224 StGB) (see Figure 9.4).

Fig. 9.4 Maltreatment: Final judgment – Distinction after offenses (in percent)

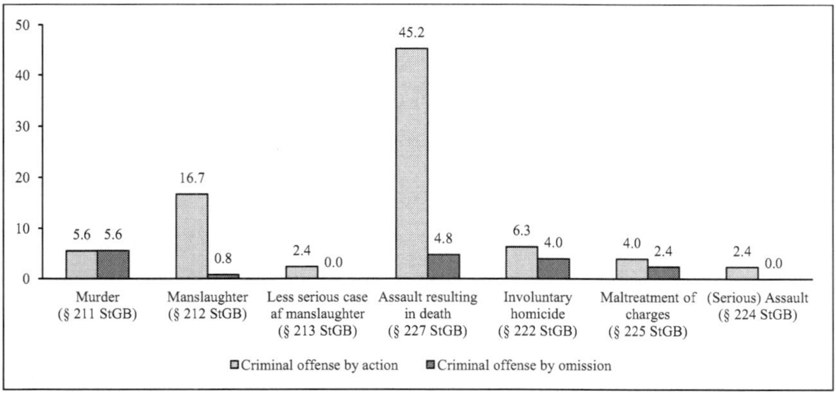

In most cases, the sentences handed down were unsuspended prison or juvenile prison sentences (68 resp.10.4 percent), more rarely suspended prison or juvenile sentences (13.6 resp. 4 percent). Only in isolated cases was a prison sentence combined with accommodation in a psychiatric hospital or drug rehabilitation centre, or a fine was imposed. With regard to sentencing severity, unsuspended prison sentences tended to be at the severe end of the range (more than six years); in 19.1 percent of cases the prison sentence was between four and six years and in 20.2 percent of cases between two and four years. The unsuspended juvenile prison sentences most frequently – in six out of 13 cases – consisted of a severe sentence of between six and ten years[31]; juvenile prison sentences of four to six years were handed down in three cases and juvenile prison sentences of between two and four years in four cases.

9.4.3 Extended suicide

This case group includes a conspicuously large number of cases with multiple victims: 11 cases featured two child victims out of the case group, making up 31.9 percent of this small subcategory. There were more completed than attempted suicides. Of the 53 perpetrators in the case group, 22 survived and 31 completed the suicide. The offenders were almost always the children's biological parents[32], with fathers slightly outnumbering mothers by 27 to 23. With regard to the age of perpetrators, the 30-40year old offenders dominated with just over 56 percent, just under 27 percent (n=4) were over 40 and only a little over 15 percent (n=8) were between 21 and 29 years old. Only one perpetrator was between 18 and 21 years old and none was under 18. Offenders in this case group were thus significantly older on average than in the other categories. Almost all surviving perpetrators underwent psychological/psychiatric assessment and for 19 it is known that they had mental problems or even mental disorders at the time of the attempt; eight had a depressive disorder and four a personality disorder. Other disorders[33] were present only in individual cases. Only very few perpetrators in this case group had a substance abuse problem and only three had problems of this kind in a period of up to one year before the suicide or suicide attempt.

The triggering event in the extended suicide case group was usually a separation conflict, where perpetrators were unable to cope with an impending or actual separation and wanted to take their own life for that reason. There were various reasons why the offenders wanted to take their

31 The maximum juvenile sentence in Germany is ten years.

32 A social father was the perpetrator in two cases and a friend of the family in one.

33 Such as bipolar disorder, PTSD or an adjustment disorder.

children with them when they died: In some cases there were altruistic motives from the perspective of the perpetrator, who for example did not want the child to be 'left behind' or grow up without an intact family; in other cases they did not want the other partner to 'get' the child; and in isolated cases there were other motives such as heavy burden of debt, and by committing the extended suicide the perpetrator wanted to save his or her family 'suffering and shame'. In some cases the suicide or suicide attempt came in connection with a mental disorder suffered by the perpetrator. There was no notable bias with regard to the age or gender of victims.

The act of homicide in this case group was often stabbing or other forms of knife injury, with over 25 percent of victims dying in this way. Just under 19 percent of victims were throttled/choked/strangled and just under 12 percent suffocated. The same number of victims was pushed over a bridge or run over by a train. Other acts of homicide tended to be found in only isolated cases (see Figure 9.5).

Fig. 9.5 Extended suicide: Acts of homicide (in percent).

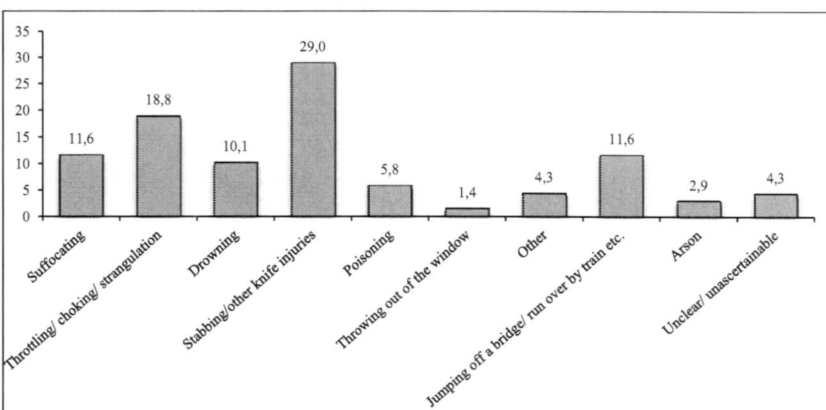

Of the 22 surviving perpetrators, ten were subsequently convicted of murder (§ 211 StGB), eight of manslaughter (§ 212 StGB) and five of less severe cases of manslaughter (§ 213 StGB). By far the majority of offenders received an unsuspended prison sentence; only one was given a suspended sentence and three were found to be exempt from criminal responsibility and were ordered to be placed in a psychiatric hospital. No juvenile sentences were handed down. With regard to sentencing severity, long and very long prison sentences dominated in this case group with nearly two-thirds of perpetrators receiving prison sentences of over six years and six perpetrators being convicted to prison sentences of over ten years; five were given life sentences.

9.4.4 Mental illness

This category includes 33 victims from the sample who were killed by 24 perpetrators, all of whom were the biological parents. A conspicuous feature is that a significantly larger number of offenders were mothers than fathers (18 mothers, six fathers). There were no very young or very old perpetrators, with all offenders falling in the 21-40year-old age group. All perpetrators in this case group underwent psychological/psychiatric assessment as part of the criminal prosecution. For 23 of the 24 perpetrators it is known that they were mentally ill before the homicide, with by far the most frequent mental illnesses being psychoses, schizophrenia or other delusional disorders; only four offenders had previously been depressive, and the remainder had personality disorders or personality accentuations. In line with the definition of the case group, at the time of the homicide all perpetrators had a mental illness under the influence of which the homicide was committed. As with past mental illnesses, the dominant form of illness consisted of psychotic disorders, in one case postpartum. Five offenders had various forms of depression and there were isolated cases of adjustment disorder, stress reaction, PTSD and other disorders. With six perpetrators, the mental illness was comorbid with a personality disorder, either from the fearful-avoidant or dramatic-emotional cluster.

In accordance with the definition of the case group, the homicide was triggered in all cases by the perpetrator's mental illness, with varying 'reasons' for the homicides in line with the various underlying disorders. Psychotic/schizophrenic/delusional offenders, for example, were paranoid or believed killing the child was the only way to protect it from other persons or from the devil. Depressive perpetrators mostly killed the child out of perceived inability to cope. Only rarely was the mental illness accompanied by other aspects that abetted the homicide such as an acute separation situation or alcohol/drug influence.

The most frequent act of homicide in the mental illness case group was suffocating (n=12). Six children were stabbed to death, four drowned, and four others died as a result of blunt force. Only in isolated cases were the children strangled, poisoned or thrown out of a window. A strong bias is visible with regard to victim age in this case group, with 14 of the 33 victims killed at an age of between one day and three months; the victim ages are distributed fairly evenly over the remaining age groups.

A majority (n=20) of perpetrators were found to be exempt from criminal responsibility under § 20 of the German Criminal Code StGB (criminal incapacity) and ordered to be placed in a psychiatric hospital subject to satisfaction of the requirements set out in § 63StGB.[34] The remaining perpetrators were merely found to have diminished criminal incapacity according to § 21 StGB; two of these were convicted of murder (§ 211 StGB), two of a less severe case of manslaughter (§ 213 StGB), and two of assault resulting in death (§ 227 StGB). No perpetrators in this case group were given a juvenile prison sentence; two were handed down a suspended prison sentence and two an unsuspended prison sentence; for one offender, in addition to the prison sentence, placement in a psychiatric hospital was ordered according to § 63 of the Criminal Code. Seventeen perpetrators were solely ordered to be placed in a psychiatric hospital; for three of these the sentence was suspended.

9.4.5 Purposeful homicide

This case group comprises 32 victims, including four cases in which two victims were killed and one case with three victims. With regard to age, this small subcategory again shows a heightened risk for children aged one day to three months, an age group in which eight victims were killed. Of the 27 perpetrators, 16 were the biological fathers and eight were the biological mothers of the children. The remaining offenders were a social father and friends of the mother. Most perpetrators were in the 21-29year-old age group (n=10) or the 30-40year-old age group (n=11); only in rare cases were they young adults, i.e. between 18 and 20 (n=2), or over 40 years old (n=4). 23 of the offenders underwent psychological/psychiatric assessment in the course of prosecution[35] and it emerged that 13 already

34 Only in one case did the court refuse to make such an order; this was determined on commencement of the main hearings as the court did not consider the perpetrator a danger to the public as § 63 StGB requires.

35 In the remaining cases, either the offenders refused to be assessed and asserted their right to remain silent in the main hearings, or, as in one case, the perpetrator was not convicted by a German criminal court, hence no information on any as-

have had mental problems or disorders prior to the homicide, in the form of drug abuse/addiction (n=5), personality disorders (n=4) and combined mental disorders (n=2). In two cases it was at least surmised that the perpetrator have had a mental illness prior to the homicide.[36] For 13 perpetrators, a mental illness/problem was diagnosed at the time of the homicide, mostly a personality disorder (n=7) or personality accentuation (n=4); one offender had a disorder belonging to the adjustment disorder/stress reaction/PTSD category and one had a psychotic disorder.

The dominant act of homicide in this case group was once again suffocation (n=13). Six victims were stabbed to death and six drowned; only in individual cases were children strangled or died as a result of blunt force, following a fall from a window or a deliberately started fire. In two cases the act of homicide remained unclear – in one the body was not found and in the second the cause of death could no longer be ascertained due to the passage of time. There were essentially two particularly frequent triggers for the homicide: One was an acute or ongoing separation conflict. In other cases the children were perceived as a 'burden' or an 'intrusion' – either as a factor encroaching on the perpetrators' general ability to get on with their lives or as a specific encumbrance, for example where the offender was required to pay maintenance. In individual cases, the child died in the context of relationship homicide against the mother, either for concealment reasons or because the child happened to come in while the mother was being murdered and the perpetrator more or less spontaneously decided to kill the child as well.

A majority (n=23) of purposeful homicide perpetrators were convicted of murder (§ 211 StGB), including two who were convicted of twofold and one of threefold murder. The conviction in the remaining cases (n=11) was for manslaughter (§ 212 StGB), with one conviction for a less severe case of manslaughter (§ 213 StGB). Except for one case, all perpetrators received unsuspended prison or juvenile prison sentences and in one case the sentence was combined with placement in a psychiatric hospital ac-

---

sessment was contained in the file. In one further case, the court refrained from obtaining an expert assessment on account of in-court expertise.

36 In these cases, a person qualified to give such an opinion (e.g. a treating physician or court-appointed expert giving an appraisal based on the file) expressed a suspicion that there was a mental disorder or that various indications (such as a suicide attempt) suggested this to be the case. The information was insufficient, however, for a precise classification to be made.

cording to § 63 StGB. The final sentences were predominately life sentences (n=16), followed by long prison sentences of more than ten years (n=7); in one case the sentence was between six and ten years. There were no shorter sentences. The picture was similar for the two perpetrators convicted as juveniles – here again, the sentences handed down were in the maximum possible range of six to ten years. There were no acquittals in this case group.

9.4.6 Neglect

This smallest case group in terms of numbers comprises 20 victims, and in contrast to most of the other case groups there is not a significant increase in risk in the first six months of a child's life. There is a slightly higher risk for children in the first 15 months, although given the small number of cases this can only be regarded as a tendency. Of the 24 perpetrators, 16 were biological mothers and seven biological fathers; in one case a grandfather was (jointly) convicted. In seven cases, both biological parents were convicted; in all other cases, the victims suffered fatal neglect at the hands of their single mothers. Most offenders were between 21 and 29 years old, four were 18-20, five 30-40 and two over 40 years old. The neglect case group did not include any perpetrators under the age of 18.

Psychological/psychiatric assessments were compiled on 20 perpetrators in the course of prosecution and nine of these were known to have had mental problems or disorders before the homicide. These included drug problems, depressions and other mental disorders. Likewise nine offenders were found to have a mental problem or disorder at the time of the homicide; personality disorders were identified in five cases and a personality accentuation was identified in one. Individual cases featured depression, drug use and a combination of disorders.

With regard to the triggering event or situation, the homicides can be divided into two groups. Firstly, there are cases were the children were more or less left entirely to their own devices. In the cases committed by single mothers, this neglect often began following separation, in some cases linked with the desire to make a new start. In such cases, the women initially failed to provide sufficiently for the children and later did not take care of them at all, spent their time increasingly and in some cases at the end entirely with friends or with a new partner and left the children behind on their own, where they then died of lack of food or liquid. Other cases consisted of medical neglect, where for example parents misjudged a known illness suffered by the child and/or omitted to obtain proper medical treatment. These cases involved chronic illnesses, where the parents failed to administer necessary medication either at all or in sufficient dosage, as well as illnesses that the parents themselves treated with alternative medicine against a doctor's advice. These children died due to failure to provide medical treatment or due to incorrect medical treatment. Where children died as a result of an acute illness, such as an infection, the parents failed to obtain treatment for the children because of a general inability to cope.[37] In some cases, parents consciously refused to obtain help because they were afraid the children would be taken away from them by social services if the circumstances came out. In isolated cases, the reason for the neglect could not be reconstructed after the event.

Seven perpetrators were convicted of assault resulting in death (§ 227 StGB), six of manslaughter (§ 212 StGB) and four of murder (one in two cases), with the murder assumed to be attended with cruelty and in two cases combined with base motives. In all cases, the parents were accused of omission. Five offenders were convicted of involuntary homicide (§ 222 StGB) and two of maltreatment of charges (§ 225 StGB), where the parents were accused of actively preventing others from looking after the children's welfare. Sentences were predominantly unsuspended, with 16 prison sentences and three juvenile prison sentences. Only in five cases were suspended sentences handed down and all of these related to prison sentences, i.e. the perpetrators were older than 21. In one case a juvenile prison sentence was combined with an order for accommodation in a drug rehabilitation centre. The severity of sentencing tended to be high with regard to the prison sentences and in the medium range of four to six years with regard to the juvenile sentences.

9.5 Summary

Homicide against children of this age group in Germany is a very heterogeneous phenomenon, with marked differences in motivation and means in some cases extending to within individual case groups. The risk is high-

---

37 For example because of a difficult family situation, numerous children and/or numerous animals.

est for children during the first six months and most of all during the first day, with a total of 38.5 percent of children in our sample killed within the first 24 hours after birth. The only case group that shows significant differences in victim gender is the maltreatment group, with 65 percent of victims being male and 35 percent female. The reasons for this heightened risk remain unclear.

The largest case group accordingly consists of neonaticides with over a third of the total, followed by death by maltreatment with upwards of a quarter. With very few exceptions, the perpetrators came from the victims' most immediate social environment and were most usually the biological or social parents. Due to the large number of neonaticides, the biological mothers predominate as offenders (56.5 percent), without this category, their proportion is just slightly higher than 40 percent, followed by the biological fathers with over 38 percent and the social fathers with some 12 percent. In most cases, the perpetrators acted alone, only in 32 cases two or more persons were called to account for the homicide of the child. The offenders were mostly between 21 and 29 years old (42.7 percent), followed by 30-40 year old persons (30.8 percent).

References

Beyer, K./McAuliffe Mack, S./Shelton, J. L. (2008). Investigative analysis of neonaticide - An exploratory study. Criminal Justice And Behavior 35, 522-535.

Bijleveld, C./Smit, P. (2006). Homicide in the Netherlands - On the Structuring of Homicide Typologies. Homicide Studies, 10, 195-219.

Bourget, D./Gagné, P. (2002). Maternal filicide in Quebec. Journal of the American Academy of Psychiatry and the Law 30, 345-351.

Bourget, D. /Gagné, P. (2005). Paternal Filicide in Quebec. Journal of the American Academy of Psychiatry and the Law 33, 354-360.

Bozankaya, Nadine (2010). Neonatizid - Die rechtliche Reaktion auf die Tötung Neugeborener - Eine strafrechtliche Untersuchung anhand von Aktenanalysen. Berlin 2010.

Brookman, F./Nolan, J. (2006). The dark figure of infanticide in England and Wales - Complexities of diagnosis. Journal of interpersonal violence 7, 869-889.

Daly, M./Wilson, M. (1988). Evolutionary Social Psychology and Family Homicide. Science 242, 519-524.

Daly, M./Wilson, M. (2001). An assessment of some proposed exceptions to the phenomenon of nepotistic discrimination against stepchildren. Annales Zoologici Fennici 38, 287-296.

Daly, M./Wilson, M. (2005). The “Cinderella effect” - Elevated mistreatment of stepchildren in comparison to those living with genetic parents. Hamilton 2005.

Daly, M./Wilson, M. (2005). The "Cinderella Effect" is no fairy tale. Trends in Cognitive Science 9, 507-508.

D'Orbán, P. T. (1979). Women who Kill their Children. The British Journal of Psychiatry, 134, 560-571.

European Foundation for the care of newborn infants. EU Benchmarking report 2009/2010: Country Highlights. (2010).

Flynn, S./Windfuhr, K./Shaw, J. (2009): Filicide - A Literature Review. Manchester 2009.

Friedman, S.H. [et al.] (2005). Filicide-Suicide - Common Factors in Parents Who Kill Their Children and Themselves. The Journal of the American Academy of Psychiatry and the Law, 33, 496-504.

Häßler, F./Bomke, A.-K./Schläfke, D. (2003). Begutachtungspraxis von Tötungsdelikten - Eine retrospektive Gutachtenanalyse. In: Häßler, F. [et al.] (Eds.). Forensische Kinder-, Jugend- und Erwachsenenpsychiatrie - Aspekte forensischer Begutachtung. Stuttgart, 61-80.

Harris, G. T./Hilton, N. Z./Rice, M. E./Eke, A. W. (2007): Children killed by genetic parents versus stepparents. Evolution and Human Behavior 28, 85-95.

Hatters Friedman, S./McCue Horwitz, S./Resnick, P. J. (2005). Child murder by mothers - a critical analysis of the current state of knowledge and a research agenda. The American journal of psychiatry 162, 1578-1587.

Hempel, Dorothea (2013). Tötungsdelikte an Neugeborenen 1997 bis 2007 in vier deutschen Regionen - Eine Analyse der Risikofaktoren der Kindsmütter. PhD Thesis, University of Jena, 2013.

Herman-Giddens, M. E./Smith, J. B./Mittal, M. [et al.] (2003). Newborns Killed or Left to Die by a Parent - A Population-Based Study. Journal of the American Medical Association 289, 1425-1429.

Hömberg, Sophia Marie (2011). Die Tötung von Kindern durch die eigenen Eltern (Infantizid) - Retrospektive Untersuchung für den Zeitraum 1994-2007. PhD Thesis, University Bonn 2011.

Mariano, T.Y./Chan, H. h./Myers, W. C. (2014). Toward a more holistic understanding of filicide: A multidisciplinary analysis of 32 years of U.S. arrest data. Forensic Science International.

Oberman, M. (2003). Understanding infanticide in context - mothers who kill, 1870-1930 and today. The Journal of Criminal Law and Criminology 92, 707-738.

Paulozzi, L./Sells, M.. (2002). Variation in Homicide Risk during Infancy - United States, 1989-1998. MMWR Weekly.

Porter, T./Gavin, H.. (2010). Infanticide and Neonaticide - A Review of 40 Years of Research Literature on Incidence and Causes. Trauma Violence and Abuse 11, 99-112.

Raic, D. (1997). Die Tötung von Kindern durch die eigenen Eltern - Soziobiographische, motivationale und strafrechtliche Aspekte. Bonn.

Resnick, P.J. (1969). Child Murder by Parents - A Psychiatric Review of Filicide. The American Journal of Psychiatry, 126, 325-334.

Resnick, P.J. (1970). Murder of a Newborn - A Psychiatric Review of Neonaticide. The American Journal of Psychiatry, 126, 1414-1420.

Schläfke, D. et al. (2003). Zur Problematik von Neonatiziden und Filiziden. In: Häßler, F. et al. (Eds.), Forensische Kinder-, Jugend- und Erwachsenenpsychiatrie - Aspekte der forensischen Begutachtung (pp. 81-102). Stuttgart.

Schlang, C. (2006). Tödlich verlaufende elterliche Gewalt. Bonn.

Schmidt, P., Graß, H., Madea, B. (1996). Child Homicide in Cologne (1985-94). Forensic Science International, 79, 131-144.

Schnitzer, P./Ewigman, B. G. (2005). Child deaths resulting from inflicted injuries - household risk factors and perpetrator characteristics. Pediatrics 116, 687-693.

Scott, P. D. (1973). Parents Who Kill Their Children. Medicine, Science and the Law - Official Journal of the British Academy of Forensic, 13, 120-126.

Stiffman, M. N./Schnitzer, P.G./Adam, P. [et al.] (2002). Household Composition and Risk of Fatal Child Maltreatment. Pediatrics 109, 615-621.

Strang, H. (1996). Children as Victims of Homicide. Trends and issus in crime and criminal justice.

Temrin, H./Buchmayer, S./Enquist, M. (2000). Stepparents and infanticide - new data contradict evolutionary predictions. Proceedings of the Royal Society 267, 943-945.

Temrin, H./Nordlund, J./Sterner, H. (2004). Are stepchildren overrepresented as victims of lethal parental violence in Sweden? Proceedings of the Royal Society 271, 124-126.

Trube-Becker, E. (1982). Gewalt gegen das Kind Vernachlässigung, Misshandlung, sexueller Missbrauch und Tötung von Kindern. Heidelberg.

Weekes-Shackelford, V. A., & Shackelford, T. K. (2004). Methods of filicide: Stepparents and genetic parents kill differently. Violence and Victims 19, 75-81.

Vanamo, T./Kauppi, A./Karkola, K. [et al.] (2001). Intra-familial child homicide in Finland 1970-1994 - Incidence, causes of death and demographic characteristic. Forensic Science International 117, 199-204.

Vock, R. (1999). Tödliche Kindesmisshandlung (durch physische Gewalteinwirkung) in der DDR im Zeitraum 1.1.1985 bis 2.10.1990. Archiv für Kriminologie, 204, 75-87.

Vock, R., Meinel, U. (2000). Tödliche Kindesvernachlässigung in der DDR im Zeitraum 1.1.1985 bis 2.10.1990 - Ergebnisse einer multizentrischen Studie. Archiv für Kriminologie, 205, 44-52.

Vock, R., Trauth, W. (1999). Tödliche Kindesmisshandlung (durch physische Gewalteinwirkung) in der Bundesrepublik Deutschland im Zeitraum 1.1.1985 bis 2.10.1990 - Ergebnisse einer multizentrischen Studie. Archiv für Kriminologie, 204, 73-85.

Vogt, K./Block, C. R. (2005). Children's risk of homicide - Victimization from birth to age 14, 1965 to 1995. Research Bulletin 4, 1-16.

10. Sexual Abuse by Catholic Clerics: Patterns of Interpretation and Coping Strategies of Victims in the Light of a Religious Socialisation

Sandra Fernau

10.1 Introduction

The phenomenon of child sexual abuse in Catholic institutions and communities gained wider public attention after many cases in the United States and Ireland became known beginning in the mid-1990s. In Germany, sexual violence in state and Church institutions came into the focus of public and academic interest following widespread media disclosure of abuse in early 2010. After former pupils of a reform school and a Catholic college first reported their experiences of victimisation, a wave of revelations of sexual abuse in state and Church contexts followed.

Both nationally and internationally, there is a lack of empirical and epidemiological research regarding sexual abuse in institutional and particularly in Church contexts. While much empirical research has been done in past decades on sexual violence in the family environment (see for an overview e.g. Finkelhor 1994, Lampe 2002), there are few international studies on sexual abuse in religious settings. The majority of studies published in this area are from the United States. Most of them are conducted with quantitative methods and from a psychological perspective. In describing child sexual abuse by Catholic clerics, researchers focus on the following aspects: On the one hand they analyse characteristics of the abusers themselves, such as their personality and possible sexual disorders, especially paedophilia and ephebophilia (cf. Laaser 1991, Haywood et al.1996a, Haywood et al. 1996b, Plante/Manuel/Bryant 1996, Doyle 2003, Plante 2003). On the other hand in the past years a few studies have been conducted that describe characteristics of victims, and the spiritual and psychological impact of the abuse, mostly with a focus on trauma symptoms (cf. Bottoms et al. 2003; Benkert & Doyle 2009; Doyle 2009; Carr et al. 2010). Two important large-scale research projects have been conducted by the John Jay College of Criminal Justice commissioned by the United States Conference of Catholic Bishops (USCCB). The first is the 'Nature and Scope' report on the prevalence of sexual abuse by Catholic priests and deacons in the years 1950 to 2002. The second is the 'Causes and Context' report, which analyses occurrences of sexual abuse within the Church from a socio-historical and psychological perspective and proposes approaches for explaining the possible causes and backgrounds to the sexual offences (cf. John Jay College Research Team 2004, Terry et al. 2011).

So far there are hardly any victimological studies available that investigate subjective experience of sexual abuse in Church contexts using a qualitative research paradigm. Yet a qualitative approach to the research field, through the reconstruction of subjective patterns of interpretation and strategies for coping with the events, enables to obtain a deeper understanding of the distinguishing features and consequences of experiences of victimisation in religious settings. The present qualitative interview study with victims of sexual abuse by Catholic clerics[1] addresses this desideratum by investigating the individual dynamics and impacts of those experiences of victimisation. The central research aim is to reconstruct biographical patterns of interpretation and attempts to cope with the experiences of abuse and to analyse them in the light of a religious socialisation.

Starting from the assumption that a Catholic upbringing and socialisation shaped the interviewee's personality development and hence their interpretation of victimisation, the approach taken in this paper can be outlined as follows: The definition of the term 'sexual abuse' is followed by a number of reflections from a sociology of religion delineating the influence and role of belief and religious practice at individual level. Next, the research design underlying the study is described together with the structure of the sample of the interview study. Besides the analyses of the subjective reception, this article focusses on the retrospective interpretation and coping with the experiences of abuse, drawing upon basic assumptions relating to religion theory and victimology. In particular, selected interview sequences are used to provide an overview of typical reaction patterns by victims.

---

1 The term 'Catholic cleric' is used here to refer to Catholic priests (including chaplains and vicars), deacons and male members of religious orders working under the auspices of the German Bishops' Conference.

10.2 Definition of sexual abuse

Criteria that are important in most definitions of sexual abuse and are applied in this study include the following:

Types of sexual acts

A first definition criterion relates to the types of sexual acts covered and includes a distinction between acts with and without physical contact (cf. Finkelhor et al. 1990, Dhaliwal et al. 1996, Wetzels 1997). These two categories, however, still cover a very wide range of forms of contact. For this reason, only those acts are classed here under the term 'sexual abuse' that, in a strict sense, directly relate to human sexuality and involve interaction with at least the individual's own or the other's body. This can include sexual activities performed with, in the presence of, or to a child or adolescent.

Relationship between offender and victim

Most normatively oriented definitions are based on the concept of 'informed consent' first formulated by Schechter and Roberge (1976). This states that children prior to a certain stage of development are not able to fully understand sexual acts and so are unable to appreciate the implications of those acts. They are therefore not capable to enter into consenting sexual relations (cf. Schechter/Roberge 1976, Finkelhor 1979, Wetzels 1997). The structure of the relationship between offender and victim is thus characterised by a competence and power difference in psychological development and social standing – a superiority of the offender. This is almost always accompanied by family interpersonal dependencies or in cases of sexual abuse within the Church by institutional interpersonal dependencies. The developmental and social asymmetry between offender and victim usually makes it unnecessary for the offender to use physical violence, which therefore has to be dropped as a definition criterion for sexual abuse. The same applies to any indication of consent by the victim, as in many cases children are unable to understand, clearly appreciate the significance, or name the acts in question (cf. Finkelhor 1979, Dhaliwal et al. 1996, Wetzels 1997).

Age limits and age differences

The power and authority imbalance between offender and victim is generally operationalized by using age limits and age differences, which vary in the relevant studies (cf. Finkelhor et al. 1990, Dhaliwal et al. 1996, Wetzels 1997). In the present study an age limit of 18 is applied as the upper limit for the potential victim group. With regard to age difference, the research field of sexual abuse within the Church invariably shows a significant age gap between offender (cleric) and victim (pupil, child in care, or altar server) that is far greater than the generally utilised age difference of at least five years.

Offender's intentions and aims in assessment of his conduct

A further common criterion likewise applied in this study is that the offender is motivated in his conduct by the desire for sexual gratification and pleasure. The adult acts here with disregard to the child's or adolescent's will or ability to understand and makes use of his developmental and social superiority to exploit the victim for the gratification of his personal sexual desire for arousal, intimacy or power. Sexual abuse is thus characterised by the sexual instrumentalisation of a child or adolescent by an adult (Baker/Duncan 1985, Wetzels 1997, p. 71f).

Sexual abuse is accordingly defined here as a sexual act, by a person significantly older than the victim, performed with or in the presence of, or to a child or adolescent, in which the offender exploits his superiority in terms of psychological development and social standing to gratify his personal sexual desires.[2]

10.3 Functions of religion and the influence of a religious socialisation on victims of sexual abuse

To investigate the dynamics and impacts of experiences of sexual abuse within the religious context, it is first necessary to present some fundamental reflections delineating the functions of religion and the influence

2 The terms 'sexual assault', 'sexual acts' or 'sexual violence' are used synonymously with the term 'sexual abuse' as just defined.

of belief and religious practice on the individual. Following classical and contemporary perspectives, religion is defined here as a system of symbols, beliefs, values and practices relating to supernatural beings, things and powers of an otherworldly sphere which are considered as holy. The core element of religion is the question of ultimate meaning – that which goes beyond the natural. As an institutional phenomenon, it prescribes spiritual doctrines and rules of conduct, ethical guidelines and moral ideals (cf. Parsons 1964 , Stark/Glock 1968, Knoblauch 1999, Hamilton 2001, Furseth/Repstad 2006).

Important sociological and sociopsychological functions of religion mentioned in numerous publications can be summarised as follows: First of all, religion has an integrative, community-building function. The formation of a religious collective by way of shared beliefs, values and ritualistic, symbolistic community experiences generates a powerful sense of mutual belonging among believers that goes as far as an 'oceanic feeling' ("ozeanisches Gefühl") (Freud 1930, p. 197). This results not only in greater willingness to take an active part in Church life, but likewise in the translation of the individual's egoistic wishes and fears into group objectives (cf. Knoblauch 1999, Hamilton 2001, Furseth/Repstad 2006, Liebsch 2010).

Furthermore, religious concepts serve to legitimize and justify the prevailing system of values and norms by endowing it with sacred significance. Doubts rose about the value consensus – for example in response to crises or threats to society – can thus be allayed by projecting the fulfilment of expectations into a transcendental sphere (cf. Parsons 1964, Knoblauch 1999, Hamilton 2001, Furseth/Repstad 2006).

At individual level, religion wields early and lasting influence on personality formation through internalisation of its system of beliefs, values and symbols in the course of a religious upbringing and socialisation. Alongside messages conveyed in language, religion also affects and deeply influences personality development at a pre-verbal, sensory-symbolic level. Religion thus plays an important part in the constitution of personal identity and its preservation in the face of change (cf. Parsons 1964, Lorenzer 1981, Knoblauch 1999, Furseth/Repstad 2006, Liebsch 2010).

As they result in an individual's experience of the world being interpreted in a way that imparts order and purpose, religious constructs also provide an orientation, interpretation and coping aid for all situations in life. Besides, the interpretation and assignment of purpose to events and personal experience helps to de-dramatize conflicts and defuse dramatic or emotionally troubling situations. The resulting encouraging or comforting thoughts lead to reduced stress, discomfort and anxiety. At the same time, especially when it comes to shocking experiences, threats or crises, unfulfilled expectations are projected into a transcendental sphere. The promise of salvation and justice in the afterlife thus compensates feelings of undeserved suffering. An interpretation that gives purpose and meaning to the individual's own actions and to life in general additionally enhances self-esteem and invokes positive feelings such as hope and joy. In this way, religious convictions serve within the individual's intrapsychic emotion and behaviour regulation processes as satisfaction of needs and coping strategies (cf. Parsons 1964, Knoblauch 1999, Grom 2007, Furseth/Repstad 2006, Liebsch 2010).

10.4 Method and sample

The qualitative interview study presented here is part of an ongoing research project at the Criminological Research Institute of Lower Saxony. Between 15 and 20 adult victims (male and female) of sexual abuse by Catholic clerics in Germany will be interviewed using a semi-structured, guideline-based approach. Study participants were recruited in two ways: Firstly, victims were able to make contact themselves by using an email address set up for the purpose. Three interviewees used this channel to say they were willing to take part. Secondly, the prevention commissioners in each diocese were asked to forward a letter from the research institute to potential interviewees known to them.[3] A further 21 victims responded to this appeal, ten of whom were selected for interview on the basis of a questionnaire they completed in advance. Interviewees were selected by a contrasting sampling method with a view to obtaining a heterogenic sample in terms of gender, age and the context of abuse so as to cover the broadest available spectrum of experience, patterns of interpretation and coping strategies.

The research instrument used is a biographical, semi-structured interview guide based with regard to his structure and organisation on the se-

3 As part of a nationwide compensation process after numerous cases of abuse in Catholic institutions and parishes became public, sexual abuse prevention commissioners were appointed in all 27 German dioceses for victims of Catholic clergy to contact.

mi-structured, guideline-based interview approach according to Helfferich (2009). This uses open questions in a flexible handling order so that interviewees, despite certain prescribed thematic focuses, can narrate within those focuses in monologue form and develop their subjective relevance systems. Starting with two diachronic guiding questions on the interviewees' childhood and youth and on their subsequent biography, the interview guide is organised in five thematic areas, each of which is introduced with open questions: 1. Family upbringing and socialisation, 2. Religious upbringing and socialisation, and contemporaneous experiences of sexual abuse, 3. Partnerships entered into by the victims, 4. Interpretation of and coping with sexual abuse, 5. Significance of religiousness and faith to the interviewees and their attitudes towards the Catholic Church.

The interviews are analysed using a combination of qualitative methods. An initial analysis providing a descriptive overview is primarily based on categorizing methods according to Grounded Theory (cf. Strauss 1987, Strauss/Corbin 1990). A second step, involving the reconstruction of biographical case studies from selected interviews to gain an extended and deeper understanding of phenomena, makes use of hermeneutic methods especially the depth-hermeneutic approach (cf. Lorenzer 1986, Bereswill/Morgenroth/Redman 2010, Salling Olesen/Weber 2012).

Of the 15 to 20 interviews planned with adult victims of sexual abuse by Catholic clerics, 13 have been conducted so far: Three with women and ten with men. These 13 interviews underlie the findings presented here and are characterised as follows: The age of interviewees ranged from 37 to 71, with an average age of 59, meaning that their experiences of victimisation lie several decades in the past. The sexual assaults took place in various contexts, with interviewees experiencing abuse in closed institutions such as children's homes and boarding schools, as altar servers and in private contexts. All acts of abuse that they reported, which differed considerably in their details, involved physical contact; in cases where the abuse was initially without touching, physical contact followed over time. Sexual activities performed with, in the presence of, and to the victims were described. The sexual assaults began when the interviewees were at ages between four and 14. On average, the abuse relationship developed from the age of ten after the entry into altar service and in most cases went on for several years (between one and nine years). There is generally a large age difference between offender and victim, which is probably characteristic for the research field of sexual abuse within the Church. In the present sample, the age difference is several decades, and the accused clerics are mostly over the age of 50.

10.5 Characteristics of patterns of interpretation and coping attempts of sexual abuse

The disclosure of traumatic experiences in the course of an interview can be generally understood as a retrospective reorganisation of reality. Within the interview context, victims create a discursive framework for the abuse that was not yet available at the time it took place (Mosser 2009). This applies to a special extent to the interviewees in the current sample: In almost all cases, they first spoke about their experiences of abuse many years later. More than half of the interviewed victims kept silent about the sexual assaults for decades. Only with the broad public disclosure of cases of abuse in state and Church institutions in 2010 did they reveal their own experiences, although in most cases only to very few selected individuals. Some of them haven't told their closer social and family milieu about the abuse to this day.

Closely bound up with these problems of disclosure are specific dynamics of sexual abuse that play an important part in the study participants' accounts and have a lasting influence on their retrospective experience, interpretation and coping with the experiences of abuse. These are predominantly expressed in several ways:

- Fear of stigmatisation and negative reactions by the family and social milieu, and frequently a related fear concerning the anticipated loss of affiliation with the Church community.
- Feelings of shame and guilt leading to self-blaming by victims.
- Trivialisation of the sexual abuse resulting in rejection resp. denial of the individual's own victim status.
- Legitimation of the incidents of abuse by adopting the offender's interpretation.
- 'Sacralisation' of the sexual assault in a religious revaluation of what happened.

In many victims' accounts it is also possible to make out an orientation towards Catholic beliefs that manifests itself in the use of religious vocabulary and recourse to internalised religious patterns of interpretation. With integration into local parish structures, taking part in rituals of the faith also plays an important part for some interviewees. Accordingly, a number of interviewees regularly attend Church on Sunday, hold unpaid offices in the parish, and also prayers (such as grace before meals, intercessions, devotions, prayers of repentance) are an integral part of their everyday life. All married victims wed in and had their children baptised into the Catholic Church, and likewise the large majority of their children are or have been altar servants.

In the following, the patterns of interpretation and coping attempts listed above are explored in more detail with special consideration of their specific manifestations in the research field of sexual abuse within the Church.

10.5.1 Fear of stigmatisation and of loss of affiliation with the Church community

The subjective experience, both at that time and now, of a large proportion of the interviewed victims is characterised by fears concerning potential consequences of disclosing their experiences. There is a deep-seated fear of rejection, blame and stigmatisation by the family and social milieu and of an associated loss of affiliation with the family and the Church community. The following two interview sequences from two victims illustrate particularly well the anticipation of negative reactions by the family and social milieu to disclosure of their experiences of abuse:[4]

> "Maybe I thought, if I say that now, then I'll somehow be pitched out of the relationship that after all I still have with my parents, then I'll be marked, then I'll be marked as a black sheep. Then you'll perhaps be, um, that is, I'll then be marked in a negative way. And then there's something terrible that happened to me, something my parents might regard as totally repugnant, and maybe they won't be able to forgive you at all or, um, there's something irreparable, something utterly negative that has happened, and maybe I also didn't want to lose what affection was left and what love was left."

Whereas these words of a 71-year-old man represent a retrospective interpretation of his subjective situation at the time of the abuse and the years

4 The quoted interview passages correspond as closely as possible to the victims' manner of expression in the original, with minor adjustments for the sake of readability prior to translation into English. Omissions resp. truncations are marked with (…).

that followed, the quotation that follows, from a now 37-year-old female victim, relate to her situation as she currently perceives it:

> "Well, I wouldn't venture anywhere any more, wherever I went they'd be saying, «Look, here she comes, the abuse victim» and the like. Well, that would be very unpleasant for me. And most of all what I'm really thinking about is my children. (…) Well, that's something I'd never expect my children to put up with. (…) That anybody out there would be pointing a finger at my children or at us, no, really. (…) They can say as often as they want that we can't help it really, but I believe people would point at you anyway. You, you're then just stuck with a kind of stigma."

Aside from concealing the abuse for fear of stigmatisation and of being blamed, both accounts show a fear that disclosure of the experiences could mean loss of affiliation. In the first passage in particular, there is evident fear of the anticipated loss of important positive elements of the relationship with the family. This fear is amplified by virtue of the fact that, as priest and hence head of the congregation, the offender held a position of power and authority in the local community that also projected into the interview's family structure. As a moral authority and guardian of virtue, his influence on this family closely integrated into the life of the community appears so great that the interviewee feared his parents would be unable to "forgive" him if the sexual assaults came into the open, that is, that he himself would be apportioned blame for the abuse.

Fear of losing important ties are also characteristic of a number of other victims, who to this day share very active participation in mostly village parish life. They refer most of all to the possibility of being ostracised from the local Church community. In general, the experiences of victimisation are not discussed or addressed in the local religious community. And while some victims reported the experienced sexual violence to the prevention commissioner for their diocese, most of those expressed the desire not to be named, i.e. to maintain their anonymity.

For such victims, any coping with the experiences of abuse in the course of disclosure and actively seeking help in the Church milieu is made difficult due to their religious socialisation and the resulting strong emotional ties and loyalty to the local religious community. A socialisation largely based on collective values makes the potential loss of ties to the Church community as a result of disclosure a predominantly menacing prospect. In this light, disclosure becomes bound up with a decision affecting the future of the victim's own social integration. It presents itself in the eyes of victims as a guilt-bound breaking off of important ties, as betrayal of the offender and the community. Hence instead of the fear of family break-up described by Summit (1983) and Crisma et al. (2004) as being characteristic of intrafamilial sexual abuse, fear of a break-up of community affiliations, of losing community support is here at the forefront of victims' subjective experience. In both cases it is the fear of a collapse of elemental relationship structures that give support and security.

10.5.2 Self-blaming by victims

As intimated in the two passages above, the described fears of stigmatisation and loss of affiliation frequently go hand in hand with strong feelings of shame and guilt in victims. These mostly lead to self-accusation, with the victims giving themselves the responsibility for the abuse.

In this sense, the female interviewee quoted above describes her thoughts and feelings towards abuse victims in general and hence also in relation to her own self:

> "You're always somehow a bit, inwardly, um, it strikes you then, well, maybe the victim went around provocatively dressed or maybe wanted it itself or only has himself to blame. I also simply can't get out of that role."

Comparing this passage with what she said further above, it also becomes clear that she directs against herself the negative reactions she fears from others. Her fear of stigmatisation is thus partly a product of and at the same time is compounded by her own self-reproaches.

The following account by a male victim aged 65 at the time of the interview likewise shows a link between fear of negative reactions from his social milieu and his own feelings of shame and guilt. In this case, however, the resulting self-blaming is given a different connotation by being embedded in a religious interpretation:

> "And, and always having to live with this mark of Cain, then they will all go and tell each other about it in the village, they'll talk, after all a village is a small place. And, always living with that, there was something going on between you and the pastor or whatever. (…) That never goes away."

In saying that he carries a "mark of Cain" visible to everyone where he lives, he not only gives expression to a guilt-bound fear of stigmatisation, but simultaneously attaches to that fear a religious, God-willed significance. His choice of words is based on the story of the brothers Cain and Abel in the Old Testament of the Bible (Genesis 4:1-16), in which Cain slayed his brother Abel and by way of punishment for the fratricide has a mark set upon him by God that brands him for the rest of his life. This has two meanings: On the one hand, the mark of Cain is the identifying mark of the murderer and hence a stigma. On the other, it is a protective mark identifying Cain as one to be judged by God alone and so saving him from violent death. In Biblical terms, then, it represents the just punishment of an offender by God.

The interviewee thus carries in his own eyes, on account of the experiences of abuse, a mark of guilt and shame that betrays and brands him as a victim. Yet the mark of Cain is not a stigma attributed by people in general or in the victim's social milieu, it is a mark given by God. There is therefore no escape from the role of the branded individual: The victim speaks of "always having to live with this mark of Cain." The interviewee's self-blaming is thus guided by the assumption of having taken upon himself a sin before God. For this reason, the stigma to be carried for that sin manifests itself as just punishment from God for the sexual abuse. Accordingly, his pattern of interpretation displays a role reversal compared with the reality of the abuse situation: The interviewee, as victim, makes himself the offender.

10.5.3 Trivialisation of the sexual abuse

In general, the occurring self-blaming by victims result in most cases from their sense of not having done enough to fend off the abuse – either physically or by avoiding contact with the offender. In this way, many victims still succumb even decades after the assaults to the suggestion of free volition and complicity. This appraisal finds expression, for example, in the passage just quoted through the words "there was something going on between you and the pastor." Another interviewee repeatedly interpreted his contact with the offender as a "relationship." Such manipulation, which is considered characteristic in the context of intrafamilial abuse (cf. Baker/Duncan 1985, Dhaliwal et al. 1996, Bange 2007, Mosser 2009) and leads to a distortion of perception patterns, is likewise inherent to typical abuse situations in the Church context.

In addition to this, especially for some male victims in the sample, self-accusation serves to protect against the feelings of helplessness and powerlessness triggered by the loss of control. By blaming themselves for the abuse, the victims can maintain the illusion of having had at least some degree of control in the past situation. The notion that they could have made it better appears to be more easily reconcilable with their male self-image than admitting their total helplessness (cf. Dhaliwal et al. 1996, Bange 2007). Their subjective interpretational scheme thus qualifies the incidents of abuse in a way that does not permit self-classification as victim.

The following two sequences from an interview with a male victim aged 66 illustrate particularly well this way of interpretation and coping:

> "Um, the bad bit, um, the reason I'm sitting here in the first place, actually I completely forgot about it, very quickly, it didn't weigh on me either, like in my childhood or in those experiences."

At the very beginning of the interview, the victim makes clear in his account that the sexual assaults did not weigh on him emotionally even at the time of the abuse. Shortly afterwards he further makes clear that he did not suffer under the experiences in any way in the time that followed either:

> "Well, it's not that I now, um, want to talk about my problems, I didn't have any problem with them. (…) It didn't, um, it didn't handicap me in my development or anything like that. So that's not the case."

As these passages show, this interviewee's coping strategy with the experiences of abuse consists of rejecting the victim status. In a number of publications on the subject, trivialisation and denial of this kind are frequently cited as common coping strategies by male victims of sexual abuse (cf. Finkelhor 1979, Baker/Duncan 1985, Dhaliwal et al. 1996, Bottoms et al. 2003, Benkert/Doyle 2009 Mosser 2009).

10.5.4 Religious neutralisation strategies among clergy offenders and their adoption by victims

The strategies with which offenders succeed in making victims pliant and ensuring that the sexual acts are kept secret play a key part in the establishment of abuse relationships. Embroilment in such relationships can come about in very different ways. The spectrum ranges from gradual, subtle customisation with an atmosphere of harassment through to drastic threats and the use of physical violence, although the last can generally be refrained from due to the social and developmental power differential between offender and victim.

Within the religious context there are additional, specific offender strategies that may be termed religious manipulation of victims. This consists of making victims pliant by exploiting religious beliefs as an explanation and justification of the sexual assaults. Alongside the gradual and subtle process of establishing the abuse relationship, these strategies supplanted, for all victims, the use of physical violence and at the same time represented a threat of catastrophic consequences in a different guise.

Examples of such religious neutralisation strategies on the part of offenders include the following: First of all, several victims reported sexual acts in the context of confession. The acts took place in most cases under the pretext of punishing sinful thoughts or unvirtuous conduct, and in isolated cases as a substitute for confession (in return for not having to confess impure phantasies). Other victims tell of the priest professing to bestow a blessing upon them through the applied sexual practices. In the case of one interviewee, for whom the sexual abuse began at the age of four, the priest attested year upon year that he had to perform the acts to drive the devil out of her. By embedding the sexual assaults in acts of exorcism, he not only lent his acts a necessity, but at the same time sparked deep feelings of shame and guilt in the purportedly possessed victim. In addition to this, acts of abuse were frequently made part of religious rituals. The sexual act was thus often followed by a form of shared repentance for the committed sin, for example by praying the rosary.

All such abuse strategies are characterised by the clerics exploiting the Catholic beliefs they inculcated in the victims in order to establish the abuse relationship. This religious manipulation amplifies the feelings of helplessness and powerlessness triggered in victims, and notably also the sense of legitimacy and normality, in some cases even necessity with regard to the acts committed by the clergy offender. Even decades after the abuse, the accounts of some interviewees still show retention of the justification strategies used by the cleric. This manifests in remarks such as "maybe I deserved it after all". There is clearly self-accusation on the part of the victim here, by means of which he lends a sense of purpose to the sexual assaults. At the same time, the victim takes over the guilt from the offender, who is thus released from his responsibility for the sexual abuse. Along with a possible desire to uphold positive elements of the relationship with the offender, the religious belief patterns internalised by interviewees lead to a distorted perception of their victimhood and of the situation at the time. In this way, a legitimation of the sexual abuse committed by the cleric takes place.

How being bound up in Catholic belief patterns makes it hard fully to renounce the mode of interpretation applied by the offender is illustrated by this extract from an interview with a male victim aged 66:

> "And, um, and in some way, I was, um, I wasn't at all aware what he wanted, «Have you sinned, have you masturbated, have you committed a sin?» And, um, well perhaps even in those days I did have a certain urge to sin."

As can be seen from the interviewee's accounts, the sexual assaults took place here under the guise of investigating sinful conduct. But though the victim today recognises this pretext for what it is, he takes on the justification pattern used by the offender almost verbatim. He thus ascribes himself an "urge to sin" and continues to speak of himself as a sinner. Through this, it is his conduct that is made to appear reproachable and not that of the priest. Furthermore the abuse becomes just punishment for his childhood transgression, and thus is legitimised in the interviewee's interpretation. The fact that he regards himself as a sinner to this day shows the lasting influence of his religious socialisation, including in relation to Catholic sexual morals: Masturbation appears to be a sin for him even today.

10.5.5 Religious interpretation of and coping with the experiences of sexual abuse

A further reaction pattern shown in a number of the interviewed victims consists of a religious revaluation of what happened. In that they retrospectively give a purpose to the experiences of sexual abuse by recourse to religious beliefs, the emotional burden triggered by the abuse is reduced: Feelings of pain, anger and sadness are compensated by the purpose-giving interpretation. In this way, the religious convictions internalised in the course of a Catholic upbringing and socialisation serve within the interviewee's intrapsychic emotion and behaviour regulation processes as a strategy for coping with their traumatic experiences.

Two remarks by a victim now aged 41 provide a particularly striking illustration of this recourse to religious interpretation models for coping with sexual abuse:

> "And the difficulties that come in accepting as well as possible and, then, um, at all seeing the divine in every other person and at all seeing in all situations in life the divine and not accident but a divine teacher who wants to tell me something. And humility, um, is when, yes, when I get it in the neck, that I

> then, um, accept it from God, simply because I have the devotion to see everything as being from God."

By the embedding of the abuse in a religious world view and the acceptance of a divine determinism, the traumatic experiences are here revaluated: In the avowal of "seeing the divine in every other person and at all seeing in all situations in life the divine and not accident but a divine teacher who wants to tell me something", the experiences are transformed into a divine test that gives the interviewee an opportunity to show himself to God as being worthy. The words "because I have the devotion to see everything as being from God" mark the interviewee's special gift of seeing the abuse as part of a divine plan intended for him. Because he humbly follows God's will, his obedience is rewarded with divine care, enabling him to draw something positive from the painful experiences. In precisely the same direction, he also explains later in the interview that despite the sexual abuse he was "given a great gift" because it also "helped me become the person I am today." This purpose-giving, positive revaluation enables the interviewee to compensate for feelings of helplessness, despair and pain invoked by the sexual abuse. All symptoms and stress reactions found in the victim even a long time after the experiences of victimisation are thus given a higher purpose and serve in his personality development.

In addition, in the course of this revaluation, the sexual assaults by the priest are given a legitimation: They no longer appear as the act of a responsible human being, but instead as part of a divine plan.

Based on the conviction that everything that happens in this life is God-given, all that happened as well as the right to judge over it is laid in God's hands. For this reason, bringing criminal charges against the priest would not have come into question for the interviewee; instead, in his interpretation, God will give him his righteous judgement:

> "It isn't up to me to make judgement here, that, um, that is for the Lord to do, maybe after death. Then he [the offender – SF] will surely reap the consequences."

These remarks provide an example of how the fulfillment of expectations is projected into a transcendental sphere by drawing upon religious beliefs – the same process outlined from a sociology of religion perspective at the beginning of this paper. Compensation for the experienced suffering and pain thus takes place through belief in divine punishment for the offender after death. Feelings of anger and aggressive impulses are also alleviated at the same time.

10.6. Summary and discussion

In the interviewed victims' upbringing and socialisation, their conduct and world view were made to be closely linked with religious classification systems and models. Both in everyday family life and through strong involvement in the life of the community, Catholic beliefs and rituals gain special significance at perceptual, cognitive and interactive level: They shape the interviewees' experience, interpretation and practical everyday conduct. This early childhood influence of the Church as a socialisation institution that also projects into the family is so enduring that it can be seen in most recounted reaction patterns to sexual abuse to this day. Many interviewees thus attempt to interpret and cope with their traumatic experiences using their internalised religious patterns of interpretation. An interesting aspect is that their Catholic faith serves them as a coping strategy: To cope with the traumatic experiences they draw upon cognitive means made available by the Church – and this despite the fact that the sexual abuse took place in the institutional context of the Church and frequently under the guise of Catholic beliefs, as became evident most of all in the religious neutralisation strategies applied by the clerics. Those offender strategies, which find expression in the exploitation of religious beliefs as an explanation and justification of the sexual assaults, represent a feature specific to the phenomenon of sexual abuse within the Church.

As the interviewees' subjective reception, interpretation and coping with experiences of abuse is shaped by their religious socialisation, it is possible to identify specific reaction patterns and coping strategies in this research field. As has been seen, the frequently encountered recourse to religious interpretation schemes has an ambivalent impact on the coping with the experienced sexual assaults: On the one hand, the interviewees' Catholic faith can tend to be helpful and facilitate interpretation and coping processes. The last-cited interview sequences in particular illustrate how religious convictions can serve within intrapsychic emotion regulation processes as a coping resource for traumatic experiences. Retrospectively assigning the sexual abuse a purpose and sacred significance alleviates feelings of helplessness and powerlessness, pain and hurt. Projection of expectations into a transcendental sphere (for example the expectation of just punishment for the offender) reduces feelings of injustice and anger. For some victims, on the other hand, their Catholic faith proves more of a handicap and hinders processes of interpretation and coping. In this connection, it was evident mainly that for some victims, it was their strong emotional affiliation and loyalty to the local Church community that impeded any coping with sexual abuse in the course of disclosure and seeking help in the Church milieu. Additionally, one interview sequence showed by way of example how being bound up in Catholic belief patterns can lead to adoption of the neutralisation strategies used by the cleric and thus make it hard fully to renounce the mode of interpretation applied by the offender.

References

Baker, A. W., Duncan, S. P. (1985). Child sexual abuse: A study of prevalence in Great Britain. Child Abuse & Neglect, 9, 457-467.

Bange, D. (2007). Sexueller Missbrauch an Jungen: Die Mauer des Schweigens. Göttingen: Hogrefe.

Benkert, M., Doyle, T. P. (2009). Clericalism, Religious Duress and its Psychological Impact on Victims of Clergy Sexual Abuse. Pastoral Psychology, 58, 223–238.

Bereswill, M., Morgenroth, C., Redman, P. (2010). Alfred Lorenzer and the depth-hermeneutic method. Psychoanalysis, Culture & Society, 15, 221-250.

Bottoms, B. L.; Nielsen, M.; Murray, R., Filipas, H. (2003). Religion-related Child Physical Abuse: Characteristics and Psychological Outcomes. Journal of Aggression, Maltreatment & Trauma, 8, 87-114.

Carr, A., Dooley, B., Fitzpatrick, M., Flanagan, E., Flanagan-Howard, R., Tierney, K., White, M., Daly, M., Egan, J. (2010). Adult adjustment of survivors of institutional child abuse in Ireland. Child Abuse & Neglect, 34, 477-489.

Crisma, M., Bascelli, E., Paci, D. & Romito, P. (2004). Adolescents Who Experienced Sexual Abuse: Fears, Needs and Impediments to Disclosure. Child Abuse & Neglect, 28, 1035-1048.

Die Bibel – The Holy Bible (2009). Übersetzung nach Martin Luther – English Standard Version Stuttgart: Deutsche Bibelgesellschaft.

Dhaliwal, G. K., Gauzas, L., Antonowicz, D. H., Ross, R. R. (1996). Adult male survivors of childhood sexual abuse: Prevalence, sexual abuse characteristics and long-term effects. Clinical Psychological Review, 16, 619-639.

Doyle, T. P. (2003). Roman Catholic Clericalism, Religious Duress, and Clergy Sexual Abuse. Pastoral Psychology 51, S. 189-231.

Doyle, T. P. (2009). The Spiritual Trauma Experienced by Victims of Sexual Abuse by Catholic Clergy. In: Pastoral Psychology 58, S. 239–260.

Finkelhor, D. (1979). Sexually Victimized Children. New York: Free Press.

Finkelhor, D., Hotaling, G., Lewis, I. A., Smith, C. (1990). Sexual abuse in a national survey of adult men and women: Prevalence, characteristics, and risk factors. Child Abuse & Neglect, 14, 19-28.

Finkelhor, D. (1994). International Epidemiology of Child Sexual Abuse. Child Abuse & Neglect, 18, 409-417.

Freud, S. (1930). Das Unbehagen in der Kultur. Studienausgabe, Band IX. Frankfurt am Main: Fischer.

Furseth, I., Repstad, P. (2006). An introduction to the sociology of religion: Classical and contemporary perspectives. Aldershot: Ashgate.

Grom, B. (2007). Religionspsychologie. 3., vollst. überarbeitete Auflage. München: Kösel-Verlag.

Hamilton, M. (2001). The Sociology of Religion: Theoretical and comparative perspectives. London: Routledge.

Haywood, T. W.; Kravitz, H. M; Grossman, L. S.; Wasyliw, O. E; Hardy, D. W. (1996a). Psychological aspects of sexual functioning among cleric and noncleric alleged sex offenders. Child Abuse & Neglect, 20, 527-536.

Haywood, T. W.; Kravitz, H. M; Wasyliw, O. E; Goldberg, J; Cavanaugh Jr., J. L. (1996b). Cycle of abuse and psychopathology in cleric and noncleric molesters of children and adolescents. Child Abuse & Neglect, 20, 1233-1243.

Helfferich, C. (2009). Die Qualität qualitativer Daten: Manual für die Durchführung qualitativer Interviews. 3., überarbeitete Aufl. Wiesbaden: VS-Verlag.

John Jay College Research Team (2004). The Nature and Scope of the Problem of Sexual Abuse of Minors by Catholic Priests and Deacons in the United States, 1950-2002. Washington, DC: United States Conference of Catholic Bishops (USCCB).

Knoblauch, H. (1999). Religionssoziologie. Berlin, New York: de Gruyter.

Laaser, M. (1991). Sexual addiction and clergy. Pastoral Psychology, 39, 213-235.

Lampe, A. (2002). The Prevalence of Childhood Sexual Abuse, Physical Abuse and Emotional Neglect in Europe. Psychosomatic Medicine and Psychotherapy, 48, 370-80.

Liebsch, K. (2010). „Symbolic interaction forms" versus "clichés". On the function and impact of religious symbolizations in the evangelical milieu. Psychoanalysis, Culture & Society, 15, 251-266.

Lorenzer, A. (1981). Das Konzil der Buchhalter: Die Zerstörung der Sinnlichkeit. Eine Religionskritik. Frankfurt am Main: Europäische Verlagsanstalt.

Lorenzer, A. (1986). Tiefenhermeneutische Kulturanalyse. In: König, H.-D., Lorenzer, A. et al. (Hrsg.), Kultur-Analysen: Psychoanalytische Studien zur Kultur. Frankfurt am Main: Fischer, S. 11-98.

Mosser, P. (2009). Wege aus dem Dunkelfeld: Aufdeckung und Hilfesuche bei sexuellem Missbrauch an Jungen. Wiesbaden: VS-Verlag.

Plante, T., Manuel, G. & Bryant, C. (1996). Personality and cognitive functioning among hospitalized sexual offending Roman Catholic priests. Pastoral Psychology, 45, S. 129-139.

Plante, T. (2003). Priests Behaving Badly: What Do We Know About Priest Sex Offenders? Sexual Addiction & Compulsivity, 9, 93–97.

Parsons, T. (1964). The Social System. 2. Aufl. New York: Free Press.

Salling Olesen, H., Weber, K. (2012). Socialization, Language, and Scenic Understanding: Alfred Lorenzer's Contribution to a Psycho-societal Methodology [73 paragraphs]. Forum Qualitative Sozialforschung / Forum: Qualitative Social Research, 13. URL: http://www.qualitative-research.net/index.php/fqs/article/view/1906/3442.

Schechter, M. D., Roberge, L. (1976). Sexual Exploitation. In: Helfer, R. E., Kempe, C. H. (Eds.), Child Abuse and Neglect: The Family and the Community. Cambridge: Ballinger, pp. 127-142.

Stark, R., Glock, C.Y. (1968). American Piety: The Nature of Religious Commitment. Berkeley: University of California Press.

Strauss, A. L. (1987). Qualitative Analysis for Social Scientists. Cambridge: Cambridge University Press.

Strauss, A. L., Corbin, J. (1990). Basics of Qualitative Research: Grounded Theory Procedures and Techniques. Thousand Oaks: Sage Publications.

Summit, R. C. (1983). The Child Sexual Abuse Accommodation Syndrome. Child Abuse & Neglect, 7, 177-193.

Terry, K. J.; Smith, M. L.; Schuth, K., Kelly; J. R. & Vollman, B. (2011). The Causes and Context of Sexual Abuse of Minors by Catholic priests in the United States, 1950-2010. Washington, DC: United States Conference of Catholic Bishops (USCCB).

Wetzels, P. (1997). Gewalterfahrungen in der Kindheit: Sexueller Mißbrauch, körperliche Mißhandlung und deren langfristige Konsequenzen. Baden-Baden: Nomos Verlagsgesellschaft.

Part IV:
Consequences of Victimisation

11. Victimisation, Fear of Crime and Life Satisfaction

Michael Hanslmaier, Stefanie Kemme, Dirk Baier

11.1 Introduction

Becoming a victim of crime has not only immediate consequences such as loss of property, physical harm and psychological distress, but is also likely to have longer-lasting consequences. Victimisation experience may also result in an elevated level of fear of crime, alter the person's defensive behaviour and lower life satisfaction.

Studies show that victimisation is related to an elevated level of fear of crime (cf. Bilsky/Wetzels 1997, Brunton-Smith/Sturgis 2011, Skogan 1987). This relationship merits further investigation, as there are other studies that find no relationship or only a weak relationship between victimisation and fear of crime (Naplava 2008, Tseloni/Zarafonitou 2008, Wittebrood 2002). The weak relationship found in empirical works may be caused by memory decay, avoiding behaviour, a rationalisation of the victimisation experience (Tseloni/Zarafonitou 2008, p. 388) – or simply by the fact that the studies relate different indicators of victimisation to different facets of fear of crime (Wittebrood 2002). This last argument is in line with findings that show that the type of crime seems to be important regarding the impact on fear of crime measures (Quann/Hung 2002, Skogan 1987, p. 151, Tseloni/Zarafonitou 2008). The connection between victimisation and fear of crime also appears to be stronger when specific victimisation experience is related to specific fear of crime (Naplava 2008, Rountree 1998, Skogan 1987). In addition, victimisation experience also seems to impact different facets of fear to differing degrees (cf. Lüdemann 2006, Gerber et al. 2010).

This aspect underscores the fact that the meaning and especially the measurement of fear of crime is not uniform. In a number of studies, fear of crime is measured with the so-called standard indicator (Hale 1996).[1]

1 The standard indicators of fear commonly use one item, targeting on fear at night in an area close to where the respondent live, for example Hale (1996, p. 85): "How

This measure has not been without criticism (cf. Bilsky and Wetzels 1997, Ferraro 1995, p. 22). It is necessary to distinguish between different meanings of fear. In general, fear comprises cognitive, affective and behavioural facets. Furthermore, fear of crime may also refer to concern about crime as a serious problem for a community or society (Skogan 1993). Disentangling the relationship between victimisation and fear of crime, therefore, requires elaborate measures of fear of crime.

However, looking at the consequences of victimisation someone should not stop at assessing victims' level of fear. Taking a broader perspective makes it possible to examine what becoming a victim means for everyday life. One way to do this is to analyse people's life satisfaction.[2] Studies have shown that becoming a victim lowers satisfaction with life in a significant way (Cohen 2008, Michalos/Zumbo 2000, Powdthavee 2005). However, crime and crime-related issues are a relatively unexplored field within life satisfaction research (Powdthavee 2005, p. 532). Dealing with life satisfaction also allows to assess the importance of victimisation for peoples' life in general and to compare it with other domains of life (e.g. work, close social relations, and income).

This paper aims to assess the impact of victimisation on fear of crime and satisfaction with life. The data base consists of a three wave nationwide representative study on crime and crime-related issues conducted in Germany in the years 2004, 2006 and 2010.

11.2 Theoretical background

11.2.1 Victimisation and fear of crime

Over the last four decades there has been much empirical research and scientific debate on fear of crime (Brunton-Smith/Sturgis 2011, p. 332,

---

safe do you feel being out alone in your neighbourhood after dark" or "is there any place around here where you feel unsafe walking at night?".

2 Throughout this paper, life satisfaction and satisfaction with life are treated as synonyms. The psychological term 'subjective well-being' is used to denote "an individual's evaluation of the extent to which he or she experiences positive and negative affect, happiness, or satisfaction with life" (Frey 2008, p. 3). The citation of empirical studies follows their terminology.

Gabriel/Greve 2003, p. 600). This section briefly reviews the findings on the relationship between victimisation experience and fear of crime.

Although there are many empirical works on fear of crime, there is no consensus on the definition of fear of crime. Throughout the empirical works, fear of crime is defined and measured in a variety of different ways. This not only makes it hard to assess the level of fear in a given population, but also leads to different findings regarding the relationship between victimisation and fear (Ferraro 1995: 21-22). One finds a surprisingly large number of works that use the 'standard indicator' to capture fear of crime, a fact that results from the availability of the indicator in large-scale social surveys.[3] Such indicators, however, focus only on specific crime situations and do not distinguish between fear and perceived risk of crime (Ferraro 1995, p. 22).

There are also authors who treat fear of crime as a multidimensional concept. Skogan (1993, p. 131) separates four different understandings of fear of crime that can be found in empirical research: concern about crime, risk of victimisation, threat of crime, and fear as behaviour. These dimensions of fear of crime have parallel concepts from other authors who distinguish cognitive, affective and behavioural components of fear (Ferraro 1995, Gabriel/Greve 2003). The present paper acknowledges the need to differentiate the facets of fear of crime and conceptualises four different measures (Franklin et al. 2008, Gabriel/Greve 2003, Gerber et al. 2010):

- Concern about crime "focuses on people's assessments of the extent to which crime is a serious problem for their community or society" (Skogan 1993, p. 132).
- The cognitive component refers to the subjective assessment of the likelihood of becoming a victim (victimisation risk).
- The affective component refers to the emotions/worries of being victimised.
- The behavioural dimension captures physical reactions and aims at avoidance behaviour.

Whereas concern about crime refers to a macro level, the other three facets are clearly related to the personal level.

---

3 For example the National Crime Survey (NCS), the General Social Survey (GSS), the European Social Survey (ESS) and the International Crime Victim Survey contain fear indicators of this kind (Ferraro 1995, p. 22, Moore 2006, p. 116, Quann/Hung 2002, p. 312).

Based on data from more than 5,000 respondents from Seattle, Rountree and Land (1996) analyse the relationship between burglary victimisation and two different indicators of fear of crime in a multilevel setting. They find a positive effect in relation to experience with household burglary both for burglary-specific fear and for the evaluation of the respondent's neighbourhood as unsafe.

Quann and Hung (2002) also find a significant impact of personal and household victimisation experience on fear of crime. The estimates are based on cross-national data from the International Crime Victim Survey (ICVS) with 39,517 respondents (year 2000 survey wave). The authors note, however, that the impact on fear of crime is not as strong as expected. Household victimisation seems to have a stronger impact on fear than personal victimisation.

A study from Athens (Tseloni/Zarafonitou 2008) with 431 respondents shows that walking alone in one's municipality and subjective victimisation risk are significantly affected by previous direct victimisation, but there is no impact on feeling safe at home at night.

Wittebrood (2002) finds in a cross-national multilevel analysis with data from the ICVS 2000 (35,000 respondents) that having been a victim of burglary or violence decreases the likelihood of feeling safe when being at home alone after dark and of feeling safe when walking in the dark in the neighbourhood. Whereas the impact of a burglary on feeling safe at home is stronger than the impact of a violent crime event, the type of victimisation does not matter when it comes to feeling safe on the streets.

The work by Rountree (1998) with Seattle data (4,638 respondents) focuses on the relationship between offence-specific victimisation experience within the last two years and offence-specific indicators of fear of crime. The results show that personal victimisation, which captures assault within one's own neighbourhood, increases fear of violence and (indirectly through perceived incivilities) fear of burglary. By contrast, burglary victimisation is only related to fear of burglary victimisation.

Shifting the focus to studies from Germany more or less confirms these findings. Naplava (2008) shows that having been a victim within the last two years significantly raises the level of fear of becoming a victim within the respondent's living area. The sample consisted of 64,000 inhabitants aged 14 years and older from the German state of North Rhine-Westphalia.

A study from Hamburg (Lüdemann 2006) finds a positive impact of the number of direct victimisation experiences on perceived likelihood of victimisation and avoiding behaviour. Feeling safe in the neighbourhood during the day is negatively related to the number of direct victimisation experiences, whereas feeling safe in the neighbourhood during darkness is not related to personal victimisation. Based on data from a representative German survey, Bilsky et al. (1995) find a correlation between violent victimisation and personal fear of crime.[4] Gerber et al. (2010) conclude in their review of the literature on insecurities about crime in Germany, Austria and Switzerland that direct and indirect victimisation experience affects the cognitive dimension of fear of crime to a stronger degree than it affects the affective component.

Another important aspect concerning the victimisation-fear relationship is time. An Italian study (Russo/Roccato 2010) shows in a two-wave longitudinal survey that victimisation experience within 12 months before T_1 does not affect fear of crime at T_2. By contrast, victimisation during the year between the two survey waves increases fear of crime. The same holds for people who have experienced multiple victimisation (i.e. victimisation at T_1 and T_2). Gale and Coupe (2005) analyse a sample of 149 victims of street robbery interviewed within four weeks of the incident (T_1) and again 9 months after the incident (T_2). Whereas the level of fear was heightened at T_1, at T_2 the level of fear during day was back down to the level before the incident. Fear at night also decreased but still remained above the initial value.

The empirical evidence presented shows that there is a connection between victimisation and fear of crime, hence the following general assumption is made:

> H_{F1}: Victims report higher levels of fear than non-victims.

However, research has shown that the relationship depends also on the type of victimisation event and the dimension of fear of crime (e.g. cognitive, affective, and conative). Not every dimension is affected in the same way. Furthermore, there seems to be a stronger connection between offence-specific victimisation and specific fear of crime.

> H_{F2}: Victimisation experience impacts the dimensions of fear of crime to differing degrees.
> H_{F3}: The relationship will be stronger between crime-specific fear and crime-specific victimisation.

4 The indicator of personal fear comprises affective and cognitive components based on an expectation*value approach (Bilsky et al. 1995, p. 96).

In addition, there is some empirical evidence that the impact of victimisation declines over time. However, it is unclear whether it comes to a complete recovery or how long this takes. Once again, therefore, a more general hypothesis is derived.

H_{F4}: The impact of a victimisation event declines over time.

11.2.2 Victimisation, fear of crime and life satisfaction

Research on life satisfaction is a growing field of research among the social sciences. It aims "to isolate what conditions affect individual and social well-being, and to what extent" (Frey, 2008, p. 4). Subjective well-being is not only a personal issue, but is also strongly affected by the living conditions and the society that shapes them (Frey/Stutzer 2002, p. vii).

Not surprisingly, personality has been found to affect subjective well-being; traits like (unrealistic) optimism and extraversion contribute to subjective well-being, as do self-esteem and genetic predisposition (Frey/ Stutzer 2002, p. 50-52). Demographic characteristics, economic situation and social relations also matter: Married people are on average happier, for example, and the unemployed report far lower satisfaction with life than employed people – controlling for loss of income (cf. Argyle 1999, Clark/Oswald 1996, Frey/Stutzer 2002, Gerlach/Stephan 1996, Oswald 1997, Winkelmann/Winkelmann 1998).

As other studies show, crime is also related to life satisfaction. Compared to the areas mentioned above there are only a few studies that deal with the consequences of crime in terms of subjective well-being (Michalos/Zumbo 2000, p. 246, Møller 2005, pp. 269-270, Powdthavee 2005, p. 532).

Michalos and Zumbo (2000) analyse the impact of fear of crime and victimisation on different satisfaction measures. Their sample consists of 737 respondents from Prince Georgia (Canada). It turns out in bivariate analysis that victims report lower scores of satisfaction with life as a whole, of satisfaction with the overall quality of life, and of happiness. However the differences are not that large. Regarding fear of crime, there is no (bivariate) relationship between the 'standard indicator', an index of defensive behaviour and the indicators of subjective well-being. However, an index of crime-related worries is negatively related to quality of life and life satisfaction. Additionally, satisfaction with personal safety and the family's safety in the neighbourhood is positively related to all three indicators of global satisfaction.

The study from Cohen (2008) analyses the effect of victimisation experience and neighbourhood safety on reported happiness based on seven survey waves from the United States General Social Survey (GSS) with more than 14,000 respondents. Individuals who rate the neighbourhood they live in as unsafe report a significantly lower happiness score. This effect disappears, however, when Cohen (2008) controls for burglary and robbery victimisation.[5] Burglary victimisation itself significantly lowers happiness.

By contrast, Moore (2006) reports a significant impact of fear of crime, but no impact of victimisation experience on happiness using data from the European Social Survey (ESS) with 25,915 respondents from 22 countries. He uses a standard indicator of fear of crime (walking alone after dark in the respondent's area). Victimisation status indicates if the respondent or a household member has been a victim of assault or burglary within the last five years.

A paper based on the European Community Household Panel reports a significant negative impact of the perception that crime is a problem in the respondent's area on the measure of subjective well-being in Germany and other European states (Pedersen/Schmidt 2009).

A study from South Africa (Powdthavee 2005) shows that victimisation experience at household level significantly lowers household satisfaction. The impact of victimisation is lower in areas with a high crime rate, which itself has a negative impact on life satisfaction. The reduction of the life satisfaction gap between victims and non-victims is explained by a reduced stigmatisation effect in areas where there are more victims (Powdthavee 2005, p. 538). A similar mechanism is discovered by Clark (2003): The well-being gap between employed and unemployed is smaller in areas with higher unemployment.

Studies that reveal the psychological consequences of fear of crime and victimisation corroborate the relationship between fear of crime, victimisation and life satisfaction. Fear of crime is associated with more distress (Ross 1993, p. 170). Studies with elderly people show that fear of crime

5 The initially large number of respondents decreases notably, however, as more variables are included in the multivariate models. It drops from 8,444 to 2,260 when victim status is included in the models. This may also account for the effect of perceived safety being rendered insignificant.

leads to less neighbourhood satisfaction and lower overall morale (Ward et al. 1986, Yin 1982). Exploring the psychological consequences of victimisation, Sorenson and Golding (1990) find that victims of crime are more likely to report increased suicidality and depression. Individuals who have been mugged or sexually assaulted report higher levels of depression. Suicidality is affected by victimisation in general and especially by having been mugged. Britt (2001) links victimisation experience to perceived health and physical well-being and shows that victimisation negatively affects health. The effects are contingent on type of victimisation (property crime vs. violent crime) and age. Norris and Kaniasty (1994) analyse the impact of victimisation on psychological symptoms and find that victims of crime are more distressed, show higher levels of depression, anxiety, somatisation, hostility, and fear. Based on longitudinal data they show that these symptoms declined over time, but this decline diminished, and even after 15 months victims still suffered more distress than non-victims.

The findings on the diminishing impact of victimisation are related to research that deals with processes of adaptation regarding subjective well-being. The extra happiness induced by new goods or an income shift wears of over time, as people adapt to the new situation (Frey/Stutzer 2002, pp. 78ff.). This is also true for events that cause a loss of subjective well-being. For example the death of a close relative or friend is associated with an increase of psychological distress, but the impact declines over time (Oswald/Powdthavee 2008). Adaptation processes are also found for people who became disabled. However, they did not recover entirely over the observation period (Oswald/Powdthavee 2008a). Based on this evidence, one would expect a declining impact of victimisation experience over time, as does Møller (2005, p. 271).[6] There might not be a total recovery of subjective well-being, however.

Based on the literature presented above, we expect a negative impact of fear of crime and victimisation experience on life satisfaction.

> H_{L1}: Victims of crime report a lower level of life satisfaction than non-victims.
> H_{L2}: Fear of crime decreases life satisfaction.

---

6 In her own analyses, Møller (2005, pp. 287-288) gives up the distinction between earlier and later victimisation, as it appears to be spurious. However, her analyses do not control for socio-demographic background (or at least it is not described), which is important in disentangling the different impacts of victimisation and social background.

In addition the assumption of a time dependent impact of victimization on life satisfaction is derived.

> H_{L3}: The impact of a victimisation experience on life satisfaction will be higher for recent victimisation than for earlier victimisation.

11.3 Empirical analysis

11.3.1 Data base and operationalisation

The sample

The empirical analyses are based on three waves of a nationwide representative survey conducted by the Criminological Research Institute of Lower Saxony in the years 2004, 2006 and 2010.[7] The target population were all German-speaking persons of 16 years and older and residing in private households. The paper-and-pencil questionnaire was sent by postal mail at the beginning of January in each year. The sampling was based on an access panel run by the German market research institute Gesellschaft für Konsumforschung (GfK). The response rate was fairly high (64 to 86 percent); this is a result of using an access panel. The 2004 and 2006 survey waves were administered by another major German market research institute, TNS Infratest. An access panel is a pool of households who are willing to participate in surveys and about whom basic socio-demographic variables are known. Participants normally receive monetary compensation for participating. Access panels receive a positive assessment in the literature (Kaase 1999, p. 42). A crucial feature of such panels is heterogeneity to ensure a representative sample. As the present analyses are about unravelling relationships, however, representativeness is a secondary concern (Diekmann 2003, pp. 368-369). It is therefore not necessary to be concerned about differences between survey waves with regard to demographic variables, and particularly employment status (see Table 11.1). Relationships should also be manifest if the sample were not to be representative. In addition, multivariate methods allow the demographic background to be controlled for.

---

7 For a more detailed description of the sample see Windzio et al. (2007) and Baier et al. (2011).

Table 11.1 Sample characteristics

	2004	2006	2010	Total sample
sample technique	Access panel	Access panel	Access panel	
survey period	8.1.-6.2.2004	5.1.-2.2.2006	7.1.-1.2.2010	
response rate	64%	70%	86%	
valid Answers	2,017	1,110	3,245	6,372
demographics				
age in years (mean)	48.3	47.6	51.3	49.7
female	54.5%	53.1%	51.1%	52.5%
low education	34.8%	27.2%	26.7%	29.3%
medium education	33.5%	32.0%	33.7%	33.3%
high education	31.7%	40.8%	39.6%	37.3%
student	7.5%	7.0%	5.4%	6.3%
retired	24.0%	22.2%	32.6%	28.1%
unemployed	6.3%	3.9%	3.5%	4.5%
employed	49.3%	57.9%	48.9%	50.4%
other	12.9%	10.0%	9.6%	10.7%
married	60.2%	57.1%	60.0%	59.6%
unmarried with partner*	7.1%	7.7%	6.4%	6.8%
unmarried without partner	16.3%	19.5%	20.4%	19.0%
divorced/separated/widowed with partner	3.1%	3.2%	1.8%	2.5%
divorced/separated/widowed w/o partner	13.3%	12.5%	11.4%	12.2%

* With partner means cohabiting with one's partner.

Dependent variables

Fear of crime was captured in an extensive manner to measure all four dimensions separately. To assess the concern about crime, participants were asked to estimate the crime trends within the last ten years before the survey for the following crimes: Crime in total, burglary, theft, and assault. They stated on a seven-point scale if in their opinion the number of crimes in general and for a specific set of offences had increased, stayed the same or decreased over the last 10 years. The conative dimension of fear (avoidance behaviour) was captured with eight items on the frequency of behaviour regarding crime, e.g. "I avoid certain parks, streets or public places". Worries about crime and subjective victimisation risk related to six different offences, so the data include the offence-specific cognitive fear (likelihood of victimisation within the next twelve months) and affective fear (frequency of worrying).[8]

Respondents were also asked to report their overall satisfaction with life ("How satisfied are you nowadays all in all with your life?") on a seven point scale ranging from (1) very unsatisfied to (7) very satisfied. The distribution is skewed to the left, as in most satisfaction with life studies (Frey/Stutzer 2002). On average, people report a score of 4.70 (6,279 respondents, SD=1.52).

This self-reported measure of life-satisfaction, as captured in large scale social surveys, "has turned out to be the best indicator of happiness. Extensive research has shown that people are capable of consistently evaluating their own state of well-being" (Frey/Stutzer 2002, p. 26). Although satisfaction may comprise several distinct domains, evidence from psychological studies shows that most aspects of subjective well-being can be reflected by a single measure (Frey/Stutzer 2002, p. 28, Kahneman 1999). Measuring subjective well-being in this way is also reliable and research has shown that reported subjective well-being has temporal stability and is sensitive to changing circumstances (Frey/Stutzer 2002, Kahneman/Krueger 2006).

Victimisation status

Participants were asked in each survey wave if they had ever been victims of theft, assault or burglary. Individuals who had been a victim stated in the next question the year of the last victimisation experience by offence. The questions described the offences in detail to separate the offences from each other.[9] In total 24.4 percent were victims of theft, 8.7 percent

8 See Table 11.2 of this paper for the wording of the question and all items.

9 The question for theft was: "Someone has stolen objects, money or other means of payment or other important documents that belonged to you or your household, without threatening you with violence or breaking into your home." Assault was captured by: "Someone has intentionally hit you, beaten you, pushed you or choked you or hurt you with a firearm, a knife, a stick, teargas, a chain or a similar object, without taking anything from you." Burglary: "Someone has entered or tried to enter your apartment without your permission, e.g. with a jimmy, a false key or through the window, and has stolen something or tried to steal (excludes breaking into basement rooms, garages, garden sheds, summerhouses, business and office premises or cars).".

were victims of assault and 8.8 percent were victims of burglary (captured in the 2004 and 2006 survey waves only).

Independent variables

Victimisation experience is not the only factor that drives fear of crime. The level of fear experienced by people who have not been victimised is explained using the concept of vulnerability (Naplava 2008). Seen from the vulnerability perspective, fear stems from three factors: increased exposure to victimisation risk, the perception of having low resources of protection and self-defence (loss of control) and anticipation of the possible consequences of victimisation as severe (Franklin et al. 2008, Hale 1996, Killias 1990, Pantazis 2000). Empirical work has confirmed the vulnerability model in general: People who perceive themselves to be physically vulnerable (e.g. senior citizens and women) or socially vulnerable (e.g. people who are poor or have lower education) report higher levels of fear (Franklin et al. 2008, Hale 1996, Kreuter 2002, Pantazis 2000, Ward et al. 1986).

Research has also revealed the impact of socio-demographic characteristics on life satisfaction. Age, sex, and educational and economic background were therefore additionally captured (see Table 11.1 for descriptives). Respondents were divided into three groups based on their school education. Individuals with no school-leaving qualification or only up to nine years of school education are classified as low education level; a medium education level is defined as a school-leaving qualification after ten years of school education; and the high education level group consists of respondents who graduated after at least twelve years of schooling. Financial situation was assessed by computing equivalent monthly income following the OECD definition (5,615 respomdents, mean = € 1442.97, SD = 1134.36). Respondents were also sorted into five occupational status groups and five family status groups. In addition, there is a dummy variable indicating whether a respondent comes from the western part of Germany including Berlin or from the eastern part of the country. This distinction would seem to be necessary considering the different histories. 82.1 percent of respondents live in western Germany and 17.9 percent in eastern Germany.

11.3.2 Victimisation, fear of crime and life satisfaction – bivariate and exploratory analyses

Victimisation and fear of crime – exploring different dimensions

The first step of the analysis has a more explorative character and relates offence-specific victimisation experience to different dimensions of fear of crime. The items cover the four dimensions of fear of crime (perception of crime trends, and affective, cognitive and conative fear) and distinguish between specific offences (Table 11.2). The analysis starts by distinguishing between victims within the last two years and non-victims within the last two years. This reference period is preliminary, as a closer look at the time dependency of the impact of a victimisation experience will be taken later.

Significant correlations exist between offence-specific victimisation and offence-specific perception of crime trends; they are rather low, but in the postulated direction. This supports the assumption of a specific relationship between victimisation and fear.

Victimisation experience has a small negative impact on the items of conative fear. This finding is rather unexpected. Perhaps people who show a higher degree of avoidance behaviour are victimised to a lesser extent (reverse causal direction), leading to the unexpected direction of the relationship.

The correlations of the affective and the cognitive component with the victimisation status are somewhat higher compared to the two other dimensions of fear and also show a tendency towards a specific relationship: Victims of burglary show the highest correlation with affective and cognitive fear of burglary, victims of theft with fear of theft, and victims of assault are most afraid of assault.

Altogether, the correlations between victimisation experience and the single item indicators are rather small. The biggest correlations are between victimisation with theft and assault and the crime specific affective and cognitive fear items. Furthermore, only some of the correlations are statistically significant at the $\alpha = 5\%$ level.

In order to test the tendency towards a specific relationship between victimisation and fear, i.e. whether victims of a specific offence are more afraid of that offence, correlation coefficients between victimisation experience and the offence-specific fear item are compared. Table 11.3 shows if the correlations between victimisation and two fear items diverge

Table 11.2 Pearson correlation between victimisation experience and dimensions of fear

	Victim within the last two years of...		
	Theft	**Burglary**	**Assault**
Perception of crime trends: "Different types of crimes are listed in the following. Please state if such crime in Germany, in your opinion, has decreased, stayed the same or increased over the last ten years; that is, between 1999 and 2009." The scale ranged from (1) has become much rarer to (7) has become much more frequent.			
Crimes in total	-0.011	0.003	0.021
Burglary	-0.017	**0.041**	-0.022
Theft in total	0.008	0.015	0.002
Assault	0.001	0.008	**0.050**
Conative fear/avoidance behaviour: "To protect themselves from crime in everyday life, people often take certain precautions. Please state how often you take the precautions named." The scale included the answer categories never, rarely, sometimes, often and always.			
I leave the house after dark only if necessary.	**-0.029**	0.000	-0.011
I avoid certain streets, places or parks.	-0.019	-0.008	-0.014
I avoid strangers I encounter during darkness if possible.	-0.019	-0.012	-0.004
I avoid using public transport at night.	-0.012	-0.022	-0.018
I avoid carrying a lot of money with me.	0.001	0.007	**-0.038**
I take care that my home does not look unoccupied during my absence.	**-0.031**	0.010	**-0.048**
I carry irritant gas, a knife or another weapon with me for self-defence.	0.024	-0.015	0.079
I additionally secure my home when absent, for example by applying an extra bolt or turning on an alarm system.	0.004	0.014	0.007
Affective fear: "If you think about yourself: how often do you have the following worries? I'm afraid that …" The scale included the answer categories never, rarely, sometimes, often and always.			
… my home may be broken into.	**0.041**	**0.073**	0.006
… I will have something stolen from me in some other way.	**0.110**	**0.062**	**0.036**
… I will be hit or hurt.	**0.034**	0.029	**0.099**
… I will be robbed.	0.013	0.018	**0.050**
… I will be sexually abused, molested or raped.	-0.010	0.014	0.022
… I may be killed in an act of violence.	0.014	0.023	**0.040**
Cognitive fear: "How likely is it, in your opinion, that these things might happen to you personally in the next twelve months?" The scale included the answer categories very unlikely, unlikely, less likely, likely and very likely.			
… my home may be broken into.	**0.045**	**0.065**	0.005
… I will have something stolen from me in some other way.	**0.122**	**0.050**	**0.040**
… I will be hit or hurt.	**0.040**	0.016	**0.126**
… I will be robbed.	0.016	0.018	0.019
… I will be sexually abused, molested or raped.	-0.010	0.015	0.015
… I may be killed in an act of violence.	-0.007	0.015	0.019

Correlations with $p < 0.05$ bold

significantly. This is done for every victimisation type separately for all significant correlations from Table 11.2. For example, the correlation between victimisation with theft and affective fear of theft is significantly stronger than the correlation between victimisation with theft and affective fear of burglary.

In sum, the tests on the heterogeneity of the correlation coefficients show that victims of theft report a significantly stronger correlation with affective and cognitive fear of theft than with fear of other offence types. Experience of assault is significantly more strongly correlated with fear of assault than with fear of other offence types, whereas there is no evidence that burglary victimisation increases fear of burglary more than fear of other forms of theft.

Table 11.3 Testing for heterogeneity in correlation coefficients

	Theft	**Burglary**	**Assault**
Affective fear			
Burglary vs. theft	-6.098***	0.711	
Burglary vs. assault	0.506		
Theft vs. assault	6.383***		-5.262***
Theft vs. robbery			-1.195
Assault vs. robbery			5.828***
Violent death vs. robbery			-0.960
Violent death vs. assault			-5.228***
Violent death vs. theft			0.264
Cognitive fear			
Burglary vs. theft	-7.697***	1.061	
Burglary vs. assault	0.397		
Theft vs. assault	7.607***		-8.021***

Test on significant differences between dependent correlation coefficients using the STATA command corcor (Goldstein 1996). Test statistic (Z) and significance for two-tailed test reported: *** $p < .001$

Another finding from the previous literature is the claim that victimisation experience more severely impacts the cognitive than the affective dimension of fear. Comparing the correlation coefficients of the cognitive and the affective dimension with victimisation experience shows no significant differences, however – with one exception: The correlation between cognitive fear of assault and having been victim of an assault is higher than the correlation with the affective item ($z = -2{,}357$, $p=0.018$).

To sum up, there is not much evidence that victimisation influences the cognitive dimension of fear more than the affective dimension. However, these two dimensions seem to depend more on victimisation than do perception of crime trends and conative fear. Regarding the offence-specific relationship between victimisation and fear of crime, the results indicate that there is a specific relationship.

It can also be seen that the relationship between victimisation experience and fear of crime is not limited to the type of offence a respondent experienced. Victims of violent crimes also report fear of property victimisation and vice versa. This leads to the question as to whether victimisation influences fear of crime in a broader manner. In the next step, therefore, the different items of fear are combined in indicators that reflect the four dimensions of fear: concern about crime, affective fear, cognitive fear and avoiding behaviour.

Factor analyses of fear of crime

The eigenvalues from the factor analysis of the items for conative fear of crime suggest a two-factor solution. The first five items load on the first factor, the sixth item loads on both and the last two items load on the second factor. This holds for all three survey waves, implying temporal stability. Based on these results, a scale is developed with the first five items that load on the first factor. Item six shows low loadings (< 0.5) on the first factor and is therefore not part of the scale. Due to the low eigenvalue and correlations, no scale is computed based on the second factor. The Cronbach's α values for the conative fear scale are satisfactory (2004: 0.79, 2006: 0.74, 2010: 0.79). The scale is derived by averaging the answers over the five items (6,364 respondents, mean = 2.94, SD = 0.92,).

Separate factor analyses for the six cognitive and six affective items for fear indicate a clear solution with one factor in each of the analysis. The Cronbach's α values for the affective scale are higher compared to the conative scale (2004: 0.87, 2006: 0.87; 2010: 0.86; N = 6,361 respondents, mean = 2.12, SD = 0.70). The same holds for the cognitive scale (2004: 0.89, 2006: 0.89, 2010: 0.89; 6,338 respondents, mean = 2.10, SD = 0.72).

Perception of past crime trends, as an indicator of crime as a concern, is measured further on via one single item that captures the perception of past trends for general crime. The mean value of 5.53 suggests that, on average, respondents think the number of crimes in total has increased over the last 10 years (6,292 respondents, SD = 1.07).

The correlations between the four dimensions of fear range from low to middle (Table 11.4), whereas it can be seen that the cognitive and the affective dimensions are particularly strongly related to each other (r = 0.665). The perception of crime trends is correlated to the other dimensions only by about 0.2, suggesting that concern about crime as a social problem may not necessarily affect more personal dimensions of fear.

Table 11.4 Pearson correlations between the different indicators of fear

	Conative Fear	Cognitive Fear	Affective Fear
Cognitive fear	0.352***		
Affective fear	0.438***	0.665***	
Perception of crime trends	0.238***	0.199***	0.215***

*** p < 0.001

Relating the scales for affective, cognitive and conative fear to the three different victimisation variables shows that victimisation experience decreases conative fear of crime (T-tests, Table 11.5). This means that victims of theft, assault and burglary report less avoidance behaviour. The differences are, however, not significant at the conventional level ($\alpha = 5\%$). By contrast, the cognitive and affective indicators of fear – both in logs to improve distribution properties – are increased by a victimisation experience. The mean differences are significant, with the exception of cognitive fear in burglary victims. This may be partly due to the small number of burglary victims.

Table 11.5 Mean comparison between victims within the last two years by offence

		Cognitive fear (log)		Conative fear		Affective fear (log)	
		Mean	N	Mean	N	Mean	N
Theft	Not a victim within last two years	0.675	5,909	2.946	5,934	0.693	5,932
	Victim within last two years	0.739	381	2.867	381	0.756	381
	t-value	3.336***		1.625		3.679***	
Assault	Not a victim within last two years	0.677	6,204	2.946	6,229	0.695	6,226
	Victim within last two years	0.797	112	2.781	113	0.819	113
	t-value	3.479***		1.881		4.008***	
Burglary	Not a victim within last two years	0.704	3,052	2.985	3,062	0.701	3,057
	Victim within last two years	0.807	38	2.896	38	0.830	38
	t-value	1.744		0.585		2.348*	

* p < 0.05, ** p< 0.01. *** p < 0.001

Victimisation experience, fear of crime and life satisfaction

One aim of the present study is to analyse the impact of victimisation events on broader measures of subjective well-being. Victimisation experience is, therefore, brought into relation with satisfaction with life. T-tests between victims and non-victims within the last two years by offence reveal significant differences for theft and assault. Individuals who have been victims of a theft or an assault report a significantly lower level of life satisfaction, and this effect seems to be stronger for assault (Table 11.6). By contrast, victims of burglary do not report less satisfaction with life than non-victims. These findings, however, are only bivariate and do not control for other important determinants of crime.

Satisfaction with life is also related to fear of crime. Bivariate Pearson correlations reveal a significant negative relationship with affective fear of crime in logs (-0.084, $p < .001$), cognitive fear of crime in logs in logs (-0.074, $p < .001$), the perception of crime trends (-0.069, $p < .001$) and conative fear (-0.042, $p < .001$).

As the bivariate analyses have shown that burglary victimisation has almost no significant impact either on fear or on life satisfaction and data on burglary are only available for part of the sample, this type of victimisation is dropped from the further analyses.

Table 11.6 Mean comparison between victims within the last two years by offence

	Theft Mean of life satisfaction	N	**Assault** Mean of life satisfaction	N	**Burglary** Mean of life satisfaction	N
No victim within last two years	4.713	5,856	4.709	6,143	4,667	3,000
Victim within last two years	4.527	374	4.150	113	4,649	37
t-value	2.299*		3.881***		0.068	

* p < 0.05, ** p< 0.01, *** p < 0.001

11.3.3 Time heals all wounds? The impact of victimisation over time

In the literature, various time spans are used for the definition of victims for the purposes of analysis. Mostly, the question relates to victimisation experience over the last one or two years, but victimisation experience may also have longer-lasting impacts, even though strong initial effects may decline over time. This section, therefore, analyses the impact of victimisation experience on fear and life satisfaction over time.

One way to analyse the impact of victimisation experience over time is to compare groups of people who differ by the length of time since the last victimisation experience. For the analysis, respondents were categorised –

by offence type – into six different groups: non-victims, victims within this or the last year, two years ago, three to five years ago, six to ten years ago and more than ten years ago (Table 11.7).[10]

Table 11.7 Years since last victimisation experience

	Theft		Assault	
	absolute	percent	absolute	percent
Non-Victim	4,801	75.94	5,804	91.42
Zero or one year	242	3.83	82	1.29
Two years	139	2.20	31	0.49
Three to five years	339	5.36	84	1.32
Five to ten years	338	5.35	118	1.86
More than ten years	463	7.32	230	3.62

The impact of the victimisation variables was assessed by entering all victimisation groups as dummies into regression models (see Figures 11.1 and 11.2). Additionally, survey wave dummies, sex and age were included as control variables. The dependent variables were satisfaction with life, and affective and cognitive fear of crime. No models were estimated for avoidance behaviour, as the bivariate analyses did not find an impact of victimisation.

Looking at the victimisation coefficients from the models for affective fear, it can be seen that all of them are significant and that the impact of the victimisation also declines over time. However, in the models for assault and theft the coefficients for victimisation two years ago have the highest values, indicating a tendency for an inverse U-shaped relationship.

Similar results are found for the impact of victimisation experience on subjective victimisation risk. But the inverse U-shaped pattern cannot be proved in a statistically significant manner.[11] The overlapping 95 percent confidence intervals give an advance indication of that finding.

10 Participants were asked for the year when the last victimisation experience happened. Based on this information and the fact that every wave was surveyed at the beginning of the year, the time of the last crime event could be computed in the same way.

11 In addition, choosing the group with the highest coefficient as reference group in each of the four models shows the only group that significantly differs from this group to be victims whose victimisation happened more than ten years ago. In the model for affective fear there is no difference between the victim groups at all.

For further multivariate analyses, two victimisation groups are computed: One group with those who became victim within the last two years, victimisation having been found to peak during that time span. The second group comprises all victimisations that are more than two years ago.

Fig. 11.1 Effect of victimisation on fear of crime by time since last event (coefficients of OLS-regression with affective/cognitive fear as dependent variable and 95 percent confidence intervals shown; models control for sex, age and survey wave)

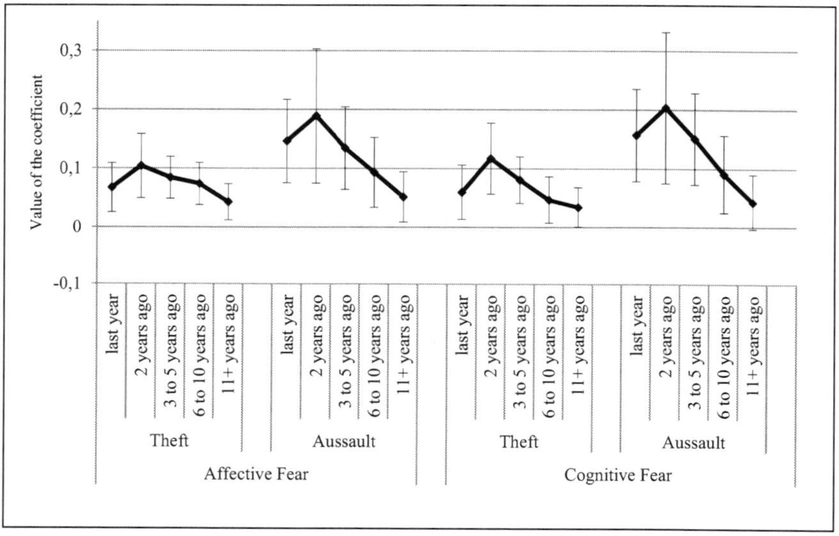

The same strategy was applied to uncover the impact of victimisation on life satisfaction over time. The results support the assumption of a declining impact of victimisation experience on life satisfaction in general (Figure 11.2). The magnitude of the coefficients for theft declines as distance from the last victimisation experience grows and only the dummy for the most recent victimisation is significant; however, there is an anomaly in the dummy indicating six to ten years.

Inspecting the model for assault more closely shows the coefficients to be declining in magnitude, producing a U-shaped pattern. The coefficients stay significant (the coefficient for victimisation experience five to ten years ago only marginally). Examining the coefficients more closely shows that there is no significant difference between individuals victimised one and two years ago and the other victim groups for assault.

Thus, the U-shaped/declining pattern of the relationship cannot be statistically confirmed.

Fig. 11.2 Effect of victimisation on life satisfaction by time since last event (coefficients of OLS-regression with life satisfaction as dependent variable and 95 percent confidence intervals shown; models control for sex, age and survey wave)

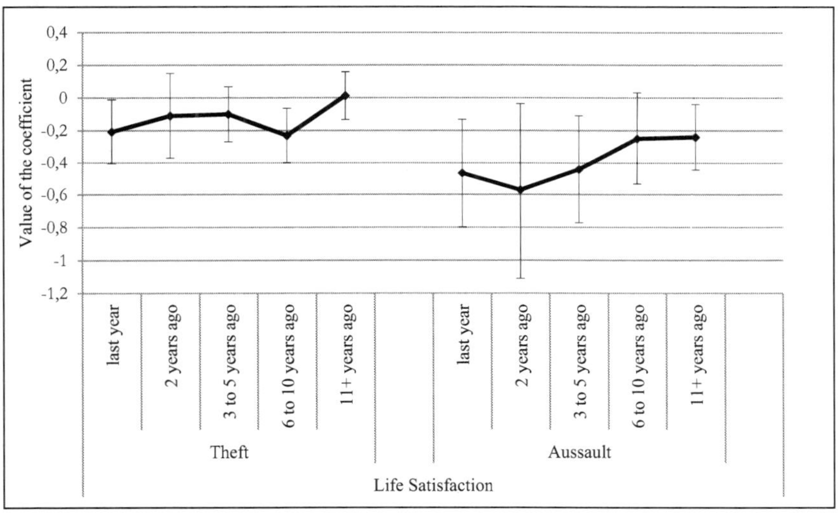

11.3.4 Multivariate regression models

Fear of crime

The final step undertaken to analyse the effect of victimisation experience on fear of crime and life satisfaction is the estimation of multivariate regression models. This step firstly makes it possible to check the robustness of the findings controlling for other relevant determinants known to influence fear and life satisfaction. Secondly, this section aims to integrate victimisation and fear of crime into a combined model explaining life satisfaction.

The control variables show quite similar effects in all models and for all four dimensions of fear of crime (Table 11.8). Women, older individuals, and people with low education levels and low incomes show higher levels of fear of crime. People from eastern Germany report a higher level of fear of crime except for the affective component. There is no difference regarding affective fear of crime between the eastern and the western part of Germany.

Table 11.8 Influencing factors of fear of crime, OLS-regression

	Affective fear of crime (log)			Cognitive fear of crime (log)			Conative fear			Perception of crime trends		
Variable	**b**		**t**	**b**		**t**	**b**		**t**	**b**		**t**
2004 survey wave (ref.)												
2006	-0.011		-0.76	-0.014		-0.93	-0.046		-1.26	-0.115	**	-2.60
2010	-0.007		0.71	-0.041	***	-3.54	-0.083	**	-3.09	-0.454	***	-13.83
Age	0.000		1.10	0.002	***	6.77	0.013	***	17.52	0.004	***	4.92
Male (ref.)												
Female	0.112	***	12.73	0.082	***	8.34	0.613	***	26.52	0.216	***	7.64
Low education (ref.)												
Medium education	-0.011		-0.99	-0.017		-1.33	-0.060	*	-2.00	-0.910	*	-2.48
High education	-0.039	**	-3.41	-0.048	***	-3.72	-0.189	***	-6.24	-0.347	***	-9.36
West (ref.)												
East	0.001		-0.06	0.025	*	2.00	0.055		1.85	0.093	*	2.58
Equivalent income (log)	-0.029	**	-3.32	-0.026	**	-2.74	-0.135	***	-5.98	-0.150	***	-5.41
Non-victim of theft (ref.)												
Victim of theft in last two years	0.078	***	4.19	0.082	***	3.99	0.012		0.24	-0.023		-0.40
Victim of theft more than two years ago	0.063	***	5.50	0.049	***	3.85	-0.065	*	-2.15	-0.045		-1.23
Non-victim of assault (ref.)												
Victim of assault in last two years	0.138	***	3.97	0.159	***	4.05	0.142		1.55	0.266	*	2.38
Victim of assault more than two years ago	0.072	***	4.02	0.067	***	3.36	0.037		0.80	0.053		0.92
Constant	0.706	***	10.61	0.631	***	8.48	2.427	***	13.90	6.375	***	29.87
Number of cases	**5,495**			**5,474**			**5,494**			**5,448**		
Adj. R^2	**0.046**			**0.037**			**0.178**			**0.095**		

*** p < .001, ** p < .01,* p < .05

When looking closer at the changes over time, there is no significant change for affective fear over the years. Looking at the perception of crime, however, it is seen that respondents in 2006 and in 2010 estimated the increase in crime less dramatically than 2004. Respondents in 2010 have the most realistic perception on crime compared to respondents in the other years, although their estimates are still far higher than in reality.

Cognitive and conative fear of crime show significant decreases between 2004 and 2010.

Two dummies for each type of crime indicate individuals who were victimised during the last two years and those where it has been more than two years since their last victimisation experience. Having been a victim of assault has a stronger effect on both affective and cognitive fear of crime than having been a victim of theft.

In addition, having been victim of theft or assault within the last two years has a stronger effect on affective and cognitive fear of crime than having been victimised more than two years ago. A closer look at the significance of these differences between the victimisation groups reveals that victims of assault report a significantly lower level of cognitive fear of crime more than two years after the victimisation than within the last two years after the victimisation. No significant differences are found for affective fear and for victims of theft.[12]

The two other indicators of fear of crime show hardly any effects of victimisation. Moreover, the coefficients for theft turn in the inverse direction, repeating the bivariate findings: Individuals who were victims of a theft more than two years ago therefore show significantly less avoidance behaviour than non-victims. The coefficients for assault are in the expected direction, but very weak. Only victims of assault within the last two years perceive the increase in crime within the past ten years more dramatically than non-victims.

Life satisfaction

For the multivariate analyses of life satisfaction, three OLS-regression models were calculated in which blocks of variables were entered stepwise. As has previously been said, age, sex, income, and occupational and family status are important factors for subjective well-being. Model II includes the categories of victimisation and Model III the fear of crime variables.

Looking at life satisfaction as a dependent variable, it is seen that life satisfaction does not change over the observed years. The significant coefficients for age and age squared confirm the U-shaped relationship be-

12 Analyses based on simply changing the reference categories.

tween age and life satisfaction (Frey/Stutzer 2002). As expected, life satisfaction grows with the education level and income. People from the eastern part of Germany and people who are unemployed are less satisfied with life. Family status shows that divorced, separated or widowed individuals without a new partner are least happy persons compared with those who are married, followed by those who are unmarried without a partner and those who are unmarried but with a partner. There is no difference between people who are married and those who are divorced, separated or widowed but have found a new partner.

Including the variables of victimisation, the models illustrate no effects for individuals who have been victims of theft. Looking at the victims of assault, however, there is a strong effect for victimisation within the last two years that declines for assaults more than two years ago. But once again, there is no significant difference between victimisation within the last two years and more than two years ago.

Adding the fear of crime variables to Model III, the adjusted R^2 gains significantly from 0.069 to 0.077. Affective fear of crime does not have an effect on life satisfaction; nor does conative fear of crime. However, subjective victimisation risk (cognitive fear) and personal perception of increasing crime levels within society lead to a less satisfied life. Controlling for fear of crime reduces the coefficients of victimisation, but the p-values remain at the same level. There seems to be a direct effect of having been a victim of assault on life satisfaction.

An unexpected finding is the insignificant effect of affective fear of crime on life satisfaction, in contradiction of the bivariate findings. This may be a result of the high correlation between affective fear and risk ($r = 0.665$). Although the VIF values for affective and cognitive fear are not too high, it is known that multicollinearity increases standard errors, and this may result in a non-significant coefficient (Urban/Mayerl 2006, pp. 229-230).

Table 11.9 Influencing factors of life satisfaction, OLS-regression

	Model I		Model II		Model III	
Variable	**b**	**t**	**b**	**t**	**b**	**t**
2004 survey wave (ref.)						
2006	0.017	2.61	0.018	0.28	0.005	0.08
2010	-0.029	-0.61	-0.045	-0.93	-0.080	-1.64
Age	-0.038***	-4.57	-0.040***	-4.81	-0.041***	-5.00
Age²	0.000***	5.17	0.000***	5.34	0.000***	5.62
Male (ref.)						
Female	0.048	1.13	0.027	0.64	0.101*	2.25
Low education (ref.)						
Medium education	0.085	1.60	0.090	1.68	0.078	1.46
High education	0.165**	3.05	0.171**	3.15	0.131*	2.41
West (ref.)						
East	-0.159**	-2.97	-0.168**	-3.14	-0.158**	-2.96
Equivalent income (log)	0.355***	8.51	0.356***	8.52	0.331***	7.93
Family status married (ref.)						
Unmarried with partner	-0.266**	-2.98	-0.249**	-2.79	-0.235**	-2.64
Unmarried without partner	-0.332***	-4.98	-0.314***	-4.71	-0.335***	-5.03
Divorced, separated, widowed with partner	-0.163	-1.22	-0.142	-1.06	-0.146	-1.10
Divorced, separated, widowed without partner	-0.352***	-5.43	-0.338***	-5.21	-0.350***	-5.42
Occupation employed (ref.)						
Student	0.099	0.93	0.096	0.90	0.086	0.81
Pensioner	-0.075	-0.99	-0.077	-1.02	-0.053	-0.71
Unemployed	-0.929***	-9.25	-0.913***	-9.09	-0.904***	-9.04
Other	0.014	0.20	0.021	0.30	0.012	0.17
Non-victim of theft (ref.)						
Victim of theft in last two years			-0.135	-1.57	-0.110	-1.28
Victim of theft more than two years ago			-0.059	-1.10	-0.048	-0.91
Non-victim of assault (ref.)						
Victim of assault in last two years			-0.491**	-2.94	-0.421*	-2.53
Victim of assault more than two years ago			-0.189*	-2.27	-0.166*	-2.00
Affective fear (ln)					-0.102	-1.17
Cognitive fear (ln)					-0.189*	-2.55
Conative fear					-0.052	-1.95
Perception of crime					-0.054**	-2.70
Constant	3.088***	8.20	3.226***	8.54	3.973***	9.87
Number of cases	**5,292**		**5,292**		**5,292**	
Adj. R²	**0.067**		**0.069**		**0.077**	

*** $p < .001$, ** $p < .01$,* $p < .05$

In order to combine the direct and indirect effects of victimisation in one model, a path model was calculated. The manifest variables of fear of crime consist of the items described earlier. The fear of crime variables were modeled as dependent variables of victimisation and as independent variables of life satisfaction. The model does not differentiate between the time since the last victimisation experience for assault/theft. Sex, age, income, education, and east-west location are included as control variables. The paths of the control variables are not mapped in Figure 11.3 as they show the expected direction and weight and the results correspond to the OLS models above.

*Figure 11.3 Factors influencing life satisfaction, path model (RMSEA = 0.023, CFI = 0.997, TLI = 0.979, 5,386 respondents, *** p < .001, ** p < .01, * p < .05, + p < .10, standardized coefficients shown)*

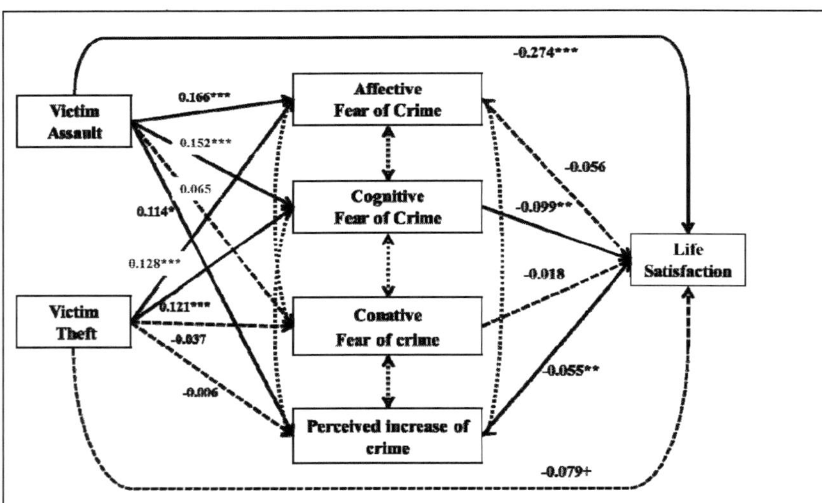

Looking at the paths from victimisation to the components of fear, the coefficients correspond to those in the regression model in Table 11.8. Having been victimised (assault or theft) leads to a higher level of affective and cognitive fear of crime. The perceived increase of crime is only affected by assault victimisation. In total, assault has higher coefficients on the fear variables compared to theft.

Looking at the determinants of life satisfaction, only cognitive fear and perception of crime have a significant negative impact on life satisfaction. In addition, there is also a direct and significant effect of victimisation experience (assault) on life satisfaction.

11.4 Conclusions

A review of existing research on victimisation and fear of crime revealed varied findings: There seems to be an impact of victimisation on fear, but the impact depends on the dimension of fear and the type of crime. The present paper, therefore, aimed to examine more closely the relationship between the dimensions of fear and victimisation experience. The study furthermore integrated the consequences of victimisation experience into a broader perspective by assessing its impact on satisfaction with life.

The analysis showed that victims report higher levels of fear, but the relationship does not hold for every dimension of fear or type of victimisation. Having been a victim of theft or assault increases the cognitive and affective component of fear of crime significantly – controlling for known covariates. These results cannot be confirmed for perception of crime trends in general; here only very weak relationships are found.

Furthermore, the relationship between victimisation and fear of crime is stronger for crime-specific fear items. Experience of assault or burglary, for example, leads to a more dramatic view on the past trend in this type of crime.

In the analyses, conative fear turns out to be decreased by the experience of theft. Having been victim of an assault does not affect conative fear at all. With a view to our hypotheses, this appears to be an unexpected result, at least at first sight. Looking closer, however, the outcome makes sense. People who show a higher degree of avoidance behaviour avoid risky situations and thereby lower their actual risk of becoming a victim. This does not rule out the possibility that victims of crime may increase their avoidance behaviour, but it is not possible to disentangle the two effects with cross-sectional data.

The effect of victimisation experience on fear of crime also declines over time. The relationship seems to be inverse U-shaped, with people victimised two years ago reporting the highest values for fear. For the affective component of fear, the multivariate model showed no significant difference between the 'last two years' and 'more than two years ago' victim groups, either for theft or for assault. Solely for the cognitive component of fear regarding the victims of assault there was evidence that 'time heals all wounds'.

Assessing the impact of victimisation on life satisfaction, the assumptions were partly confirmed. Victims of assault report lower satisfaction with life than non-victims in the multivariate model. For victims of theft, there is only an impact in the bivariate model and a statistically weak effect in the path model. No impact for victims of burglary is found. This may be due to unexplained heterogeneity that affects victimisation as well as life satisfaction. Perhaps the low number of burglary victims leads to a lack of statistical power.

The hypothesis on the declining impact of victimisation experience on life satisfaction over time could not be confirmed statistically; however, a tendency towards a declining impact is showed for assault.

The bivariate analyses revealed a negative correlation between the four dimensions of fear of crime and life satisfaction: A higher level of fear leads to less satisfaction. But a closer look shows that this does not hold for every dimension of fear. In the multivariate model, affective fear did not impact life satisfaction. Only perception of crime and cognitive fear lowered life satisfaction significantly. Perhaps life satisfaction is more affected by cognitive evaluations of the situation and therefore affective fear does not have an influence on it.

The reason for the lack of significance for affective fear may also lie in the fact that affective fear and cognitive fear are highly correlated, so the two dimensions cannot be properly disentangled. A possible solution to this problem, appropriate when the interest lies in fear as an independent variable, would be to combine the two indicators into a single construct that measures personal fear of crime (Bilsky/Wetzels 1997).

Conative fear also does not impact life satisfaction. It can be assumed that a higher level of avoidance behaviour leads to a feeling of safety and control which tends to result in more satisfaction with life.

In sum, the impact of victimisation and fear of crime on life satisfaction has to be compared to other determinants of life satisfaction. The impact of unemployment is more than twice as large, for example, as the coefficient for 'victim of assault in the last two years'.

The empirical analyses are not without shortcomings. On the one hand, the data base is only cross-sectional. It is not therefore possible to determine if victimisation itself increased fear or if victims had a higher level of fear even before the victimisation event. This is not implausible as a higher fear of crime may be a reaction to an elevated actual level of victimisation risk. Also, the hypothesis of a declining effect of victimisation on fear of crime and life satisfaction could be better studied in a longitudinal setting. In addition, the present paper focuses on the consequences of victimisation. Other determinants of fear, namely disorder and the impact of the media were consequently not controlled for.

References

Argyle, M. (1999). Causes and Correlates of Happiness. In: D. Kahneman, E. Diener, N. Schwarz (Eds.), Well-Being. The Foundations of Hedonic Psychology (pp. 353-373). New York: Russel Sage Foundation.

Baier, D., Kemme, S., Hanslmaier, M., Doering, B., Rehbein, F., Pfeiffer, C. (2011). Kriminalitätsfurcht, Strafbedürfnisse und wahrgenommene Kriminalitätsentwicklung. Ergebnisse von bevölkerungsrepräsentativen Befragungen aus den Jahren 2004, 2006 und 2010. KFN: Forschungsbericht Nr. 117.

Bilsky, W., Wetzels, P. (1997). On the Relationship Between Criminal Victimisation and Fear of Crime. Psychology, Crime & Law, 3, 309-318.

Bilsky, W., Wetzels, P., Mecklenburg, E., Pfeiffer, C. (1995). Subjektive Wahrnehmung von Kriminalität und Opfererfahrung. In: G. Kaiser, J.-M. Jehle (Eds.), Kriminologische Opferforschung. Neue Perspektiven und Erkenntnisse. Teilband II (pp. 73-106). Heidelberg: Kriminalistik Verlag.

Britt, C.L. (2001). Health Consequences of Criminal Victimisation. International Review of Victimology, 8, 63-73.

Brunton-Smith, I., Sturgis, P. (2011). Do Neighborhoods Generate Fear of Crime? An Empirical Test Using the British Crime Survey. Criminology, 49, 331-369.

Clark, A.E. (2003). Unemployment as a Social Norm: Psychological Evidence from Panel Data. Journal of Labor Economics, 21, 323-351.

Clark, A.E, Oswald, A.J. (1996). Satisfaction and Comparison Income. Journal of Public Economics, 61, 359-381.

Cohen, M.A. (2008). The Effect of Crime on Life Satisfaction. Journal of Legal Studies, 37, 325-353.

Diekmann, A. (2003). Empirische Sozialforschung. Grundlagen, Methoden, Anwendungen. 10th Ed. Reinbek: Rowohlt.

Ferraro, K.F. (1995). Fear of Crime. Interpreting Victimisation Risk. Albany: State University of New York Press.

Franklin, T.W, Franklin, C.A., Fearn, N.E. (2008). A Multilevel Analysis of the Vulnerability, Disorder, and Social Integration Models of Fear of Crime. Social Justice Research, 21, 204-227.

Frey, B.S. (2008). Happiness. A Revolution in Economics. Cambridge: MIT Press.

Frey, B.S., Stutzer, A. (2002). Happiness and Economics: How the Economy and Institutions Affect Well-Being. Princeton: Princeton University Press.

Gabriel, U., Greve, W. (2003). The Psychology of Fear of Crime. Conceptual and Methodological Perspectives. British Journal of Criminology, 43, 600-614.

Gale, J.-A., Coupe, T. (2005). The Behavioural, Emotional and Psychological Effects of Street Robbery on Victims. International Review of Victimology, 12, 1-22.

Gerber, M.M., Hirtenlehner, H., Jackson, J. (2010). Insecurities About Crime in Germany, Austria and Switzerland: A Review of Research Findings. European Journal of Criminology, 7, 141-157.

Gerlach, K., Stephan, G. (1996). A Paper on Unhappiness and Unemployment in Germany. Economics Letters, 52, 325-330.

Goldstein, R. (1996). Testing Dependent Correlation Coefficients. STATA Technical Bulletin, 32, 18.

Hale, C. (1996). Fear of Crime: A Review of the Literature. International Review of Victimology, 4, 79-150.

Kaase, M. (1999). Qualitätskriterien in der Umfrageforschung. Denkschrift. Berlin: Akademie Verlag.

Kahneman, D. (1999). Objective Happiness. In: D. Kahneman, E. Diener, N. Schwarz (Eds.), Well-Being. The Foundations of Hedonic Psychology (pp. 3-25). New York: Russel Sage Foundation.

Kahneman, D., Krueger, A.B. (2006). Developments in the Measurement of Subjective Well-Being. The Journal of Economic Perspectives, 20, 3–24.

Killias, M. (1990). Vulnerability: Towards a Better Understanding of a key Variable in the Genesis of Fear of Crime. Violence and Victims, 5, 97-108.

Kreuter, F. (2002). Kriminalitätsfurcht: Messung und methodische Probleme. Opladen: Leske+Budrich.

Lüdemann, C. (2006). Kriminalitätsfurcht im urbanen Raum: Eine Mehrebenenanalyse zu individuellen und sozialräumlichen Determinanten verschiedener Dimensionen von Kriminalitätsfurcht. Kölner Zeitschrift für Soziologie und Sozialpsychologie, 58, 285-306.

Michalos, A.C, Zumbo, B.D. (2000). Criminal Victimisation and the Quality of Life. Social Indicators Research, 50, 245-295.

Moore, S.C. (2006). The Value of Reducing Fear: An Analysis Using the European Social Survey. Applied Economics, 38, 115-117.

Møller, V. (2005). Resilient or Resigned? Criminal Victimisation and Quality of Life in South Africa. Social Indicators Research, 72, 263-317.

Naplava, T. (2008). Kriminalitätsfurcht und registrierte Kriminalität. Monatsschrift für Kriminologie und Strafrechtsreform, 91, 56-73.

Norris, F.H., Kaniasty, K. (1994). Psychological Distress Following Criminal Victimisation in the General Population: Cross-Sectional, Longitudinal, and Prospective Analyses. Journal of Consulting and Clinical Psychology, 62, 111-23.

Oswald, A.J. (1997). Happiness and Economic Performance. The Economic Journal, 107, 1815–1831.

Oswald, A.J., Powdthavee, N. (2008). Death, Happiness, and the Calculation of Compensatory Damages. Journal of Legal Studies, 37, 217-252.

Oswald, A.J., Powdthavee, N. (2008a). Does Happiness Adapt: A Longitudinal Study of Disability with Implications for Economists and Judges. Journal of Public Economics, 92, 1061-1077.

Pantazis, C. (2000). Fear of Crime, Vulnerability and Poverty. British Journal of Criminology, 40, 414-436.

Pedersen, P.J, Schmidt, T.D. (2009). Happiness in Europe : Cross-Country Differences in the Determinants of Subjective Well-Being.

Powdthavee, N. (2005). Unhappiness and Crime: Evidence from South Africa. Economica, 72, 531-547.

Quann, N., Hung, K. (2002). Victimisation Experience and the Fear of Crime: a Cross-National Study. In: P. Nieuwbeerta (Ed.), Crime Victimisation in a Comparative Perspective. Results from the International Crime Victim Survey, 1989-2000 (pp. 301-316). Den Haag: Boom Juridische uitgevers.

Ross, C.E. (1993). Fear of Victimisation and Health. Journal of Quantitative Criminology, 9, 159-175.

Rountree, P.W. (1998). A Reexamination of the Crime-Fear Linkage. Journal of Research in Crime and Delinquency, 35, 341-372.

Rountree, P.W., Land, K.C (1996). Perceived Risk versus Fear of Crime: Empirical Evidence of Conceptually Distinct Reactions in Survey Data. Social Forces, 74, 1353-1376.

Russo, S., Roccato, M. (2010). How Long Does Victimisation Foster Fear of Crime? A Longitudinal Study. Journal of Community Psychology, 38, 960-974.

Skogan, W.G. (1987). The Impact of Victimisation on Fear. Crime & Delinquency, 33, 135-154.

Skogan, W.G. (1993). The Various Meanings of Fear. In: W. Bilsky, C. Pfeiffer, P. Wetzels (EDs.), Fear of Crime and Criminal Victimisation (pp. 131-140). Stuttgart: Enke.

Sorenson, S.B., Golding, J.M. (1990). Depressive Sequelae of Recent Criminal Victimisation. Journal of Traumatic Stress, 3, 337-350.

Tseloni, A., Zarafonitou, C. (2008). Fear of Crime and Victimisation: A Multivariate Multilevel Analysis of Competing Measurements. European Journal of Criminology, 5, 387-409.

Urban, D., Mayerl, J. (2006). Regressionsanalyse: Theorie, Technik und Anwendung. 2nd revised Ed. Wiesbaden: VS Verlag.

Ward, R.A., LaGory, M., Sherman, S.R. (1986). Fear of Crime Among the Elderly As Person/Environment Interaction. The Sociological Quarterly, 27, 327-341.

Windzio, M., Simonson, J., Pfeiffer, C., Kleimann, M. (2007). Kriminalitätswahrnehmung und Punitivität in der Bevölkerung – Welche Rolle spielen die Massenmedien? Ergebnisse der Befragungen zu Kriminalitätswahrnehmung und Strafeinstellungen 2004 und 2006. KFN: Forschungsbericht Nr. 103.

Winkelmann, L., Winkelmann, R. (1998). Why Are the Unemployed so Unhappy? Evidence from Panel Data. Economica, 65, 1–15.

Wittebrood, K. (2002). Fear of Crime and Victimisation in Western Industrialized Countries. A multilevel Analysis. In: P. Nieuwbeerta (Ed.), Crime Victimisation in a Comparative Perspective. Results from the International Crime Victim Survey, 1989-2000 (pp. 285-300). Den Haag: Boom Juridische uitgevers.

Yin, P. (1982). Fear of Crime as a Problem for the Elderly. Social Problems, 30, 240–245.

12. How Violent Victimisation Affects Moral Cognitions, Moral Emotions and Moral Motivation

Bettina Doering, Dirk Baier

12.1 Theoretical background

A key focus of criminological research is to explain delinquent behaviour. Such behaviour constitutes a deviation from the norm, i.e. it breaches the law. The law is, to a great extent, an expression of social consensus on tolerable and intolerable behaviour. That consensus in turn is based on shared moral values. Laws that prevail without any moral reference can be perceived as arbitrary and are thus often ignored. People whose personal moral values mirror those on which laws are based tend to adhere to those laws. People's moral values should thus be a key influencing factor of delinquent behaviour.

Surprisingly, there are only few criminological research approaches that have focused on the link between morality and delinquent behaviour. One exception is the work of Wikström on the Situational Action Theory of Crime Causation (cf. Wikström 2009, Wikström et al. 2010, Wikström/ Treiber 2009). Here, the assumption is that all criminal behaviour is based on morality. People engage in criminal activity because they perceive criminal behaviour as an action alternative and choose it as one of many possible types of behaviour. This two-step process is driven by a person's propensity and by the criminogenic factors (exposure) of a given situation. Propensity depends on a person's moral standards and values and their self-control, and also on the interplay between the two. High moral standards and values result in certain alternative courses of action being left out of consideration. People with high morality do not seek to solve interpersonal conflict with violence; rather, when attempting to mediate in a conflict situation, they choose other behaviours such as talking, withdrawing, and so on. This theory is supported by empirical analysis. The 'propensity' factor, meaning low morality and self-control, significantly increases criminal behaviour (cf. Wikström 2009). Other empirical studies also confirm that the higher a person's moral standards and values, the lower their risk of delinquent behaviour (cf. Barriga et al. 2001, Krettenauer/Eichler 2006, Murray-Close et al. 2006, Stams et al. 2006).

One key problem in existing studies is their vague definition of morality. Wikström (2006) places moral standards and values on an equal footing with abiding by the law. This is particularly evident when operationalising morality: Svensson et al. (2001, p. 741) ask whether it is right to do something illegal as long as one is not caught. Here, an illegal act is evaluated on the basis of whether the perpetrator gets away with it. It is not the moral standpoint but the fear of being caught that is operationalised. Moral standards and values describe, by way of contrast, underlying principles which have universal, categorical, non-partisan application (Celikates/Gosepath 2009, Nunner-Winkler 1991), and which although partly enshrined in law must still be seen as separate from the legal system.

To conduct empirical analysis of the role of morality in explaining delinquent behaviour and the socialisation factors connected with morality, it therefore appears necessary to define morality in a way that goes beyond law abidance (cf. Doering 2013, 2013a). In general, individual morality is to be seen as the degree of abidance with fundamental principles that demonstrate the stated characteristics. This abidance can be divided into three components (cf. Rest 1983): the cognitive, the emotional and the motivational. With regard to the cognitive component, the work of Kohlberg in particular analysed people's ability to exercise moral judgement. Barriga et al. (2001) further developed this research tradition, and also developed a measure for standardised surveys. In contrast with Kohlberg's Kantian approach, Barriga et al. (2001) look at moral traits, thus taking a more virtue-ethics position as used by Aristotle. When it comes to an individual's sense of self, these traits are important in different ways. The more important they are thought to be – especially when compared to non-moral traits – the more embedded moral principles are in the cognitive structure of a person.

The emotional component is, for example, emphasised in the works of Braithwaite (1989), who looks at the role of feelings of shame. Breaking the rules can evoke such feelings. However, Braithwaite's focus lies primarily on the sanctions involved in such breaches rather than the factors that tend to prevent them. Krettenauer and Eichler (2006) also look at moral emotions. Their findings show that adolescents who anticipate feelings of guilt or shame after breaking the rules demonstrate less delinquency. These findings may show that the adolescents concerned demonstrate greater feelings of empathy. Empathy is discussed as a key influencing factor of delinquency (cf. Hosser/Beckurts 2005), and is defined as "an affective response that stems from the apprehension or comprehension of another's emotional state or condition and is similar to what the other person is feeling or would be expected to feel" (Eisenberg 2002, p. 135). Acts of violence are thus prevented by empathy because it is anticipated that there could be serious consequences for the other party.

A further decisive component of morality agreed upon in current research alongside these first two components is moral motivation (Pratt et al. 2003). According to Nunner-Winkler (2008, p. 103f), moral motivation comprises a person's willingness to accept the consequences of doing what they believe to be right. Morally motivated individuals accept that moral principles take priority over personal needs. Less morally motivated people tend to put their personal needs first, making them more likely to adopt delinquent behaviour that can bring them short-term benefits. Unlike the cognitive and emotional components, moral motivation thus involves the degree to which moral knowledge and moral emotion are perceived as binding.

Up to now, the relationship between the three components of moral standards and values has not been sufficiently studied, hence it must be assumed that they are similar in serving as behavioural indicators and are similarly influenced by socialisation factors. Independent of the concrete relationship between the components of morality, it can be helpful in empirical analysis of the causes and consequences to draw on a more nuanced concept of morality.

As with most personality traits, the socialisation factors of individual morality are many and varied. The role of victimisation experience is a case in point. Focus is placed on this factor because research has shown victimisation to be a drastic, life-shaping experience. In an American study, Kahn (1984) showed that victimisation experience goes hand in hand with depression, anxiety, feelings of shame, and a range of other psychological problems. Experience of serious victimisation can also trigger post-traumatic stress disorder (cf. North et al. 1994). Apart from internalising behaviours, victims can also display externalising behavioural disorders. Various authors point to the fact that people with experience of victimisation display aggressive behaviour in inappropriate situations because they chronically accuse the other people involved of having negative intentions and can only react to them in an aggressive way (Dodge 1993, Staub 1998). Findings on intrafamilial violence showing that victims of this violence have a greater risk of violent behaviour in adolescence underline the link to externalising disorders (cf. Baier/Pfeiffer 2011).

One theoretical explanatory model for the stated relationships is provided by the social information processing model (Crick/Dodge 1994), which attempts to explain people's ability to adjust socially and to stand out. When one person meets another, these basic prerequisites shape the interaction between them. On the one hand, these prerequisites are biological abilities; while on the other, they constitute what is known as the 'data base' of past experience, meaning specific memories which, among other things, dictate social skills and shape social models. The data base is used in each step of the social information process. Crick and Dodge (1994) describe six different sub-processes of information processing. In the first two (encoding and interpretation), people selectively acknowledge individual situational stimuli and begin to construe a mental representation of a situation. Steps three and four (classification of cues and response access or construction) involve target selection and construction of a potential response. Choice of behaviour occurs in step five (response decision), while the chosen behaviour is executed in step six (behavioural enactment). The experiences stored in the data base influence each and every step of the process.

As already shown, people with aggressive or delinquent behaviour display a cronic 'hostile attribution error' (Dodge 1980) and thus a general tendency to accuse others more frequently of having negative intentions. Apart from the effects on encoding and interpretation of situational stimuli, aggressive models contained in the data base also affect other processes. For example, it has been shown that aggressive behaviour is regarded as positive because it is seen to promise success. As a result, people with such learning experiences also tend more frequently to aggressive behaviour (Perry et al. 1986). Also, the experiences of aggressive people limit their behavioural spectrum to the extent that fewer socially acceptable behavioural alternatives are available to them (Slaby/Guerra 1988).

Experience of violence can alter the data base as described. Dodge et al. (1990) note that, among other things, experience of abuse can result in the social environment being perceived as dangerous and threatening. Under learning theory, it can also be assumed that the experience of violence leads to modelling. From parental example, for instance, a child or adolescent learns that aggression and violence can be used to resolve conflicts as well as to achieve personal goals and protect personal interests. Thus, aggressive schemas, content and emotions are all stored in the data base. In the past, such influence of violent victimisation has mainly been substantiated on the basis of domestic violence; for children and adolescents, however, it is also just as plausible that experience of violence outside the family leads to negative personality traits, thus hindering the development of positive traits. It is also to be assumed that frequent experience of violence or of severe violent victimisation is particularly impactful. Baier et al. (2011, p. 95ff) show, for example, that people with experience of repeated victimisation display an especially intense fear of crime. It is important to note here that the effect of repeated victimisation cannot be verified with the data provided in the following because repeated violent victimisation occurs too seldom in the sample. Only the effects of severity of victimisation can be verified. That an effect is assumed can be justified in that such offences are thought to be particularly salient and thus of particular importance.

Few empirical studies have been conducted on how violent victimisation influences a person's morality. Studies only support a negative relationship for the emotional component: Experience of violence reduces empathy (Malti et al. 2010, Wilmers et al. 2002, p. 244 ff). In such cases, a circular process must be assumed: Victimised children and adolescents find it difficult to put themselves in their opposite number's place. They react by rejecting offers of contact, which in turn results in them accusing the others of being unfriendly. Thus, contact, which is central to the exercise of perspective-taking and empathy (Arsenio/Lemerise 2001), does not occur. Although these relationships can only be confirmed for empathy, it is assumed here that the other components of moral standards and values are also less well developed in individuals who have experienced violence. When analysing this issue, focus is placed on adolescents who are in the identity-building phase of their psychological development.

The influencing factors of morality and any delinquency-reducing effect of moral identity should apply equally to different groups of individuals. Males and females should differ on this score just as little as natives and foreigners or highly educated and poorly educated individuals. Especially in respect of gender, a range of studies show significant differences of degree, with girls seen as having higher morality (especially in teenage years), committing fewer violent acts and less frequently becoming victims of violence (see Doering 2013, 2013a; Baier 2011). Experience of violence, however, should be equally as bad for the moral development of girls as for that of boys.

Based on the theoretical assumptions and empirical findings presented so far, a number of hypotheses can be formulated for the analyses that follow:

- Hypothesis 1: Victims of violence demonstrate lower morality than non-victims.
- Hypothesis 1a: Experience of serious violence significantly reduces morality in comparison to experience of mild violence.
- Hypothesis 1b: Boys and girls do not differ in respect of the stated relationships.
- Hypothesis 2: Adolescents with high morality commit fewer acts of violence than those with lower morality.
- Hypothesis 2a: Morality mediates the relationship between victimisation and violent delinquency.

12.2 Methodology

12.2.1 Sample

To test the hypotheses, a school survey of ninth graders was conducted in May and June 2010 in the district of Emsland (cf. Doering/Baier 2011). Emsland is located in the northern German State of Lower Saxony, and displays a number of interesting characteristics: It is a largely rural area, where unemployment and receipt of welfare benefit is significantly lower than in other parts of the country or the region. Almost three-quarters of adolescents belong to the Catholic Church, while the national average is less than half. The number of adolescents who have experienced parental separation is also lower than in other regions. The conditions for growing up in this district are thus seen as more intact than in other parts of Germany.

A representative, standardised, administered school survey was conducted, using a written questionnaire which was given out to the various classes during lessons. 4,014 pupils were taught in 177 ninth grade classes in Emsland during school year 2009/2010. The aim was to involve all classes and all pupils in the survey. After some schools refused to take part as well as pupils and/or their parents, and due to absences on account of illness and for other reasons, a total of 2,891 pupils in 145 classes were finally surveyed. This represented a response rate of 72.0 percent. The non-responses mostly involved pupils at lower-level type schools rather than those at mid-level and higher schools (Doering/Baier 2011, p. 58).

The pupils had an average age of 15.18 years. A little more than half of those surveyed were girls (51.3 percent). The vast majority were of German descent (84.2 percent); 16.8 percent had immigrant backgrounds, mostly from countries in the former Soviet Union. The share of immigrants in the ninth grade for the whole of Germany is 27.4 percent, serving to underline the particular social structure of the survey region. Pupils with immigrant backgrounds were defined as those who do not posses German citizenship or were not born in Germany or for whom one of these criteria applies to at least one biological parent.

12.2.2 Measurement instruments

Three concepts are specified in the hypotheses: Victimisation, morality and violent delinquency. These were operationalised as follows:

Victimisation: Two different forms of victimisation were surveyed. Respondents were first asked about experience of parental violence in childhood and then about other violent victimisation experience which could be categorised as criminal offences. This dual instrument had several advantages: On the one hand, early experience was compared with later experience. On the other, experience of events in a very specific context, the family, are placed in contrast with those largely expected in public spaces.[1] With regard to parental violence, respondents were asked about their experience of six different types of parental behaviour. Pupils were asked to state whether, before they were twelve years old, their parents had shown behaviour towards them such a clip round the ear, rough handling/shoving, throwing an object at them, striking with an object, punching/kicking, or beating. The survey used the Strauß (1979) conflict-tactic scale. While the violent behaviour of the father and the mother were documented separately, the presentation in the following does not differentiate

---

1 Analyses show that only 12.7 percent of criminal violent victimisation occurs at home or with relatives; it occurs significantly more frequently in school/on the way to school, in the disco/youth centre, at bus stops/on public transport, on the sports field, etc. – meaning in places that can be described as 'public spaces' (Doering and Baier 2001, p. 64 f). This also means that an overlap exists, albeit a small one, between the victimisation variables.

between violence exercised by the father and that exercised by the mother. Instead, the maximum value is used; this means that if a pupil experienced only paternal violence and was not exposed to violence from the mother, the answer for the father is taken into account. The frequency of each violent act was to be rated on a scale of '1 = never' to '6 = several times a week'. The first three types of behaviour were described as 'mild violence', the last three as 'severe violence'. Initially, a new maximum score was calculated for each of these two forms of violence. If a respondent had, for example, received a clip round the ear from the father and/or the mother, but had not been roughly handled/shoved, the answer regarding the clip around the ear determines the score on the index 'mild violence'. A delineation was only made in the end between pupils who had experienced violence and those who had not, because high frequencies of parental violence only featured on rare occasions. Finally, both types of violence were combined to form three groups of pupils: Those with no experience of violence, those who had at most experienced mild violence, and those who had (also) experienced severe violence.

Criminal acts of violent victimisation were surveyed by asking respondents about their experience of four offences: Assault ("someone deliberately hit you so hard that they injured you" – for example, a bleeding wound or a black eye), aggravated assault ("you were deliberately injured with a weapon or an object or several people deliberately hit you so hard that you were injured"), robbery ("someone used violence in snatching something from you or threatened you with violence while taking something from you, such as your bag or money") and extortion ("someone tried to make you give them money or things (say a jacket or a watch) and threatened you with violence if you refused to give them what they wanted"). The aim was to document the lifetime prevalence, with the adolescents only given the choice of 'yes' or 'no' answer. Given the description of the offences and the frequency distribution[2], a differentiation was made between mild and serious offences (assault versus aggravated assault, robbery, and extortion), resulting in a three-part variable: Adolescents who have never experienced criminal violent victimisation, adolescents who

2 Assault were experienced by 20.4 percent of adolescents; the other offences by 5.0 percent at most.

have at most experienced mild violence, and adolescents who have (also) experienced serious victimisation.[3]

Morality: In accordance with the cited definition of morality, it is necessary to delineate between the cognitive, emotional and motivational components. Three different measurement instruments are used. The cognitive component is measured via the centrality of moral traits. To measure moral centrality, the 'good-self assessment scale' (Arnold 1993, Barriga et al. 2001, Harter/Monsour 1992, Nunner-Winkler et al. 2006, Pratt et al. 1999, Pratt et al. 2003) was used in a shortened and adapted version. Pupils were asked to rate on a scale of '1 = not important at all' to '4 = extremely important' the importance they place on possessing four moral traits (fairness, honesty, willingness to help others, consideration of others) and four personal traits (popularity, sense of humour, athleticism, intelligence). Table 12.1 shows factor loadings and item item-total correlation for the items in question. The 'sense of humour' item shows a low factor loading and item Item-total correlation and is thus excluded from the analyses. The remaining items can be combined into two scales due to the good scale reliability. The correlation between the two scales is -.01 (not significant). The deciding factor is that in the analyses, it is not the scale values that are considered but the difference between the moral and personal traits. This is necessary, because the moral traits prove popular across the board and thus the difference between them and the personal traits is the deciding factor. A positive difference indicates a higher level of importance is placed on moral compared with personal traits. A negative difference points, by way of contrast, to personal traits being seen as more important. The average of the difference variable 'centrality of moral traits' is 0.84 (standard deviation: 0.77); overall, 12.5 percent of respondents achieved a negative difference rating, while 83.5 percent achieved a positive difference rating (at 4.0 percent, the difference in zero).

The emotional components of morality were identified via empathy using a reduced, four-item instrument based on Stadler et al. (2004; see Table 12.2). Respondents were asked to rate their answers on a scale from '1 = does not apply' to '4 = fully applies'. The mean values thus show that most pupils are empathetic. The scale can be considered reliable. The overall mean is 2.96 (standard deviation: 0.63).

3 A positive relationship exists between experience of parental violence and criminal violent victimisation (Spearman's Rho = .27, $p < .001$).

Table 12.1 Statistics for items measuring centrality of moral traits

		Mean	Standard deviation	Factor 1[a]	Factor 2	Item-total correlation	Cronbach's alpha
Moral values	Fair	3.51	0.57	.68		.43	.68
	Honest	3.72	0.50	.62		.37	
	Helpful	3.40	0.59	.75		.52	
	Considerate	3.33	0.61	.79		.55	
Personal	Popular	2.52	0.82		.74	.43	.64[b]
	Sense of humour	3.32	0.66		.34	.18	
	Athletic	2.68	0.94		.77	.48	
	Intelligent	2.73	0.80		.73	.42	

[a] Factor loading in an explorative factor analysis (principal component analysis) with varimax rotation (only loadings > .30 are shown)
[b] reliability without 'sense of humour'

Table 12.2 Statistics for items measuring empathy

	Mean	Standard deviation	Item-total correlation	Cronbach's alpha
I bothers me when I see someone being made fun of.	2.82	0.76	.66	.83
I find it very upsetting when I see someone cry.	2.94	0.82	.63	
I feel sorry for pupils who are often teased.	3.09	0.78	.71	
I often feel for those who are worse off than myself.	2.99	0.75	.61	

The motivational component of morality is identified using a measure to analyse 'moral motivation'. This is based on Nunner-Winkler et al. (2006), and attempts to illustrate motivation based on 'hypothetical decisions on how to act and potential emotions in moral conflicts' (p. 66). In the use of moral conflict, unlike in the case of moral dilemma, it is not two moral values that stand in contradiction to one another, but a moral value and a personal need. The construction of moral conflict follows three criteria: Firstly, pupils need to be familiar with the structure of the described situations, and secondly, they need to be readily able understand the moral dimension. Thirdly, it should not be too difficult for them to make immoral decisions. The following conflict (bike conflict) was presented using the following wording: "Imagine you offered your bike for sale. You want to sell it for 400 Euro. A pupil is interested. He bargains with you and you agree on 320 Euro. Then he says: 'Sorry, I don't have the money on me; I'll quickly run home to get it. I'll be back in half an hour.' You say:

'Agreed, I'll wait for you.' Shortly after he is gone, another customer shows up who is willing to pay the full price." The pupils are then asked to state what they would do in this situation, how they would justify their actions, how they would feel at the time, and why they would feel that way. The open answer format was chosen because what are known as 'production measures' rather than 'recognition measures' can reduce the degree of socially desired answers (Elm/Weber 1994).

The open answers given by the pupils were coded and evaluated using an evaluation strategy based on Nunner-Winkler et al. (2006) and Malti and Buchmann (2010). Because, for the first time, moral conflict was used not in a verbal interview but in a written questionnaire, a manipulation check was applied to verify that the pupils had understood the conflict: 2.2 percent of them incorrectly marked the manipulation check and were excluded from subsequent analyses. The collected data were coded by two trained students. The coding was done using an inductive categorisation system. The system and its reliability were tested on 9.5 percent of the cases prior to application. The interrater reliability (Cohen's Kappa) was over .70 for all categories, which is seen as a good consensus (Bortz/Döring 2005, p. 277). For the ensuing analyses, a global rating was formed from the decisions, justifications and emotions: On the one hand, the 'victimiser' category, meaning those who sold the bike to the second customer and felt good or bad in doing so, and who gave pragmatic reasons for the decision; on the other, the 'moralists' who sold to the bike to the first customer, had either positive or negative feelings about it, and gave moral-based reasons for their decision. Some 47.0 percent of the pupils belonged to the victimizer group, and 53.0 percent to the moralists. In contrast to the measurement instruments presented thus far, the number of missing values is very high (21.7 percent of all respondents). This can be explained by the open answer format (with a higher number of uncodable entries) and the use of the manipulation check.

The three components of morality are not mutually exclusive, while the correlations only lie in the middle range, thus confirming that different dimensions of morality are represented. The correlations (Pearson's r) are .29 ($p < .001$) between moral centrality and empathy, .20 ($p < .001$) between moral centrality and moral motivation and .18 ($p < .001$) between empathy and moral motivation.

Violent delinquency: In contrast to criminal victimisation, respondents were asked whether they had committed four types of violent acts (assault, aggravated assault, robbery, and extortion). Rather than lifetime prevalence, the analysis looked at twelve-month prevalence. This shows the proportion of adolescents who had committed at least one violent act in the past twelve months. Twelve-month prevalence is used to bring out a causal structure: Parental violence and victimisation in the form of violent criminal offences in respondents' lives to date had largely occurred prior to the past twelve months. In the case of parental violence, this is ensured by the wording of the question ('before you were 12 years old'); with the other three types of victimisation, it can be assumed because respondents' average age at first victimisation involving the four offences is 11.3 years, meaning long before their fifteenth birthday.

12.3 Findings

Table 12.3 contains descriptive statistics on the model variables used, some of which have been mentioned in the preceding section. With the exception of experience of parental violence, significant gender differences are evident, making it necessary to take account of the gender variables in multivariate analyses. Boys have significantly more frequent experience of violent criminal offences, both as victims and as perpetrators. Girls, by contrast, show a significantly higher mean for the three dimensions of morality. Overall, it was found that 40.2 percent of respondents experienced violence during childhood, with one in four experiencing serious violence. 24.3 percent of respondents reported experience of violent criminal offences as victims (9.6 percent serious violence). Six percent of the adolescents surveyed said they had committed a violent offence in the past twelve months.[4]

The assumptions in Hypotheses 1, 1a and 1b were tested for the three components by linear regression. The findings are shown in Table 12.4. To verify whether experience of serious violence has a greater influence than that of mild violence, adolescents with experience of mild violence form the reference group; if Hypothesis 1a holds true, adolescents with no experience of violence should demonstrate significantly higher morality, while those with experience of serious violence should show significantly lower morality. In order to analyse whether the correlations are the same for both

4 The mean for this variable and for the moral motivation variable can be seen as a percentage because the two variables are dichotomous and can be treated as interval-scaled variables.

Table 12.3 Descriptive statistics of the survey variables by gender

		N	%/mean (standard deviation)	Boys (%/mean)	Girls (%/mean)	Cramer's V/t-value
Parental violence in childhood	Never	2836	59.8	58.1	61.3	.034
	Mild		29.6	31.1	28.2	
	Serious		10.6	10.8	10.4	
Victimisation via violent criminal offences	Never	2857	75.7	68.3	82.8	.169***
	Mild		14.7	19.2	10.5	
	Serious		9.6	12.5	6.8	
Moral centrality		2875	0.84 (0.77)	0.63	1.05	-15.278***
Empathy		2870	2.96 (0.63)	2.69	3.22	-24.456***
Moral motivation		2265	1.53 (0.50)	1.44	1.61	-8.004***
Violent delinquency		2791	0.06 (0.24)	0.10	0.03	7.894***

* $p < .05$, ** $p < .01$, *** $p < .001$

genders, gender and the interaction variables between gender and experience of violence are also specified; these should have no significance if Hypothesis 1b holds true.[5]

The models show that, when controlled for victimisation experience, female respondents show significantly higher morality than male respondents, with the strongest effect in relation to empathy. Victimisation experience, almost across the board, has no influence on respondents' level of morality. Experience of criminal victimisation plays no role at all, while experience of parental violence is at least seen to have a significant link with moral motivation: Adolescents who were exposed to serious parental violence display lower levels of moral motivation than those who experience mild or no parental violence. Of the twelve specified interaction effects, nine are not significant. The effect for the remaining three significant effects is more or less negligible. Because the main effects are not significant, the interaction effects should not be looked at in any detail. There is evidence that the influence of the experience of violence on moral motivation tends to be greater in female respondents than in male respondents.[6]

5 To avoid multicollinearity when introducing interaction variables, all variables were mean-centered before being multiplied (cf. Jaccard/Turrisi 2003).

Table 12.4 Influencing factors of morality (OLS regressions; coefficient: Beta)

	Model: Moral centrality	Model: Empathy	Model: Moral motivation
Gender: Female (a)	.27 ***	.42 ***	.15 ***
Parental violence: Mild	*Reference*	*Reference*	*Reference*
Parental violence: None (b)	.03	-.01	.04
Parental violence: Serious (c)	-.03	.01	-.05 *
Criminal violent victimisation experience: Mild	*Reference*	*Reference*	*Reference*
Criminal violent victimisation experience: Never (d)	-.01	.01	.04
Criminal violent victimisation experience: Serious (e)	-.02	.02	.01
Interaction a * b	.01	.05 *	.06 *
Interaction a * c	.03	.03	-.01
Interaction a * d	.01	-.01	-.02
Interaction a * e	-.05 *	.00	-.03
Number of cases	**2787**	**2784**	**2208**
R^2	**.076**	**.177**	**.035**

* p < .05, ** p < .01, *** p < .001

Because victimisation experience is only marginally linked with the various components of morality, there is no need to test Hypothesis 2a. The findings of the test are nonetheless shown in Table 12.5. Binary logistic regression analyses were conducted using violent delinquency (in the last twelve months) as the dependent variable. The first model confirms a significant relationship between experience of violent victimisation and violent delinquency: Adolescents with no experience of parental violence and no experience of criminal violent victimisation are significantly less likely to commit violent offences than those with experience of mild violence. Additionally, at least when it comes to parental violence, there is evidence that adolescents with experience of serious violence are significantly more

6 This can be illustrated by the example of moral motivation and parental violence: The means for boys are 1.45 (no parental violence), 1.45 (mild violence) and 1.39 (serious violence), with the differences not significant (F = 0.723, p > .05). For girls, by contrast, there are significant differences between the three groups (means: 1.66, 1.56 and 1.47; F = 10.510, p < .001). Post-hoc testing (Scheffé test) shows that the group with no experience of violence differs significantly from the other two groups (p < .01).

likely to commit violent offences than those with experience of mild violence. Additionally, fewer girls than boys commit violent offences.

The second model takes in the morality variables. Little change is seen regarding the coefficients of the victimisation variables, meaning that no mediation occurs. Given that the coefficients hardly change, a mediation test was not performed. Of the morality variables, empathy and motivation prove to be significant. Greater empathy and greater moral motivation reduce the risk of violent delinquency. Moral centrality has, by way of contrast, no influence on violent delinquency. It is interesting that with the inclusion of the morality variables, the influence of gender drops significantly. That female adolescents commit fewer violent acts than male adolescents is thus partly due to their higher morality.

Table 12.5 Influencing factors of violent delinquency (binary logistic regression; coefficient: Exp(B))

	Model I	**Model II**
Gender: Female	0.302 ***	0.497 **
Parental violence: Mild	*Reference*	*Reference*
Parental violence: None	0.643 *	0.610 *
Parental violence: None	1.925 **	1.898 *
Criminal violent victimisation: Mild	*Reference*	*Reference*
Criminal violent victimisation: Never	0.184 ***	0.188 ***
Criminal violent victimisation: Serious	0.884	0.871
Moral centrality		1.059
Empathy		0.467 ***
Moral motivation		0.525 **
Number of Cases	**2154**	**2154**
Nagelkerkes R^2	**.203**	**.249**

* $p < .05$, ** $p < .01$, *** $p < .001$

Supplementary analysis: Victimisation and other personality traits

The findings presented above were unable to confirm the central hypotheses. In discussing these findings, it is possible to focus either on substantive aspects or on distinguishing features of the specific dataset. As noted when describing the sample, the area where the survey was conducted offers more intact conditions for growing up compared with the national average. The sample may display too little variance in the experience of violent victimisation for any stable relationships to be identified – especially when it comes to serious violence. Before non-confirmation of the hypotheses is put down to the sample, however, it would appear useful to see if other personality factors that attract greater focus in criminological research similarly lack any systematic relationship with victimisation experience. If not, then the hypotheses should be subjected to substantive discussion.

Table 12.6 Statistics for items measuring risk-seeking and affinity to violence

	Mean	Standard deviation	Item-total correlation	Cronbach's alpha
I like to test my limits by doing something dangerous.	2.19	0.91	.75	.90
I find it exciting sometimes to do things that are potentially dangerous.	2.19	0.95	.79	
Excitement and adventure are more important than safety.	2.12	0.88	.75	
It's fun to take risks.	2.34	0.94	.80	
Scale "risk-seeking"	**2.21 (Boys: 2.44, Girls: 1.99, t = 15.222***)**			
The man is the head of the family. Women and children have to do as he says.	1.83	0.85	.36	.74
If a woman betrays her husband, he's allowed to hit her.	1.12	0.45	.34	
A man should be ready and willing to use violence to defend his wife and children.	2.69	1.02	.43	
A man who isn't willing to use violence when someone insults him is a weakling.	1.56	0.84	.54	
The man is the head of the family and is allowed to use violence when necessary.	1.27	0.61	.41	
Men should be allowed to own firearms in order to protect their families and property.	1.60	0.89	.48	
A real man is willing to hit out if someone speaks badly about his family.	1.63	0.87	.59	
A real man is strong and protects his family.	3.01	0.90	.35	
Scale "affinity to violence"	**1.84 (Boys: 2.00, Girls: 1.68, t = 18.766***)**			

* $p < .05$, ** $p < .01$, *** $p < .001$

Two additional personality factors were investigated in the survey: Risk-seeking as a dimension of low self-control, and affinity to violence. For both personality traits, other studies report correlations with experience of parental violence and violent delinquency (among others Baier at al. 2006, p. 148 ff and p. 156 ff, Fuchs et al. 2005, p. 145 ff and 314 ff, Wetzels et al. 2001, p. 253 ff). Risk-seeking was documented using four items. These are shown in Table 12.6 and are based on a proposal by Grasmick et al.

(1993). When investigating affinity to violence, an eight-item scale was used which measures physical violence, to which men are far more prone (see Enzmann et al. 2004). Both scales show adequate reliability. Male adolescents achieve significantly higher mean scores on both scales.[7]

Analyzing victimisation experience as an influencing factor of both personality traits using OLS regressions produces the findings shown in Table 12.7. For affinity to violence, the coefficients fully match expectations: Adolescents with no experience of parental violence and/or with no experience of criminal violent victimisation demonstrate significantly lower affinity than those with experience of mild violence; school students with experience of serious violence also tend to have a greater affinity to violence than those with experience of mild violence. When it comes to risk-seeking, there is evidence that the dividing line runs between the group without and the group with experience of violence, meaning that the degree of violence is less relevant. Adolescents with no experience of violence demonstrate significantly lower risk-seeking than those with experience of mild or serious violence.

Table 12.7 Influencing factors of affinity to violence and risk-seeking (OLS regressions; coefficient: Beta).

	Model: Affinity to violence	**Model: Risk-seeking**
Gender: Female	-.31 ***	-.25 ***
Parental violence: Mild	*Reference*	*Reference*
Parental violence: None	-.10 ***	-.06 **
Parental violence: Serious	.05 **	.02
Criminal violent victimisation: Mild	*Reference*	*Reference*
Criminal violent victimisation: Never	-.08 **	-.12 ***
Criminal violent victimisation: Serious	.04 *	.02
Number of cases	**2783**	**2777**
R^2	**.147**	**.102**

* $p < .05$, ** $p < .01$, *** $p < .001$

7 The correlations between the personality traits and the moral dimension are moderate but all significant ($p < .001$). The correlation with affinity to violence is -.24 for moral centrality, -.27 for empathy and -.22 for motivation. The correlations for risk-seeking are -.22 (centrality), -.21 (empathy) and -.17 (motivation).

The personality factors are significant influencing variables of violent delinquency (Table 12.8). Adolescents who accept violence and are prone to take risks show a significantly higher risk of violent delinquency. To a certain extent, the personality factors also mediate the influence of victimisation experience. This is especially evident for the group of adolescents with experience of serious parental violence. In Model I, these show a significantly greater risk of violence than those with experience of mild violence; in Model II this significant effect disappears. Full mediation of the influence of violent experience, however, does not occur. Experience of violence can thus affect a person's affinity to violence independent of the associated changes in the personality structures.

Table 12.8 Influencing factors of violent delinquency (binary logistic regressions; coefficient: Exp(B))

	Model I	**Model II**
Gender: Female	0.295 ***	0.547 **
Parental violence: Mild	*Reference*	*Reference*
Parental violence: None	0.552 **	0.579 **
Parental violence: Serious	1.645 *	1.408
Criminal violent victimisation: Mild	*Reference*	*Reference*
Criminal violent victimisation: Never	0.194 ***	0.225 ***
Criminal violent victimisation: Serious	0.639	0.817
Affinity to violence		2.682 ***
Risk-seeking		1.805 ***
Number of cases	**2697**	**2697**
Nagelkerkes R^2	**.198**	**.272**

* $p < .05$, ** $p < .01$, *** $p < .001$

12.4 Discussion

Based on the results for affinity to violence and risk-seeking, the findings relating to morality cannot be ascribed solely to specific characteristics of the sample. In relation to established concepts in criminological research, expectations regarding the influence of violent victimisation are confirmed. Neither the sample nor the operationalization used in relation to morality should be criticised because established methods were applied that demonstrate adequate reliability. The constructs can also be assumed to have adequate validity from their moderate inter-correlation and from their expected negative correlation with delinquent behaviour. In the following, therefore, the findings will be discussed substantively in relation to the presented hypotheses.

Hypothesis 1 assumes that victims of violence have lower morality than non-victims. This is not confirmed in a multidimensional analysis of morality (cognitive, emotional and motivational). There is only one point where serious parental violence is shown to have a significant effect on moral motivation. In contrast, multiple significant correlations are evident between victimisation and other personality traits. Socialisation conditions relating to morality differ in some ways to socialisation conditions relating to other personality traits. Negative experiences foster the development of negative traits; they do not, however, prevent the development of positive traits to the same degree. In terms of the social information processing model (Crick/Dodge 1994), this means that the data base and in particular adherence to/knowledge of social rules are not influenced by victimisation. A lack of negative experience is thus not sufficient to foster positive personality traits. Resilience factors – which the findings on influencing factors of violent delinquency show to include morality – are not fostered by the absence of violent experience. The findings thus indicate that in order to explain resilience factors, it is necessary to develop specific models and to subject them to empirical study; it is not enough to merely investigate the generic risk factors of delinquent behaviour and its predictors. Resilience factors are no doubt also to be found in children's and adolescents' key socialisation areas of family, school and friends.

Because Hypothesis 1 was refused, Hypotheses 1a and 1b must also go unconfirmed. The degree of violence experienced adds nothing to the explanation of morality. Of more importance is whether or not an individual has experienced violence; this also applies in respect of violent delinquency. Recurrence of violence was not analysed for. This is possibly more important than the degree of violence experienced. Given the low number of adolescents with multiple experience of violence, however, such a hypothesis cannot be tested at this point.

As victimisation has no significant influence on morality, there is no need to investigate its influence by gender. This was still done, however, although no major differences were found regarding the effect of victimisation. There is, however, evidence of a somewhat stronger effect for girls. This is also confirmed by the findings of another study on the influence of parental violence on violent behaviour (Baier 2011). Experience of parental violence has a potentially greater impact for girls because girls are generally more family orientated; they tend to seek more parental closeness and trust than boys. Experience of violence could thus lead to greater feelings of hurt, which is compensated by a range of different behaviours.

On the subject of gender, one finding was brought out for which no hypothesis was specified. In the sample, as in many other studies, it was confirmed that boys demonstrate violent behaviour more frequently than girls. A range of explanations can be put forward for this purpose (cf. Scheithauer 2003). The analyses show that morality is a central explanatory factor. Female respondents display greater empathy and greater moral motivation, which in turn significantly influences violent behaviour. Against this backdrop, studies that focus on the influencing factors of morality must thus attempt to identify factors that significantly differ between boys and girls.

Given the non-existent relationship between victimisation and morality, it is not possible to confirm Hypothesis 2a – of morality having a mediating effect with regard to violent delinquency. Only moral centrality shows no relationship with violent delinquency in the multivariate model. Moral cognitions do not, therefore, prevent an individual from engaging in violence. It is possible that people for whom fairness, helping others and so on is important, believe the use of violence is still appropriate and legitimate in specific situations. For people with great empathy, this is almost certainly not an option because the negative feelings experienced by a victim of violence lie at the centre of decisions to act. The in some respects differing impacts of the dimensions of morality make it necessary to give greater consideration to the relationship between cognitive, emotional and motivational components of morality. Are, for example, the cognitive and emotional dimensions predictors of the motivational dimension or are all three dimensions of equal weighting? This question can only be answered using longitudinal studies.

The findings also highlight a further research question. Up to now, it has been assumed that one reason why victimisation affects violent delinquency is a change in personality. At least for affinity to violence and risk-seeking, this can be confirmed to a marginal extent. Victims and non-victims still differ from one another significantly in their risk of violence, when these factors are taken into account. This might of course be due to other personality factors not included here in the analysis. It is possible that the direct relationship can have other causes. More recent studies point, for example, to cerebral changes in individuals who have been subjected to violence (cf. Teicher et al. 2012). This suggests a need for research investigating the systematically different mediators for the relationship between victimisation and violent delinquency, and also looking at potentially recursive relationships.

References

Arnold, M. L. (1993). The Place of Morality in the Adolescent Self. Harvard University, Cambridge, MA: unpublished thesis.

Arsenio, W. F., Lemerise, E. A. (2001). Varieties of Childhood Bullying: Values, Emotion Processes, and Social Competence. Social Development, 10, 59-73.

Baier, D. (2011). Jugendgewalt und Geschlecht – Erkenntnisse aus Kriminalstatistik und Dunkelfelduntersuchungen. Zeitschrift für Jugendkriminalrecht und Jugendhilfe, 4/2011, 356-364.

Baier, D., Kemme, S., Hanslmaier, M., Doering, B., Rehbein, F. Pfeiffer, C. (2011). Kriminalitätsfurcht, Strafbedürfnisse und wahrgenommene Kriminalitätsentwicklung. Ergebnisse von bevölkerungsrepräsentativen Befragungen aus den Jahren 2004, 2006 und 2010. KFN: Forschungsbericht Nr. 117.

Baier, D., Pfeiffer, C. (2011). Wenn Opfer nicht zu Tätern werden. Beeinflussen Bedingungen der Schulklasse den Zusammenhang von innerfamiliären Gewalterfahrungen und eigener Gewalttäterschaft? Trauma und Gewalt, 5, 6-19.

Baier, D., Pfeiffer, C., Windzio, M., Rabold, S. (2006). Schülerbefragung 2005: Gewalterfahrungen, Schulabsentismus und Medienkonsum von Kindern und Jugendlichen. Abschlussbericht über eine repräsentative Befragung von Schülerinnen und Schülern der 4. und 9. Jahrgangsstufe. KFN.

Barriga, A. Q., Morrison, E. M., Liau, A. K., Gibbs, J. C. (2001). Moral Cognition: Explaining the Gender Difference in Antisocial Behavior. Merrill-Palmer Quarterly, 47, 532-562.

Bortz, J., Döring, N. (2005). Forschungsmethoden und Evaluation für Human- und Sozialwissenschaftler (4. Auflage). Berlin: Springer.

Braithwaite, J. (1989). Crime, Shame and Reintegration. Cambridge: Universtity Press.

Celikates, R., Gosepath, S. (2009). Philosophie der Moral. Texte von der Antike bis zur Gegenwart. Frankfurt am Main: Suhrkamp.

Crick, N. R., Dodge, K. A. (1994). A Review and Reformulation of Social-Information Processing Mechanisms in Children´s Social Adjustment. Psychological Bulletin, 115, 74-101.

Dodge, K. A. (1980). Social Cognition and Child's Aggressive Behavior. Child Development, 51, 162-170.

Dodge, K. A. (1993). Social Cognitive Mechanisms in the Development of Conduct Disorder and Depression. Annual Review of Psychology, 44, 559-584.

Dodge, K. A., Bates, J. E., Pettit, G. S. (1990). Mechanisms in the Cycle of Violence. Science, 250, 1678-1683.

Doering, B. (2013). The Development of Moral Identity and Moral Motivation in Childhood and Adolescence. In K. Heinrichs, F. Oser (Eds.), Theoretical Perspectives and Empirical Results on Moral Motivation. Rotterdam: Sense Publishers (in press).

Doering, B. (2013a). Die Bedeutung Moralischer Motivation bei der Erklärung delinquenten Verhaltens im Jugendalter (in press).

Doering, B., Baier, D. (2011). Jugendliche als Opfer und Täter von Gewalt im Landkreis Emsland. KFN-Forschungsbericht Nr. 113. Hannover: KFN.

Eisenberg, N. (2002). An Affective Response that Stems from the Apprehension or Comprehension of Another's Emotional State or Condition, and That is Similar to What the Other Person is Feeling or Would be Expected to Eeel. In R. J. Davidson, A. Harrington (Eds.), Empathy-related Emotional Responses, Altruism, and their Socialization (pp. 131-164). London: Oxford University Press.

Elm, D. R., Weber, J. (1994). Measuring Moral Judgement: The Moral Judgement Interview or the Defining Issue Test. Journal of Business Ethics, 13, 341-355.

Enzmann, D., Brettfeld, K., Wetzels, P. (2004). Männlichkeitsnormen und die Kultur der Ehre. In D. Oberwittler, S. Karstedt (Eds.), Soziologie der Kriminalität (pp. 240-263). Wiesbaden: VS Verlag für Sozialwissenschaften.

Fuchs, M., Lamnek, S., Luedtke, J., Baur, N. (2005). Gewalt an Schulen: 1994 - 1999 - 2004 (1. Auflage). Wiesbaden: Verlag für Sozialwissenschaften.

Grasmick, H.G., Tittle, C.R., Bursik, R.J., Arneklev, B.J. (1993). Testing the Core Empirical Implications of Gottfredson and Hirschi´s General Theory of Crime. Journal of Research in Crime and Delinquency, 30, 5-29.

Harter, S., Monsour, A. (1992). Developmental Analysis of Conflict Caused by Opposing Attributes in the Adolescent Self-Portrait. Developmental Psychology, 28, 251-260.

Hosser, D., Beckurts, D. (2005). Empathie und Delinquenz. KFN-Forschungsbericht Nr. 96. Hannover: KFN.

Jaccard, J., Turrisi, R. (2003). Interaction Effects in Multiple Regression. Thousand Oaks: Sage.

Kahn, A. (1984). Victims of Violence: Final Report of APA Task Force of Victims of Crime and Violence Washington: American Psychological Association.

Krettenauer, T., Eichler, D. (2006). Adolescents' Self-attributed Moral Emotions Following a Moral Transgression: Relations With Delinquency, Confidence in Moral Judgment and Age. British Journal of Developmental Psychology, 24, 489–506.

Malti, T., Buchmann, M. (2010). Socialization and Individual Antecedents of Adolescents´ and Young Adults´ Moral Motivation. Journal of Youth and Adolescence, 39, 138-149.

Malti, T., Perren, S., Buchmann, M. (2010). Children's Peer Victimization, Empathy, and Emotional Symptoms. Child Psychiatry and Human Development, 41, 98-113.

Murray-Close, D., Crick, N. R., Galotti, K. M. (2006). Children's Moral Reasoning Regarding Physical and Relational Aggression. Social Development, 15, 345-372.

North, C.S., Smith, E.M., Spitznagel, E.L. (1994). Post-traumatic Stress Disorder in Survivors of a Mass Shooting. American Journal of Psychiatry, 151, 82-88.

Nunner-Winkler, G. (1991). Weibliche Moral. Die Kontroverse um eine geschlechtsspezifische Ethik. Frankfurt am Main, New York: Campus.

Nunner-Winkler, G. (2008). Zur Entwicklung moralischer Motivation. In J. Schneider (Ed.), Entwicklung von der Kindheit bis zum Erwachsenenalter: Befunde der Münchner Längsschnittstudie LOGIK (pp. 103-123). Weinheim: Beltz.

Nunner-Winkler, G., Meyer-Nikele, M., Wohlrab, D. (2006). Integration durch Moral: Moralische Motivation und Ziviltugenden Jugendlicher. Wiesbaden: VS Verlag für Sozialwissenschaften.

Perry, D. G., Perry, L. C., Rasmussen, P. (1986). Cognitive Social Learning Mediators of Aggression. Child Development, 57, 700-711.

Pratt, M. W., Arnold, M. L., Pratt, A. T., Diessner, R. (1999). Predicting Adolescent Moral Reasoning from Family Climate: A Longitudinal Study. Journal of Early Adolescence, 19, 148-175.

Pratt, M. W., Hunsberger, B., Pancer, S. M., Alisat, S. (2003). A Longitudinal Analysis of Personal Values Socialization: Correlates of a Moral Self-ideal in Late Adolescence. Social Development, 12, 563-585.

Rest, J. R. (1983). Morality. In J. Flavell, E. Markman (Eds.), Handbook of Child Psychology: Vol.3. Cognitive Development (pp. 556-628). New York: Wiley.

Scheithauer, H. (2003). Aggressives Verhalten von Jungen und Mädchen. Göttingen: Hogrefe.

Slaby, R. G., Guerra, N. G. (1988). Cognitive Mediators of Aggression in Adolescent Offenders: 1. Assessment. Developmental Psychology, 24, 580-588.

Stadler, C., Janke, W., Schmeck, K. (2004). IVE – Inventar zur Erfassung von Impulsivität, Risikoverhalten und Empathie bei 9- bis 14jährigen Kindern. Göttingen: Hogrefe.

Stams, J. G., Brugman, D., Dekovic, M., Rosmalen, L., Laan, P., Gibbs, J. C. (2006). The Moral Judgment of Juvenile Delinquents: A Meta-analysis. Journal of Abnormal Child Psychology, 34, 697–713.

Staub, E. (1998). Breaking the Cycle of Genocidal Violence: Healing and Reconciliation. In J. Harvey (Ed.), Perspectives on Loss (pp. 231-238). Washington: Taylor and Francis.

Straus, M. A. (1979). Measuring Intrafamily Conflict and Violence: The Conflict Tactic Scales. Journal of Marriage and The Family, 41, 75-88.

Svensson, R., Pauwels, L., Weerman, F. M. (2010). Does the Effect of Self-control on Adolescent Offending Vary by Level of Morality? A Test in Three Countries. Criminal Justice and Behavior, 37, 732- 743.

Teicher, M.H., Anderson, C.M., Polcari, A. (2012). Childhood Maltreatment is Associated With Reduced Volume in the Hippocampal Subfields CA3, Dentate Gyrus, and Subiculum. Proseedings of the National Acadamy of Sciences of the United States of America, 109, E563-E572.

Wetzels, P., Enzmann, D., Mecklenburg, E., Pfeiffer, C. (2001). Jugend und Gewalt. Eine repräsentative Dunkelfeldanalyse in München und acht anderen deutschen Städten. Baden-Baden: Nomos.

Wikström, P.-O. H. (2006). Individuals, Settings, and Acts of Crime: Situational Mechanisms and the Explanation of Crime. In P.-O. H. Wikström, R. J. Sampson (Eds.), The Explanation of Crime: Context, Mechanisms and Development (pp. 61-107). Cambridge: University Press.

Wikström, P.-O. H. (2009). Crime Propensity, Criminogenic Exposure and Crime Involvement in Early to Mid Adolescence. Monatsschrift für Kriminologie und Strafrechtsreform, 92, 253-266.

Wikström, P.-O. H., Ceccato, V., Hardie, B., Treiber, K. (2010). Activity Fields and the Dynamics of Crime. Advancing Knowledge About the Role of the Environment in Crime Causation. Journal of Quantitative Criminology, 26, 55-87.

Wikström, P.-O. H., Treiber, K. H. (2009). Violence as Situational Action. International Journal of Conflict and Violence, 3, 75-96.

Wilmers, N., Enzmann, D., Schaefer, D., Herbers, K., Greve, W., Wetzels, P. (2002). Jugendliche in Deutschland zur Jahrtausendwende: Gefährlich oder gefährdet? Baden-Baden: Nomos.